THE END OF
THE CHURCH AGE
...AND AFTER

THE END OF
THE CHURCH AGE
...AND AFTER

By Harold Camping

Family Stations, Inc.

Published and printed by
Family Stations, Inc.
Oakland, California 94621
U.S.A.

First Edition 12-02
Second Edition 06-03

On the Internet:
www.familyradio.com

CONTENTS

Contents

PREFACE

The thought that the church age would come to an end is a shocking idea to those of us who have been taught the so-called amillennium or the postmillennium idea of the return of Christ. In both of these schools of thought the concept that the churches and congregations would be here and would be functioning as God's people all the way to the end of the world and the return of Christ has been thoroughly ingrained into our thinking.

However, in the churches that have been taught the so-called premillennial idea of the return of Christ, it is amazing to note that they have been taught that there would come a time when the church age would come to an end prior to the end of the world. True, they did not use the language that there would come a time when the church age would come to an end. However, effectively this is what they were saying when they taught the concept that there would come a time when the believers would be raptured. In fact, while many details of the closing events of this world's history have been grossly misunderstood by this pre-mil concept it is remarkable that they had correctly been given a faint glimpse of much of the Biblical outline of the events that must unfold before the world ends. A comparison of the basic pre-mil teaching with the true Biblical teaching shows:

Pre-mil teaching	True Biblical teaching
1. Church Age will come to an end	Church Age will come to end
2. At end of Church Age, true believers will be raptured	At end of Church Age, true believers will be driven from churches and/or commanded to depart from churches.
3. End of Church Age coincides with beginning of great tribulation	End of Church Age coincides with beginning of great tribulation
4. During tribulation the Jews who are blood descendants of Abraham will evangelize the world	During tribulation the spiritual Jews, the true believers from every nation will evangelize the world. A great multitude which no man can number will be saved.

5. The tribulation period is a time when judgment is upon the world	The tribulation season is a time when judgment is upon the churches
6. The true believers will not experience God's judgment upon the churches because they have been raptured	The true believers will not experience God's judgment upon the churches because they are outside of the churches
7. The tribulation period is a literal seven years and is divided into two parts	The tribulation period is typified by a seventy year period and is divided into two parts.
8. The tribulation period ends with the coming of Christ to this earth to reign for 1000 years	The tribulation period ends with the coming of Christ and the end of the world

Given the fact that the events concerning the end of the world have been sealed (Daniel 12:9) until the time of the end, it is indeed amazing that the pre-mil position is as accurate as it is. (We should note that amongst the wrong teachings of the pre-mil position is that the rapture would occur before the end of the world. There is much proof in the Bible that the rapture occurs at the end of the world. For more information see Appendix C: When Is The Rapture?)

However, by God's mercy the end of the world is very near so that we can now know with far greater accuracy the details of God's program leading up to the end of the world.

It should also be noted that heretofore, any theological position concerning details of the end of the world could be considered and accepted intellectually. Because each and every position, whether a-mil, post-mil, or pre-mil, taught that the end of the world would take place at some unknown time in the future, no action except intellectual assent on the part of the believer was required.

However, as the Biblical details of the end of the world as set forth in this study are considered, it should be emphatically noted that action on the part of the reader is required. Thus, this study should not be considered simply as an eschatological position that discusses the great event of the end of the world as coming some unknown time in the future. Rather, it is a very carefully developed Biblical eschatological position that requires immediate decisive action on the part of the believers who understand the truth of this study and who have an intense desire to be obedient to all the commands of the Bible.

As this study will show, we are now in that time of history when the church age has come to an end. Consequently, God has commanded each and every believer to leave his local church and continue to serve God as His ambassador outside of the churches and congregations. This is the action required by God for any and all who truly tremble before the Word of God.

Thus, this study will be very offensive to some readers. But it can also be a great blessing in the lives of those who will understand the Biblical truth that it sets forth.

May God have mercy on each reader of this study so that the result in his life may be a fervent readiness to do the will of Almighty God.

PLEASE NOTE   The phrase "The End of the Church Age" is in no way speaking of the end of the eternal church which is made up of only truly saved individuals. The eternal church which began when the first person in the world became saved will continue forever. As long as this world exists, God will be adding to it.

The church age that has come to an end is the external representation of the kingdom of God which exists as local congregations. We will learn in this study that for more than 1950 years beginning with Pentecost in A.D. 33, the external representation of the kingdom of God was the local churches. Throughout the church age the true believers who are eternal citizens of the eternal church were to be members of these local congregations. This eternal church is an invisible church because only God knows for certain who the true believers are.

Examples of these local churches are the seven churches named in Chapters 2 and 3 of Revelation. These congregations consisted of both saved and unsaved individuals. For example, one of these, the church of Sardis, had only a few true believers within it (Revelation 3:4). Thus, while it was a local church externally representing the kingdom of God on this earth, in actuality it had only a few people who had become members of God's eternal church.

As we will learn in this study it is the era of these local congregations and churches that has come to an end. The true believers who are included in the membership of these local churches have either already been driven out or are commanded to come out.

Thus, the local churches all over the world will finally have only unsaved people as members.

However, the invisible eternal church will continue to grow and flourish outside of these local churches which for more than 1950 years have been the divine institution that God raised up to be the caretaker of the Gospel. Since the beginning of the Great Tribulation, the eternal church no longer has any identification with the local churches.

Therefore, a better title for this book could be,

"The End of the Institution of the Local Churches and After."

Introduction.
The Bible Is The Final Authority

This book is entitled "The End of the Church Age and After." However, the essential issue that is being presented is not the subject of the end of the church age. The essential issue is the authority of the Bible. Is the Bible truly the ultimate and final authority to which every true believers is subject?

The big question each one must face is: Do I have such a fear of God that I tremble before Him if I suspect a doctrine I hold may be contrary to the Word of God?

Or is it possible that I feel altogether secure with God because I faithfully obey each and every doctrine that my church teaches. Do I realize that some of the doctrines held by my church may not be faithful to the Bible? In turn, do I trust that everything my church teaches is altogether true to the Bible?

If I discover that a doctrine my church teaches is not faithful to God's Word, do I tremble in fear?

To say it another way, if I discover that a doctrine my church teaches is not faithful to God's Word, do I tremble in fear? We must remember that any doctrine we hold that is not faithful to the Bible is a lie. It is something developed by men. Therefore, to believe that this doctrine is true, when in actuality, it is not true to the Bible, is to place our trust in men rather than in God. Actually, it is a sin equivalent to that committed by ancient Israel as they worshipped God in Jerusalem but also worshipped other gods at the high places. This was such a serious sin that God finally destroyed Israel in 709 B.C. and Judah in 587 B.C. As we will discover in this book, it is such a serious sin of our day that God's judgment is upon today's churches.

The same principle must be applied to this study. Has every effort been made to be sure that everything presented in this book is altogether faithful to the Bible? The teachings and the conclusions must have nothing to do with visions or voices or dreams. They are to be unrelated to human speculation. They must be carefully founded on the Bible alone.

It must be admitted that at times, it is very difficult to obey the Bible. That is, sometimes as we carefully read the Bible we find that God is giving us a command for some kind of action. And sometimes we don't like that command. We don't like it at all. Then comes the big question that each of us must personally ask: In my fear of God, am I ready to be obedient to the command even though I don't like it? The answer has to be, "If I am a true child of God, I want to be obedient to each and every command. My delight is to do the will of God." If I keep hesitating to obey, I must ask myself the fair question, "Am I truly a child of God?"

The Saved Person Is a New Creation

The reason why that is the spiritual mentality of the true believer is because at the moment he became saved, he became born again. He experienced from heaven above a new resurrected soul in which he never desires to sin again. In I John 3:9, God assures us of this as He declares:

Whosoever is born of God doth not commit sin; for his seed remaineth in him: and he cannot sin, because he is born of God.

The seed that remaineth in him is Christ (Galatians 3:16).

Therefore, the true believer has become a new creature in Christ (II Corinthians 5:17). At death, which could come moments after salvation or years after salvation, in his soul existence, he goes immediately, without any change, into heaven to live and reign with Christ. Because he was given his new resurrected soul, God can say of him in I John 2:3-4:

And hereby we do know that we know him, if we keep his commandments. He that saith, I know him, and keepeth not his commandments, is a liar, and the truth is not in him.

He can also understand Romans 7:22:

For I delight in the law of God after the inward man:

He is in accordance with the testimony of Romans 7:24, **"who shall deliver me from the body of this death?"** He deplores the fact that he must still live in a sin-cursed body that will also become saved when Christ comes on the last day.

Frankly stated, if a highly successful pastor or a Biblical theologian or I do not find an intense desire in my life to be obedient to all the Bible commands, so that I tremble before God lest I teach something contrary to the will of God, I may have evidence that I am not saved. Ordination or acclaim that I am a

> *Ordination or acclaim that I am a faithful Bible teacher*
> *or elder or pastor, in themselves, give no guarantee that*
> *I have become saved.*

faithful Bible teacher or elder or pastor, in themselves, give no guarantee that I have become saved.

Unfortunately, those who are not saved may not be able to understand these truths. They may conclude that these statements concerning a new resurrected soul are merely the opinion of the writer of this study. In fact, that judgment can extend to this whole study so that the reader may conclude that this study is merely the opinion of the writer.

The best this writer can hope for is that each one who reads this book will carefully and diligently check the Bible for the validity of each conclusion that is taught in this study.

Progressive Revelation

The Bible is the complete revelation of God's Word to the human race. We are not to add to it. We are not to take away from it. It alone and in its entirety is the Word of God.

However, when we consider how we receive truth from the Bible, we have another matter altogether. God insists that there is a timetable known only to God by which He reveals the truths of the Bible to mankind.

For example, Jesus clearly told his disciples that the time would come when He would be killed and after three days, He would rise again. Mark 8:31 declares:

And he began to teach them, that the Son of man must suffer many things, and be rejected of the elders, and of the chief priests, and scribes, and be killed, and after three days rise again.

Even though this is a plain, clear statement, it was not understood at all by the disciples. It was only after His resurrection, as the disciples were reminded by the two men in shining garments, who stood outside the empty sepulchre, that they understood. Luke 24:6-8 informs us:

He is not here, but is risen: remember how he spake unto you when he was yet in Galilee, Saying, The Son of man must be delivered into

the hands of sinful men, and be crucified, and the third day rise again. And they remembered his words,

God had given them the revelation that Christ was to be killed and rise again, but it was not a revelation that became a part of their understanding until Christ had risen.

Likewise, we read in Ephesians 3:3-5:

How that by revelation he made known unto me the mystery; (as I wrote afore in few words, Whereby, when ye read, ye may understand my knowledge in the mystery of Christ) Which in other ages was not made known unto the sons of men, as it is now revealed unto his holy apostles and prophets by the Spirit;

God is indicating that a mystery was made known to the Apostle Paul, "That the Gentiles should be fellowheirs, and of the same body, and partakers of his promise in Christ by the gospel" (verse 6). However, this truth was repeatedly written about in the Bible, for example, Abram's name was changed to Abraham because he would be the father of many nations (Genesis 17:5-7).

Many years earlier, Jesus had told the disciples in Matthew 28:19:

Go ye therefore, and teach all nations, baptizing them in the name of the Father, and of the Son, and of the Holy Ghost:

The truth that those whom God would save would include people from all nations of the world is taught in many places in the Bible. But while this truth was included in God's revelation to mankind, only when Saul of Tarsus had become saved was it truly revealed to the minds of the apostles.

This principle of progressive revelation is especially emphasized in Daniel 12:8, 9:

And I heard, but I understood not: then said I, O my Lord, what shall be the end of these things? And he said, Go thy way, Daniel: for the words are closed up and sealed till the time of the end.

In God's revelation, which is the Bible, God has a great many things to say about the end of the world and the details that lead up to the end of the world. But God has a timetable for the giving of understanding of these truths.

> *God has a timetable for the giving of understanding of these truths.*

The true meaning of these end-time statements is not to be revealed to the minds of men until near the time of the end. This is why many devout, God-fearing theologians of the past have endeavored to explain the meaning of Biblical end-time passages, but they have not even come close to the truth. This was not a failure on their part. It was simply not time for God to reveal the meaning of these end-time passages.

Thus, we can expect that in our day, when the signs are showing that we must be close to the end of time, the meaning of a great many Biblical passages should become revealed to the minds of careful, diligent students of the Bible. The very fact that we can find great harmony in our understanding of Biblical passages that heretofore have been very obscure greatly encourages us that God has placed us on the right track. We can expect, therefore, that many passages of the Bible which in earlier times have been somewhat mysterious, can now be understood.

The Bible- the supreme law book

It must also be emphasized that the Bible is a book of law. It is the supreme law book by which God governs all mankind. Even as each political government has written laws by which the rulers govern so, too, God who is King of kings and Lord of lords, has a written law by which He governs. Moreover, rulers of nations are subject to the written law of their land. So, too, God is subject to the written law, the Bible, by which He governs the nations. This principle is set forth in the language of Psalm 138:2:

I will worship toward thy holy temple, and praise thy name for thy lovingkindness and for thy truth: for thou hast magnified thy word above all thy name.

We stand amazed at the idea that the Word of God is above all His Name. But when we understand that the Word of God is a synonym for the law of God we learn that God, too, is subject to all of the laws He has written in the law book, the Bible. When we read the 176 verses of Psalm 119, for example, in each of more than 170 of these verses we find a reference to words such as law, precept, commandment, word, testimony, statute, etc. Each of these words is a synonym for the word "law."

The Bible is a law book that God uses to govern the nations, and it also indicates there will be a trial to discover the guilt or innocence of those whom God governs - the whole human race. We read in II Corinthians 5:10:

For we must all appear before the judgment seat of Christ; that every one may receive the things done in his body, according to that he hath done, whether it be good or bad.

God has declared that this trial is to be at the end of the world. Revelation 20:11, 12 describes this trial:

And I saw a great white throne, and him that sat on it, from whose face the earth and the heaven fled away; and there was found no place for them. And I saw the dead, small and great, stand before God; and the books were opened: and another book was opened, which is the book of life: and the dead were judged out of those things which were written in the books, according to their works.

A trial requires a judge, and throughout the Bible God has repeatedly indicated that God in the person of the Lord Jesus Christ is the Judge. We read, for example in Psalm 9:7, 8:

But the LORD shall endure for ever: he hath prepared his throne for judgment. And he shall judge the world in righteousness, he shall minister judgment to the people in uprightness.

The law of God (the Bible) also reveals the penalty that will be required of those who are found guilty. That penalty is eternal damnation. God warns in II Thessalonians 1:8, 9:

In flaming fire taking vengeance on them that know not God, and that obey not the gospel of our Lord Jesus Christ: Who shall be punished with everlasting destruction from the presence of the Lord, and from the glory of his power;

The fact that essentially the Bible is a book of law is normally not apparent to the reader of the Bible. This is because God declares His laws in the context of history, in the context of examples of peoples and nations that disobeyed His laws and suffered the consequence of their sins. God's laws are frequently hidden because God sometimes spoke utilizing metaphors and parables. But in the measure we begin to understand these obscure passages, we always find that the basic truth being brought is the law of God.

An integral part of God's law book is that He declares His purpose and plans to publish the teachings of His law book to all the world. Moreover, a most important part of God's law are the laws that govern God's salvation plan - a plan that is required to maintain the integrity of God's law.

Because God is subject to the laws set forth in the Bible, He cannot have a people for Himself eternally unless their sins (their violations of the law of God) have been adjudicated (these individuals have stood for trial) and the penalty demanded by the law (eternal damnation) has been paid. Therefore, when God the Father gave to Christ those whom He had elected to salvation (John 6:37) it meant that Christ must somehow first satisfy the requirements of the law of God as it applied to these individuals. That is, the penalty for the sins of these elect individuals had to be paid before they could be forgiven so they could eternally be with Christ

This is why Jesus had to become sin for them, be brought to trial as their stand-in, as their substitute, on their behalf. This is what the cross is all about. There Christ was found guilty because all of the sins of the elect were laid on Him. It was at that time God poured out His wrath on Him on behalf of those He came to save. Because God is under the same law that mankind is under He had to suffer sufficiently so that His suffering would be perfectly equal to each of these elect persons spending an eternity in Hell. Only because He was God as well as man could God so intensify the punishment on Him that is was equal to a perfect satisfaction of the law's demands.

Once we have learned this tremendously important principle that the Bible is God's Supreme Law Book we should tremble as we read it. God, in the Bible, is constantly declaring the laws by which we are to live. Violation will absolutely bring about the penalty of eternal damnation. Therefore as we read in the Bible God's laws that govern the church age, that relate the end of the local church age and the bringing in of the final harvest, we should carefully study God's law book, the Bible, to know God's Will. It cannot be emphasized too strongly the seriousness of disobeying God's laws as they are set forth in this divine lawbook, the Bible.

Because God Himself is subject to the laws of the Bible, He must bring to completion the punishments He has decreed that are to be experienced by any human - even church leaders and local congregations that transgress His laws.

Chapter 1.
What is going on?

We see churches falling away from the truth of the Bible

Everywhere we look, we see that the churches are increasingly falling away from the truth of the Bible and following their own wisdom. They are departing from the rules of the Bible and developing their own rules. Also, we see that there are very few in the churches who are concerned about the faithfulness of their church or of their own doctrines. There may be concern that "those liberal churches" are unfaithful to God or that this "cult" is bad. However, when it comes to individuals looking at their own doctrinal positions or the positions of their church, we do not see much of this. In many churches, effectively, the confessions are the highest authority. The confessions have been around so long the church leaders will not change them. Any new idea is tested against the confessions rather than the Bible. If the idea does not square with what the church believes or the confessions, it is rejected.

A few believers in a church may get nervous and speak with their pastor or an elder, but their suggestions do not have much impact. In fact, these people will probably find that their church continues to depart further in doctrine and practice from the truths of the Bible.

If we honestly examine our own church or the churches in general, we find many areas in which the truths of the Bible have been set aside. If we made the same examination 50 or 100 years ago, we would have to conclude that most of the churches then were much more faithful. Here are a sampling of areas in which the churches have departed from the Bible. A careful examination could add many more items to this list.

(a) **Divorce and remarriage.** The Bible clearly commands that the husband is bound to his wife until death (I Corinthians 7:39, Romans 7:1-3). Therefore, there is not to be divorce and remarriage. Passages like Matthew 5:32 and 19:9 are being used to teach that divorce and remarriage are permissible. However, a careful study of the Bible shows that this is not the case. The church traditionally has correctly understood this, but in the last 50 years, this rule has been completely set aside, so that the divorce rate is as high in the churches as in the secular world. Virtually every denomination has made provision for divorce, and the result of this has been great damage upon society. There are broken homes, mixed-up children, single parents, etc.

However, no denomination is dealing with the root problem, namely, how can we stop the divorce plague and return to the sanctity of marriage? The solution is to go back to the Biblical rules of no divorce and remarriage, but we do not see this happening. (For more information about the Biblical rules for marriage, please contact Family Radio and ask for the booklet, "What God Hath Joined Together")

(b) **Sunday Sabbath.** God has established Sunday as the New Testament Sabbath day. It is the Lord's Day, a day to be used entirely for the things of the Lord. It is a day for worship, evangelizing, training our children in the things of the Lord, Bible study, visiting those who need encouragement, etc. The churches have historically kept this day exclusively for the Lord's things. They may not have fully understood the Sunday Sabbath, and confused it with the seventh-day Sabbath of the Old Testament, but nevertheless, it was kept pretty much according to the Bible. However, in the past 50 years, this day has been turned into a day of pleasure, a day for our pleasure, and not for God's pleasure. God warned about this in Isaiah 58:13-14. Virtually every church has departed from God in this area. (For a detailed explanation of the Bible verses that explain the Sunday Sabbath, please contact Family Radio and request the booklet, "Sunday: The Sabbath")

(c) **Gospels of signs and wonders.** In the past 50 years, the churches that feature "tongues" as described in I Corinthians 12, 13, and 14 have increased enormously, to the point that almost every denomination has been impacted. Tongues are frequently a part of those churches that are the fastest growing in our day, and it is very difficult to find pastors who will say definitively that this is not from God. Tongues are a world-wide phenomenon, showing up in the fastest growing churches worldwide.

In addition to tongues, many of these churches also feature other kinds of miracles, including the miracle called "falling down backward." However, God completed His divine revelation when He completed the last chapter of the last book of the Bible. In Revelation 22:18-19, God indicates that there is not to be any addition or removal from this "book." The "book" in view can only be the Bible (Revelation 22:9-10, Hebrews 10:7). Therefore, once the Bible was completed in approximately A.D. 95, that ended all divine revelation. This means that the phenomenon of speaking in tongues in the church at Corinth would have ended. With it would have ended the other signs and wonders that occurred during Bible days. However, mankind by nature is not satisfied with a gospel of just trusting the Bible, he seeks something more, something such as a miraculous message from God. God will not accommodate this desire, but Satan, as he is taking his seat (rulership) in the corporate body, will provide supernatural messages (II Corinthians 11:13-14, II Thessalonians 2:1-4). God warns that one of the signs that we are near the end is the appearance of these false christs coming with gospels of signs and wonders (Matthew 24:24). We will cover this subject in much more detail later on this study.

(d) **Rulership and the place of women in the church.** Women's place in the church is another example of the decision by the church to change God's law to suit man's ideas. There is tremendous pressure to accept women in the pulpit and women who rule and have authority in the church. This is absolutely contrary to the law of God (I Corinthians 14:34, I Timothy 2:12). Also, God has given strict rules regarding the leadership in the church (I Timothy 3). Not only must the leaders be men, but they must be married with children, giving evidence that they can rule their own home. Also, many other qualifications are given for these rulers. Therefore, most men do not qualify for leadership, and yet churches today are appointing single men and married men without children. The churches have chosen to go their own way and to disregard God's law.

(e) **Music.** For hundreds of years, the church has been blessed by Godly Christian music, in which both the words and the music were God glorifying. The words of the music expressed important spiritual principles. These words helped encourage believers in the truths of the Bible. As believers would think about these words, they would be built up in the Word of God. However, today it is different. There is much less substance to the words today. Often times anthems are sung that just repeat short phrases. These phrases tend to be very shallow in spiritual content. Also, the sound is patterned after the music of the world. Very often worldly music is chosen, such as rock-and-roll, and the words are just changed to words from the Bible. One has difficulty telling the music of the world from the contemporary Christian music since it is difficult to understand the words. The Christian music has effectively just become the music of the world because you cannot tell the two apart.

However, the Bible indicates that music is associated with worship and should reflect the holy nature of God. In both the Old Testament and the New Testament, the word "worship" identifies with bowing down. That is, when we worship God, we are bowing down before God, we are acknowledging His rulership over us. We are showing that we should be trembling before God because He is holy God. This is the proper setting for the music of the church. Christian music should reflect the holy nature of God. It should be music that reflects the idea of "bowing down" before God, the idea that God is His eternal majesty who is to be feared and held in awe. The music of the church through the ages has generally reflected this in both its words and sounds. However, today the music of the church is closely patterned after that of the world.

(f) **Salvation is by grace alone.** The law of God has been changed in that it is widely taught that salvation is not altogether dependent on God's grace alone. It is taught that God has provided for the salvation of every individual in the human race and that salvation thus depends upon man to be the decision maker. Of his own free will, some say, man can accept or reject salvation. Thus, salvation would ultimately be a joining of Christ's work on the cross and man's work in accepting Christ - both would have contributed to the individual's salvation.

This perverse teaching disregards all kinds of laws of the Bible. No recognition is given to the Bible's teaching that man is spiritually dead and has no desire to seek God (Ephesians 2:1-5, Romans 3:10-11). It denies the truth that Christ went to the cross to save *His* people from their sins (Matthew 1:21), and the rest of the world must stand at Judgment Day and give an account of their sins (II Corinthians 5:10). This teaching fails to face statements such as Revelation 17:8, which teaches that only some people have their names written in the book of life from the foundation of the world.

Moreover the Bible tells us to believe on the Lord Jesus Christ, that is, we are to trust Him for all that He has done for our salvation, and that includes the fact that from the foundation of the world, God chose those whom He would save, and therefore has obligated Himself to save those whom He has chosen (Ephesians 1:4-10).

Those, however, who believe that man has a free will effectively are indicating that they do not trust Christ to save them in His time and in His manner. They want a salvation in which they, themselves, are the guarantor, that is, they can become saved any time they wish by simply reaching out and accepting Christ. In this way, they do not have to wait for God to act. Thus, effectively, they do not trust God at all. But if they do not trust Christ who is eternal God then they are not saved, for they do not believe on Him. The result of God saving us is that we believe on Him, that our will has been broken, and we trust everything in the Bible that God has declared concerning salvation.

To some degree, the pernicious teaching of free will has plagued the church throughout New Testament history, but in our day it has invaded almost every congregation. Thus, these congregations no longer have God's salvation plan. The salvation they offer is designed by men and will save no one from the wrath of God. What a terrible situation the church has come into. (For further information, please contact Family Radio and request the book, "Baptism: The Washing Away of Our Sins" or the book "God's Magnificent Salvation Plan.")

(g) **Today's gospel - a social gospel.** All people have three aspirations: 1) political freedom, 2) economic security, and 3) freedom from disease. All of mankind desires these blessings, and pastors and teachers increasingly incorporate these desires into their gospels. The social gospel, which has great concern for the physically hungry, is becoming the number one priority. Preachers say that the Christian ethic demands that all men have political freedom. It is believed that the church must do all it can to provide medicine and doctors to the world, and it is also believed that the church can expect God to provide good health (even miraculous healings), to those who claim the name of Jesus.

These aspirations have nothing to do with the Gospel of the Bible. This is proven by the parable of the rich man and Lazarus (Luke 16). The rich man with all his money could buy many, many freedoms that were denied others. He could afford the finest doctors and medicines. Certainly he had economic security.

Lazarus, on the other hand, was a beggar. He had sores that were licked by dogs. He had no economic security, and he had poor health. His political freedom was of no consequence. Which of these two men most badly needed the Gospel? According to today's social gospel, it is obvious that Lazarus had the greater need, but did he? Both the rich man and Lazarus equally need the Gospel. God strips the curtain of eternity aside and the rich man is seen in hell and Lazarus is in Abraham's bosom, a figure which signifies heaven. The beggar, Lazarus, had everything in this life because he was saved. The rich man had nothing because he was unsaved. Surely this teaches that the social-political gospel has nothing to do with the Gospel of salvation.

The Gospel is concerned with the spiritual needs of mankind.

The Gospel is concerned with the spiritual needs of mankind. Only within the congregation does the Gospel concern itself with physical needs.

Many doctrines and practices that are prevalent today present evidence that the church has rewritten the laws of the Bible. Indeed, congregations are being encouraged to follow a salvation program different from that which is found in the Bible.

(h) **Preaching the full counsel of God: hell and damnation.** One frightening thing is that there is so little preaching about hell and damnation, but hell is that from which we are saved. All kinds of salvation messages are being presented with the general theme of God's love, the idea being that it would be salutary and wise to become identified with the Lord Jesus Christ. These messages imply that by accepting Him, things are going to go well and life will have purpose and meaning.

How can anyone become saved if he does not know what he is being saved from? How can he know what he is saved from unless it is thoroughly discussed and diligently taught that because of sins he is under the wrath of God. He is subject to eternal damnation. He ought to be taught from what he needs to be saved from.

One can rightly fear eternal damnation only if the Bible's disclosures of the awful nature of hell are taught. God did not place multitudinous Biblical references to the awfulness and certainty of His wrath just to fill up space. These warnings are to be read, taught, discussed, and should instill fear in mankind. If these passages are neglected, it is not the whole counsel of God (Acts 20:26-27). It will be man's gospel and not the true Gospel.

These are just a few of the areas in which churches have fallen away from the truths of the Bible. If anyone takes a close examination of their own church, they will see other areas in which their church has departed from the Bible.

Does the Bible speak about this Falling Away?

We have seen some of the areas in which the churches of today have departed from the Bible. There are many more items that could be added to this list. We are seeing that the Bible is no longer the final authority. When a concerned church member comes with a verse that disagrees with something that his church teaches and asks his pastor or elder about the verse, the response is not encouraging. We would expect that pastors and elders would tremble before the Word of God if they discovered that they are holding a doctrine contrary to the Bible. But, generally, we do not find this.

So, the question is: Does the Bible speak about this falling away? Does the Bible predict what we are seeing today? The answer is Yes! The Bible definitely speaks about this falling away. The Bible definitely predicts that this falling away would come. As we will see in this study, Matthew 24 as well as many other passages are definitely discussing this time. We read in verses 21 and 24 of Matthew 24:

> **For then shall be great tribulation, such as was not since the beginning of the world to this time, no, nor ever shall be.**

> **For there shall arise false Christs, and false prophets, and shall shew great signs and wonders; insomuch that, if *it were* possible, they shall deceive the very elect.**

Verse 21 tells us of a future time of great tribulation. It is a tribulation that is so great that there has never been such a tribulation in the history of the world. Then verse 24 tells us the character of this tribulation. It is a spiritual tribulation that plagues the churches. Notice that false christs are arising. Since Christ has worked in the churches, these false christs, of whom Satan is the chief, will work in the church. That is why they are called false christs. These false christs are coming with all of their false doctrines, which is what we see in the churches today.

Notice the signpost that God gives us. Namely, they come with signs and wonders. As mentioned above, gospels of signs and wonders, including tongues, are prevalent in the church today, like no other time in history. This is a big evidence. As we continue in this study, we will learn much more about these gospels of signs and wonders.

God also indicates that there will come a time in history in which Satan will be victorious over the body of believers. We read in Revelation 13:7:

> **And it was given unto him to make war with the saints, and to overcome them: and power was given him over all kindreds, and tongues, and nations.**

The saints are those in the churches and congregations. It was given to Satan to make war with the corporate body and to overcome it. Notice that it was "given unto him." God has given him this victory. We read in Revelation 9:1-3:

> **And the fifth angel sounded, and I saw a star fall from heaven unto the earth: and to him was given the key of the bottomless pit. And**

he opened the bottomless pit; and there arose a smoke out of the pit, as the smoke of a great furnace; and the sun and the air were darkened by reason of the smoke of the pit. And there came out of the smoke locusts upon the earth: and unto them was given power, as the scorpions of the earth have power.

The "star" here is a reference to the Lord Jesus Christ, He is the only one with the key to the bottomless pit. The bottomless pit is a reference to hell. Christ is the one that loosed Satan to come against the church. This explains what we read in II Thessalonians 2:1-4, which tells us that the man of sin (Satan) will take his seat in the temple. From I Corinthians 3, we know that the temple is a reference to the corporate body, the churches and congregations, and the man of sin is Satan, and finally to take ones "seat" is to rule. We will go into more details on these verses later in this study.

The Old Testament Book of Daniel also speaks of this time. We know this because God has directed us to look back into the Book of Daniel in Matthew 24:15. We read in Daniel 7:21 and 25:

I beheld, and the same horn made war with the saints, and prevailed against them;

And he shall speak *great* words against the most High, and shall wear out the saints of the most High, and think to change times and laws: and they shall be given into his hand until a time and times and the dividing of time.

Verse 21 is very similar to Revelation 13:7. Satan is the "little horn" who will make war with the churches and will prevail. The changing of "times and laws" refers to Satan working in the churches to change the rules of the Bible. This identifies exactly with what we have seen. In the short listing above, we can see many areas in which the churches have changed the laws of the Bible to suit their own desires.

> *God has not only allowed the churches to fall away,*
> *but has appointed Satan as the ruler of the churches.*

Therefore, we can see from this short sampling of verses that the Bible does speak of this time, and that it is a dreadful time, because God has not only allowed the churches to fall away, but has appointed Satan as the ruler of the churches. We must remember that to "sit" or to take one's "seat" means to rule.

Therefore, we can see that the Bible is not silent about the falling away that we see today. The Bible actually has a whole lot to say about what is happening today. As we proceed in this study, we will see that the "Great Tribulation" that we are experiencing today is very well documented in the Bible. There are many more passages that describe the time in which we are living.

What is God's Response to the Churches Falling Away?

We have seen that the churches and congregations have departed from the truths of the Bible, and that there appears to be little or no fear of God in the hearts of church leaders today. As we have compared what churches do and teach versus the Bible, we see the flippant disregard for the laws of God. We have also seen that the Bible is not silent about this time, but rather that God has declared that this time would come, and that it would be a dreadful time. We have seen these two important points, and now we are faced with the next logical question: What is God's response to this open rebellion? Is God just going to sit idle while all of this is occurring? Has God simply written about this so that the believers are not in shock when this happens? Is God going to allow all of this without any response?

We will find that the Bible answers these questions with a definite NO! Let us look briefly at a few passages to get an introduction to this topic. First, we read in I Peter 4:17-18:

> **For the time *is come* that judgment must begin at the house of God: and if *it* first *begin* at us, what shall the end *be* of them that obey not the gospel of God? And if the righteous scarcely be saved, where shall the ungodly and the sinner appear?**

Just as God will examine all of the unsaved of the whole world on the last day, as we read in Revelation 20:11-15 and in other passages, God is insisting in I Peter 4:17 that His judgment begins in His own house, in His churches and congregations. Now, just as in the final judgment on the last day when God will show no mercy, we will see in this study that there is no mercy in God's judgment upon the church. This is truly a dreadful situation; it is a situation of such magnitude that God speaks about it in many parts of the Bible. For example, God speaks about this same judgment in Jeremiah

25. In Jeremiah 25, God expands the explanation of I Peter 4:17. We read in Jeremiah 25:15-26:

> **For thus saith the LORD God of Israel unto me; Take the wine cup of this fury at my hand, and cause all the nations, to whom I send thee, to drink it. And they shall drink, and be moved, and be mad, because of the sword that I will send among them. Then took I the cup at the LORD'S hand, and made all the nations to drink, unto whom the LORD had sent me: *To wit*, Jerusalem, and the cities of Judah, and the kings thereof, and the princes thereof, to make them a desolation, an astonishment, an hissing, and a curse; as *it is* this day; Pharaoh king of Egypt, and his servants, and his princes, and all his people; And all the mingled people, and all the kings of the land of Uz, and all the kings of the land of the Philistines, and Ashkelon, and Azzah, and Ekron, and the remnant of Ashdod, Edom, and Moab, and the children of Ammon, And all the kings of Tyrus, and all the kings of Zidon, and the kings of the isles which *are* beyond the sea, Dedan, and Tema, and Buz, and all *that are* in the utmost corners, And all the kings of Arabia, and all the kings of the mingled people that dwell in the desert, And all the kings of Zimri, and all the kings of Elam, and all the kings of the Medes, And all the kings of the north, far and near, one with another, and all the kingdoms of the world, which *are* upon the face of the earth: and the king of Sheshach shall drink after them.**

If we examine this language carefully, we see that it must be talking about Judgment Day. Notice how God emphasizes judgment upon all of the nations of the world. He lists many known nations at that time and then transitions to speaking about all of the nations that are "**upon the face of the earth.**" This can only be the final judgment, Judgment Day at the last day. Notice also where this judgment begins. It begins at Jerusalem and Judah. This parallels I Peter 4:17. Also, look at verses 28 and 29:

> **And it shall be, if they refuse to take the cup at thine hand to drink, then shalt thou say unto them, Thus saith the LORD of hosts; Ye shall certainly drink. For, lo, I begin to bring evil on the city which is called by my name, and should ye be utterly unpunished? Ye shall not be unpunished: for I will call for a sword upon all the inhabitants of the earth, saith the LORD of hosts.**

Notice God's response if the peoples of the world complain that judgment has come for them. God declares that those in the world who have had no connection with the churches of God will be judged because God has first begun with His own house. God is insisting that He is not a respecter of persons. His judgment upon the unsaved in the churches is no less severe than those outside. We see the exact parallel between Jeremiah 25 and I Peter 4:17-18. Judgment begins first with the corporate body, the people of God, the churches and congregations, then it transitions to the whole world. No one will be able to complain that God is unfair because He began with His own people.

So, God is using two parallel passages to indicate that when the final judgment comes, it begins with the churches and congregation. They are the visible House of God that we can see in the world today.

Therefore, God is teaching in these two passages that He is not silent in all of this falling away. Rather, God's judgment has already begun, and it has begun in the churches. We will see this more as we proceed in this study. God's response is that the time has come for judgment to begin at the house of God.

As further evidence that God is not silent, we can examine how God has dealt with His people in the past. We can see God's patience with national Israel in the Book of Judges. We see God's continued patience in I and II Samuel and I and II Kings. This is really parallel to God's patience with the New Testament churches and congregations. As we study Revelation 2 and 3, we can see that most of these seven churches were already in trouble with God, indicating that even back to the beginning of the New Testament era, there were problems in the churches. However, God persisted with the New Testament churches for over 1900 years, just like He did with Israel. However, there came a time that judgment fell upon Israel for their increasing wickedness. For the ten northern tribes, it came in 709 B.C. and for the two southern tribes, known as Judah, it came in 587 B.C.

We read in Hebrews 13:8:

Jesus Christ the same yesterday, and to day, and for ever.

So, we know that as Jesus Christ dealt with His people in the Old Testament, we can expect the same thing for His people, the churches and congregations, in the New Testament. Therefore, we have further Biblical evidence that the judgment of God has come upon the church.

One thing we want to note is that when God judged His corporate body in the past, it was a complete judgment. He completely destroyed Israel, the ten northern tribes in 709 B.C. Then, in 587 B.C., He completely destroyed

Jerusalem and the temple. We can therefore expect a similar complete destruction of the corporate body again.

As we continue in this study, we will see abundant Biblical evidence that the churches are under the judgment of God.

What Does God Expect from the Believers?

We are beginning to see that the churches and congregations are under the judgment of God. This explains why we see the falling away that we do, and why pastors, elders, and church officers are not really concerned about being altogether faithful to the Word of God. This is why when an individual in the congregation gets nervous about how his church is departing from the Bible and speaks to his pastor, he is pretty much ignored or rebuffed.

Now, we must face the question: Given all of this falling away and given that the time of God's judgment has begun for the churches, what is God's expected response from the believer? Does He expect anything from me? Should I continue to attend my church as I have always done? Is God only directing His judgment upon the "liberal" churches? Surely my church is still under the blessing of God and my pastor is still preaching from the Bible, so I should not have to worry too much about these things.

Actually, God has a lot to say to the believer today, and He has a big expectation of the believer. However, in order to understand God's command for the believer today, we are going to back up and study God's whole plan of salvation throughout time. We are going to see that what is happening today is not an isolated situation, but rather that it fits neatly into God's plan of "times and seasons." Let's continue our study now by looking at God's salvation plan throughout the history of the world.

Chapter 2.
Times and Seasons

This world has existed now for 13,000 years. As we shall clearly see in this study, we, by God's divine providence, have come very near to the end of the world's existence. Because we are so near the end, many truths of the Bible, which God had sealed, are now being revealed. This is particularly true of those things that are an integral part of the end-time revelation. We might recall that God prophesied in Daniel 12:9:

And he said, Go thy way, Daniel: for the words *are* closed up and sealed till the time of the end.

Thus, we can expect that many passages of the Bible, which heretofore, have been somewhat mysterious, can now be understood.

For example, in Acts 1:7, the disciples ask Jesus if the time has come for Him to restore the kingdom to Israel. We can speculate that they had the same notion that appeared to be popular in that day amongst the Jews. That is, they expected that when the Messiah would come, He would reign as a king in Jerusalem and free them from Roman rule (see John 6:15).

We have been taught by the Bible that the kingdom of God is a spiritual kingdom. It will only be completed when all of the elect have become saved. We see this implied in Jesus' answer to them in Acts 1:7, 8:

And he said unto them, It is not for you to know the times or the seasons, which the Father hath put in his own power. But ye shall receive power, after that the Holy Ghost is come upon you: and ye shall be witnesses unto me both in Jerusalem, and in all Judaea, and in Samaria, and unto the uttermost part of the earth.

Effectively, Jesus is telling the disciples that it is not for them to know the details of God's program to evangelize the world. Their task was to get busy proclaiming the Gospel to the world, and of course, all believers who followed them were to witness to the whole world the commands of the Gospel to believe on the Lord Jesus Christ.

> *The proclamation of God's salvation plan is in some mysterious way divided into times and seasons.*

However, as Jesus answered them, He made a very mysterious statement. **"It is not for you to know the times or the seasons."** Jesus, in this statement, is telling us that the proclamation of God's salvation plan is in some mysterious way divided into times and seasons. Again in I Thessalonians 5:1, we read of times and seasons. I Thessalonians 5:1, 2 records:

> **But of the times and the seasons, brethren, ye have no need that I write unto you. For yourselves know perfectly that the day of the Lord so cometh as a thief in the night.**

What can this mean? We, of course, must find our answer in the Bible. One clue that helps us to understand this statement is James 5:7:

> **Be patient therefore, brethren, unto the coming of the Lord. Behold, the husbandman waiteth for the precious fruit of the earth, and hath long patience for it, until he receive the early and latter rain.**

The ultimate husbandman in view here is God Himself. In James 5:7, God is emphasizing that there is an early rain and a latter rain. In Deuteronomy 32:2, God explains that rain is a picture of the Gospel coming from heaven. There we read:

> **My doctrine shall drop as the rain, my speech shall distil as the dew, as the small rain upon the tender herb, and as the showers upon the grass:**

Thus, we can know, based on James 5:7, that there are at least two seasons that identify with bringing of the Gospel to the world.

Three Distinct Seasons of Rain

As we continue to examine the Bible carefully seeking information concerning the early and latter rain, we find a beautiful outline of God's entire worldwide program of sending forth the Gospel. It is set forth in Joel 2:23 and is further developed in other places in the Bible. Joel 2:23 declares:

> **Be glad then, ye children of Zion, and rejoice in the LORD your God: for he hath given you the former rain moderately, and he will**

**cause to come down for you the rain, the former rain, and the latter
rain in the first month.**

The Hebrew word translated "moderately" is more accurately
translated "righteously." Secondly, the verb "hath given" should be more
properly translated "gives." Thirdly, the final phrase "the latter rain in the
first month" is more accurately translated "after the first." Thus, the verse
should read:

**Be glad then, ye children of Zion, and rejoice in the LORD your
God: for he gives you the former rain "righteously" and he will
cause to come down for you the rain, the former rain, and the latter
rain after the first.**

In this verse we read about three rains. The first is described as former
or early. Following this first early rain there is additional rain that is divided
into early and latter rain. Both the second early rain and the latter rain are
rain that comes after the first early righteous rain.

Thus far, we have learned that there are three seasons: an early
righteous rain of bringing the Gospel, an early rain after this first rain, and
a latter rain after the first. The purpose of spiritual rain is to bring forth a
spiritual harvest. This is indicated by Joel 2:24-26, which declares:

**And the floors shall be full of wheat, and the fats shall overflow with
wine and oil. And I will restore to you the years that the locust hath
eaten, the cankerworm, and the caterpiller, and the palmerworm,
my great army which I sent among you. And ye shall eat in plenty,
and be satisfied, and praise the name of the LORD your God, that
hath dealt wondrously with you: and my people shall never be
ashamed.**

Three Rains Bring Three Harvests

Continuing to examine the Bible for information that might relate to
harvests being brought forth, we find that God speaks of three harvests. We
shall discover that these three harvests can be identified with the three
seasons of rain described in Joel 2:23.

In Leviticus 23:10, 11 the Bible indicates:

Speak unto the children of Israel, and say unto them, When ye be

come into the land which I give unto you, and shall reap the harvest thereof, then ye shall bring a sheaf of the firstfruits [*Hebrew "reshith"*] of your harvest unto the priest: And he shall wave the sheaf before the LORD, to be accepted for you: on the morrow after the sabbath the priest shall wave it.

These verses speak of a time of harvest when the firstfruits are brought to the priest and waved before the Lord. These firstfruits are distinguished from the firstfruits that would be brought in after 50 days at Pentecost by calling them by the Hebrew word *reshith*. Later, we will learn that the firstfruits that were brought in at Pentecost were called by the Hebrew word *bikkur*. The time this (*reshith*, firstfruits) harvest was to take place was when Israel first came into the land of Canaan. It was a harvest that they did not plant. It was produce that was already there when they came into the land of Canaan. In Joshua 4:19 we read that Israel crossed the Jordan River into the land of Canaan on the tenth day of the first month and kept the Passover feast four days later on the fourteenth day of the month (Joshua 5:10). It would have been at that time, therefore, that this first harvest took place. This harvest was also called "the first [*reshith*] of the firstfruits [*bikkur*]" (Exodus 23:19) That is, it was a harvest of firstfruits that anticipated the Pentecostal harvest of firstfruits (*bikkur*) that came 50 days later. Leviticus 23:15-17 speaks of this Pentecostal harvest:

And ye shall count unto you from the morrow after the sabbath, from the day that ye brought the sheaf of the wave offering; seven sabbaths shall be complete: Even unto the morrow after the seventh sabbath shall ye number fifty days; and ye shall offer a new meat offering unto the LORD. Ye shall bring out of your habitations two wave loaves of two tenth deals: they shall be of fine flour; they shall be baken with leaven; they are the firstfruits unto the LORD.

These verses are speaking of Pentecost, which came 50 days after the Passover. Pentecost is also spoken as the feast of harvest, the firstfruits (*bikkur*) of thy labors (Exodus 23:16). Please note the Hebrew word firstfruits concerning the Pentecostal harvest is a different word from the Hebrew word "firstfruits" used in Leviticus 23:10, 11, which describes the earliest harvest that was identified with the Passover.

A third harvest is also spoken of and it is called the feast of ingathering, which was at the end of the year (Exodus 23:16). This feast was also called the feast of tabernacles and was observed at the time of the final harvest. This harvest was never described as firstfruits. The Bible simply describes it as a feast of ingathering at the end of the year.

These three harvests were so important that God declared in Deuteronomy 16:16:

> **Three times in a year shall all thy males appear before the LORD thy God in the place which he shall choose; in the feast of unleavened bread, and in the feast of weeks, and in the feast of tabernacles: and they shall not appear before the LORD empty:**

The feast of unleavened bread began with the Passover when "the first [*reshith*] of the first fruits [*bikkur*]" were brought into "the house of the Lord thy God."

We must remember that harvest is a consequence of rain. We can see the beautiful parallel that exists between the rain of Joel 2:23 and these three harvests.

Christ, the First Harvest Coming from the Early Righteous Rain

First there will be the early rain called the righteous rain in Joel 2:23. This first early righteous rain must be identified with the Gospel as God ministered it in national Israel, beginning with Abraham and ending with Christ being announced as the Lamb of God. The harvest that resulted from this first early righteous rain was the Lord Jesus Himself. When John the Baptist announced "behold the Lamb of God that taketh away the sins of the world" he was announcing that the Passover Lamb had come. The first of the firstfruits had arrived.

> *The announcement that Jesus the Passover Lamb was here effectively declared that the first early righteous rain had done its work.*

The announcement that Jesus the Passover Lamb was here effectively declared that the first early righteous rain had done its work. It had brought the Lord Jesus into the world as the Passover Lamb. He was the harvest that must come before the early and latter rain that would follow could come. It is Jesus who is the firstfruits that we read about in I Corinthians 15:23:

But every man in his own order: Christ the firstfruits; afterward they that are Christ's at his coming.

He was typified by the *reshith* firstfruits of the Old Testament. He is also the firstfruits that we read about in Romans 8:23:

And not only they, but ourselves also, which have the firstfruits of the Spirit, even we ourselves groan within ourselves, waiting for the adoption, to wit, the redemption of our body.

Thus, the Passover was identified with this first early righteous rain because Christ is our Passover. He, therefore, is the first of the firstfruits.

The Church Age -- The Pentecostal Harvest Coming from the Early Rain

This early harvest when the first (*reshith*) of the firstfruits, Christ Himself, has been brought in is followed by the second harvest. It too, is called a harvest of firstfruits (*bikkur*). But as we learned, in the Old Testament, a different Hebrew word was used for the first of the firstfruits that identified with Christ as the Passover from the firstfruits identified with the Pentecost.

This second harvest, in which the firstfruits identified with the Pentecost is brought in, is pointing to the entire New Testament church age. It began with the Pentecost in A.D. 33 when about 3,000 individuals became saved in one afternoon. It was a product of the early rain that came after the first early righteous rain that had brought Christ as the Passover Lamb. This Pentecostal rain of the Gospel in the entire world continued for more than 1900 years. It produced churches and congregations all over the world as external evidence of the existence of the kingdom of God. All of those who became saved as these churches preached the Gospel were the firstfruits. In fact, in James 1:18 the believers are called firstfruits. There, God declares:

Of his own will begat he us with the word of truth, that we should be a kind of firstfruits of his creatures.

James 1:18 speaks of the believers as a kind of firstfruits. There were two kinds of firstfruits, the first of the firstfruits and the Pentecostal firstfruits. The church age was not the first (*reshith*) of the firstfruits (*bikkur*). The churches were the Pentecostal firstfruits (*bikkur*).

In Revelation 14 God speaks of the 144,000, which we will learn later in our study identify with all those who have been saved during the church age. There too, in verse 4, they are called the firstfruits. Revelation 14:4 declares:

These are they which were not defiled with women; for they are virgins. These are they which follow the Lamb whithersoever he goeth. These were redeemed from among men, being the firstfruits unto God and to the Lamb.

We thus have seen two distinct seasons of the Gospel.

SEASON	DESCRIPTION	HARVEST
1. The Old Testament era of national Israel.	First early righteous rain.	Harvest is Jesus who is announced as Passover Lamb. He is first of firstfruits.
2. The church age beginning with Pentecost A.D. 33.	Early rain.	Harvest is all of those who are saved during church age. They are called firstfruits.

These two seasons were in view when Jesus told the disciples in Acts 1:7:

And he said unto them, It is not for you to know the times or the seasons, which the Father hath put in his own power.

The Season of the Latter Rain

But there is still another season that must be considered. It identifies with the term "latter rain." The early Pentecostal rain, which identifies with the Pentecostal firstfruits that came into the kingdom of Christ during the church age, is followed by the latter rain.

> *This latter rain identifies beautifully*
> *with the harvest of ingathering*

This latter rain identifies beautifully with the harvest of ingathering, which is brought in at the end of the year. In Exodus 23:14-16, we read:

> **Three times thou shalt keep a feast unto me in the year. Thou shalt keep the feast of unleavened bread: (thou shalt eat unleavened bread seven days, as I commanded thee, in the time appointed of the month Abib; for in it thou camest out from Egypt: and none shall appear before me empty:) And the feast of harvest, the firstfruits of thy labours, which thou hast sown in the field: and the feast of ingathering, which is in the end of the year, when thou hast gathered in thy labours out of the field.**

These verses speak of the feast of ingathering in the end of the year. The word "firstfruits" is never used in connection with this feast or harvest of ingathering because this feast celebrates the final completion of the harvest. It, therefore, must identify with the final gathering in of the believers. The final gathering in or harvesting of the believers must identify with the latter rain. Later we will learn that this latter rain identifies with the great multitude which no man can number that becomes saved during the Great Tribulation period (Revelation 7:9-14).

We thus have now learned that there are three seasons which God has in view of Acts 1:7.

SEASON	DESCRIPTION	HARVEST
1. The Old Testament era of national Israel.	First early righteous rain	Harvest is Jesus who is announced as Passover Lamb. He is first of firstfruits.
2. The church age beginning with Pentecost A.D. 33.	Early rain	Harvest is all of those who are saved during church age. They are called firstfruits.
3. A great multitude coming in after church age.	Latter rain	Harvest is those who are saved during Great Tribulation period.

As we study the three rains set forth in Joel 2:23, we discover a very interesting and significant truth. Between each of the seasons of rain there is a brief time of intense spiritual famine. It is not a famine of the failure of the true Word of God being preached. It is a famine of hearing the Word of God.

The Famine of Elijah's Day

This spiritual famine of hearing the Word of God was typified by a physical famine in Elijah's day. We might recall that in I Kings 17:1 we read:

> **And Elijah the Tishbite, who was of the inhabitants of Gilead, said unto Ahab, As the LORD God of Israel liveth, before whom I stand, there shall not be dew nor rain these years, but according to my word.**

This famine occurred in Israel when the wicked man Ahab who was married to the exceedingly wicked Jezebel was reigning over Israel. According to James 5:17, 18, we learn that this famine continued for three years and six months. There we read:

> **Elias was a man subject to like passions as we are, and he prayed earnestly that it might not rain: and it rained not on the earth by the space of three years and six months. And he prayed again, and the heaven gave rain, and the earth brought forth her fruit.**

According to Deuteronomy 11:13-17, the withholding of rain so that there is spiritual famine is a result of great wickedness. We read:

> **And it shall come to pass, if ye shall hearken diligently unto my commandments which I command you this day, to love the LORD your God, and to serve him with all your heart and with all your soul, That I will give you the rain of your land in his due season, the first rain and the latter rain, that thou mayest gather in thy corn, and thy wine, and thine oil. And I will send grass in thy fields for thy cattle, that thou mayest eat and be full. Take heed to yourselves, that your heart be not deceived, and ye turn aside, and serve other gods, and worship them; And then the LORD'S wrath be kindled against you, and he shut up the heaven, that there be no rain, and that the land yield not her fruit; and lest ye perish quickly from off**

the good land which the LORD giveth you.

In the situation that existed in Elijah's day, the famine of rain ended after Elijah called down fire from heaven, which consumed the bullock on the altar and the altar itself. Following this event and the killing of the 450 prophets of Baal, the famine came to an end as a great rain began to fall.

This dramatic event occurred on Mount Carmel when Elijah challenged the 450 prophets of Baal to call down fire from heaven. Fire from heaven is a picture of God bringing judgment. The 450 prophets of Baal, who were emissaries of Satan, could not bring judgment; only God could do that. The bullock was a picture of Christ who came under the judgment of God for our sins. This event was actually a representation of what would happen when Christ went to the cross. Christ, represented by the bullock and the altar, came under the wrath of God because He had been laden with all the sins of those He came to save. The 450 prophets of Baal were killed by Elijah (I Kings 18:40), typifying the fact that Satan was vanquished by the death and resurrection of Christ. It was at the cross that judgment came on Satan. The three and a half years of famine, which preceded this dramatic even on Mount Carmel, typifies the three and a half years during which Jesus preached. Later, we will examine this Mount Carmel event in greater detail.

The Famine of Jesus' Day

Significantly, we will learn later in our study that during the time Jesus preached, hardly anyone became saved. There was a grievous spiritual famine of hearing the Word of God. Later, we will learn that the period of time from the announcing of Jesus as the Lamb of God until He was crucified was three years and six months. Thus, it was a spiritual famine that was parallel to the physical famine of Elijah's day.

We have learned that the early righteous rain continued until Jesus was announced as the Passover Lamb. We also learned that a few weeks after the cross the spiritual famine dramatically ended as the spiritual rain began to fall as indicated by about 3,000 individuals becoming saved at Pentecost. Indeed, the prophecy of Deuteronomy 11 was fulfilled. The spiritual apostasy that existed at the time Jesus came resulted in a period of an intense famine of hearing the Word of God. This was followed by the early rain season that identifies with the church age. This early rain Pentecostal church age season would continue for over 1900 years until the beginning of the Great Tribulation.

The Famine Beginning with the Great Tribulation

The beginning of the Great Tribulation signaled another time of spiritual famine. This time of spiritual famine is also identified with a time of three and a half years. But whereas the physical famine of Elijah's day and the spiritual famine of Jesus' day were a literal three and a half years, the spiritual famine that began at the beginning of the Great Tribulation was symbolically three and a half years. We might remember that this time continues for 42 months as indicated by the language of Revelation 11:2:

> **But the court which is without the temple leave out, and measure it not; for it is given unto the Gentiles: and the holy city shall they tread under foot forty and two months.**

In Revelation 11:9 and 11, it is spoken of as three and a half days:

> **And they of the people and kindreds and tongues and nations shall see their dead bodies three days and an half, and shall not suffer their dead bodies to be put in graves. . . .**

> **And after three days and an half the Spirit of life from God entered into them, and they stood upon their feet; and great fear fell upon them which saw them.**

Later we will learn that three and a half days may be understood as three and half years because the Bible in a number of places used a day for a year. In all likelihood, it is the literal period 2300 evening mornings spoken of in Daniel 8.

This time of spiritual famine is followed by the latter rain which completes the Great Tribulation time and which is immediately followed by the time of the return of Christ at the end of the world.

In Acts 1:7, Jesus spoke of times and seasons in connection with His Gospel program. We are now beginning to understand these times and seasons.

1. Season of righteous early rain – Old Testament period beginning with Abraham and ending with the announcement of Jesus as the lamb of God.

2. Time of spiritual famine – three and a half years during Jesus' ministry.

3. Season of early rain – Church age which continues more than 1950

years beginning with the resurrection in A.D. 33 and ending at the beginning of the Great Tribulation.

4. Time of spiritual famine – First part (half hour) of Great Tribulation (three and a half days or forty two months)

5. Season of latter rain – Last part of Great Tribulation when a great multitude, which no man can number, is being saved.

6. Time of judgment, at end of world when Christ returns.

We will examine this truth as we continue our study. We will discover that the Bible approaches the question of God's three season salvation program from the vantage point of a vineyard which God planted.

One Vineyard - Two Caretakers

The principle that God has divided His program of evangelizing the world into seasons and times is demonstrated and taught in many ways in the Bible. In this study we will become acquainted with a number of these. Presently, we will examine God's use of the figure of a vineyard in illustrating the division of God's Gospel program into seasons.

We find in the Bible numerous references to a vineyard. However, two parables featuring a vineyard stand out. One is related in Matthew 21 and the other in Isaiah 5. We will examine these two parables looking at their similarities and their differences. We will learn that the vineyard described in Matthew 21 is speaking about the kingdom of God as it was externally represented by the nation of Israel. They were God's special people but the relationship ended when they crucified the Lord Jesus. Likewise, we will learn that Isaiah 5 is using the same vineyard as that of Matthew 21. But in Isaiah 5 it is speaking about the kingdom of God as it was represented by the local congregations throughout the church age. The church age became dramatically in evidence on the day of Pentecost when about 3,000 were saved (Acts 2).

That a vineyard represents people is clearly seen by verses such as the following.

John 15:1   **I am the true vine, and my Father is the husbandman.**

Isaiah 5:7   **For the vineyard of the Lord of hosts is the house of Israel, and the men of Judah his pleasant plant: and he looked for judgment, but behold oppression; for righteousness, but behold a cry.**

Matthew 21:45   **And when the chief priests and Pharisees had heard his parables, they perceived that he spake of them.**

Not only do these verses identify the vineyard with people, but it is representing a special people who are to be identified with Christ Himself.

Both Matthew 21 and Isaiah 5 are
speaking of the same vineyard

Fact is, we will learn that both Matthew 21 and Isaiah 5 are speaking of the same vineyard but of its existence in two different periods of time. Both vineyards are established and owned by Christ.

Isaiah 5:1   **Now will I sing to my well beloved a song of my beloved touching his vineyard. My well beloved hath a vineyard in a very fruitful hill:**

Matthew 21:33   **Hear another parable: There was a certain householder, which planted a vineyard, and hedged it round about, and digged a winepress in it, and built a tower, and let it out to husbandmen, and went into a far country.**

Both have God's protection and care.

Isaiah 5:2   **And he fenced it, and gathered out the stones thereof, and planted it with the choicest vine, and built a tower in the midst of it, and also made a winepress therein: and he looked that it should bring forth grapes, and it brought forth wild grapes.**

Matthew 21:33   **... and hedged it round about, and digged a winepress in it, and built a tower...**

Both have caretakers or husbandmen who are given responsibility to bring forth a harvest. They must answer to the owner of the vineyard.

Isaiah 5:7   **... he looked for judgment but behold oppression ...**

Matthew 21:33   **... and let it out to husbandmen, that they might receive the fruits of it.**

In both vineyards the caretakers fail their responsibility.

Matthew 21:34 and 35 declare:

And when the time of the fruit drew near, he sent his servants to the husbandmen, that they might receive the fruits of it. And the husbandmen took his servants, and beat one, and killed another, and stoned another.

Isaiah 5:2 declares:

... and he looked that it should bring forth grapes, and it brought forth wild grapes.

But there is a dramatic difference in the reaction of the owner of the vineyard (God Himself) to the failures of the caretakers of the vineyard. In Matthew 21 the vineyard is not harmed or damaged by God. It is simply given to another group of husbandmen. Matthew 21:41 records:

They say unto him, He will miserably destroy those wicked men, and will let out his vineyard unto other husbandmen, which shall render him the fruits in their seasons.

On the other hand, the vineyard of Isaiah 5 is utterly and ruthlessly destroyed by its owner (God Himself). Isaiah 5:5, 6 declares:

And now go to; I will tell you what I will do to my vineyard: I will take away the hedge thereof, and it shall be eaten up; and break

down the wall thereof, and it shall be trodden down: And I will lay
it waste: it shall not be pruned, nor digged; but there shall come up
briers and thorns: I will also command the clouds that they rain no
rain upon it.

This is the language of total and complete destruction. It means that God
is forever finished with this vineyard. But why did God deal so ruthlessly with
this vineyard?

Why did God destroy the vineyard of Isaiah 5 and not the vineyard of
Matthew 21? We must remember the purpose of the vineyard is to produce
fruit. The vineyard of Isaiah 5, instead of producing good fruit, produces wild
grapes. The Hebrew word translated in this passage as wild grapes is a word
that is translated elsewhere as "stink" (See Isaiah 34:3 and Joel 2:20).
Therefore, the vineyard produced a stench, something altogether evil. It,
therefore, was completely destroyed by its owner.

On the other hand, in Matthew 21 God made no comment concerning a
failed fruit production. He only refers to the treatment the husbandmen gave
to the owner of the vineyard. We read in Matthew 21:37-39:

But last of all he sent unto them his son, saying, They will reverence
my son. But when the husbandmen saw the son, they said among
themselves, This is the heir; come, let us kill him, and let us seize on
his inheritance. And they caught him, and cast him out of the
vineyard, and slew him.

Because of their terrible conduct in finally killing the owner's son, the
vineyard is taken from them and given to other husbandmen.

Spiritually, we can immediately see that the husbandmen who killed the
owner's son can only refer to the nation of Israel who wanted Jesus to be
crucified. Even though they were used of God, they as a nation did not want
the Gospel.

Remember John 1:11 declares:

He [*Jesus*] came unto his own, and his own received him not.

The Jews to whom Jesus was speaking in Matthew 21 understood very
clearly that Jesus was speaking about them. Matthew 21:45 states:

And when the chief priests and Pharisees had heard his parables,
they perceived that he spake of them.

The Fruits of the Vineyard

But why did God not destroy the vineyard of Matthew 21. The answer should be clear. The vineyard that was the nation of Israel which represented the kingdom of God during the Old Testament did produce the good fruits that God intended it to produce. Those fruits were Christ Himself and the Gospel that flows from Him. It was necessary that the Jews kill the owner of the vineyard. Had Jesus Christ not been killed there would be no salvation, no Gospel, no Savior, and therefore, no fruits from the vineyard.

> *The fruit of the vineyard was Christ Himself*
> *together with the Gospel.*

The fruit of the vineyard was Christ Himself together with the Gospel. By bringing forth its intended harvest of Christ and the Gospel, the vineyard had served its purpose. Therefore, once Christ was killed, the vineyard which represented the kingdom of God was transferred from the Jewish nation to the New Testament church age. The temple, the synagogues, the Old Testament ceremonial laws, the high priest, and the other priests all ceased to function in any sense as representing the kingdom of God. The kingdom of God was transferred to the church age with its pastors, elders, deacons, and the New Testament ceremonial laws of water baptism and the Lord's Supper. The New Testament churches were now appointed to be the caretakers of the kingdom of God. They also were given the mandate to bring the Gospel to the whole world.

Thus, the vineyard of Isaiah 5 is the very same vineyard as that of Matthew 21. The difference is that the caretakers of the vineyard had dramatically shifted from the nation of Israel with its temple and the synagogues to the New Testament church age.

Unfortunately, the new caretakers of the vineyard already from their beginning began to bring forth some fruit that was not good fruit but instead that which would be a stink in God's nostrils. Even though the church age was still in its infancy, God warned the church in Ephesus He would remove their candlestick if they did not return to their first love (Revelation 2:5). And for example, the church in Sardis had already become a dead church with only a few believers within it (Revelation 3:5).

We may safely equate the stinking fruit of the church age with the high places of Old Testament Israel. We will learn in this study that these high places of the Old Testament were the worship of heathen gods alongside the worship of Jehovah God. We will learn in this study that the holding and teaching of false doctrines that are not faithful to the Bible are the spiritual high places of the church age. These have been evident in churches throughout the church age but have been accelerated in our day as we will discover in this study.

They, to use the language of Isaiah 5,
are a stench.

These high places, teachings from the mind of men rather than from God, are not good fruit from the vineyard. They, to use the language of Isaiah 5, are a stench. It is indeed remarkable that for more than 1950 years, God put up with this stinking fruit. It is a testimony to the patience and mercy of God that He allowed this situation to exist for so long a period of time.

However, there is an end to God's patience. Isaiah 5:5, 6 describes the end of the vineyard. God Himself destroys it. As we are learning and will continue to learn in this study, God uses Satan to assist in the destruction of all the churches that are in existence at the end of the church age.

No Longer an Earthly Organization

Significantly, at the end of the church age, God does not assign the care taking of the vineyard to another corporate external representation of the kingdom of God. There is a major shift in God's divine economy from the use of institutions like old Testament Israel or the churches and congregations of the New Testament. True, the kingdom of God continues to flourish but it is no longer under the care or responsibility of an earthly organization. This is indeed a major change in God's method of evangelizing the world. After destroying the vineyard of Isaiah 5, God does not plant another vineyard. God no longer uses an organized body of believers under the supervision of God-ordained priests, or pastors, or elders, or deacons. During the season of the latter rain that follows the destruction of the vineyard described in Isaiah 5, the task of sending the Gospel into the world is assigned to individual believers. God, utilizing individual believers, is finishing the task of evangelizing the world.

For the first 9500 years of the history of the world, God did not utilize any divine institutions like Israel or the local congregations to represent the kingdom of God in the world. The largest institution that existed was the family. But then for about 3500 years God used an earthly institution to corporately represent the kingdom of God. From the time Israel came out of Egypt in 1447 B.C. until Pentecost of A.D. 33, it was the nation of Israel. Then at Pentecost in A.D. 33, God shifted the representation of the kingdom of God from the nation of Israel to another God-ordained institution the local churches that existed throughout the church age.

During the time of God's use of the nation of Israel God developed a legal entity with priests and a temple and synagogues. During the time of God's usage of the church age He developed a divine God ordained entity which was the local church. It, too, by God's commands had church overseers such as elders and deacons and pastors and teachers.

However, with the end of the church age the vineyard was totally destroyed. Never again would God use an earthly institution to externally represent the kingdom of God. During the final season, during which time the final harvest of believers would be brought in, God would only use individual believers.

Assembling Together of Ourselves

This agrees with the statement of Hebrews 10:25 where God commands that as Judgment Day approaches, we are not to neglect the assembling of ourselves together. The word "ourselves" surprises us. During the church age, we would expect to see the word "church" or "congregation" rather than the word "ourselves." However, during the latter rain, God does not use an earthly organization as He had used national Israel in the Old Testament or as He used the local congregations throughout the church age. He uses individual believers.

It is true that believers can come together in an organization such as Family Radio to facilitate the sending forth of the Gospel into the world. But Family Radio has no membership. It has no spiritual rule over those who support it. It has no Biblical standing as a God-ordained organization. Because we know that it is God who works in the believer to will and to do of His good pleasure, we know that only God can raise up an organization like Family Radio. We must give God all the glory for whatever successes it may have as it sends the Gospel into all the world. But it must be simply looked at as a convenient vehicle by which individual believers can be used of God to accomplish the task of evangelizing the world during the season of the latter rain. By bringing together the resources of a number of believers, radio stations and other means can be owned and operated to assist with the task of evangelization. This can be done on a scale that would be impossible for a single believer to do.

The truth that during the later rain season the Gospel mandate is strictly carried out by individual believers therefore agrees with the statement of Hebrews 10:25 where God commands that as Judgment Day approaches, we are not to neglect the assembling of ourselves together. However during the latter rain season God does not use an earthly organization such as national Israel which He used during the Old Testament or such as the local churches which He used throughout the church age. The vineyard which God had planted and which externally represented the Kingdom of God which was first under the care of national Israel and then under the care of the churches has ceased to exist.

More than One Season

It should be noted that in Matthew 21:41 the Bible records:

They say unto him, He will miserably destroy those wicked men, and will let out his vineyard unto other husbandmen, which shall render him the fruits in their seasons.

The fact that the word "seasons" is plural tells us that God is anticipating more than one season which would come after the vineyard was taken from the nation of Israel. We have already learned that the first season that would follow was the church age season during which the harvest of the Pentecostal firstfruits was brought in. After that season was finished, the true believers, who are typified by the two witnesses of Revelation 11, are driven out and/or are commanded to come out of the churches. To use the language of Revelation 11, they are killed.

The two witnesses of Revelation 11:11 had been killed. By the language of John 16:2 we can understand that to be killed is equivalent to being driven out of the churches. John 16:2 records:

They shall put you out of the synagogues: yea, the time cometh, that whosoever killeth you will think that he doeth God service.

However, there is one more season. It is the season of the latter rain during which the final harvest is brought in. This final season which brings forth fruit is typified by the two witnesses as they stand on their feet as the Holy Spirit comes upon them. Revelation 11:11 records:

And after three days and an half the Spirit of life from God entered into them, and they stood upon their feet; and great fear fell upon them which saw them.

This language parallels that which we find in Ezekiel. In Ezekiel 2, Ezekiel is commanded to bring God's Word to Israel.

We read in Ezekiel 2:1, 2, and 4:

And he said unto me, Son of man, stand upon thy feet, and I will speak unto thee. And the spirit entered into me when he spake unto me, and set me upon my feet, that I heard him that spake unto me. ... For they are impudent children and stiffhearted. I do send thee unto them; and thou shalt say unto them, Thus saith the Lord GOD.

It is parallel language to that which documents God's command to Saul of Tarsus who became the Apostle Paul. We read in Acts 26:16:

But rise, and stand upon thy feet: for I have appeared unto thee for this purpose, to make thee a minister and a witness both of these things which thou hast seen, and of those things in the which I will appear unto thee;

Thus, we can be sure that when the two witnesses are commanded to stand on their feet as the Spirit enters into them, it refers to the true believers who have been driven our of the churches. However, they continue to be used by God to bring the Gospel.

Fear of God Comes upon those who Spiritually Hear the Gospel

Revelation 11:11 also indicates that great fear came upon them that beheld them. This must be speaking of those who became saved. They are the ones who truly fear God because they have become saved. They are the ones who see that the two witnesses are bringing the Gospel.

Thus, we know that these two witnesses represent the true believers who are driven out of the churches or in obedience to God's command come out of the churches. As individuals without membership in an earthly spiritual organization like ancient Israel or a local congregation, without titles such as priest, pastor, elder, or deacon, they send out the Gospel into the world during the final season of the latter rain. Of course, each one who becomes saved during the latter rain season also becomes an ambassador of Christ to assist in sending forth the Gospel during the latter rain season.

Thus, we have learned that God planted a vineyard and placed it under the care of Old Testament Israel. Their era ended when the harvest which consisted of the Lord Jesus Christ Himself together with the Gospel was produced. Following this God took the vineyard, the external corporate representation of the kingdom of God away from national Israel. The era of the temple in Jerusalem, the synagogues and the ceremonial law activities of the Old Testament came to an end.

God then transferred the vineyard, the corporate external representation of the kingdom of God, to another body. That body was the New Testament churches that expanded into all the world.

However, finally, because of the stench, the evil, the high places, the wrong doctrines that constantly were a weakness throughout the church age, God destroyed His vineyard. That is, He has brought judgment upon all of the churches throughout the world. We will learn much more about this sad fact as we continue this study.

However, it was not a part of God's divine economy to replace the institution of the church age with another visible external institution representing the kingdom of God. Once the vineyard God had planted was completely destroyed, we do not read anywhere in the Bible that God would plant another vineyard.

Instead, He completes the evangelization of the world utilizing individual believers without the help of a God-ordained external body. This, we are learning, is God's methodology of completing His work of bringing in the full number of the elect. God speaks of this final harvest of believers as the season of the latter rain.

Significantly, the opening verses of Revelation 20 also relate to the subject of the latter rain. We shall now examine these verses.

The Little Season

The opening verses of Revelation 20 have intrigued and fascinated believers throughout the time of the church age. Now that we are very near the end of time, God is opening up the understanding of true believers so that we can know what God is teaching in these verses.

When we look carefully at the first seven verses, we will find that God makes reference to the church age as the time when Satan is bound. And He makes reference to the latter rain by calling it a little season. The terms church age and latter rain are not found in these verses, however, when we carefully examine these verses we will find that these terms are definitely in view.

In these verses, three times we find the phrase "a thousand years" being used with the information that it is a period of time that has a fulfilment or comes to an end. On the other hand, the term a thousand years is used twice with no indication that it has an end. Let us study these verses to see why this is so and at the same time discover the church age and the latter rain hidden within these verses.

Revelation 20 opens with the verses 1 to 3, which declare:

And I saw an angel come down from heaven, having the key of the bottomless pit and a great chain in his hand. And he laid hold on the dragon, that old serpent, which is the Devil, and Satan, and bound him a thousand years, And cast him into the bottomless pit, and shut him up, and set a seal upon him, that he should deceive the nations no more, till the thousand years should be fulfilled: and after that he must be loosed a little season.

Immediately we must ask, when was Satan cast into, or when will Satan be cast into, a bottomless pit so that he could not deceive the nations for a thousand years?

We know that the Greek word *abussos* which is translated "bottomless pit" in Revelation 20, and as "deep" in Luke 8:31 and Romans 10:7, is a reference to hell. Romans 10:7 declares:

Or, Who shall descend into the deep? (that is, to bring up Christ again from the dead.)

In this verse the word "deep" (Greek *abussos*), is equated with Christ's death. We know that Christ's death means He suffered the penalty of eternal damnation (hell) on behalf of those He came to save. Therefore, we can know that Satan was cast into hell.

But is there other information in the Bible that refers to a past or future time when Satan would be cast into hell? Let us search the Bible.

In fact, there are no references that can be found in the Bible concerning a <u>future</u> time when Satan will be cast into hell and following that, he will be loosed from hell. But there are two passages that clearly show that before the Bible was completed, Satan had been cast into hell. The first of these is found in II Peter 2:4, where God declares:

For if God spared not the angels that sinned, but cast them down to

hell, and delivered them into chains of darkness, to be reserved unto judgment;

This verse is in the past tense, as are the next two verses of II Peter 2, which speak of the historic judgment of God by the flood of Noah's day and the judgment of Sodom and Gomorrah, which were destroyed in Abraham's day.

The second verse is Jude 1:6 where God reports:

And the angels which kept not their first estate, but left their own habitation, he hath reserved in everlasting chains under darkness unto the judgment of the great day.

This judgment is also in the past tense. It, too, is in the setting of two other historic judgments. The first is recorded in Jude verse 5 and speaks of God's judgment on Israel when they died in the wilderness rather than entering into the land of Canaan. The second is Jude verse 7 which again records the historic judgment that came on Sodom and Gomorrah.

These verses of II Peter 2 and Jude are recording judgments that were already accomplished at the time Peter and Jude were writing. Even as the judgments on Sodom and Gomorrah and on the world in Noah's day were past history at the time this was being written, so, too, it appears that the judgment on the angels was past history at the time this was written. Therefore, we suspect that the judgment on the angels must have somehow occurred when Jesus went to the cross. But how can that be. Don't we read in I Peter 5:8 that the devil goes about as a roaring lion. And doesn't Ephesians 6 speak of our adversary, the devil?

The answer to these questions can be known if we understand what hell is. We must learn what hell is by searching the Bible. In Ephesians 4:8, 9 we read:

Wherefore he saith, When he ascended up on high, he led captivity captive, and gave gifts unto men. (Now that he ascended, what is it but that he also descended first into the lower parts of the earth?

The phrase "lower parts of the earth," like the phrase "heart of the earth" of Matthew 12:40, surely refers to hell. Thus, Ephesians 4:8, 9 can only mean that Christ went into hell (that is, He experienced the wrath of God), to deliver those who were in hell (those who were under the wrath of God). No one today can be in a literal place called hell. This is true because no one has yet been tried at the judgment throne of God. At the time the unsaved are judged at the judgment throne of God, hell will be a literal place because this universe will have become new heavens and new earth. The new heavens and new earth will be a wonderful place where no one can be under the wrath of God. Therefore, we can understand that the first three verses of Revelations 20 are teaching that at the time of the cross, Satan was put under the wrath of God (the bottomless pit which is a synonym for hell). This was also the time that he was cast out of heaven. During the Old Testament, he had access into heaven as we read in the first chapter of Job. But Revelation 12 records his expulsion from heaven. There we read that he was defeated by the blood of the Lamb. We read in Revelation 12:9 and 11:

> **And the great dragon was cast out, that old serpent, called the Devil, and Satan, which deceiveth the whole world: he was cast out into the earth, and his angels were cast out with him. . . . And they overcame him by the blood of the Lamb, and by the word of their testimony; and they loved not their lives unto the death.**

Returning to Revelation 20:1-3, we read that Satan was cast into the bottomless pit (hell) so that he could no longer deceive the nations.

Satan Can No Longer Deceive the Nations

What does it mean that the devil could no longer deceive the nations? We have learned that during the time Jesus preached the Gospel, very few people became saved. At the same time, Satan was very active. Is there a connection between few people being saved and a very active Satan? The passage of Luke 8, verses 11 and 12 helps us. There we read:

> **Now the parable is this: The seed is the word of God. Those by the way side are they that hear; then cometh the devil, and taketh away the word out of their hearts, lest they should believe and be saved.**

From these verses we learn that the prime method that Satan uses to assault Christ is to stop the growth of the kingdom of God. The devil is a liar and the father of lies. Mankind is fair game for his wiles as God declares in Romans 3:4, **"let God be true, but every man a liar."**

But something wonderful happened seven weeks after Christ went to the cross. On the day of Pentecost, Peter preached one sermon and about 3,000 individuals became saved. In one day, 3,000 came out from under the tyranny and deception of Satan. Satan had been bound so that he could not deceive the nations any longer. And ever since, throughout the church age, all over the world people have been coming into the kingdom of God.

Thus, we can be sure that the binding of Satan had to have happened at the time of the cross. No wonder then that we see the parallel between, on the one hand, the language of II Peter 2:4 and Jude 6, and on the other hand, the language of Revelation 20:1-3.

However, that means that the words "a thousand years" must be understood metaphorically rather than literally. In this study we will learn that Satan was loosed at the beginning of the Great Tribulation. And that was almost 2,000 years after the cross.

Thus, in this context the term "thousand years" must be understood spiritually as saying the "completeness of time." The completeness of time for the church age began with the binding of Satan at the time of the cross and continued for over 1950 years.

Satan Is Loosed

This period of time ended with Satan being loosed. The loosing of Satan coincided with the beginning of the Great Tribulation. True, while Satan was bound he was able to intimidate, to threaten, to kill believers. Throughout this period he had been able to go about as a roaring lion. But he could not stop the forward advance of the kingdom of God. Even though he killed Christians, he was not the winner. Verse 4 of Revelation 20 declares:

And I saw thrones, and they sat upon them, and judgment was given unto them: and I saw the souls of them that were beheaded for the witness of Jesus, and for the word of God, and which had not worshipped the beast, neither his image, neither had received his mark upon their foreheads, or in their hands; and they lived and reigned with Christ a thousand years.

Those who were martyred simply changed residency. As disembodied souls, they reigned with Christ a thousand years. Please note the language carefully. **"I saw the souls of them that were beheaded."** It does not say "I saw the souls who had been beheaded." It says I saw the souls of them that were beheaded. This is parallel language to a statement like, "I saw the hand of the man who had been killed." I am seeing only the hand of the man that was killed. Likewise, when Christians leave their bodies, in their soul existence they go to live and reign with Christ in heaven. II Corinthians 5:8 declares:

We are confident, I say, and willing rather to be absent from the body, and to be present with the Lord.

Thus, God in Revelation 20 is showing us a vision in which we see the believers reigning with Christ after they had been killed.

We have learned that the term "a thousand years" in this context signifies the completeness of time. Earlier we noted that three times in Revelation 20 the thousand years have a beginning and an end. Therefore, the phrase a thousand years must identify with the period that began with the binding of Satan when Christ went to the cross and ended with the loosing of Satan at the beginning of the Great Tribulation. Thus, it must encompass the same period of time as that of the New Testament church age. However, the vision of the souls of the disembodied martyrs shows them reigning a thousand years with no ending or completion in view. That can readily be understood if we keep in mind that true believers at the time they became saved were given eternal life. Thus, they begin to reign with Christ the moment they are saved (Ephesians 2:5) and will continue to reign with Him forevermore. In their case, the thousand years cannot have an end because it goes on eternally.

The Rest of the Dead

That brings us to verse 5 of Revelation 20, where we read:

But the rest of the dead lived not again until the thousand years were finished. This is the first resurrection.

Who are the rest of the dead who lived not again until the thousand years are finished. Since the finishing of the thousand years identifies with the loosing of Satan, which identifies with the beginning of the Great Tribulation, we can know that these dead come to life at the end of the church age after the beginning of the Great Tribulation. The term "lived not again" implies that they had previously lived. Could this refer to the unsaved who had previously lived on earth and who will be resurrected to stand for judgment on the last day? The problem with this conclusion is that it does not fit very well into the context (the rest of these verses are speaking of those who are saved). Secondly, ordinarily when the Bible speaks of life or living it is speaking of eternal life or salvation. The unbelievers who are resurrected on the last day are not resurrected to eternal life. They are resurrected so they can experience eternal damnation which the Bible calls the second death. Indeed, verse 5 of Revelation 20 reminds us of the truth we read in I Corinthians 15:22. There God declares:

For as in Adam all die, even so in Christ shall all be made alive.

In Adam, each and every human has become dead in his sins. Spiritually, before we are saved we are dead. But in Christ there is a time when the elect of God do become spiritually alive. They become alive again because before Adam sinned, they were alive. When Adam sinned, they became dead. Since we all came from Adam, in a sense, we were in the loins of Adam when he was on earth.

Returning to Revelation 20:5 we now can understand that after Satan has been loosed, that is, after the thousand years are finished, the rest of those who had died in Adam and were to be made alive in Christ would become alive again. That is, they would become saved during the time of the Great Tribulation.

Now we can understand why Revelation 20:3 states:

... till the thousand years should be fulfilled: and after that he must be loosed a little season.

Outside of the churches, a great multitude is being saved. But within the churches, Satan is reigning because he has been loosed to be used of God to deceive those within the churches.

Thus, the little season must coincide with the season of the latter rain. It is the season when the great multitude which no man can number are being saved (Revelation 1:9-14).

This is why Revelation 20, verse 5, speaks of the first resurrection, and then in verse 6 describes the characteristics of those who have become saved. The first resurrection is experienced at the moment of salvation when we receive our brand new eternal soul. This implies a second resurrection for the believers. That will be on the last day when we receive our eternal resurrected spiritual bodies.

Thus, we have learned that Revelation 20:1-7 can be clearly understood when we realize that God is speaking of the church age as the time when Satan had been bound. Further, He is speaking of the season of the latter rain as a little season during which Satan has been loosed and the rest of those who are to become saved (the great multitude which no man can number), do become saved.

Before we leave Revelation 20 we must ask the question: How can it be that at the time of the cross, Satan was bound and cast into hell and then later on, he is set free, and as we will learn later in this study, he is set free to rule in the churches. Fact is, we read in Revelation 9:1-3:

And the fifth angel sounded, and I saw a star fall from heaven unto the earth: and to him was given the key of the bottomless pit. And he opened the bottomless pit; and there arose a smoke out of the pit, as the smoke of a great furnace; and the sun and the air were darkened by reason of the smoke of the pit. And there came out of the smoke locusts upon the earth: and unto them was given power, as the scorpions of the earth have power.

In this passage, the star who came from heaven to open the bottomless pit can only be Christ. We read in Revelation 1:18:

I am he that liveth, and was dead; and, behold, I am alive for evermore, Amen; and have the keys of hell and of death.

Furthermore, in Revelation 13:3 Satan is typified by a dragon with seven heads and ten horns and we read in verse 3:

And I saw one of his heads as it were wounded to death; and his deadly wound was healed: and all the world wondered after the beast.

We know, of course after the guilty have been judged and sentence is passed, nothing can change that sentence. By Christ's victory over death, as Jesus suffered death for the elect, Satan was given a death blow. He was sentenced to hell forever more. Significantly, when we read of the great white throne, where Jesus sits to judge the unsaved, we do not read of Satan being judged. This is because he was judged and effectively sentenced to hell forevermore by Christ's victory over death at the time of the cross. Therefore, we read in Revelation 20:10-12 of this sequence of events:

And the devil that deceived them was cast into the lake of fire and brimstone, where the beast and the false prophet are, and shall be tormented day and night for ever and ever. And I saw a great white throne, and him that sat on it, from whose face the earth and the

heaven fled away; and there was found no place for them. And I saw the dead, small and great, stand before God; and the books were opened: and another book was opened, which is the book of life: and the dead were judged out of those things which were written in the books, according to their works.

The beast and the false prophets are pictures of Satan as he rules in the churches during the Great Tribulation.

Thus, while on the one hand, Satan remains in hell (that is, remains under the eternal wrath of God), in another sense, he is temporarily loosed from hell because God still has some work for him before the world comes to an end. That work is to rule in the churches during the Great Tribulation. He is allowed to rule there as a judgment of God upon these churches.

The Souls under the Altar

We have learned that the words "little season" as we find them recorded in Revelation 20 identify with the season of the latter rain during which the final harvest is brought in. This term is also used in Revelation 6 in connection with the opening of the fifth seal. There the Bible declares in Revelation 6:9-11:

And when he had opened the fifth seal, I saw under the altar the souls of them that were slain for the word of God, and for the testimony which they held: And they cried with a loud voice, saying, How long, O Lord, holy and true, dost thou not judge and avenge our blood on them that dwell on the earth? And white robes were given unto every one of them; and it was said unto them, that they should rest yet for a little season, until their fellowservants also and their brethren, that should be killed as they were, should be fulfilled.

Now we are able to have a clearer understanding of these verses.

It can be shown that the earlier verses of Revelation 6 are detailing the sending forth of the Gospel during the church age. The rider on the white horse going forth to conquer can only be a picture of Christ sending forth the Gospel throughout the church age. The rider on the red horse who wishes to take peace from the earth can refer only to Satan as he goes about as a roaring lion. By persecution and physical killing, he attempts to frustrate God's Gospel plan.

The rider on the black horse is a warning to the churches that if they do not remain faithful, God will begin to take the Gospel away from them. This parallels the language of Leviticus 26:23-26:

> **And if ye will not be reformed by me by these things, but will walk contrary unto me; Then will I also walk contrary unto you, and will punish you yet seven times for your sins. And I will bring a sword upon you, that shall avenge the quarrel of my covenant: and when ye are gathered together within your cities, I will send the pestilence among you; and ye shall be delivered into the hand of the enemy. And when I have broken the staff of your bread, ten women shall bake your bread in one oven, and they shall deliver you your bread again by weight: and ye shall eat, and not be satisfied.**

It parallels the language of Isaiah 3:1:

> **For, behold, the Lord, the LORD of hosts, doth take away from Jerusalem and from Judah the stay and the staff, the whole stay of bread, and the whole stay of water,**

The rider on the pale horse is a final warning to the churches that judgment will come upon them. It parallels the language of Leviticus 26:27-30:

> **And if ye will not for all this hearken unto me, but walk contrary unto me; Then I will walk contrary unto you also in fury; and I, even I, will chastise you seven times for your sins. And ye shall eat the flesh of your sons, and the flesh of your daughters shall ye eat. And I will destroy your high places, and cut down your images, and cast your carcases upon the carcases of your idols, and my soul shall abhor you.**

Thus, these first four riders are declaring God's intentions for and warnings to the churches during the church age.

1. The Gospel will be victorious.

2. Satan will attempt to restrain the Gospel.

3. If the church is not faithful, the true Gospel will be severely curtailed.

4. Finally, the churches will be destroyed.

Revelation 6:9 then declares:

And when he had opened the fifth seal, I saw under the altar the souls of them that were slain for the word of God, and for the testimony which they held:

The slain in these verses must refer to the believers throughout the church age in the sense of Romans 8:36, where we read:

As it is written, For thy sake we are killed all the day long; we are accounted as sheep for the slaughter.

This identifies with Satan going about as a roaring lion seeking whom he may devour (I Peter 5:8), and with the language of Matthew 10:28, which declares:

And fear not them which kill the body, but are not able to kill the soul: but rather fear him which is able to destroy both soul and body in hell.

The desire of these souls of Revelation 6:10 is that God's perfect justice will be done. They are under the altar. This is a figure of speech that we can understand to mean they have been covered by the blood of Jesus. Therefore, justice has already been accomplished on their behalf because Christ is their Savior. But what about the unsaved who continue in rebellion against Christ. Justice will not be done until they stand before the judgement throne of God on the last day. But the last day cannot come until God's plan of evangelizing the world has been completed. There is still a little season which we have learned is the season of the latter rain when believers will be killed. They will be killed in the same sense as the believers throughout the church age were killed.

Only when the little season, the season of the latter rain, has ended will God bring forth His perfect justice. Then all of the unsaved will stand for trial at God's great white throne. They will be found guilty and cast into eternal damnation.

Thus, we have learned that the words "little season" are used as a synonym for the final harvest season which is also called the latter rain. Both in Revelation 6 and in Revelation 20, God speaks of this little season.

We will now continue our study as we look again at the early rain season of the Old Testament as it brought forth the harvest of Christ and the Gospel.

Chapter 3.
The First Season. Early Righteous Rain

We have learned that in God's program of the Gospel, there are three seasons that God has planned. We should now look with some detail at the first season. It is the season identified with the early righteous rain. It is the season of rain that produced a most significant harvest. That harvest was the Lord Jesus Himself as the Lamb that was to be offered.

The beginning of this season of rain in one sense can go all the way back to the beginning of time. From the moment Adam and Eve fell into sin, the Gospel was available to save. Remember that in the Gospel context, God's use of the word "rain" was to describe the Gospel like rain from heaven to provide spiritual life in the lives of those whom Christ came to save.

> *It was on the Lord Jesus Christ who is the first early harvest. He was the first of the firstfruits.*

In the situation of the early righteous rain, we learned that the focus of the spiritual harvest was not on those who would become saved. Instead, it was on the Lord Jesus Christ who is the first early harvest. He was the first of the firstfruits. He was identified with the Passover that was kept by Israel at the time they first came into the land of Canaan, immediately after they crossed the Jordan River. Remember we read in Leviticus 23:10-11:

Speak unto the children of Israel, and say unto them, When ye be come into the land which I give unto you, and shall reap the harvest thereof, then ye shall bring a sheaf of the firstfruits of your harvest unto the priest: And he shall wave the sheaf before the LORD, to be accepted for you: on the morrow after the sabbath the priest shall wave it.

The harvest that was gathered at that time was called the first of the firstfruits. The first of the firstfruits was the Lord Jesus Christ. Remember we learned that in the New Testament, Christ is called the firstfruits in I Corinthians 15:23 and in Romans 8:23. This harvest also identified with the land of Canaan, which is a representation of the kingdom of God. Because Jesus came as the Passover Lamb, the kingdom of God, typified by Canaan, became a reality. Before Jesus was announced, John the Baptist was preaching that the kingdom of God was at hand (Matthew 3:2). It was at hand because Jesus, the very essence of the kingdom of God, was about to be announced at the Messiah.

The Old Testament — The Season of Early Righteous Rain

The season of the early righteous rain, which ended when Jesus was announced, identifies very closely with the Old Testament. As was already indicated, in one sense this early righteous rain of the Gospel goes to the very beginning of time. All that is reported in the first eleven chapters of Genesis are important events that were already preparing this world for the great and wonderful harvest of the first of the firstfruits, the Lord Jesus.

The creation of the world, the fall of mankind into sin, the multiplication of sin in the world, the saving of Noah and his family from the waters that destroyed the entire world of Noah's day, the confusion of tongues, and the division of the continent in Peleg's day all had their place as God was preparing for the Messiah to come. Even the information giving the life spans of so many individuals was part of the necessary preparations for the bringing forth of Jesus as the harvest. This would help us to understand that Jesus came in the fullness of time.

However, in another sense, the beginning of the early righteous rain began with the circumcision of Abraham in the year 2068 B.C. This marked the official beginning of the nation of Israel from whom Christ came. The occupying of the land of Canaan, the birth of Isaac in Sarah's old age, and the sacrifice of Isaac were all historical events that particularly focused on God's plan of salvation.

These historical events that served as marvelous pictures of God's salvation program multiplied throughout the history of the nation of Israel. Coming out of Egypt under the leadership of Moses, crossing the Red Sea, obtaining the manna from heaven and water from the rock were great and wonderful events that served as indicators pointing to the harvest that was to come. Remember the harvest was the Lord Jesus as the sacrificial lamb.

Moreover, God gave a host of laws that helped to focus the eyes of Israel on the character and work of the coming Messiah. Laws concerning feast days, sabbaths, burnt offerings, blood sacrifices, and all the other ceremonial laws pointed to the coming of the Lord Jesus as the Savior.

Indeed, throughout the season from Abraham to the announcement of Christ by John the Baptist, God not only illustrated the nature of the coming harvest, which was the Lord Jesus, but He also provided by means of Israel a spoken Word concerning this harvest. It was in the setting of Israel's history and by the use of Israelites that the whole Old Testament was given to us. It was from Israel that holy men of old spoke as they were moved by the Holy Spirit. In fact, all the things that are recorded in the Old Testament were necessary ingredients to provide the super wonderful harvest of our Messiah who is the first of the firstfruits.

Some Were Saved throughout Old Testament History

True, there were people who did become saved throughout the first 11,000 years of history and especially during the 2100 year season of the history of Israel beginning with Abraham. Noah found grace in the eyes of the Lord. Enoch the seventh from Adam was saved. Even before him, Abel the second son of Adam was saved.

The Bible gives names of some who were saved during Israel's history. Men like Moses, Aaron, Joshua, Caleb, Samuel, David, Ebedmelech, and the family of the Rechabites are some of those named by God. Some of the women who were saved included Ruth the Moabitess, Rahab, Sarah, Huldah, and the queen of Sheba.

However, there is no evidence of many becoming saved. Fact is, we have the information given to us in Hebrews 3 that Israel perished in the wilderness because of unbelief. The largest number we can find in the Old Testament was the report by God to Elijah that at that time, there were 7,000 who had not bowed the knee to Baal. If we estimate that Israel may have numbered as many as two million people at that time, 7,000 would be only about one-third of one percent of the nation. Surely there may have been other times when even a larger percentage of the nation of Israel was saved, but God does not give us clear language concerning this matter.

The Coming Messiah, the First of the Firstfruits Harvest

Instead, the constant focus of the Old Testament must be understood to be on the coming Messiah. Until He came as the first of the firstfruits, as the very first harvest, there would not be salvation for the world. We must remember that the primary focus of the Gospel is not on the nation of Israel. The primary focus of the Gospel is on the Lord Jesus Christ who would provide salvation for all the elect who are spread throughout the world.

It is also true that substantial portions of the Old Testament focus on the early and latter rain of the New Testament. This can be understood if we remember that Jesus is both Savior and Judge of all the earth. He is the

Judge of all the earth who emptied Himself of His glory to become the suffering servant who would be the first of the firstfruits, the very earliest harvest. But He never ceased being eternal God who is Judge and King of all the earth.

> *The primary focus of the Gospel*
> *is on the Lord Jesus Christ*

Therefore, the Old Testament provides a great amount of information concerning the nature and impact of God's salvation plan. But it also provides a great amount of information concerning God's judgments to come. Since the final judgment begins with God's judgment on the churches and congregations, we can expect and do find much information in the Old Testament concerning the Great Tribulation of our day. As we proceed in this study, we will see this.

This early righteous rain season that produced Christ as the first of the firstfruits harvest was followed by a time of great spiritual famine. That time was the three and a half years during which Jesus ministered in the land of Israel. We will look very carefully at that three and a half year period in the next chapter.

Chapter 4.
Time No. 1. Famine and Judgment During Jesus' Ministry

We learned in Chapter 3 that immediately following the first Gospel season that produced Christ as the first of the firstfruits harvest, there would be three and a half years of spiritual famine. Remember that season was the season of the early righteous rain that would bring in the harvest of the first of the firstfruits, Jesus Christ Himself. That first Gospel season was called by God "early righteous rain" (Joel 2:23). It was the whole Old Testament period, and more particularly, the period that began with Abraham. It ended with the announcing of Jesus as the Lamb of God in the year A.D. 29. That announcement together with the ceremonial washing of Jesus in the Jordan River signaled that the sacrifice was ready and the high priest (also the Lord Jesus) was prepared to offer the sacrifice. But it also signaled that the first of the times that identify with the term "times and seasons" had begun.

One would immediately suppose that now that Christ had been announced, a time of great spiritual awakening would occur. After all, here now was God Himself in the person of the Lord Jesus Christ. Surely, the people would flock to Him as the Savior.

A Time of Great Spiritual Famine of Hearing the Word

Amazingly, the exact opposite occurred. Everywhere in the Gospels that record the activities of Jesus before He returned to heaven, we read of spiritual famine. This sad information begins with John 1:11, where we read:

He came unto his own, and his own received him not.

It continues in Luke 4:16-30. Early on, after He preached in the synagogue of Nazareth where He grew up, the towns people's reaction is recorded in Luke 4:28-29:

And all they in the synagogue, when they heard these things, were filled with wrath, And rose up, and thrust him out of the city, and led him unto the brow of the hill whereon their city was built, that they might cast him down headlong.

It is emphasized in the statement of Jesus in Luke 9:22:

Saying, The Son of man must suffer many things, and be rejected of the elders and chief priests and scribes, and be slain, and be raised the third day.

This sad situation is vividly disclosed to us in the language of Matthew 11:23-24:

And thou, Capernaum, which art exalted unto heaven, shalt be brought down to hell: for if the mighty works, which have been done in thee, had been done in Sodom, it would have remained until this day. But I say unto you, That it shall be more tolerable for the land of Sodom in the day of judgment, than for thee.

Capernaum was a village on the shore of the Sea of Galilee. Jesus spent much time preaching and healing there. But in this revealing passage, He is indicating that the inhabitants of Capernaum were far more rebellious against God than those of Sodom. Remember only Lot and his two daughters escaped God's judgment on Sodom. How sinful and blind the people of Capernaum must have been if they were more blind than the people of Sodom.

We would expect that if anyone was spiritual, it would be amongst the spiritual teachers and priests. Therefore, we are shocked to read of Jesus' assessment of their spiritual condition in the whole chapter of Matthew 23. Almost every verse of the 39 verses of this chapter is an indictment against them. For example, Jesus said in verse 33:

Ye serpents, ye generation of vipers, how can ye escape the damnation of hell?

Serpents are a reference to Satan. This verse echoes the awful judgment of Jesus upon the Jews as He was teaching in the temple. We read in John 8:44:

Ye are of your father the devil, and the lusts of your father ye will do. He was a murderer from the beginning, and abode not in the truth, because there is no truth in him. When he speaketh a lie, he speaketh of his own: for he is a liar, and the father of it.

> *Satan in some sense was ruling*
> *in the temple and synagogues.*

If the Jews in the temple, which would include the religious teachers, are spiritually of their father the devil, it means that Satan in some sense is ruling in the temple and synagogues. And since virtually no one is being saved at this time, it means that the Holy Spirit is not present.

Therefore, the spiritual condition in the temple and synagogues at the time Jesus was ministering is virtually identical to that which we will learn later in this study is the situation in the churches during the Great Tribulation that comes just before the end of the world. No wonder Jesus said in Matthew 23:37-38:

O Jerusalem, Jerusalem, thou that killest the prophets, and stonest them which are sent unto thee, how often would I have gathered thy children together, even as a hen gathereth her chickens under her wings, and ye would not! Behold, your house is left unto you desolate.

Moreover, we read in John 6 that a great multitude followed Him (verse 2). This is when Jesus fed the 5,000 men plus women and children (verse 10), so we can know there was a very large crowd following Him. But when He began to speak about the spiritual implications of a relationship with Him, we read in verses 66 and 67:

From that time many of his disciples went back, and walked no more with him. Then said Jesus unto the twelve, Will ye also go away?

Although these two verses do not specifically say that only the twelve apostles remain, they give the strong impression that not many more than the twelve remained. Basically, all the rest had left.

A Famine of Hearing the Word of God

The reason for this blindness in Israel at the time Jesus ministered is given in Matthew 13:13-15:

Therefore speak I to them in parables: because they seeing see not; and hearing they hear not, neither do they understand. And in them is fulfilled the prophecy of Esaias, which saith, By hearing ye shall hear, and shall not understand; and seeing ye shall see, and shall not perceive: For this people's heart is waxed gross, and their ears are dull of hearing, and their eyes they have closed; lest at any time they should see with their eyes, and hear with their ears, and should understand with their heart, and should be converted, and I should heal them.

The problem was that there was a famine of hearing the Word of God. True, with their physical ears they heard the finest preaching possible. After all, Jesus is God Himself. No one could preach as accurately and wisely as Jesus. Surely, we would expect a great number of believers as a result of people hearing such a perfect preacher. Don't we read in Isaiah 55:11:

So shall my word be that goeth forth out of my mouth: it shall not return unto me void, but it shall accomplish that which I please, and it shall prosper in the thing whereto I sent it.

> *The problem was that there was a*
> *famine of hearing the Word of God.*

The preaching was perfect. The physical hearing was quite adequate. What was wrong? What was the problem? The problem was that there was a famine of hearing the Word of God. God was not giving the hearers spiritual ears to hear the Word of God. They could only receive spiritual ears so that they could hear the Word and become saved if God the Holy Spirit was applying the spoken Word to the hearts of those who were to become saved. When Jesus was preaching, the Holy Spirit was not doing this. Jesus told His disciples in John 14:17:

Even the Spirit of truth; whom the world cannot receive, because it seeth him not, neither knoweth him: but ye know him; for he dwelleth with you, and shall be in you.

Three Requirements for Salvation

We must know that there are three requirements that must be met before someone becomes saved. The first requirement is that Jesus must have paid for the sins of that individual. Since Jesus only paid for the sins of the elect, that individual would necessarily have been chosen by God before the foundation of the world. (For more information, contact Family Radio for the book, "God's Magnificent Salvation Plan".) The second requirement is that a person whom God plans to save must be under the physical hearing of the Word of God. Romans 10:17 discloses:

So then faith cometh by hearing, and hearing by the word of God.

The third requirement is the action of God the Holy Spirit applying that Word to the heart of the one God is saving. The only reason anyone becomes saved is because God applies the Word of God to the heart and life of those He has elected to salvation. In John 14:17, Jesus effectively is instructing us that while Jesus was preaching the perfect Word of God, the Holy Spirit was not in them, that is, He was not in their midst to apply the spoken Word to anyone's heart so they would become saved.

Later, in Acts 2, the Holy Spirit was poured out into the midst of those assembled in Jerusalem on Pentecost day and about 3,000 were saved. The Holy Spirit had come into the midst of these people for the express purpose of applying the spoken Word to the hearts of those present so that many of them would become saved. Thus, we can know that there will always be a famine of hearing the Word of God if the Holy Spirit is not present to apply the Word of God to the lives of those who are to become saved. For God's own purposes during the three and a half years that Christ ministered, the Holy Spirit saved hardly anyone.

True, there was the woman taken in adultery (John 8:1-11) who became saved. There was the man let down through the roof (Luke 5:20) who became saved. And of course, there was the thief on the cross. Possibly, there were a few others, but all of these were exceptions, probably occurring to assist us in understanding salvation. However, the rule was a spiritual famine of hearing the Word of God.

Jesus explained this in somewhat different words in Matthew 13:13-15, which we looked at a bit earlier. God blinded Israel of that day because of the wickedness of their hearts.

We do know that there were people living at this period of time who gave evidence of salvation. The apostles except for Judas were saved. Mary, Martha, Lazarus, and Mary Magdalene were saved. Perhaps the seventy who were sent out two by two were saved. Perhaps all of the 120 in the upper room at Pentecost were saved. Likewise, it is possible that most if not all of the 500 to whom Christ appeared in Galilee after His resurrection (I Corinthians 15:6) were saved. But all of these are very small numbers when compared with the about 3,000 who were saved on Pentecost afternoon. Moreover, it could well be that most of these, if not all of the apostles, the seventy, the 120, the 500, were already saved before Jesus was announced as the Messiah. Remember, the period before the announcement of Jesus was the season of the early righteous rain. Certainly, if Christ said such ugly things about Capernaum, which was most blessed by the presence of Jesus, the rest of the land of Israel at that time was in a total spiritual famine of hearing the Word of God.

The Spiritual Famine Prepared for the Crucifixion of Jesus

The reason for this spiritual famine in the first place is because of the wickedness of Israel of that day. However, there is another major reason why this famine continued throughout the ministry of Jesus. That reason has to do with God's plan of salvation. Jesus had to be rejected by His people because He had to be crucified. We read in Romans 11:12 and 15:

Now if the fall of them be the riches of the world, and the diminishing of them the riches of the Gentiles; how much more their fulness?

For if the casting away of them be the reconciling of the world, what shall the receiving of them be, but life from the dead?

Israel fell in their rebellion against God in that they bound Jesus and had Him crucified. But this was absolutely necessary in order for salvation to be possible for all of God's elect throughout the world. Thus, this time of spiritual famine was a time of judgment. That judgment focused on the Lord Jesus Christ who is the first of the firstfruits harvest of the first season — the early righteous rain. This harvest resulted in Jesus being announced as the Lamb of God. This announcement, that signified that the first season, that of the early righteous rain, had come to an end, was immediately followed by a three and a half year period of spiritual famine during which Jesus was under judgment. He was experiencing the dreadful event of being the sacrificial lamb. Thus, we can know that the first season, the season of the early righteous rain, is followed by a time of judgment. The sacrificial lamb was killed. Christ was rejected by man and finally, He was rejected by God. **"My God, my God, why hast thou forsaken me?"** (Matthew 27:46)

Satan Was Conquered

There was another judgment that identifies with this same time of spiritual famine, and that was the judgment that came upon Satan. Throughout the season of the early righteous rain, Satan was relatively free to bind the hearts of people. He was even allowed to be in heaven and make accusations concerning God's relationship with the believers (Job 1).

Certainly, during Jesus' ministry Satan was particularly arrogant as he tempted Jesus for 40 days in the wilderness and as he entered into Judas so that he could bind Jesus in an effort to kill Him. As we already learned, Satan to a high degree ruled in the temple and the synagogues, as indicated by Jesus' assertion that the Jews in the temple were of their father the devil.

But something happened to Satan when Jesus went to the cross. It was anticipated at the time the seventy returned to Jesus saying, **"Lord, even the devils are subject unto us through thy name"** (Luke 10:17). Jesus replied to them in verses 18 and 19:

And he said unto them, I beheld Satan as lightning fall from heaven. Behold, I give unto you power to tread on serpents and scorpions, and over all the power of the enemy: and nothing shall by any means hurt you.

It is further stated in Revelation 12:7-11:

And there was war in heaven: Michael and his angels fought against the dragon; and the dragon fought and his angels, And prevailed not; neither was their place found any more in heaven. And the great dragon was cast out, that old serpent, called the Devil, and Satan, which deceiveth the whole world: he was cast out into the earth, and his angels were cast out with him. And I heard a loud voice saying in heaven, Now is come salvation, and strength, and the kingdom of our God, and the power of his Christ: for the accuser of our brethren is cast down, which accused them before our God day and night. And they overcame him by the blood of the Lamb, and by the word of their testimony; and they loved not their lives unto the death.

---

*Michael is the Lord Jesus Christ. He defeated
Satan by shedding His blood*

Michael is the Lord Jesus Christ. He defeated Satan by shedding His blood, that is, by giving His life in the atonement experience. By going to the cross, Jesus not only paid for the sins of the elect, He also brought judgment on Satan. Revelation 20:2-3 declares:

And he laid hold on the dragon, that old serpent, which is the Devil, and Satan, and bound him a thousand years, And cast him into the bottomless pit, and shut him up, and set a seal upon him, that he should deceive the nations no more, till the thousand years should be fulfilled: and after that he must be loosed a little season.

Revelation 13:3 informs us that one of the seven heads of the beast (Satan) was wounded to death.

All of this language indicates that at the time of the cross, Satan was sentenced to eternal damnation, and since the time of the cross, he has been and will be under the wrath of God till the end of time. Fact is, at the end of time, Satan will be immediately cast into the lake of fire (Revelation 20:10). No statement is made anywhere in the Bible that Satan will be judged on the last day. This is because effectively, he was judged at the cross. On the other hand, all of mankind who have not become saved will be judged on the last day (Revelation 20:11-15).

Thus, we see that the three and a half year time following the season of early righteous rain was a time of spiritual famine of hearing the Word of God. And it was a time when God brought judgment both on Christ and on Satan.

We might note that when the three and a half year famine of Elijah's day ended, judgment was brought on the sacrifice, which represented Christ, as fire from heaven destroyed it. However, judgment also came upon the 450 prophets of Baal who were a representation of Satan. All of them were killed by Elijah who in that historical parable represents God as the Judge.

Three and a Half Years

This sorry time of Jesus' ministry, during which there was a spiritual famine of hearing the Word of God, can be shown to be a period of three and a half years. In Daniel 9:27, we read:

And he shall confirm the covenant with many for one week: and in the midst of the week he shall cause the sacrifice and the oblation to cease, and for the overspreading of abominations he shall make

it desolate, even until the consummation, and that determined shall be poured upon the desolate.

Christ is the one to confirm the covenant. Officially, He was declared as the Messiah, that is, He has come to confirm the covenant, when John the Baptist baptized Him. In the middle of the week that followed, that is, three and a half years later, sacrifice and offering ceased. Sacrifice and offering ceased when Jesus was crucified. He was the sacrifice to which all previous sacrifices were pointing. Thus, this time that followed the early righteous rain season was precisely three and a half years. The time was identical in length to the three and a half years of famine of Elijah's day. We might recall that it was very near the end of that famine that fire came down from heaven and destroyed the sacrificial bullock and the altar. That event was pointing to the judgment that was to fall on Christ when He was crucified. The parallelism between that event and the time of Jesus' ministry ending with His crucifixion is very exact.

We thus far have learned in our study of the times and seasons that God speaks of in Acts 1:7 and I Thessalonians 5:1, that immediately following the season of the early righteous rain, which produced the harvest of the Lord Jesus Christ Himself, there was a time of judgments. This time was precisely three and a half years in duration and ended with Jesus experiencing the judgment of God as payment for all the sins of those whom He had elected to save. It indeed was a time of a great spiritual famine of hearing the Word of God and it was a time of judgment.

According to the time line indicated by Joel 2:23, God taught us that after the early righteous rain there would follow additional rain, which was divided into early rain and latter rain. It is this season of early rain that we must now examine as we turn to the next chapter of this study.

Chapter 5.
Early Pentecostal Rain: the Church Age

We learned that the three and a half year famine in Elijah's day ended with fire from heaven consuming the sacrifice prepared by Elijah on Mount Carmel. We know that this represented God's judgment on Christ. We also saw, in parallel fashion, judgment falling on the 450 prophets of Baal who represented Satan. But what happened immediately following this dreadful judgment experience? We read in I Kings 18:44-45:

And it came to pass at the seventh time, that he said, Behold, there ariseth a little cloud out of the sea, like a man's hand. And he said, Go up, say unto Ahab, Prepare thy chariot, and get thee down, that the rain stop thee not. And it came to pass in the mean while, that the heaven was black with clouds and wind, and there was a great rain. And Ahab rode, and went to Jezreel.

Likewise, following the resurrection of Christ, there was a great rain. No, it was not physical, literal rain. It was the water, the rain of the Gospel bringing forth an abundance of spiritual fruit. The season of the early Pentecostal rain had begun.

This season was to continue for more than 1950 years, and its purpose was to bring in the entire Pentecostal harvest of the firstfruits.

It began in earnest on the day of Pentecost. During that great and wonderful day, the Holy Spirit was poured out. That is, God the Holy Spirit was in the midst of the congregation, applying the preached Gospel message to the hearts and lives of those who were elected to salvation. The promise of John 14:17 that the Holy Spirit would be in you (that is, in your midst), had come to pass. The consequence was that on that Pentecostal afternoon, about 3,000 were saved.

This consequence of people becoming saved would be in evidence wherever there was any reasonably faithful preaching of the Word. We must define reasonable preaching as that which was not perfect (only Jesus was the perfect preacher), but, as a minimum, it was in the setting of the Bible alone and in its entirety being the Word of God. This situation of people being saved would continue for more than 1950 years and would end only when the work of the churches was finished.

Later, we will see that the work of sending the Gospel into the world was finished during the time of the Great Tribulation.

In the first years of this spiritual season of the early Pentecostal rain, the temple in Jerusalem was still used by the New Testament church. But after a few decades, the Bible no longer speaks of the New Testament church as having any identification with the temple. Fact is, the temple was completely destroyed in A.D. 70. Insofar as the synagogues are concerned, except for the synagogue in Berea (Acts 17:10-12), they would have nothing to do with having Jesus as their Savior.

The Transition from the Synagogues to the Churches

> *The transition from the temple and*
> *the synagogues was very traumatic.*

The transition from the temple and the synagogues was very traumatic. The spiritual leaders were filled with anger at those who left the synagogues to follow Christ. Very quickly their anger caused Stephen to be stoned to death by the temple leaders. Moreover, one of the Pharisees, named Saul of Tarsus who later became the Apostle Paul, brought Christians, who had left the synagogues, to be killed if they would not repent. We read in Acts 8:3-4:

As for Saul, he made havock of the church, entering into every house, and haling men and women committed them to prison. Therefore they that were scattered abroad went every where preaching the word.

The enmity of the synagogue leaders against the New Testament church accomplished two things. First, it caused all the believers in Christ to be driven from the synagogues. Secondly, it drove the fledgling New Testament church away from Jerusalem and into all of Judea and even into countries outside of Israel. This greatly helped the early church to carry out Christ's command to go into all the world with the Gospel. The enmity of the synagogue leaders was so intense that after Saul of Tarsus became saved, they continually tried to kill him.

By this means, God effectively made a complete break between the early righteous rain season, when the spiritual focus was on the temple and the synagogues, and the early Pentecostal season, when the focus was on the churches and congregations which were entirely outside and independent of the synagogues. Never again would true believers be found in the synagogues. Before the Bible was even finished, already seven churches were in full bloom. We read about them in Revelation 2 and Revelation 3. By that time, the church age had been well established.

In preparation for the church age, which we have learned identifies totally with the early Pentecostal rain and its harvest of firstfruits, God wrote the first four books of the New Testament, Matthew, Mark, Luke, and John. These books provided rule after rule for the church age. An outstanding activity that the churches were to be engaged in during the church age was evangelizing the world. In preparation, the twelve apostles as well as the 70 were trained in this activity as they were sent out two by two with the Gospel.

Jesus gave instructions concerning the character and nature of the Sunday Sabbath that was instituted the Sunday morning Jesus arose from the dead. God underscored that all of the Old Testament ceremonial laws were ended by rending in two the great curtain that separated the holy of holies from the holy place. This signaled the fact that the Old Testament ceremonial laws, which all pointed to some aspect of the Gospel, had been completed by Christ who is the very essence of the Gospel.

God Established Rules for the Church Age

As the Bible was being completed, God laid down many rules which were to be observed throughout the church age. There was to be spiritual oversight by elders and deacons. The qualifications of these elders and deacons were very detailed. Rules concerning offerings and congregational worship were set forth. Two new ceremonial laws were introduced into the churches. The first was water baptism and the second was the communion service.

Because the chief task of the church during the church age was the evangelization of the world, much more information was introduced into the Bible as the New Testament was written. This included such important things as describing the nature of salvation, the authority of the Bible and how it is to be interpreted, the believers' relationship to Christ, and Christ's relationship to God the Father and to the Holy Spirit.

> *For the first 1400 years or so of the church age, there was no printing press.*

When we ponder the awesome task of evangelizing the world, which God assigned to the truly saved during the season of the early Pentecostal rain, we can understand at least some of the reasons why God established the churches the way He did. We must remember that at least for the first 1400 years or so of the church age, there was no printing press. Therefore, the only Bibles that were available were handwritten and exceedingly few in number. Most of the people were illiterate. Therefore, God structured the church age in such a way that illiterate people could be served with the Gospel. Qualified men who could teach (that is, they had access to the Scriptures and could read and study them), were appointed as elders, deacons, evangelists, and pastors. They were to be the means by which the written Word of God could be taught to the people of the congregation.

After each congregation was established, qualified men were sent out from that congregation to establish other congregations. God details this in Acts 13, where we read of Paul and Barnabas being sent forth as missionaries from the church that had been established in Antioch of Syria.

As churches faithfully carried out the rules set forth in the Bible for the church age, the people who attended the church were placed under the spiritual care of those who had the spiritual oversight of the congregation. At the same time, this external evidence of the kingdom of God in the world reached out into the distant lands of the world so that by the time the church age had come to an end, churches had been established in a very high percentage of the cities and villages throughout the world.

It was God's good pleasure to continue this method of reaching the world with Christ until God had securely put in place the ability of believers to reach whole continents for hours each day with the true Gospel. That is, God guided men to establish worldwide communication by radio, by Internet, by satellite broadcasting, etc. We will examine this phenomenon more fully in Chapter 9 of this study.

The Temple, Israel, Jerusalem, Judah

Symbolically, God speaks of the churches of the church age as the temple, as Israel, as Jerusalem, and as Judah. Unless we understand this, a number of passages that help us to understand the times and the seasons will remain obscure. Therefore, before we continue this study, we will look at the verses that set forth this symbolism.

First of all, the Bible clearly identifies the true believers as Jews in the spiritual sense. That is the reason why, in turn, He identifies them with a temple, Israel, Jerusalem, and Judaea. All of these entities originally were identified only with the Jews. In Romans 2:28-29, God declares:

For he is not a Jew, which is one outwardly; neither is that circumcision, which is outward in the flesh: But he is a Jew, which is one inwardly; and circumcision is that of the heart, in the spirit, and not in the letter; whose praise is not of men, but of God.

> *A true Jew by God's definition*
> *is anyone who has become saved.*

In these important verses, God is showing us that in God's sight a true Jew is not a blood descendant of Abraham, who shows this by physical circumcision, but a true Jew by God's definition is anyone who has been circumcised in the heart. That is, his sins have been cut off. That means a true Jew by God's definition is anyone who has become saved. This truth is reinforced by the language of Galatians 3:7:

Know ye therefore that they which are of faith, the same are the children of Abraham.

Abraham was the progenitor of the physical nation of Jews. In this verse God is reiterating what we already read in Romans 2:28-29, that a true Jew is someone who has begun to trust in the Lord Jesus.

To be sure that we understand this, the Bible declares in Galatians 3:26-29:

For ye are all the children of God by faith in Christ Jesus. For as many of you as have been baptized into Christ have put on Christ. There is neither Jew nor Greek, there is neither bond nor free, there is neither male nor female: for ye are all one in Christ Jesus. And if ye be Christ's, then are ye Abraham's seed, and heirs according to the promise.

In this passage, God is indicating that each and every believer whether physically a Jew or a Gentile is spiritually a descendant of Abraham, thus making him spiritually a Jew. This is easily understood if we recognize that those who believe are sons of God, as we read in Romans 8:14:

For as many as are led by the Spirit of God, they are the sons of God.

As sons of God we are sons of Christ who in His flesh was the son of David, the son of Abraham (Matthew 1:1). Since Christ is the son of David who was a Jew, and we are sons of Christ, then we who are saved are also sons of David, and therefore, we are also Jews.

We can now understand why Jesus identifies the believers with the temple, with Israel, with Jerusalem, and with Judah. These are all entities entirely identified with Jesus.

Let us therefore, first of all, learn what the Bible says of believers being the temple. In I Corinthians 3:16, we read:

Know ye not that ye are the temple of God, and that the Spirit of God dwelleth in you?

The context of this verse begins in verse 9, where we read:

For we are labourers together with God: ye are God's husbandry, ye are God's building.

The foundation of the temple is indicated in verse 11:

For other foundation can no man lay than that is laid, which is Jesus Christ.

The building blocks that are built into this temple are indicated in verse 12:

Now if any man build upon this foundation gold, silver, precious stones, wood, hay, stubble;

It should be immediately apparent that the true believers are typified by gold, silver, and precious stones. They are the lively (living) stones who are built up into a spiritual house (I Peter 2:5).

Truly Saved and Apparently Saved in the Churches

On the other hand, the wood, hay, and stubble must relate to the church members who are still unsaved. Fire does not destroy gold or silver, but fire will utterly destroy wood, hay, and stubble. Thus, the Bible is teaching that the spiritual temple is a spiritual house representing the churches and congregations, but within those churches there are people who are truly saved (gold, silver, and precious stones), and those who are not saved (wood, hay, and stubble).

The churches that have existed throughout the season of the church age are also typified as spiritual Israel. In Galatians 6:16, we read of believers that they are the Israel of God. In Revelation 7, God speaks of 144,000 of all the tribes of Israel who were sealed (Revelation 7:4). The Bible then names 12,000 from each of twelve tribes of Israel, but the tribe of Dan is not named. One tribe had to remain unnamed because in actuality, there were thirteen tribes. There were twelve sons of Jacob who became the heads of tribes, but Joseph was given the two tribes of Ephraim and Manasseh, who were the sons of Joseph. Therefore, the total number of tribes was thirteen.

Therefore, when Revelation 7:4 speaks of 144,000 of <u>all</u> the tribes of Israel, it is immediately apparent that the twelve tribes named are actually the complete fullness of the Israel of God, which includes all the churches of the church age. The numbers 12,000 and 144,000 symbolically represent the complete fullness of all those who would become saved in the early Pentecostal rain season of the New Testament church era.

It might be noted that the 144,000 are presented in Revelation 14 as those who have their Father's name written on their foreheads (Revelation 14:1), they were redeemed from the earth (Revelation 14:3), and they are the firstfruits (Revelation 14:4). Remember we learned earlier in this study that the firstfruits are the harvest of the early Pentecostal rain.

Later in this study, we will look at the significance of the statement that these 144,000 were sealed.

These same twelve tribes are spoken of in James 1:1:

James, a servant of God and of the Lord Jesus Christ, to the twelve tribes which are scattered abroad, greeting.

These twelve tribes are also called firstfruits in James 1:18:

Of his own will begat he us with the word of truth, that we should be a kind of firstfruits of his creatures.

> *The book of James particularly focuses upon*
> *those in the churches during the church age season.*

We have learned thus far that the members of the churches and congregations throughout the church age are typified as a spiritual temple and by a spiritual Israel consisting of 12 tribes. The reason that the Book of James speaks of "firstfruits" is that this book is particularly focused upon those within the congregation during the church age. Of course, every book of the Bible is for all believers, including those saved during the latter rain. However, the Book of James particularly focuses upon those in the churches during the church age season. It is harsh language is to help those in the churches examine if they are truly saved. Also, we read the accusation that those in the churches are **"adulterers and adulteresses"** (James 4:4). The unsaved in the churches are still in spiritual fornication against the law of God (Romans 7:1-3). So, God provides the Book of James as a warning particularly to those in the churches. With this in mind, we can see why James 1:18 was written the way it was.

We also know the members of churches and congregations were typified by Jerusalem and Judea. In Revelation 21:2 we read:

And I John saw the holy city, new Jerusalem, coming down from God out of heaven, prepared as a bride adorned for her husband.

This verse is speaking of the whole body of believers, throughout eternity future we are called the new Jerusalem.

In Galatians 4:25-26, the Bible speaks of a present Jerusalem:

For this Agar is mount Sinai in Arabia, and answereth to Jerusalem which now is, and is in bondage with her children. But Jerusalem which is above is free, which is the mother of us all.

The context shows that the Jerusalem which now is consists of individuals who are still in spiritual bondage. That is, they have not become saved even though God calls them a Jerusalem. But these verses also speak of a Jerusalem above. This Jerusalem can only relate to those who have become saved. We read in Ephesians 2:4-6:

But God, who is rich in mercy, for his great love wherewith he loved us, Even when we were dead in sins, hath quickened us together with Christ, (by grace ye are saved;) And hath raised us up together, and made us sit together in heavenly places in Christ Jesus:

In principle, the true believers are seated in the heavenlies with Christ even though we live on this earth serving as ambassadors of Christ.

Thus, the body of believers on earth is made up of Jerusalem above (those who are saved), and Jerusalem which now is (those who think they are saved but are still in bondage to sin). These individuals make up the churches and congregations. Therefore, the churches are spiritually called Jerusalem.

Thus, we see a parallel as God speaks of the churches as a temple and as Jerusalem. In the temple those who were saved were called gold, silver, and precious stones. They are called the Jerusalem above. However, also in the temple there are those who are called wood, hay, and stubble. They are called the Jerusalem which now is.

The churches are also called Judea because Jerusalem was the capital of Judea. We read in Luke 21:20-21:

And when ye shall see Jerusalem compassed with armies, then know that the desolation thereof is nigh. Then let them which are in Judaea flee to the mountains; and let them which are in the midst of it depart out; and let not them that are in the countries enter thereinto.

These verses link Jerusalem and Judea together. As we continue in this study, we will look very carefully at these verses.

Unfaithful Churches

There was a major problem that continued throughout the church age. It was already in evidence just a few decades after the beginning of the season of early Pentecostal rain. That problem was a lack of faithfulness to the teachings of the Bible. God tells us about this in Revelation 2 and Revelation 3, where the Bible speaks about the seven churches that flourished even before the Bible was completed.

> *So God tells them if they don't repent,*
> *He will remove their candlestick.*

In the Biblical account of the spiritual condition of these congregations we read that already the church in Ephesus had lost its first love. To love God is to keep His commandments (John 14:21, 24). Thus, they were already beginning to teach doctrines that were not based faithfully upon the Bible. So God tells them if they don't repent, He will remove their candlestick. If their candlestick is removed, it means there is no light of the true Gospel coming from that church. They will have become a dead church.

In fact, the church of Sardis had already become a dead church even though some true believers were still a part of it (Revelation 3:1).

God was almost ready to vomit the church of Laodicea out of His mouth (Revelation 3:16). The church of Thyatira was troubled by a spiritually adulterous woman God called Jezebel (Revelation 2:20). The church at Pergamos had allowed a wicked group called the Nicolaitans to operate in the church.

Indeed, these have been the kinds of problems that have existed in the churches throughout the church age. At times, it would become so bad that the churches were entirely removed. The seven churches of Revelation, for example, finally ceased to exist. However, because the churches were God's method of evangelizing the world, new churches would be established even as some churches ceased to function. God in His mercy and patience continued to use churches as His means to get the Gospel into the world.

Spiritual High Places

Fact is, the spiritual situation that prevailed throughout the church age in many ways paralleled the situation that prevailed during the 344 years that Judah existed as a nation. Judah had its high places. They were small places of worship constructed on a convenient hill. But the one who was worshipped was not Jehovah. They were places where false gods were worshipped. Thus, Judah was engaging in spiritual harlotry.

Even when faithful, God-fearing kings reigned, with two exceptions the high places were never removed from the land of Israel. God overlooked this obvious spiritual adultery, but He warned them that eventually, God would bring judgment on Israel and Judah because of the existence of those high places. As our study continues, we will look more carefully at this.

Amazingly, the same situation has prevailed throughout the church age. Doctrines that were held and taught by churches that were not faithful to the Bible are the equivalent of those Old Testament high places. This is true because any church doctrine that is obeyed by the members of the church is an act of worship of the one who commanded that this doctrine be obeyed. When we obey God's commandments, it is an indication that we are surrendering our will to the one who asked for obedience to that command. Thus, if the congregation obeys doctrines that were designed in the minds of church theologians, and those doctrines do not come from the Bible, then in a real sense, the minds of those theologians are being worshipped. Obedience to that false doctrine becomes the equivalent of a high place of the Old Testament.

> *Obedience to that false doctrine becomes the*
> *equivalent of a high place of the Old Testament.*

Amazingly, God has overlooked these spiritual high places that have existed throughout the church age. In spite of them, for more than 1950 years, God used defective churches to do God's work of reaching the elect with the Gospel.

It is true that at times during the season of the Pentecostal early rain, which we call the church age, the spiritual condition of the churches was very weak. But at other times, glorious chapters were written into the history of the church age as believers were willing to be burned at the stake rather than be unfaithful to their Savior.

However, even as the Old Testament season of the early righteous rain ended with a three and a half year time of hearing the Word of God, which was also a time that identified with severe judgment, so, too, the church age season ended with a time symbolized by three and a half years during which there was also an intense spiritual famine together with God's judgment. We will look carefully at this sad fact as we continue this study.

Chapter 6.
Time No. 2. The Great Tribulation

Thus far in our study, we have examined:

The season of the early righteous rain of the Old Testament that brought as its first of the firstfruits harvest the Lord Jesus Christ.

The time of three and a half years that immediately followed the early righteous rain. The time was a time of spiritual famine of hearing the Word of God and a time of judgment on Christ and Satan.

The season of the early Pentecostal rain that continued for more than 1950 years and brought in the Pentecostal firstfruits harvest of all those who became saved throughout the church age.

We are now ready to examine in some detail the time of spiritual famine of hearing the Word of God that began with the beginning of the Great Tribulation. We will discover that it was symbolized by a time of three and a half years. It, too, was a time of judgment, the judgment falling on the churches of the church age.

When God made the transition from the Old Testament early righteous rain season to the three and a half year time of Christ's ministry, during which there was a time of spiritual famine of hearing the Word of God, in the historical setting, it impacted a very small percentage of the world's population. Most of the peoples of the world knew nothing at all about what was happening in the nation of Israel. Likewise, when God transitioned from this three and a half year time of spiritual famine and judgment to the season of the early Pentecostal rain, that is, to the season of the church age, a very small percentage of the world's population was impacted by it. Only those cities in which a Jewish synagogue was located, and they were few in number compared to the number of all the cities of the world, were impacted in any way by this transition.

A Worldwide Trauma

But in our day, when God has transitioned from the season of the early Pentecostal rain, the church age, to the time of Great Tribulation, the impact is worldwide. Churches are located in cities and villages all over the world.

Hundreds of millions of people are members of churches. Therefore, a sudden transition to a time of spiritual famine of hearing the Word, a time of judgment upon those churches, is an enormous event in the history of God's Gospel program.

Therefore, this transition to the time of Great Tribulation is written about exceedingly extensively in the Bible. Because this huge event took place very near the end of time, the numerous Bible references to it were not understood even by the finest God-fearing theologians. God explains this in Daniel 12, where God was explaining some of the end-time events, and He declared in Daniel 12:9:

And he said, Go thy way, Daniel: for the words are closed up and sealed till the time of the end.

But now we are very near the time of the end, and God is revealing from the Bible a great many things to believers that previously had been hidden from God's people. We now find that all the way from Genesis to Revelation there is information concerning the transition from the church age to the Great Tribulation. We find that amongst the extensive Biblical references to this traumatic event are the following passages.

Genesis 45 in which God tells of the famine in Joseph's day that caused his father to go into the land of Egypt.
The strange account of Judges 19 which describes the killing of the concubine by the men of Benjamin.
A great many chapters in the Book of Isaiah.
A great many chapters in the Book of Jeremiah.
Almost all of the Book of Lamentations.
Many of the first 39 chapters of Ezekiel.
Daniel 7, Daniel 8, Daniel 11, and Daniel 12.
Portions of the Book of Hosea.
Almost all of the Book of Joel.
Much of the Book of Amos.
Portions of the Book of Micah.
Much of the Book of Nahum.
Much of the Book of Habakkuk.
Parts of the Book of Zechariah.
Matthew 24.
Mark 13.
Parts of Luke 17.

Luke 21.
The last seven chapters of the Book of Acts.
II Thessalonians 2.
Revelation 7, 8, 9, 10, 11, 13, 14, 17, 18, 20.

This is not a complete list but it is sufficient to show that the transition to the Great Tribulation is very extensively documented in the Bible. In this study, we will examine a number of these passages to show the harmony that exists between them.

As we study a number of these passages, we will discover that they all fit into a plan wherein at a precise time in history, the end of the church age did occur. It was immediately followed by a time of Great Tribulation which symbolically continues for three and a half years. In actuality, it is probably the literal time of 2300 days spoken of in Daniel 8.

At the end of the symbolic three and a half years, the final season of the latter rain did commence. This latter rain season that will bring in the final harvest of believers will be a very short season during which the judgment of God will remain on the churches. The churches will continue to experience a spiritual famine of hearing the Word of God, and they will continue to be under the judgment of God. This very short season of the latter rain will be followed by the final time, that of the judgment at the end of the world.

We shall now begin to examine some of the evidence in the Bible that describes this transition from the season of the early Pentecostal rain, the church age, to the time of the Great Tribulation.

The Bible shows that a time would come when God would no longer use the churches and congregations to bring the Gospel to the world. They instead would come under the wrath of God.

The Old Testament Anticipates the Great Tribulation

To see this plan, we will first carefully examine Old Testament Israel. They, without any question, typify the New Testament church which the Bible speaks of as the Israel of God (Galatians 6:16). As we discover how God related to national Israel, we will learn how God interrelates with the churches of the New Testament.

Old Testament Israel began with the patriarchs Abraham, Isaac, and Jacob. It reached its highest glory during the reigns of David and Solomon.

It was a nation brought out of Egypt, into the land of Canaan under the leadership of first Moses and then Joshua. God bestowed His love upon this nation making it His people. Deuteronomy 7:6-8 beautifully records this fact:

> **For thou art an holy people unto the LORD thy God: the LORD thy God hath chosen thee to be a special people unto himself, above all people that are upon the face of the earth. The LORD did not set his love upon you, nor choose you, because ye were more in number than any people; for ye were the fewest of all people: But because the LORD loved you, and because he would keep the oath which he had sworn unto your fathers, hath the LORD brought you out with a mighty hand, and redeemed you out of the house of bondmen, from the hand of Pharaoh king of Egypt.**

And so, Israel continued for hundreds of years under the patient guidance of God. Again and again when they went astray God sent judges or prophets or priests or kings to bring them back to a more obedient faithfulness to God.

The Problem of High Places

> *One problem did persist and became a continuous problem. That was the problem of high places.*

One problem did persist and became a continuous problem. That was the problem of high places. High places were places outside of Jerusalem where false god's were worshipped. It was already a serious problem when Moses received the law at Mount Sinai. The golden calf worship was similar to later high place worship. However, until the temple was constructed by Solomon, the correct worship of Jehovah God was also observed at high places. But once the temple was built, any worship at high places was always the worship of false gods.

The division of the kingdom upon the death of Solomon in 931 B.C. stimulated the worship of false gods. The first king of the nation of Israel, which consisted of ten tribes of Israel, built worship centers in Dan and Bethel that featured the worship of calves. This sad condition never changed throughout the history of the ten tribes of Israel. In the nation of Judah, which consisted of the two tribes of Judah and Benjamin, the situation was somewhat better in that many of the kings who reigned were God-fearing men. Even so with the exception of two kings, Hezekiah and Josiah, to some degree high places were always in evidence in the land.

These high places were obviously an act of rebellion against the law of God. Yet for hundreds of years, God tolerated them and especially blessed Judah in spite of them. But they were not unnoticed by God. In Leviticus 26:27-31, God solemnly warned:

And if ye will not for all this hearken unto me, but walk contrary unto me; Then I will walk contrary unto you also in fury; and I, even I, will chastise you seven times for your sins. And ye shall eat the flesh of your sons, and the flesh of your daughters shall ye eat. And I will destroy your high places, and cut down your images, and cast your carcases upon the carcases of your idols, and my soul shall abhor you. And I will make your cities waste, and bring your sanctuaries unto desolation, and I will not smell the savour of your sweet odours.

Note in this warning God is specifically talking about the high places. This warning was given before Israel entered the land of Canaan.

The High Places Will Be Destroyed

But how and when would God destroy the high places. Remember in Leviticus 26 God had declared that He had chosen them to be a special people. He had set His love upon them. Surely God would be very gentle with Israel when and if He carried out His threat to remove the high places.

But also remember, God had said **"I will make your cities waste and bring your sanctuaries unto desolation"** (verse 31). Would God really do this. Yes, He would. And He did do that.

In the year 709 B.C., disaster struck the ten tribes of Israel. This nation that God loved was entirely destroyed by the Assyrians. Except for the city of Jerusalem, at the same time the ten tribes were destroyed, much of the nation of Judah was also destroyed. Only because Hezekiah the king of Judah removed all of the high places was Jerusalem spared. How could God bring this horrible disaster on the people to whom He had pledged His love.

But there was more. One hundred years later, in the year 609 B.C., the nation of Judah was again struck with disaster. King Josiah, the most God-fearing king who ever ruled over Judah, was killed in battle when he was only 39 years of age.

One hundred years earlier, King Hezekiah had destroyed the high places and so Jerusalem was spared at the time the ten tribes were destroyed. But following Hezekiah, his son and then his grandson reigned, and during their reigns they rebuilt the high places. Thus, Judah continued in its rebellion against God.

And then Josiah became king. Truly, he was a wonderful king. God declared concerning King Josiah in II Kings 23:25:

> **And like unto him was there no king before him, that turned to the LORD with all his heart, and with all his soul, and with all his might, according to all the law of Moses; neither after him arose there any like him.**

King Josiah's godly acts were wonderful. The Bible records in II Kings 22 and 23 and in II Chronicles 34 and 35 all of the righteous acts of this great king. Included among his acts was the destruction of all of the high places.

But it was too late. When God warned in Leviticus 26 that He would destroy all of the high places, He gave sufficient information so that we can know precisely when this occurred. He had said in Leviticus 26:33-34:

> **And I will scatter you among the heathen, and will draw out a sword after you: and your land shall be desolate, and your cities waste. Then shall the land enjoy her sabbaths, as long as it lieth desolate, and ye be in your enemies' land; even then shall the land rest, and enjoy her sabbaths.**

God identifies the time when the land would enjoy its sabbaths as a time of seventy years. He states in II Chronicles 36:21, **"the land had enjoyed her sabbaths: for as long as she lay desolate she kept sabbath, to fulfil threescore and ten years."**

The Bible shows us that this seventy years began with the death of Josiah in 609 B.C. and ended with the conquering of Babylon by the Medes and the Persians in 539 B.C.

The fulfillment of this prophecy required the death of King Josiah because the year 609 B.C. was to be the beginning of the seventy years that had been prophesied. Indeed, now God's wrath began to be poured out upon Judah.

Although four more kings would reign, they were all wicked. During their reign, first Egypt assailed them and then Babylon began to destroy them. Finally, in the year 587 B.C., twenty three years inclusive after King Josiah was killed in battle, the end came.

> *This terrible end came on the people whom*
> *God loved.*

And what an end. Jerusalem, the temple, the holy of holies were all destroyed. This terrible end came on the people whom God loved, who had been chosen as a special people. God carried out His warning that He would destroy the high places. He did so first in 709 B.C. and then completed the task in 587 B.C. Truly, God does not give empty or idle warnings.

But how does this relate to the church and the New Testament era, the congregations and denominations by means of which God has sent the Gospel into all the world during the past more than 1900 years?

High Places: A Warning to the Church

When we begin to consider the plight of the churches and congregations in our day, at least four facts became abundantly evident.

1. The eternal church made up of all true believers will never be destroyed.

2. The corporate or external church as represented by the various denominations and local congregations that have existed during the past more than 1950 years could be destroyed even as the seven churches of Revelation 2 and Revelation 3 were eventually destroyed.

3. Ancient Israel that was loved by God and protected by God for hundreds of years was finally destroyed, the nation of Israel in 709 B.C., the nation of Judah in 587 B.C.

4. An insistent cause of their destruction was their persistence in maintaining places of worship, called high places, where heathen gods were worshipped.

With this background in view, we must ask the logical question: What does the destruction of ancient Israel in 709 B.C. and 587 B.C. have to do with us today? The answer must come to us loud and clear. What God did to ancient Israel has everything to do with this matter. In Hebrews 13:8, the Bible declares, **"Jesus Christ the same yesterday, and to day, and for ever."** Jesus is Jehovah God of the Old Testament. As we view His treatment of ancient Israel, we can know how He deals with the New Testament Israel, the churches and congregations that exist all over the world.

The logical conclusion then might be: Since the high places of Israel were a dominant cause of the destruction of ancient Israel, it appears that the churches of today are safe from God's judgment because we do not have high places where heathen gods are worshipped.

Today's Churches Have Their High Places

But is it true, that our churches are free of high places? The Bible shows us that the churches of today are not at all free of the high places. The Bible defines the nature of the New Testament high places in II Corinthians 10:4-6. There we read:

> **For the weapons of our warfare are not carnal, but mighty through God to the pulling down of strong holds; Casting down imaginations, and every high thing that exalteth itself against the knowledge of God, and bringing into captivity every thought to the obedience of Christ; And having in a readiness to revenge all disobedience, when your obedience is fulfilled.**

In this very revealing passage, God has set forth His plans for the New Testament church. And as we shall see they are parallel to His plan for ancient Israel. We can readily see this parallelism if we recognize the nature of the Old Testament high places. True worship faithfully identified with a careful following of the laws of God set forth in the Bible. But many in Israel had their own ideas concerning the nature of true worship.

Out of their own imaginations and rationalizations they designed places of worship to gods that they felt should be honored as Jehovah God was honored. So, they designed and constructed their high places. They were probably called high places because these places, where false gods were worshipped, normally were built on the top of a hill.

In the New testament era, it was not fashionable to construct places of worship to false gods. But the New Testament individual has the same kind of thoughts and imaginations as the Old Testament believer. He, too, has opinions as to the proper worship of God that frequently includes ideas from his own mind rather than from the Bible.

During the Old Testament days, it took serious thought as to how to properly design and build a high place in order to make the overall worship scene more complete. In the New Testament, serious men have carefully thought about teachings they felt were pleasing to God. They reasoned together in solemn meetings such as church councils, consistories, and synods. After prayerful consideration, they adopted doctrines that were not always true to the Bible. Some of the erroneous conclusions were even written into and became a part of very prestigious confessions. This was so even though they had arrived at conclusions that were not taught in the Bible. Conclusions such as there can be divorce for fornication, baptismal regeneration, our faith is an instrument that God uses to bring us to salvation, a future millennium, women can pastor a church, universal atonement, and our acceptance of Christ is a requirement for salvation, are typical of many doctrines solemnly adopted by churches. But these are high places in that they have come from the exalted minds of men, not from God.

> *These are high places in that they have come from the exalted minds of men, not from God.*

At the beginning of this study, we briefly examined some high places in the churches. We saw that there were quite a number of high places in our churches today. Churches have rewritten the rules concerning divorce and remarriage, the Sunday Sabbath, gospels of signs and wonders, the tongues phenomenon, the role of women in the church, music, and preaching about hell and damnation. These are all high places that have grown extensively in the churches in the past fifty years.

We must never forget that the pillar and ground of truth cannot be the church (I Timothy 3:15). The pillar and ground can be only God. Therefore, any doctrine held by a church must come under the careful scrutiny of the Bible. Fact is, the teaching that is held by a great number of churches that the church is the pillar and ground of truth is in itself an enormous high place because it makes the church and that which it teaches an authority at least equal to God.

The New Testament High Places Will Be Destroyed

For over 1950 years, God has overlooked these spiritual high places even as for many hundreds of years He overlooked the high places of Israel and Judah.

But remember, God had warned ancient Israel that eventually He would destroy the high places. This destruction commenced when Judah began to go into bondage at the time their last good king, King Josiah, was killed in 609

B.C. The destruction was completed in 587 B.C. when Jerusalem and the temple were entirely destroyed, twenty three years inclusively after 609 B.C.

Ominously, the passage in II Corinthians 10:4-6 which speaks of the New Testament high places also warns of a time when God will destroy the high places. Remember, God said, **"For the weapons of our warfare are not carnal, but mighty through God . . . having in a readiness to revenge all disobedience, when your obedience is fulfilled."** In this very revealing passage, God is declaring that punishment will come when the obedience of the churches has been fulfilled, that is, when their work of sending the Gospel into the world has been finished, God would begin to bring judgment upon them. This coincides with the warning of Revelation 11 that the time will come when the work of the church to bring the Gospel, as typified by the two witnesses, is finished. When it is finished, the two witnesses will be killed. Revelation 11:7 declares:

> **And when they shall have finished their testimony, the beast that ascendeth out of the bottomless pit shall make war against them, and shall overcome them, and kill them.**

Earlier in Revelation 11, God had explained in verse 4 that the two witnesses are the two olive trees and the two candlesticks standing before the God of the earth. Remember in Revelation 1:20 and Revelation 2:1 God had indicated that each church is represented by a candlestick. This is so because within each church or congregation, there are true believers. They individually are light bearers of the Gospel. Because they are an integral part of the congregation, the church itself as an entity becomes a light bearer. In this way throughout the church age, the churches that have remained reasonably faithful to the Bible have been represented by a candlestick.

However, when these true believers are silenced within the congregation or are driven from the congregation, effectively, they have been killed. John 16:2 declares:

> **They shall put you out of the synagogues: yea, the time cometh, that whosoever killeth you will think that he doeth God service.**

This killing of the witnesses can occur only when the work of the church to bring the Gospel has been finished. It is only God who determines when that work is finished. As we continue our study, we will learn that the end of the time of the work of the church to bring the Gospel to the world coincides with the beginning of the Great Tribulation. One thing is certain, when the two witnesses are killed because their work had been finished, it means that the church is dead - the candlestick no longer can give light. That is, God is no longer using the church to bring the Gospel.

> *That is, God is no longer using*
> *the church to bring the Gospel.*

Therefore, we see clearly that God has predetermined a time during the New Testament era when punishment would come against high things and the exalted reasoning of men. This punishment would take place when the obedience of the churches was fulfilled. We have already seen that the obedience was fulfilled when the work of the two witnesses was finished.

This identifies with the warning of I Peter 4:17, **"For the time is come that judgment must begin at the house of God."** The event of this judgment on the churches is a terrible blow to them. In a way it is as traumatic and awful as the destruction of ancient Judah by the Babylonians in 587 B.C. Therefore, God speaks of this event as a time of Great Tribulation. In Matthew 24:21, the Bible declares there will be Great Tribulation such as this world has never known or ever shall know.

How terrible when God's blessings no longer rest on the churches and congregations which only a few years earlier were still God's evangelists to the world.

But now we ask the big question. Has this Great Tribulation of Matthew 24:21 already begun? We also wonder if a church removes its high places, can it avoid this judgment? Moreover, how does God bring judgment upon the churches?

Chapter 7.
The Church Age Has Come to an End

The Bible discloses the fact that following the season of the early Pentecostal rain (the church age), which has brought in the harvest of the firstfruits, there would be a time of a spiritual famine of hearing the Word of God. This would also be a time of judgment on the churches. This time symbolically would be three and a half years in duration. It is called the time of Great Tribulation. This time of Great Tribulation will be immediately followed by the return of Christ and the end of the world. We read in Matthew 24:21:

For then shall be great tribulation, such as was not since the beginning of the world to this time, no, nor ever shall be.

And in Matthew 24:29, God declares:

Immediately after the tribulation of those days shall the sun be darkened, and the moon shall not give her light, and the stars shall fall from heaven, and the powers of the heavens shall be shaken:

This Great Tribulation period is not only described in Matthew 24 and Mark 13, but it is also described in the language of Revelation 13, Daniel 7, Daniel 8, and many other Scriptures.

It is typified by the seventy year period beginning with the death of King Josiah in 609 B.C. and ending with the conquering of Babylon by the Medes and Persians in 539 B.C.

It is a time typified by God bringing judgment upon Judah because they refused to remove the high places where heathen gods were worshipped. God warned in Leviticus 26:30:

And I will destroy your high places, and cut down your images, and cast your carcases upon the carcases of your idols, and my soul shall abhor you.

He reiterated this warning in Ezekiel 6: 3, 4:

And say, Ye mountains of Israel, hear the word of the Lord GOD; Thus saith the Lord GOD to the mountains, and to the hills, to the

rivers, and to the valleys; Behold, I, even I, will bring a sword upon you, and I will destroy your high places. And your altars shall be desolate, and your images shall be broken: and I will cast down your slain men before your idols.

The character of the events occurring in the seventy year period from 609 B.C. to 539 B.C. was the total rule of Babylon over Israel. When the Israelites were taken captive into Babylon they had no temple, no holy city, and no priesthood. They were entirely separated from Jerusalem and all the sacred activity that had previously been taking place there.

Likewise, the character of the Great Tribulation spoken of in Matthew 24 is that Satan has occupied the churches and has become victorious over the saints. In Revelation 13:7, we read:

And it was given unto him to make war with the saints, and to overcome them: and power was given him over all kindreds, and tongues, and nations.

In Daniel 7:25 God prophesied:

And he shall speak great words against the most High, and shall wear out the saints of the most High, and think to change times and laws: and they shall be given into his hand until a time and times and the dividing of time.

In Daniel 8:11, 12 the Bible declares:

Yea, he magnified himself even to the prince of the host, and by him the daily sacrifice was taken away, and the place of his sanctuary was cast down. And an host was given him against the daily sacrifice by reason of transgression, and it cast down the truth to the ground; and it practised, and prospered.

These passages clearly show that the time was to come that God would give Satan the victory over the churches and congregations. This is the end of the church age, when Satan is given complete victory over the external church.

When we understand that Satan is given victory over the external church which consists of all the local congregations, we wonder how this can be. Don't we read in Revelation 20:2, 3:

And he laid hold on the dragon, that old serpent, which is the Devil, and Satan, and bound him a thousand years, And cast him into the bottomless pit, and shut him up, and set a seal upon him, that he should deceive the nations no more, till the thousand years should be fulfilled: and after that he must be loosed a little season.

> *This is the end of the church age, when Satan*
> *is given complete victory over the external church.*

We do know that Satan was bound in the sense that he could no longer frustrate the purpose of the Gospel to save people. During the ministry of Jesus, virtually no one became saved. On the one hand, the Holy Spirit was not at work applying the preached Word of God to the lives of those who were to be saved. And on the other hand, Satan appeared to be present almost everywhere Jesus preached. As Luke 8:12 indicates, the devil took the Word out of the hearts of those who heard the Word lest they should believe and be saved.

The fact that about 3,000 were saved seven weeks after the time of the cross indicates that this was the dominant meaning of the truth that Satan had been bound. It was at the cross that Satan was given the death blow and was bound so that he could no longer deceive the nations. Beginning at the time he was bound and all through the church age, people all over the world did become saved.

We must, therefore, ask the question: How is it possible that Satan is able to gain victory over the churches during the Great Tribulation? Did he finally figure out a plan whereby he could do this? The answer is, No! It is God who loosed Satan as a judgment upon the churches. We read about this loosing of Satan in Revelation 9:1-4:

And the fifth angel sounded, and I saw a star fall from heaven unto the earth: and to him was given the key of the bottomless pit. And he opened the bottomless pit; and there arose a smoke out of the pit, as the smoke of a great furnace; and the sun and the air were darkened by reason of the smoke of the pit. And there came out of the smoke locusts upon the earth: and unto them was given power, as the scorpions of the earth have power. And it was commanded them that they should not hurt the grass of the earth, neither any green thing, neither any tree; but only those men which have not the seal of God in their foreheads.

The star that fell from heaven can only be Christ. He alone has the key that opens and shuts (Revelation 3:7). Very deliberately Christ loosed Satan in the sense that He again allowed Satan to frustrate the preached Word so that it could not save. The time was coincidental with the withdrawal of the Holy Spirit from the churches. Once he was loosed, Satan, as the constant enemy of Christ, of course could be expected to immediately attack the body of Christ which was found in the local churches all over the world.

Thus, we can know that it is only because God is orchestrating the details of the Great Tribulation and the end of the world that Satan can become so victorious during the time of Great Tribulation.

The Two Witnesses

When we look at the sending forth of the Gospel during the church age, we must take note of the two witnesses of Revelation 11. These two witnesses represent the true believers. Initially, they identify with the true believers in the churches during the church age. The command to go into all the world with the Gospel had been given at the beginning of the church age. The carrying out of this command was typified by the two witnesses of which the Bible speaks in Revelation 11. Revelation 11:3, 4 declares:

And I will give power unto my two witnesses, and they shall prophesy a thousand two hundred and threescore days, clothed in sackcloth. These are the two olive trees, and the two candlesticks standing before the God of the earth.

The two witnesses are identified in Revelation 11:4 as two olive trees and two candlesticks. The two olive trees identify with the olive tree of Romans 11:16-24. This underscores that these two witnesses represent true believers.

The two witnesses identify with the two candlesticks. This immediately identifies with the church age. Revelation 1:20 and Revelation 2:1 teach us that symbolically, each church is represented by a candlestick amongst which Christ walks. The candlestick represents the light of the Gospel as it is sent out into the world during the church age by the churches and during the latter rain by the true believers who are altogether outside of the churches.

The number two (two witnesses, two olive trees, two candlesticks), identifies with true believers who faithfully bring the Gospel. Remember Jesus sent the twelve disciples out two and two (Mark 6:7) and the seventy two and two (Luke 10:1).

We see the end of the church age in the death of these two witnesses, as we read Revelation 11:7, which declares:

And when they shall have finished their testimony, the beast that ascendeth out of the bottomless pit shall make war against them, and shall overcome them, and kill them.

The death of the two witnesses identifies with the destruction of the church. Satan is loosed at the beginning of the Great Tribulation and is allowed by God to destroy the churches.

The Churches Will Be Judged

Even as God finally destroyed Judah and Jerusalem in 587 B.C. because they had not removed the high places, God indicates that the church, too, will be destroyed because it does not remove the high places. Remember we read in II Corinthians 10:4-6:

For the weapons of our warfare are not carnal, but mighty through God to the pulling down of strong holds; Casting down imaginations, and every high thing that exalteth itself against the knowledge of God, and bringing into captivity every thought to the obedience of Christ; And having in a readiness to revenge all disobedience, when your obedience is fulfilled.

As we learned earlier, the high places of the church are the doctrines held and taught by the church which are not true to the Bible. Some of these are imbedded in the Confessions but additional wrong doctrines are also taught. Divorce for fornication is an example of such a perversion of the law of God.

Even as Israel refused to permanently destroy its high places, so, too, the churches and denominations of our day refuse to remove from their Confessions and from other teachings those doctrines which are not true to the Bible. As we learned earlier, this refusal to remove wrong doctrines from their Confessions and other doctrinal teachings of the church may be a result of the false notion that the church is the pillar and ground of truth. Later in our study, we will learn that only God can be the pillar and ground of truth.

Thus, both Revelation 11:7 and II Corinthians 10:4-6 teach that there comes a time when the work of the church is finished (Revelation 11:2), its obedience has been fulfilled (II Corinthians 10:6), and then follows judgment upon the church. This is so even as God's judgment came upon Old Testament Israel and Judah.

It is true that during the 322 year duration of Judah from the death of Solomon in 931 B.C. until the death of Josiah in 609 B.C., God tolerated and overlooked the high places.

Likewise, throughout the New Testament era, God has overlooked and tolerated the high places in the churches. Even though many churches and denominations insist that the Bible is the only infallible Word of God, they cling to a number of doctrines of men rather than submit entirely to the truth of the Bible. We have learned that these doctrines are equivalent to the high places of ancient Judah.

As we have seen, the Great Tribulation of Matthew 24 was typified by the destruction of Jerusalem in the period 609 B.C. to 587 B.C. Therefore, we can expect that even as Judah and Israel were destroyed because they would not remove their high places, so, too, the New Testament Israel, because high places are found in the churches and congregations throughout the world, will also be destroyed during the Great Tribulation.

The destruction of the churches is not a physical literal destruction as was the situation in 587 B.C. Instead, it is a spiritual destruction as God allows the true believers to be driven out. The churches become spiritually desolate because as we will learn later in this study, the Holy Spirit no longer works in the churches and Satan rules in them.

This destruction of the churches is made evident by the declaration of Revelation 11:7:

> **And when they shall have finished their testimony, the beast that ascendeth out of the bottomless pit shall make war against them, and shall overcome them, and kill them.**

It is seen in the language of II Corinthians 10:6:

> **And having in a readiness to revenge all disobedience, when your obedience is fulfilled.**

II Thessalonians 2:3, 4 speaks of it in this way:

> **Let no man deceive you by any means: for that day shall not come, except there come a falling away first, and that man of sin be revealed, the son of perdition; Who opposeth and exalteth himself above all that is called God, or that is worshipped; so that he as God**

sitteth in the temple of God, shewing himself that he is God.

> *All of these passages tell us in different ways*
> *that the end of the church age will come.*

All of these passages tell us in different ways that the end of the church age will come. We see the believers in the churches killed in Revelation 11:7. God will "revenge" the disobedience of the churches after their work is done. The phrase **"when your obedience is fulfilled"** matches Revelation 11:7, which says, **"when they shall have finished their testimony."**

The II Thessalonians 2 passage tells us the death of the churches comes with Satan ruling in the churches. So, all of these passages are telling us the same thing, namely, that the end of the church age will come at some point. As we will see in this study, that time is now.

The Beast that Comes from the Sea

Let us examine some verses in Revelation 13 to better understand this Great Tribulation time and the end of the church age. We will start with verses 1-3:

> **And I stood upon the sand of the sea, and saw a beast rise up out of the sea, having seven heads and ten horns, and upon his horns ten crowns, and upon his heads the name of blasphemy. And the beast which I saw was like unto a leopard, and his feet were as the feet of a bear, and his mouth as the mouth of a lion: and the dragon gave him his power, and his seat, and great authority. And I saw one of his heads as it were wounded to death; and his deadly wound was healed: and all the world wondered after the beast.**

This beast is a representation of Satan. But it is looking particularly at the rule of Satan over all of the unsaved during the Great Tribulation of our day. We know this to be so for at least two reasons. The first is that he comes out of the sea. In the Bible, the sea frequently represents hell. Remember that Satan was cast into hell (he became eternally subject to the wrath of God), at the cross. But remember, too, that Revelation 20 teaches that just before the end, Satan would be loosed from his prison so that he would go out to deceive the nations of the world (Revelation 20:7, 8). That is why

Revelation 13:3 declares his death wound was healed.

This beast has seven heads and ten horns but the ten horns are crowned. This indicates the rule of Satan during the Great Tribulation period. In Revelation 17:12, we read:

And the ten horns which thou sawest are ten kings, which have received no kingdom as yet; but receive power as kings one hour with the beast.

We will discover later on that the phrase "one hour" or "one day" refers very particularly to the entire time of the Great Tribulation period. (See Appendix A.)

Returning to Revelation 13:2, we read that this beast, who we now know represents the rule of Satan during the Great Tribulation, was like a leopard, a bear, and a lion. It is a picture of Satan coming as a savage wild beast to destroy. Verses 4 and 5 continue:

And they worshipped the dragon which gave power unto the beast: and they worshipped the beast, saying, Who is like unto the beast? who is able to make war with him? And there was given unto him a mouth speaking great things and blasphemies; and power was given unto him to continue forty and two months.

The unsaved all over the world worship Satan during this time of Great Tribulation. It might be noted that in our day, the intense interest in the occult and in days like Halloween indicates the enormous adulation that Satan is receiving. Verses 6 and 7 state:

And he opened his mouth in blasphemy against God, to blaspheme his name, and his tabernacle, and them that dwell in heaven. And it was given unto him to make war with the saints, and to overcome them: and power was given him over all kindreds, and tongues, and nations.

Because he has been loosed by God to again deceive the nations, his chief attack is against the believers in Christ. This is so because they are the body of Christ and Christ is the chief enemy of Satan whom he wishes to destroy.

God has loosed Satan to prepare the world for the judgment of the last day. But in God's divine arrangement, judgment is to begin at the house of

God (I Peter 4:17). Therefore, verse 6 teaches that Satan blasphemes, that is, he mocks, ridicules, and speaks scandalously against the true believers and he was able to overcome the saints (the true believers).

> *How can Satan overcome the saints?*
> *Aren't they forever safe with Christ?*

How can Satan overcome the saints? Aren't they forever safe with Christ? True, but he overcomes them in the sense that they are driven from the churches and congregations. Remember John 16:2:

They shall put you out of the synagogues: yea, the time cometh, that whosoever killeth you will think that he doeth God service.

During the Great Tribulation, as we will presently see, Satan will be ruling in the congregations, and the true believers will be killed (driven out of the churches). This identifies with Revelation 11:7:

And when they shall have finished their testimony, the beast that ascendeth out of the bottomless pit shall make war against them, and shall overcome them, and kill them.

Thus, during the Great Tribulation, except for the true believers who no longer are a part of the churches and congregations, Satan will rule over all, both in the churches and outside of the churches. Satan ruling in the churches corresponds with the end of the church age, God is no longer using the churches to evangelize the world.

Thus far we have learned that the beast that comes out of the sea represents Satan as he rules during the Great Tribulation period of our day. Continuing with Revelation 13, we read in verses 11, 12:

And I beheld another beast coming up out of the earth; and he had two horns like a lamb, and he spake as a dragon. And he exerciseth all the power of the first beast before him, and causeth the earth and them which dwell therein to worship the first beast, whose deadly wound was healed.

The Beast that Comes Out of the Earth

God now is speaking of a beast coming out of the earth. We know that this beast also is Satan. However, Satan now is presented as antichrist, that is, he looks and acts like Christ. He has two horns like a lamb (that is, like Christ the Lamb of God). Yet we are not to be deceived, "he spake as a dragon." It is Satan masquerading as Christ as he takes over the rulership of the churches and congregations during the Great Tribulation of our day. This identifies with the language of II Thessalonians 2:3, 4:

> **Let no man deceive you by any means: for that day shall not come, except there come a falling away first, and that man of sin be revealed, the son of perdition; Who opposeth and exalteth himself above all that is called God, or that is worshipped; so that he as God sitteth in the temple of God, shewing himself that he is God.**

> *During the Great Tribulation, Satan will be sitting (that is, ruling) in these churches.*

The temple of God is the churches and congregations. But during the Great Tribulation, Satan will be sitting (that is, ruling) in these churches. God the Holy Spirit will no longer be in the midst of the congregations. Satan has overcome the true believers by driving them out (they are killed), and now he is free to rule as he pleases. Those who remain in these churches think they are worshipping God, but in actuality, they are worshipping Satan. Thus, this beast that comes out of the earth also represents Satan. More particularly, it represents Satan as he rules in the churches and congregations during the Great Tribulation period of our day. Later on, in Revelation 19:20, he is called the false prophet. He is called the false prophet because it is Satan ruling in the churches and congregations.

Fire from Heaven

Returning to Revelation 13, we next read, in verses 13, 14:

> **And he doeth great wonders, so that he maketh fire come down from heaven on the earth in the sight of men, And deceiveth them that dwell on the earth by the means of those miracles which he had**

power to do in the sight of the beast; saying to them that dwell on the earth, that they should make an image to the beast, which had the wound by a sword, and did live.

We read here in Revelation 13:13-14 that Satan will be calling down fire from heaven. However, as we study the Bible, we learn that Satan cannot literally call down fire from heaven. This is proven by the contest between the 450 prophets of Baal, who were Satan's emissaries, and Elijah. We can read about this in I Kings 18. But God gave Satan a demonstration that showed that causing someone to fall backward was equivalent to calling down fire from heaven.

In Numbers 16 we read of the rebellion against Moses that was led by three men, Korah, Dathan, and Abiram. We read in Numbers 16:2-3:

And they rose up before Moses, with certain of the children of Israel, two hundred and fifty princes of the assembly, famous in the congregation, men of renown: And they gathered themselves together against Moses and against Aaron, and said unto them, Ye take too much upon you, seeing all the congregation are holy, every one of them, and the LORD is among them: wherefore then lift ye up yourselves above the congregation of the LORD?

The consequences of this rebellion were that the earth opened up and swallowed the families of the three men and the destruction by fire of the 250 men who rebelled. Numbers 16:35: "And there came out a fire from the LORD, and consumed the two hundred and fifty men that offered incense." The next day the Israelites complained. Numbers 16:41: "But on the morrow all the congregation of the children of Israel murmured against Moses and against Aaron, saying, Ye have killed the people of the LORD." As a result of this added rebellion on the part of Israel, God sent a plague into Israel that began to kill the Israelites in great numbers. Only the timely intervention of Aaron in making an atonement for Israel kept God from killing all of Israel. We read of this terrible judgment and its remedy in Numbers 16:45-48:

Get you up from among this congregation, that I may consume them as in a moment. And they fell upon their faces. And Moses said unto Aaron, Take a censer, and put fire therein from off the altar, and put on incense, and go quickly unto the congregation, and make an atonement for them: for there is wrath gone out from the

LORD; the plague is begun. And Aaron took as Moses commanded, and ran into the midst of the congregation; and, behold, the plague was begun among the people: and he put on incense, and made an atonement for the people. And he stood between the dead and the living; and the plague was stayed.

In this account, rebellious Israel is representative of mankind who has rebelled against God. The plague that killed a great many of the Israelites and the fire that came down and destroyed the 250 men point to the judgment of God that will destroy all of the unsaved. The atonement offered by Aaron as well as Aaron himself, as he stood between the dead and the living, represent Christ who stopped the wrath of God from falling on all those for whom He made atonement. Thus, we see much of the Gospel of salvation in this account.

Does Satan Make Fire Come from Heaven?

We read again in Revelation 13:13, that the beast **"maketh fire come down from heaven on the earth in the sight of men."** Does this mean that at some point in time, Satan will be able to literally make fire come down from heaven? Actually, we can see that this phenomenon is presently happening worldwide, but it is not a literal fire, it is an activity that is the equivalent of calling down fire from heaven. Let us search the Bible to see how this can be.

In two outstanding examples in which Satan, through his emissaries, threatened believers, fire came down from heaven to destroy the wicked ones.

In II Kings 1, we read of the wicked king of Israel sending a captain with fifty men to take Elijah. In the face of Satan's open assault on believers, Elijah, who represents believers, called down fire from heaven and the captain and fifty men were destroyed.

In Revelation 20, we read of Satan assaulting the camp of the saints by means of the nations from the four corners of the earth, and fire came down from heaven to destroy these nations.

There was another time when Satan assaulted the kingdom of God and fire should have been called down from heaven to destroy him. Instead, a different action was taken to show that Satan could have been destroyed by fire. That action, therefore, became the equivalent of calling down fire from heaven.

The event was when Jesus was in the Garden of Gethsemane, and Judas and the temple soldiers came to take Jesus. Satan himself was there, because a bit earlier, he had entered into Judas (Luke 22:3). Satan was so much a part of what followed that Christ called Judas a "devil" (John 6:70-71). Jesus asked Judas and the temple soldiers, "Whom seek ye? And they said, Jesus of Nazareth." Jesus then answered, "I am" (John 18:4-5).

At that moment, following the action of Elijah as recorded in II Kings 1, and the action against the forces of evil as recorded in Revelation 20, Jesus should have called down fire from heaven to destroy the enemies who would bind Him, but Jesus could not take this action. He declared to the temple soldiers, **"this is your hour, and the power of darkness"** (Luke 22:53). Christ could not destroy these enemies because it was necessary that He be bound and go to the cross to pay for our sins. Only then could He be our Savior.

Jesus showed that He was willingly being bound and that it was God's will that He be taken, but Christ could have destroyed these enemies. Instead of bringing fire from heaven, when Jesus said, "I am," He caused them to reel backward and fall to the ground (John 18:6). This was a substitute action to show that He had the power to destroy them.

The Bible also instructs us that Satan cannot make fire come down from heaven.

We learned from Revelation 13:13 that Satan will cause fire to come down from heaven, but the Bible also instructs us that Satan cannot make fire come down from heaven. Do you recall the contest between Elijah and the prophets of Baal (I Kings 18)? The 450 prophets of Baal, whose head is Satan, tried all day to cause fire to come down to the altar they had made. But they failed totally to accomplish this. Elijah, on the other hand, prayed that God would send fire on the altar that Elijah had built, and fire came down and consumed the offering, the wood, and even the stones of the altar.

Therefore, Satan cannot literally call down fire from heaven. Satan was present when Jesus caused those who came to take Him to fall backward as a substitute for calling down fire from heaven (John 18). This is the solution to the prophecy that Satan would call down fire from heaven: He causes people to fall backward to the ground under some supernatural power as the equivalent of calling fire from heaven. Thus, this could be the manner through which Revelation 13:13 finds its fulfillment. Among the false gospels of our day, there is an extensive phenomenon going on in which many people fall backward by some supernatural power. Among some, this is called "being slain in the spirit." Since Satan himself cannot literally call down fire from heaven, he follows the lead of Jesus and causes people to fall backward, which is a substitute for calling down fire from heaven.

Falling Backward Equals Fire from Heaven

Thus, this miracle of people falling backward to the ground which is occurring all over the world is clear evidence that we are now in the Great Tribulation period of Revelation 13 and Matthew 24. This supernatural activity is one of the signs Satan employs to assure those in these churches that Christ is still active within these churches. Satan wishes to be like God. God is the judge of all the earth. God shows His right and ability to judge by calling down fire to destroy the one being judged. Satan is not the judge in any sense, but he tries to show he is judge by causing people to fall backward. That is why the churches in which he does this speak of it as being "slain in the spirit." Additionally, other supernatural activities, such as Satan giving messages to people in many churches by means of visions and the supernatural activity of tongues, are given by Satan to try to assure those in these churches that Christ is still ruling there.

In these verses, God tells us that Satan, as he comes as the beast out of the earth or as the false prophet, causes those who dwell on the earth to **"make an image to the beast, which had the wound by a sword, and did live"** (Revelation 13:14). That is, to make an image of Satan. Furthermore, concerning this image, we read in Revelation 13, verse 15:

> **And he had power to give life unto the image of the beast, that the image of the beast should both speak, and cause that as many as would not worship the image of the beast should be killed.**

How are we to understand this image of Satan to which life has been given? This is a very important question because in Revelation 14:9, we read about those who worship his image. And remember in Revelation 14:7 we read the warning that we are to worship only God the Creator.

The Image of the Beast

Making an image is the same as making a likeness of any entity. The image or likeness is not the entity but it represents the entity. The true

believer, for example, has become the image of Christ. We read in II
Corinthians 3:18:

**But we all, with open face beholding as in a glass the glory of the
Lord, are changed into the same image from glory to glory, even as
by the Spirit of the Lord.**

We read in Colossians 3:10:

**And have put on the new man, which is renewed in knowledge after
the image of him that created him:**

And in Romans 1:23 we read:

**And changed the glory of the uncorruptible God into an image
made like to corruptible man, and to birds, and fourfooted beasts,
and creeping things.**

Studying these verses assures us that the image of God is the true
believers. The image of Satan is all the unsaved. This agrees with Jesus'
assessment of the Israel of His day. He declares in John 8:44:

**Ye are of your father the devil, and the lusts of your father ye will
do. He was a murderer from the beginning, and abode not in the
truth, because there is no truth in him. When he speaketh a lie, he
speaketh of his own: for he is a liar, and the father of it.**

Thus, we can understand that the image of Satan consists of the unsaved
within the churches. They have been given life only in the sense that they
have contact with the supernatural as they receive messages by means of
tongues or voices or visions. They have contact with the supernatural by
falling backwards. Of course, it is false life, but to those who experience these
things, the experiences assure them that they must be alive in Christ.

What then could the Bible mean when it speaks about worshipping the
image of the beast? We worship the one who is our master, the one we look
to as our authority. To worship means to bow down before the one to whom
we have surrendered our will. Thus, as true believers, our will has been
surrendered to Christ because we worship Him as our Lord and our God.

The question must be posed: In any church or congregation, who is the
authority that should rule our life. Is it the Bible, the Bible alone? Or is it the

theologians and Bible teachers of the denomination to which we belong.

In any conservative church of today, the answer comes very quickly. The Bible alone is our authority. But is that really so! Who developed doctrines such as the one that we must accept Christ to become saved, or that we must be baptized in water as a condition for salvation, or that faith is an instrument God gives us so we might become saved, or that water baptism seals us in some way, or that one can divorce an adulterous husband, etc. Since these doctrines did not come from God, they could only have come from the minds of men.

Some or all of these doctrines are adhered to and effectively obeyed in virtually every church and congregation of our day.

If these doctrines came from the minds of men, the lofty thinking of theologians, they did not come from God. The very fact that they dare to hold these doctrines as truth when they are not truth means that they are trusting a lie. That in turn means that ultimately, they are worshipping the father of lies, who is Satan. And they themselves are the image of Satan.

We must remember, of course, that throughout the history of the New Testament church, many of these false doctrines existed in churches that God used to further the great commission of evangelizing the world. However, we must also remember God is a long-suffering God. He has tolerated these New Testament high places for a long, long time. We have seen that same patience of God as He tolerated the high places of Israel and Judah for hundreds of years.

But there is an end to God's patience. He has decreed there would come a time when He would destroy the high places. He did this by destroying Israel in 709 B.C. and Judah in 587 B.C. He did this by loosing Satan so that he would rule in the temple, in the churches and congregations of our day.

> *Significantly, in virtually every church that exists*
> *anywhere in the world,*
> *the image of the beast is worshipped.*

Significantly, in virtually every church that exists anywhere in the world, the image of the beast is worshipped. That is, doctrines developed out of the minds of men are regarded as God's truth.

Fact is, this matter of regarding any doctrines spawned by the thinking of theologians as God's truth betrays the mentality that the corporate church effectively rules over the Bible. Protestants fault the Roman Catholics because they plainly contend that the church rules over the Bible. The reality is that the same condition prevails in the Protestant churches. This is another way of saying that the image of Satan, that is, the minds of corruptible man is being worshipped.

Worship the Image of the Beast or Be Killed

Remember we read in Revelation 13:15, **"that as many as would not worship the image of the beast should be killed."** The evidence of the reality of this statement is seen in a startling fashion in our day. In any conservative church of our day, which we may have always considered to be most faithful to the Bible, if we try to remain there as a member but take serious issue with statements of the confessions of that denomination, statements that can be shown to be in violation of the Bible, take issue with that church's stand on marriage and divorce, ordinarily, such action will cause that individual to be driven out. Spiritually, he will be killed. If a pastor of such a church begins to object to the doctrines his church holds, and which he can show to be in violation of the Bible, he will be driven out of that denomination. Spiritually, he will be killed.

Returning to Revelation 14:7, now we can understand why God is warning that the Gospel we are to proclaim during the latter rain should emphasize that we are to worship God who **"made heaven, and earth, and the sea, and the fountains of waters."** Trusting our church, our theologians, or any entity of any kind rather than God the Creator will no longer be tolerated by God.

In fact, this is a solemn warning to a ministry like Family Radio, that we better be sure that the doctrines we bring to the world are as Biblical as possible. As we have already learned, we are to be especially concerned that the salvation message does not in the slightest way teach that any work that we do assisted in our salvation.

Continuing a bit longer in Revelation 13, we read in verses 16 and 17:

And he causeth all, both small and great, rich and poor, free and bond, to receive a mark in their right hand, or in their foreheads: And that no man might buy or sell, save he that had the mark, or the name of the beast, or the number of his name.

These two verses introduce more questions. What is signified by the mark of the beast? What does it mean to buy or sell?

Satan ruling in the temple, that is, ruling in the churches and congregations during the Great Tribulation, causes everyone present there to receive Satan's mark. We must understand this to simply mean that those who are not saved carry the ownership brand of Satan. Like a cattleman puts his ownership brand on his cattle so there is no question about who owns the cattle, so Satan spiritually has his mark or brand on those who worship him or his image.

Similarly, we read in Revelation 14:1 that the 144,000, who are the complete fullness of all who became saved during the church age, have an identification mark on them. They have their Father's name written on their forehead. We know, of course, that a name is not literally placed on each believer's forehead. Rather, it is language to show that these 144,000 are eternally owned by God and they are citizens of His kingdom. Later in our study, we will look again at these 144,000.

What Does Buy or Sell Mean?

But what does the phrase "buy or sell" signify?

This is a crucial question because verse 17 declares that no one can buy or sell unless he has the mark of the beast.

When we search the Bible to help us understand the phrase "buy or sell," we find that God employs language that identifies Jesus as a merchant. In Matthew 13:45, 46 we read:

Again, the kingdom of heaven is like unto a merchant man, seeking goodly pearls: Who, when he had found one pearl of great price, went and sold all that he had, and bought it.

The merchant in this parable can only be Christ. The pearl is the kingdom of God. Christ sold all that he had, that is, He emptied Himself of His glory and became the suffering servant in order to obtain the kingdom of God.

In Isaiah 55:1 we read:

Ho, every one that thirsteth, come ye to the waters, and he that hath no money; come ye, buy, and eat; yea, come, buy wine and milk without money and without price.

This language is also the language of a merchant who has the Gospel for sale. It is a Gospel that can be bought without money and without price. In other references, the sending forth of the Gospel is typified by merchant ships (for example, the ships of Tarshish) that bring to Jerusalem gold, silver, and all manner of precious things.

The virtuous woman of Proverbs 31:18, **"perceiveth that her merchandise is good,"** and Proverbs 31:14 says, **"She is like the merchants' ships."** Proverbs 31:24, **"She maketh fine linen, and selleth it."** She can be shown to be a picture of the believers as we buy without money the Gospel and sell it to others who buy from us without money. Thus, buying and selling has entirely to do with sending forth the Gospel.

Returning to Revelation 13:17, we read that in the churches and congregations that have come under the rule of Satan, no one can buy or sell; that is, no one can bring the Gospel there unless they have the mark of the beast.

What terrible information this is. Effectively, God is saying that in these churches and congregations where Satan now rules, no one can preach or teach there unless they are not saved. What is even worse is that, since everyone in the congregation believes they have a prophetic office to declare the Word of God based upon passages like Acts 2:17, the ominous warning of Revelation 13:17 in principle can apply to everyone in the congregation.

This information dramatically increases the problem that pastors and Bible teachers in churches face. It cannot mean that each and every pastor ministering in any church is automatically proven to be unsaved. But it does mean when a pastor or any believer within that church is faced with the Biblical information concerning the Great Tribulation and then insists that this is not the time to flee from his church, or if he insists that somehow his church is the exception and he can continue to minister in this congregation, or if he offers any other rationale as to why he should not leave, the serious question must be raised, "How then does this pastor or believer answer to this terrible warning of Revelation 13:17?" Indeed, these are extremely serious verses. The serious nature of these warnings is further set forth in Revelation 14:9-11:

> **And the third angel followed them, saying with a loud voice, If any man worship the beast and his image, and receive his mark in his forehead, or in his hand, The same shall drink of the wine of the wrath of God, which is poured out without mixture into the cup of his indignation; and he shall be tormented with fire and brimstone in the presence of the holy angels, and in the presence of the Lamb: And the smoke of their torment ascendeth up for ever and ever: and they have no rest day nor night, who worship the beast and his**

image, and whosoever receiveth the mark of his name.

These verses are so clear they need no further explanation.

As we have studied these verses in Revelation 13, we have seen more and more evidence that the beginning of the Great Tribulation spoken of in Matthew 24 corresponds with the end of the church age. Revelation 13 shows that during the Great Tribulation, the churches will be under God's judgment and that God has given the churches over to Satan. With the churches under God's wrath and under Satan's rulership, we can see clear proof that the beginning of the Great Tribulation signifies that we are at the end of the church age.

Chapter 8.
More on the Great Tribulation

A Famine of Hearing the Word of God

We have learned that in God's predetermined plan for the world that we have finally come to that time which God calls the time of Great Tribulation. It is the time when the work of the corporate external church has been finished. It is no longer being used of God to do the work that had been assigned to it as its principle endeavor. That work is to evangelize the world. For more than 1950 years, even though the churches and congregations have had many imperfections and doctrinal failures, God has used them as a divine organism, as a God blessed institution to spread the Gospel to every area of the world.

But now the time has come when the era of the church age has come to an end. The time has come for others to complete the task of world evangelization. And simultaneously with the end of the church age, God has brought His judgment upon the churches. For more than 1950 years God has tolerated the wrong doctrines even as He tolerated the high places of Old Testament Israel. But now God has loosed Satan and through his deceptions, churches all over the world have become apostate, following the desires of men rather than those of God. Satan has been allowed to marshal his forces to surround Jerusalem and destroy it. We will learn that the terms "Jerusalem" and "Judea" can only refer to the corporate external church.

But the question once more must be raised: If a church earnestly tries to remove all of its wrong doctrines (its spiritual high places), and if it still has true believers within it, why can't it continue as a viable God-blessed congregation?

> *The primary purpose of the church is to evangelize.*

One answer to this question has to do with the nature and purpose of the church. The primary purpose of the church is to evangelize. Preaching should be such that first of all, those who attend the church, including the children, might hear the true Gospel and that God would bless the Word in the lives of those who are the hearers. In this manner, a great many who are a part of that church might become saved. Additionally, it was to send out missionaries both locally in their cities but also into all the world. As this was faithfully done, God's program was to bless these activities so that all of His elect could become saved.

But then we read Amos 8:11:

Behold, the days come, saith the Lord GOD, that I will send a famine in the land, not a famine of bread, nor a thirst for water, but of hearing the words of the LORD.

The Book of Amos is speaking of the very time in which we are now living. And this verse is very pertinent to this time. God is speaking of a famine that is to come. It is not a famine of bread and water. Spiritually, bread identifies with Jesus who is the bread of life. Water has to do with the true Gospel. Thus, God is declaring this is not a time when there is a famine of the declaration of the true Gospel. That is, in the churches that exist today there may be pastors who still faithfully bring the true Gospel to their congregations. There may be missionaries who are sent out by these faithful churches who are still faithfully bringing the Gospel to the lost of the world.

However, it is the next phrase that is so ominous, a famine "**of <u>hearing</u> the words of the LORD.**" Why is that so ominous. We must remember, there are two very important ingredients in God's plan of saving the elect. First of all, they must be under the hearing of the Word of God. Faith cometh by hearing and hearing by the Word of God (Romans 8:17).

Secondly, God must apply that faithful Word to the hearts of those He plans to save. God opened the heart of Lydia (Acts 16:14). That is, if God is going to save someone, He must give that person spiritual ears to hear the Word spoken.

Jesus, for example, the perfect preacher declared the Gospel for three and a half years and yet at the end of His ministry, there were only 120 believers in Jerusalem and a little more than 500 in Galilee. And many of these were already saved before Christ began to preach. Jesus tells us why this was so in Matthew 13:13, 14:

Therefore speak I to them in parables: because they seeing see not; and hearing they hear not, neither do they understand. And in them is fulfilled the prophecy of Esaias, which saith, By hearing ye shall hear, and shall not understand; and seeing ye shall see, and shall not perceive.

For three and a half years, there had been the most faithful preaching possible, but God was not applying that Word to the hearts of those who were hearing it. But when Peter preached one sermon at Pentecost, about 3,000 were saved. Obviously, it is not the faithful preaching alone that God uses a means to save people. It also requires that the Holy Spirit apply that Word to the hearts of those God plans to save.

The Holy Spirit Is Taken from the Midst

The Bible approaches this issue from a different vantage point in II Thessalonians 2:3-12. There God is speaking of the time when the man of sin will take his seat in the temple of God and will be worshipped as God. The man of sin can only be Satan. He is called a man because he is typified by the king of Babylon. Isaiah 14 prophesies that the king of Babylon who is also called Lucifer would desire to be like the most High (Isaiah 14:14). It also declares that he wanted to sit, that is reign, upon the mount of the congregation (Isaiah 14:13).

This desire of Satan (Lucifer) was fulfilled during the time of the Great Tribulation even as II Thessalonians declares that the man of sin would sit (reign) in the temple of God.

Returning to II Thessalonians 2, we read verse 7, which warns:

For the mystery of iniquity doth already work: only he who now letteth will let, until he be taken out of the way.

The word "letteth" is an old English word that would better be translated "restraineth." The word "way" in the phrase "taken out of the way" is altogether incorrect. It is a Greek word that is found many times in the Bible but never, except here, is it translated as "way." It is most commonly translated "midst."

Many Bible scholars have correctly seen that the "he" who now restraineth must be the Holy Spirit. **"The mystery of iniquity doth already work"** tells us there has always been sin or iniquity in the temple (the New Testament churches). But this mystery of iniquity has been restrained by God binding Satan (Revelation 20:2).

However, the time was to come when the one who restrains, who can be none other than the Holy Spirit, would be taken out of the midst. The question is, which midst is the Holy Spirit removed from to allow Satan to rule in the churches and congregations.

Obviously, the only possibility is that the Holy Spirit would be taken from the midst of the temple.

In Matthew 18:20, the Bible declares:

For where two or three are gathered together in my name, there am I in the midst of them.

This verse is anticipating the season of the church age when God would be present in the midst of the believers, however small in number they might be. In John 14:17, Jesus anticipated this condition during the church age by declaring:

Even the Spirit of truth; whom the world cannot receive, because it seeth him not, neither knoweth him: but ye know him; for he dwelleth with you, and shall be in you.

In this verse, Jesus is anticipating Pentecost when the Holy Spirit would be in the midst of the believers.

We must remember the Holy Spirit is always present within the life of the true believer. Romans 8:9 informs us that if we do not have the Spirit, we are none of His. Throughout history a characteristic of every true believer is that at the moment of salvation, he became indwelt by the Holy Spirit. However, in John 14:17, Jesus is referring to the situation that existed during the ministry of Jesus. While the true believers were indwelt by the Holy Spirit, the Holy Spirit was not in them in the sense of being in their midst to save. We know this to be true because earlier in our study, we learned that very few people became saved during the time of Christ's ministry. John 14:17 then declares that He will be in you. That is, when the Holy Spirit was poured out at Pentecost, the Holy Spirit was in the midst of the believers in order to save.

In I Corinthians 3, the Bible discusses the building of the temple. Within it are gold, silver, and precious stones (the true believers). But also within it are wood, hay, and stubble (those who believe they are saved but obviously are not saved).

In I Corinthians 3:16, God speaks of the temple being made of many individuals:

Know ye not that ye are the temple of God, and that the Spirit of God dwelleth in you?

The word "ye" in this verse is plural. That is, the temple consists of many individuals who together are the temple. The verse continues by declaring "the Spirit of God dwelleth in you." Again, the word "you" is a plural word indicating, therefore, that the Spirit of God indwells the congregations as they are being used of God to evangelize.

As we learned earlier, when Jesus preached, very few became saved. During the time Jesus preached, the Holy Spirit was not in the midst of the believers to apply the Word to the lives of the unsaved. But at Pentecost, the Holy Spirit was poured out and about 3,000 were saved, and ever since then, in the New Testament era, people are saved as the Gospel is sent out.

However, II Thessalonians 2 indicates there will be a time when the Holy Spirit will be taken out of the midst. We must understand then that the Holy Spirit will be taken out of the temple. That is, He will remove Himself from the congregations and denominations that had become a part of the temple of God.

> *We must understand then that the*
> *Holy Spirit will be taken out of the temple.*

The presence of the Holy Spirit is to guide the work of the church. More importantly, He is to apply the Word of God as it is faithfully preached to the hearts of those whom God has elected to salvation.

The Holy Spirit Restrains Satan

But the question must be asked: Why does God speak of someone (the Holy Spirit) who restrains being taken out of the midst? We can find our answer if we look at the parable of the sower. Remember the seed was the Word of God. The seed fell by the wayside and the fowls of the air devoured it (Luke 8:5). Jesus explained the meaning of this in Luke 8:12:

Those by the way side are they that hear; then cometh the devil, and taketh away the word out of their hearts, lest they should believe and be saved.

When Satan has taken his seat (become the ruler) in the temple (the churches and congregations) and the Holy Spirit is no longer in the midst of the congregation, there is no longer anyone to restrain Satan from taking the Word of God, however faithfully it has been preached, out of the listeners' hearts so that they may become saved. Therefore, if the Holy Spirit is no longer working in the church, it means no one can become saved as the result of the preaching in that church. This is so because God is no longer present to apply the Word to the hearts of the unsaved. Effectively, the candlestick has been removed, and that is why the believers are commanded to come out of Judea and Jerusalem. This is so even though there is still plenty of spiritual bread and water, there is still faithful preaching.

Now we can understand more plainly verse 19 of Matthew 24, where we read:

And woe unto them that are with child, and to them that give suck in those days!

The terrible truth is that children born in that congregation may be under the hearing of good preaching, but if the Holy Spirit is not in the midst of that congregation, they will not become saved. That family has a serious problem that can be remedied only by leaving the congregation. We can now understand the sad verses recorded in Lamentations 2:11, 12 where we read:

Mine eyes do fail with tears, my bowels are troubled, my liver is poured upon the earth, for the destruction of the daughter of my people; because the children and the sucklings swoon in the streets of the city. They say to their mothers, Where is corn and wine? when they swooned as the wounded in the streets of the city, when their soul was poured out into their mothers' bosom.

These sorrowful words are part of a lament that the Holy Spirit spoke through Jeremiah as Judah was experiencing the judgment of God following the death of King Josiah in 609 B.C.

"Where is corn and wine?" Corn and wine are words pointing to the Gospel. Jesus is the bread of life. He has provided His blood (the wine) for our salvation. But now there is no corn and wine, no salvation possible. This is because there is a famine of hearing the Word of God. The Holy Spirit is no longer working in the congregations.

The true Gospel may still be faithfully preached. Those who are saved may believe they experience blessings, but what about the infants and the children. If the Holy Spirit is not applying the Word of God by giving these children spiritual ears, they will remain spiritually dead. How awful this is. This is a frightening truth that parents must face. If they truly love their children and are praying for their salvation, they must consider this problem very seriously.

Jeremiah is Speaking about the Churches of Our Day

The Book of Jeremiah has been in the Bible for more than 2,000 years. However, most pastors and Bible teachers have paid little or no attention to this book. This is a result of the very negative character of most of the book. It is also a result of the fact that much of it was difficult to understand. This was caused by the fact that it, like many other parts of the Bible, teaches truth concerning the very end of time. We have learned that there are parts of the Bible that have been sealed up until the end of time. That is, God will not give true believers a clear understanding of the Gospel message contained in these passages until we have come very near to the end of the world.

This is the situation that prevails with the Book of Jeremiah. We will discover that almost the entire book is pointing to the time of the Great Tribulation of our day. True, it is recording the experiences of Judah at the time it was destroyed by Babylon in 587 B.C. But we will discover that the destruction of Judah was given as an example or as an illustration of what the church can expect during the Great Tribulation of our day.

There are at least three proofs in the Book of Jeremiah that its focus is primarily on our day.

The First Proof

The first of these proofs is in the language of Jeremiah 2:2. There we read:

Go and cry in the ears of Jerusalem, saying, Thus saith the LORD; I remember thee, the kindness of thy youth, the love of thine espousals, when thou wentest after me in the wilderness, in a land that was not sown.

This verse is speaking of a Jerusalem that was in the wilderness, in a land that was not sown. We know that ancient Israel was in the wilderness for 40 years immediately after they left Egypt. This verse emphasizes that while in this wilderness, there was some very fine spiritual conduct that was in evidence and which God remembers. **"I remember thee, the kindness of thy youth, the love of thine espousals."** The word "youth" certainly can apply to Israel in the wilderness. That was the time they were first formed as a congregation. The same is true of the word "espousals." It is a word that identifies with the beginning of a marriage. The Bible clearly teaches that God became spiritually married to Israel.

But what about the words "kindness" and "love"? Does the Bible teach anywhere that these attributes were ever in view when Israel was in the wilderness? The Hebrew word translated "kindness" is also frequently translated in the Bible as "mercy," "goodness," and "loving kindness." Does the Bible speak anywhere of the mercy, the goodness, the kindness, or the loving kindness of Israel when they were in the wilderness? This is a word that must identify with true believers. Fact is, throughout the Bible, it is a word that most often is attributed to God Himself.

Search as we might, we cannot find anywhere in the Bible where this word is associated with Israel in the wilderness. Instead, we constantly read of Israel complaining and rebelling against God. Hebrews 3:17-19 sums up the spiritual condition of Israel in the wilderness. We read there:

But with whom was he grieved forty years? was it not with them that had sinned, whose carcases fell in the wilderness? And to whom sware he that they should not enter into his rest, but to them that believed not? So we see that they could not enter in because of unbelief.

In Numbers 14:29, 30, God assures us that this included virtually the whole nation. These verses tell us:

Your carcases shall fall in this wilderness; and all that were numbered of you, according to your whole number, from twenty years old and upward, which have murmured against me, Doubtless ye shall not come into the land, concerning which I sware to make you dwell therein, save Caleb the son of Jephunneh, and Joshua the son of Nun.

Thus, we wonder about the phrase recorded in Jeremiah 2:2, **"I remember thee, the kindness of thy youth."** It surely does not appear to apply to Israel during their forty years in the wilderness.

The same problem applies to the phrase, "the love of thine espousals." Nowhere do we find the concept of Israel's love for God in connection with their forty year wilderness sojourn.

The Churches Are Jerusalem

How then are we to understand Jeremiah 2:2? What other Jerusalem was there to which Jeremiah was to cry? What other Jerusalem identifies with the wilderness? There is a Biblical answer to these questions. Remember we learned earlier in our study that the churches and congregations of our day are called Jerusalem. Remember they are composed of true believers, who are called the Jerusalem above in Galatians 4, and in I Corinthians 3 they are called gold, silver, and precious stones. These churches also have within them the Jerusalem which now is and it is in bondage with her children (Galatians 4:25). These are those in the churches who are still in bondage to sin. They identify with the wood, hay, and stubble of I Corinthians 3.

This Jerusalem had its beginning at the beginning of the church age. This is the Jerusalem that identifies with the woman of Revelation 12 who dwelt in the wilderness (Revelation 12:6, 14).

However, if the churches that existed throughout the church age are the Jerusalem that is in view in Jeremiah 2:2, can the other statements in this verse properly relate, **"the kindness of thy youth, the love of thine espousals"**?

The fact is, these statements agree perfectly with the Jerusalem that is identified with the church age. When was the church age in its youth? And what was its spiritual condition at its beginning? We know the church age began immediately following the resurrection of Christ. As we look at the seven churches of Revelation 2 and Revelation 3, we see their spiritual condition when the church age was still in its youth. Revelation 2:2, 3 declares:

> **I know thy works, and thy labour, and thy patience, and how thou canst not bear them which are evil: and thou hast tried them which say they are apostles, and are not, and hast found them liars: And hast borne, and hast patience, and for my name's sake hast laboured, and hast not fainted.**

Revelation 2:4 informs μs that there was love for God in the early church:

> **Nevertheless I have somewhat against thee, because thou hast left thy first love.**

In Revelation 2:9, 19 and in Revelation 3:8, 10 are additional statements indicating the faithfulness of the early church.

> **Revelation 2:9: I know thy works, and tribulation, and poverty, (but thou art rich) and I know the blasphemy of them which say they are Jews, and are not, but are the synagogue of Satan.**

Revelation 2:19: I know thy works, and charity, and service, and faith, and thy patience, and thy works; and the last to be more than the first.

Revelation 3:8: I know thy works: behold, I have set before thee an open door, and no man can shut it: for thou hast a little strength, and hast kept my word, and hast not denied my name.

Revelation 3:10: Because thou hast kept the word of my patience, I also will keep thee from the hour of temptation, which shall come upon all the world, to try them that dwell upon the earth.

Can we say however that they were espoused, that is, were married to Christ? They were not married to Him as a corporate external representation of the kingdom of God. But within the church there were both believers and unbelievers, Jerusalem above and Jerusalem which now is. Those who were the true believers are the bride of Christ. They were espoused to Christ. They were those who could identify with kindness and love.

This youthful church had not yet been sown as Jeremiah 2:3 indicates. It was just taking form, but it had not yet gone into all the world to sow the seeds of the Gospel.

Thus, we must come to the inescapable conclusion that the Book of Jeremiah is addressed to the church age and its end. Jeremiah 2:2 has no possibility of identifying with ancient Israel in the wilderness.

A Second Proof

Moreover, God gives us additional proofs that the Book of Jeremiah is mainly focused on the churches and congregations at the end of the church age. In Jeremiah 3:3, we read:

Therefore the showers have been withholden, and there hath been no latter rain; and thou hadst a whore's forehead, thou refusedst to be ashamed.

The key word in this verse is the word "latter" rain. In this study of the end of the church age, repeatedly we have seen that the words latter rain focus on the final spiritual season of sending the Gospel into the world. Thus, when this verse indicates there has been no latter rain, it can only have in view the spiritual drought of hearing the Word of God that came immediately when Satan was loosed at the end of the church age and the latter rain had not yet begun. Remember, the latter rain is the final sending out of the Gospel into the world during the last part of the Great Tribulation. Thus, by the language of Jeremiah 3:3 we are again assured that the Book of Jeremiah primarily has in view the end of the church age.

A Third Proof

There is another very important truth that we must now examine that we can learn from a study of this seventy-year tribulation of the nation of Judah. This truth is that the Bible clearly shows that this seventy-year period is identified with the end of the world. Thus, this is a third proof that the Book of Jeremiah is first of all focused on the Great Tribulation of our day.

Chapter 25 of Jeremiah shows us this truth. As we examine Jeremiah 25, we will find that the timing and the cause for the judgment at the end of the world are tightly tied to God's judgment on the churches and congregations that had been commissioned to bring the Gospel to the world.

In Jeremiah 25:3-7, God gives the warning and sets the stage for what is going to follow:

> **From the thirteenth year of Josiah the son of Amon king of Judah, even unto this day, that is the three and twentieth year, the word of the LORD hath come unto me, and I have spoken unto you, rising early and speaking; but ye have not hearkened. And the LORD hath sent unto you all his servants the prophets, rising early and sending them; but ye have not hearkened, nor inclined your ear to hear. They said, Turn ye again now every one from his evil way, and from the evil of your doings, and dwell in the land that the LORD hath given unto you and to your fathers for ever and ever: And go not after other gods to serve them, and to worship them, and provoke me not to anger with the works of your hands; and I will do you no hurt. Yet ye have not hearkened unto me, saith the LORD; that ye might provoke me to anger with the works of your hands to your own hurt.**

Having given the warning, God then declares what is to happen. Jeremiah 25:8-9 warns:

> **Therefore thus saith the LORD of hosts; Because ye have not heard**

my words, Behold, I will send and take all the families of the north, saith the LORD, and Nebuchadrezzar the king of Babylon, my servant, and will bring them against this land, and against the inhabitants thereof, and <u>against all these nations round about</u>, and will utterly destroy them, and make them an astonishment, and an hissing, and <u>perpetual desolations</u>.

Please notice the character of this warning. Because of Judah's refusal to obey, not only is God going to bring the king of Babylon against Judah but he is going to bring him against all the nations round about. Later in Jeremiah 25, we will learn that all the nations included all the nations in the entire world.

The second truth we learn from this verse is that this judgment is to result in total and perpetual, that is, ever lasting destruction. The words "perpetual" or "everlasting" destruction identify with the end of the world and the lake of fire.

Verse 10, which follows, states:

Moreover I will take from them the voice of mirth, and the voice of gladness, the voice of the bridegroom, and the voice of the bride, the sound of the millstones, and the light of the candle.

The phrases, "the voice of mirth [*joy*]," "the voice of gladness, the voice of the bridegroom," and "the voice of the bride, the sound of the millstones, and the light of the candle," all identify with the true Gospel. Historically, these phrases identify with the land of Judah and Jerusalem, which had been entirely destroyed. However, earlier we learned that near the end of time, Judah and Jerusalem represent the external evidence of the kingdom of God as it is found in the churches and congregation. In them there is the famine of hearing the Word of God because the Holy Spirit is no longer in their midst.

Continuing with Jeremiah 25, the prophecy of this chapter relates to the 70 years we are presently studying, and we read in verses 11-13:

And this whole land shall be a desolation, and an astonishment; and these nations shall serve the king of Babylon seventy years. And it shall come to pass, when seventy years are accomplished, that I will punish the king of Babylon, and that nation, saith the LORD, for their iniquity, and the land of the Chaldeans, and will make it perpetual desolations. And I will bring upon that land all my words which I have pronounced against it, even all that is

written in this book, which Jeremiah hath prophesied against <u>all</u> <u>the nations</u>.

In these verses, we learn that the king of Babylon will reign over all of the nations for the entire 70 years, but at the end of the 70 years, judgment will come upon Babylon. And again we are taught that this judgment is to come upon all the nations.

In verses 15-17, God reiterates that judgment is to come upon all the nations. God says in verses 15-17:

For thus saith the LORD God of Israel unto me; Take the wine cup of this fury at my hand, and cause all the nations, to whom I send thee, to drink it. And they shall drink, and be moved, and be mad, because of the sword that I will send among them. Then took I the cup at the LORD'S hand, and made all the nations to drink, unto whom the LORD had sent me:

Please note the phrase "all the nations." This is a very important and outstanding truth. This is so because the judgment upon all the nations is at the end of the world. Therefore, we can be sure that Jeremiah 25 is particularly looking to the time of the end of the world.

The End of the World

To say it a bit differently, the language of Jeremiah appears to be speaking about the 70 years from 609 B.C. to 539 B.C., but in actuality, it is speaking about the end of the world. As it speaks about the end of the world, it uses the experiences of Judah, Jerusalem, and Babylon to assist us in understanding God's program for the end of the world.

As we continue to study Jeremiah 25, we see that the judgment God has in view begins with His judgment on Jerusalem and Judah. Verse 18 prophesies:

To wit, Jerusalem, and the cities of Judah, and the kings thereof, and the princes thereof, to make them a desolation, an astonishment, an hissing, and a curse; as it is this day;

We will find that verses 18 to 26 detail God's plan for judgment, but it begins with judgment upon Jerusalem and Judah. Earlier we learned that the only entity that can identify with Jerusalem and Judah are the churches and congregations of our day, which are the external, corporate representation of the kingdom of God. Therefore, Jeremiah 25:18 is giving the same truth that we find in I Peter 4:17, where we read, **"For the time is come that judgment must begin at the house of God."** We are being assured that when judgment falls on the churches and congregations, this judgment is going to transition into the final judgment upon the whole world.

Jeremiah 25:18 goes on to say that Jerusalem and Judah will become a desolation and a curse. This matches the language of II Thessalonians 2 where God indicates that the man of sin (Satan) will take his seat (he will rule) in the temple (the churches and congregations). At the same time, II Thessalonians 2 teaches that He who restrains (the Holy Spirit restrains sin), will be taken out of the midst. That is, within the churches, God the Holy Spirit will no longer be applying the Word of God to the lives of those who are present. There will be a famine of hearing the Word of God.

All Nations Must Drink of the Wrath of God

Jeremiah 25 then lists a great many nations of the world of Jeremiah's day as illustrative of all the nations of the world that will exist at the end of time. The fact that this is so is clearly seen by the precise language of verse 26:

> **And all the kings of the north, far and near, one with another, and <u>all the kingdoms of the world</u>, which are upon the face of the earth: and the king of Sheshach shall drink after them.**

No one can argue with the phrase in this verse, **"and all the kingdoms of the world, which are upon the face of the earth."** Without question, this is a reference to the final judgment when Christ comes at the end of the world.

This verse concludes with the statement, **"and the king of Sheshach shall drink after them."** Sheshach is another name for Babylon. We have learned that the king of Babylon typified Satan whom God loosed near the end of time to prepare the churches and the world for Judgment Day. At Judgment Day, Satan will be cast into the lake of fire along with the unsaved who have been judged and found guilty.

The certainty of this judgment is emphasized by the language of Jeremiah 25:27:

> **Therefore thou shalt say unto them, Thus saith the LORD of hosts, the God of Israel; Drink ye, and be drunken, and spue, and fall, and rise no more, because of the sword which I will send among you.**

This is the language of eternal damnation.

Judgment Begins at God's House

As we continue to examine Jeremiah 25, we read two very significant verses. They are verses 28 and 29:

> **And it shall be, if they refuse to take the cup at thine hand to drink, then shalt thou say unto them, Thus saith the LORD of hosts; Ye shall certainly drink. For, lo, I begin to bring evil on the city which is called by my name, and should ye be utterly unpunished? Ye shall not be unpunished: for I will call for a sword upon all the inhabitants of the earth, saith the LORD of hosts.**

In these verses, God is giving His rationale as to why judgment has begun with the house of God. He is declaring that in His perfect justice, He will bring judgment upon the city which is called by His name. The city that is called by His name are the churches and congregations that for over 1950 years were the external representation of the kingdom of God on this earth. This is where the Christians were found. "Christian" is a word that signifies "of the family of Christ." This is the entity that is called the holy place. This is the divine institution wherein God the Holy Spirit was present. This is the holy organism that God used to evangelize the world.

> *This is the holy organism that*
> *God used to evangelize the world.*

From man's point of view, it would appear that this would be the last place where God's judgment would fall. After all, in the churches that feature Jesus Christ as Savior, we find that most people are fine examples of decent morality who claim they trust in Christ and are ready to obey Christ.

But God is demonstrating the perfection of His holy integrity, His perfect justice. We, of course, can see this in the atonement when Jesus was punished in absolutely equal measure, according to what was demanded by God's justice, what should have been experienced by those He came to save. Now again, God is demonstrating His perfect justice as He shows in His perfect righteousness that no one can escape the perfect justice of God. Even those who have identified so closely with the kingdom of God that they are called Christians, or they have appeared to live so righteously before God, if they are not saved, they are still under the wrath of God. Even the divine organism, the church, of which they are a member, cannot escape the wrath of God.

God in His perfect righteousness demonstrates His perfect integrity by beginning His judgment upon the house of God. Thereby He shows His perfect justice as He follows up with judgment upon the whole world.

We thus have learned that the seventy-year period spoken of in the Bible was a literal period that focused on the nation of Israel and Jerusalem. However, this judgment on Jerusalem was a definite picture or representation of God's judgment on the churches and congregations during the Great Tribulation that immediately precedes the end of the world.

In another sense, Jeremiah 25 and the seventy years are focused entirely and only on our day. This is so because in the year 539 B.C., which was the end of the seventy years, all of the world did not come into judgment. Therefore, when we find any references in the Bible to this seventy-year period, we can know that the primary focus, and at times the only focus, is upon the Great Tribulation of our day.

We have carefully examined three proofs that show that the Book of Jeremiah is intimately involved with our day. In the process of setting forth these proofs, we have also learned why God brings about the final judgment of the world by beginning with the churches and congregations of our day. Throughout this study, we will learn much more about the judgment.

It might be noted that the Book of Jeremiah is so intensely involved with our day that a verse by verse study of many of its chapters would almost bring about the conclusion that it is today's newspaper. We have already seen a suggestion of this as we outlined the three proofs that the Book of Jeremiah identifies with the churches and congregations of our day.

God Instructs Us to Look in the Book of Daniel

The Bible gives further proof of the teaching of the Great Tribulation and its awful impact upon the end time churches and congregations. This is set forth by the language of Matthew 24:15, 16. There God declares:

When ye therefore shall see the abomination of desolation, spoken

of by Daniel the prophet, stand in the holy place, (whoso readeth, let him understand:) Then let them which be in Judaea flee into the mountains.

These verses unquestionably are concerned with the Great Tribulation which we have been discussing at length. Verse 21 assures us that this is so for there we read:

For then shall be great tribulation, such as was not since the beginning of the world to this time, no, nor ever shall be.

However, in verse 15, God takes us into the Book of Daniel. Verse 15 declares:

When ye therefore shall see the abomination of desolation, spoken of by Daniel the prophet, stand in the holy place, (whoso readeth, let him understand:)

By this verse God is instructing us to go into the Book of Daniel to learn more about the Great Tribulation period. In the Book of Daniel, we find further proof that the Great Tribulation is at the end of time. This is taught by Daniel 12:8-10:

And I heard, but I understood not: then said I, O my Lord, what shall be the end of these things? And he said, Go thy way, Daniel: for the words are closed up and sealed till the time of the end. Many shall be purified, and made white, and tried; but the wicked shall do wickedly: and none of the wicked shall understand; but the wise shall understand.

We will also discover that the Book of Daniel points to other prophecies of the Great tribulation that are recorded in the Old Testament.

The Abomination of Desolation

When we turn to the Book of Daniel, we must find the verses that relate to Matthew 24:15. The key phrases are "abomination of desolation" and "standing in the holy place."

Two verses in the Book of Daniel identify with these phrases. The first is Daniel 11:31, where we read:

And arms shall stand on his part, and they shall pollute the sanctuary of strength, and shall take away the daily sacrifice, and they shall place the abomination that maketh desolate.

In Daniel 11:31 the Bible is prophesying concerning a time when the sanctuary of strength would be polluted, and the daily would be taken away, replaced by the abomination of desolation. We know that the sanctuary of strength must be where God is worshiped. It is here that the daily sacrifices and the daily candlesticks are being utilized in service to God. The only place that can be in view is the temple. But according to this verse at some future date the worship of God would be replaced by the abomination of desolation.

Matthew 24:15 instructs us that this dreadful event must identify with the Great Tribulation that comes just before the end of the world. We will also learn that Daniel 12 will give further proof that this is at the end of the world.

But why does the Bible tell us to look at the Book of Daniel concerning the abomination of desolation standing in the holy place. We have just concluded that the holy place must be the same entity as the sanctuary of strength where the daily sacrifices and daily lamp stands were burning. Thus, we can know that the holy place is the temple because, as we have learned, that is where the true believers are ordinarily found. That is where the Holy Spirit is present.

Near the end of time, the temple that God speaks of is the corporate external body of believers as they are found in churches and congregations. While the churches do not offer daily sacrifices, they should have a daily or continual candlestick giving the light of the Gospel to the world. They, without question, are the only holy place that can be in view. It is the local church that has been given the Bible together with the commission to send the Gospel into the whole world. But from Daniel 11:31, we know that the daily will be taken away when the abomination of desolation is set up. This information agrees with that which we previously learned concerning the fact that during the Great Tribulation, the Holy Spirit will no longer be in the midst. That is, the candlestick will be removed from the churches and congregations. Moreover, Satan will be reigning in the churches. He is the very essence of desolation.

There is a second reference in the Book of Daniel that speaks of the abomination of desolation standing in the holy place. In Daniel 12:11, we read:

And from the time that the daily sacrifice shall be taken away, and the abomination that maketh desolate set up, there shall be a thousand two hundred and ninety days.

When we look at this reference to the abomination of desolation recorded in the Book of Daniel, there is much more we can learn about the Great Tribulation. First of all in this verse, there is a time reference. The time reference is 1290 days. What time could this be.

Daniel's Prophecies Are Not to be Understood Until the End of Time

To begin with, there are conclusions to which we can quickly come. The first is that an understanding of the time that is in view was not to be understood until very near the end of time. This we can know to be true because of the context in which Daniel 12:11 is placed. Verses 8 to 10 record:

And I heard, but I understood not: then said I, O my Lord, what shall be the end of these things? And he said, Go thy way, Daniel: for the words are closed up and sealed till the time of the end. Many shall be purified, and made white, and tried; but the wicked shall do wickedly: and none of the wicked shall understand; but the wise shall understand.

> *God has a timetable for revealing the understanding of truth recorded in the Bible.*

God has a timetable for revealing the understanding of truth recorded in the Bible. All that mankind is to ever learn from God prior to the end of the world is recorded in the Bible. However, we cannot understand the meaning of the Biblical account unless God opens our spiritual eyes.

Thus, for example, even though Jesus repeatedly told the disciples He would be killed and that He would rise again, they did not understand any of this until after Jesus had risen from the dead. (See Luke 19:31-34.)

The same principle is true concerning the end-time events. Daniel 12:8-10 is disclosing to us that the nature of the-end time events will not be understood until the world is very close to the end. This is the time our knowledge of the end-time events should be greatly increased.

A Day Equals a Year

The second conclusion we can come to in our desire to understand Daniel 12:11 is that the 1290 days cannot be literal days. A careful search of the Bible does not reveal any time period between two events or concerning the duration of an event that equals 1290 literal days. We will learn that the 1290 days is referring to 1290 years. But we must justify the conclusion that the word "day" is a veiled reference to a period of a year. Several examples of this substitution can be found in the Bible.

In Ezekiel 4 the prophet Ezekiel is commanded to take certain actions for periods of days which represent years. For example, verse 6 records:

> **And when thou hast accomplished them, lie again on thy right side, and thou shalt bear the iniquity of the house of Judah forty days: I have appointed thee each day for a year.**

In Numbers 14:34 God is utilizing the same substitution of a day for a year as He declares to Israel:

> **After the number of the days in which ye searched the land, even forty days, each day for a year, shall ye bear your iniquities, even forty years, and ye shall know my breach of promise.**

In Revelation 11 we read of the two witnesses being dead for three and a half days (Revelation 11:9 and 11). This period is the same period spoken of in Revelation 11:2 where God indicates the holy city would be trodden under foot forty two months. Forty two months equals three and a half years. The three and a half days are the same period of time as the forty two months (three and a half years). Thus, again God is equating a day with a year.

Moreover, when we look in the Bible for events associated with the idea of 1290 years, we will learn that we are correct in substituting the word year for the word day.

By God's mercy, in this time of history when we are so near the end of the world, we have been given precise understanding concerning the calendar of history. (The reader is invited to contact Family Radio and request the book *Adam When?* which details the Bible's calendar of history.) Without a very accurate calendar, no one would be able to understand the 1290 days (years) spoken of in Daniel 12:10.

Two Significant Historical Events are Separated by 1290 Years

A search of the calendar of earth's history reveals that there are two historical events, both identified with the Great Tribulation, that are exactly 1290 years apart.

The first event is that of Jacob and his entire family being directed by God to go into Egypt to escape the seven year famine that was **"over all the** face of the earth" (Genesis 41:56). This event is spoken of as great affliction in Acts 7:11. In the original Greek language of the Bible, the English word translated "affliction" is the identical word translated "tribulation" in Matthew 24:27. Acts 7:11 declares:

> **Now there came a dearth over all the land of Egypt and Chanaan, and great affliction [*great tribulation*]: and our fathers found no sustenance.**

Please note the fact that the experience of Jacob in leaving the land of Canaan to go into Egypt is called Great Tribulation. Thus, God is unquestionably paralleling Jacob's experience to the end time Great Tribulation.

The time of this very traumatic event was the year 1877 B.C. If this event occurred at the beginning of a period of 1290 years, what event was exactly 1290 years after it. The year 1877 B.C. minus 1290 years brings us to the year 587 B.C.

This first event, that took place in 1877 B.C., is called "great tribulation." It was a dramatic historical portrait of the Great Tribulation of Matthew 24. We have also learned that there was a dramatic historical event that occurred in 587 B.C. that is altogether parallel to the Great Tribulation of our day.

The year 587 B.C. was the precise year that Jerusalem and the temple were entirely destroyed by the Babylonians and the remnant was commanded to go as captives into Babylon. The wicked nation of Babylon, headed up by the king of Babylon, became the ruler of Jerusalem and all of Judea. Because the temple was destroyed, there was no longer a holy of holies. Jerusalem had become occupied by the abomination of desolation. We, therefore, are certain that these two events must identify with the prophecy of Daniel 12:11.

But Matthew 24:15-21 in which God gave us the signpost to go to the Book of Daniel is speaking of a Great Tribulation that will occur as a last worldwide event before the end of the world. Is there a 1290 year relationship between, on the one hand, the Great Tribulations of 1877 B.C. and 587 B.C. and, on the other hand, the Great Tribulation spoken of in Matthew 24?

One Third, Two Thirds

There is! We can see this when we examine a principle God uses in bringing Biblical truth. That is the principle of one third, two thirds relationships. This is seen, for example, in Zechariah 13 wherein God symbolically divides the peoples of the world into two fractions. The saved of the world are identified with the fraction one third. The unsaved of the world are identified with the fraction two thirds. In Zechariah 13:8, 9 we read:

> **And it shall come to pass, that in all the land, saith the LORD, two parts therein shall be cut off and die; but the third shall be left therein. And I will bring the third part through the fire, and will refine them as silver is refined, and will try them as gold is tried: they shall call on my name, and I will hear them: I will say, It is my people: and they shall say, The LORD is my God.**

Another illustration relates three important events by these same fractions. In I Kings 6:1 we read:

> **And it came to pass in the four hundred and eightieth year after the children of Israel were come out of the land of Egypt, in the fourth year of Solomon's reign over Israel, in the month Zif, which is the second month, that he began to build the house of the LORD.**

Israel going out of the land of Egypt represents God's salvation plan. God declares, **"I am the LORD thy God, which have brought thee out of the land of Egypt, out of the house of bondage"** (Exodus 20:2). That is, I am Jehovah who has saved you. This physical representation of salvation occurred 430 years after the time Jacob went into the land of Egypt (Exodus 12:40, 41). It was the year 1447 B.C.

According to I Kings 6:1, it was exactly 480 years later, that is, 480 years after 1447 B.C., the year 967 B.C., when Solomon began to build the temple. We have learned that the temple of the Old Testament was a representation of the New Testament congregations and churches. It was also a representation of Christ Himself. Remember He told the Jews, **"Destroy this temple, and in three days I will raise it up"** (John 2:19).

When did Jesus, the spiritual temple, come to this earth to be the temple? While we do not have absolute proof that Jesus was born in the year 7 B.C., all of the circumstantial evidence points to 7 B.C. as the year of His birth. And 7 B.C. is exactly 960 years after Solomon's temple foundation was laid in 967 B.C. Thus, the total period from the going out of Egypt in 1447 B.C. to the birth of Christ in 7 B.C. is 1440 years. The 480 year period is one third of this 1440 years. The 960 years is two thirds of this 1440 years.

One Third, Two Thirds Brings Us to the Great Tribulation

When we carefully examine the great tribulations of the Bible in the light of this one third, two thirds principle we discover that the year A.D. 1994 fits perfectly into God's plan. The year 1994 is two times 1290 years after the year 587 B.C., which was the year the total destruction of Jerusalem and the temple occurred.

Let us look a moment at the arithmetic.

We must add 587 to 1994 and subtract 1 because there is no year 0 in going from B.C. years to A.D. years. Thus, 587 + 1994 - 1 = 2580 years = 2 x 1290 years.

Thus, the entire period from the great tribulation Jacob experienced in 1877 B.C. to 1994 A.D. is 1877 + 1994 - 1 = 3870 years. The 1290 years from 1877 B.C. to 587 B.C. is one third of this 3870 years. The 2580 years from 587 B.C. to 1994 A.D. is two thirds of this 3870 years.

The fact that in the year 1994 there already existed great evidence that the time of the Great Tribulation was here convinces us that we have correctly applied this one third, two thirds principle. It might be noted that this same one third, two thirds principle is seen beginning with the great tribulation of 1877 B.C. when Jacob and his family went into Egypt. Precisely 430 years after Jacob went into Egypt that tribulation period came to an end. That took place when Israel went out of Egypt in 1447 B.C. Exactly 860 years later (2 times 430) Israel again went into great tribulation when Jerusalem and the temple were destroyed in 587 B.C.

The year 1877 B.C. was the official year that Israel (Jacob and family) left the land of Canaan to go into the wicked world of Egypt. But it was also the year when they came under the care and protection of Joseph who was able to supply them with sufficient food. It was the year that ended the first phase of the seven-year famine.

The year 587 B.C. was the official year that Jerusalem was destroyed which ended the first phase of the seventy-year tribulation of those days.

In parallel fashion then we could conclude that 1994 was the official end of the church age which ended the first phase of the Great Tribulation. This first phase was typified by the symbolic forty two months of Revelation 11:2 during which the holy city was trodden under foot and the symbolic three and a half days that the two witnesses lay dead in the streets (Revelation 11:9), and the likely literal period of 2300 days of Daniel 8:13, 14 during which the sanctuary and host were trodden under foot. It also would then indicate that it ended the half hour of silence from heaven which is spoken of in Revelation 8:1. It, therefore, would also be the official year of the beginning of the season of the latter rain.

This information concerning the one third, two thirds principle thus further assists us in seeing the parallels that exist between the two historical great tribulations (1877 B.C. and 587 B.C.), and the Great Tribulation of our day.

Many lessons can be learned by examining these two great historical events that should greatly help us in understanding the present tribulation time and how we as believers are to relate to it. Therefore, as we continue this study we will examine some of the more important lessons God is teaching us.

The Preterit Position

Before we continue our study, we should look at the contention of those who insist that the teaching of Matthew 24 concerning the destruction of the temple was completely fulfilled in A.D. 70. In that year, the Roman Titus completely destroyed Jerusalem. Their contention is, therefore, that we are not to look at Matthew 24 or any other chapters of a similar nature to assist us with an understanding of the events in the church or the world near the end of time. This is theologically called the preterit position. Preterit simply means that which has already happened. The preterit position was held by many theologians in years gone by.

When we look at Matthew 24 carefully, we know that the preterit position is not possible. Let us see why this is so. Matthew 24:1-2 declares:

And Jesus went out, and departed from the temple: and his disciples came to him for to shew him the buildings of the temple. And Jesus said unto them, See ye not all these things? verily I say unto you, There shall not be left here one stone upon another, that shall not be thrown down.

While it is true that the temple was destroyed in A.D. 70, it is not true that not one stone was left upon another. The present western wall together with the temple foundation still exist today. These structures were an essential part of the temple buildings.

Secondly, in Matthew 24:3, Jesus points us to the time of the fulfillment of this prophecy as He records a question from the disciples. We read:

And as he sat upon the mount of Olives, the disciples came unto him privately, saying, Tell us, when shall these things be? and what shall be the sign of thy coming, and of the end of the world?

Definitely, this verse points us to the end of time for the fulfillment of this prophecy.

Moreover, verse 15 calls our attention to the abomination of desolation spoken of by Daniel the prophet. When we follow this signpost, it points to the end of time, as we will learn in this study.

Furthermore, verse 21 speaks of a great tribulation such as was not since the beginning of this world. Then verses 29 and 30 tell us that the Great Tribulation will be followed immediately by the destruction of the universe and the return of Christ.

Thus, we must understand that the so-called preterit position has no Biblical validity of any kind. We must understand that the whole chapter is discussing the Great Tribulation and the end of the world.

Chapter 9.
The Third Season. The Latter Rain

In this study, we have learned that God has a carefully developed plan to evangelize the world. It consists of three seasons and three times. Thus far in our study we have examined in some detail the first two times, that is, the three and a half year famine of Jesus' day and the spiritual famine of hearing the Word of God during the Great Tribulation.

We also examined in some detail the first season called the early righteous rain which was the Old Testament era that resulted in the harvest of Jesus Christ Himself as the Messiah. We then examined the second season which was called the early Pentecostal rain. It began when Jesus arose from the grave and continued for more than 1950 years as the church age. It brought forth a spiritual harvest of Pentecostal firstfruits, the complete fullness of which is typified by the number 144,000 which God speaks of in Revelation 7 and Revelation 14. Later we will examine the 144,000 in greater detail to see why they are the complete fullness of the church age.

We are now ready to consider the third and final season, that is, the season of the latter rain. We will discover that it is a time that coincides with the last part of the Great Tribulation.

In the Bible, the use of the word "rain" can be teaching God's curse or God's blessing. When God destroyed the world in Noah's day, much of the water that came upon the earth came as rain. We read that it rained forty days and forty nights. That rain was a judgment upon the earth. On the other hand, we frequently read of rain upon the earth as an expression of the salvation message, the true Gospel, coming from heaven to earth. Deuteronomy 32:1-3 teaches this principle:

Give ear, O ye heavens, and I will speak; and hear, O earth, the words of my mouth. My doctrine shall drop as the rain, my speech shall distil as the dew, as the small rain upon the tender herb, and as the showers upon the grass: Because I will publish the name of the LORD: ascribe ye greatness unto our God.

As we learned earlier in this study, this rain of the Gospel is divided particularly into two seasons during the New Testament era. These seasons of rain and the time between these seasons of rain are so important that we will again review some of the material presented thus far.

First of all, there is the early or first Pentecostal rain and following this there is the latter rain. In Deuteronomy 11:14, 15 we read:

That I will give you the rain of your land in his due season, the first rain and the latter rain, that thou mayest gather in thy corn, and thy wine, and thine oil. And I will send grass in thy fields for thy cattle, that thou mayest eat and be full.

In James 5:7, the same principle is stated:

Be patient therefore, brethren, unto the coming of the Lord. Behold, the husbandman waiteth for the precious fruit of the earth, and hath long patience for it, until he receive the early and latter rain.

This is also taught in Jeremiah 5:24:

Neither say they in their heart, Let us now fear the LORD our God, that giveth rain, both the former and the latter, in his season: he reserveth unto us the appointed weeks of the harvest.

In Hosea 6:3 we find another reference to this principle:

Then shall we know, if we follow on to know the LORD: his going forth is prepared as the morning; and he shall come unto us as the rain, as the latter and former rain unto the earth.

That there is the early or former rain and the latter rain each in its season instructs us that God anticipates the sending forth of the Gospel in more than one season. This accords with the teaching of Jesus in Acts 1:6, 7:

When they therefore were come together, they asked of him, saying, Lord, wilt thou at this time restore again the kingdom to Israel? And he said unto them, It is not for you to know the <u>times</u> or the <u>seasons</u>, which the Father hath put in his own power.

The restoration of the kingdom to Israel is accomplished as the Gospel goes forth. Those who become saved become an eternal part of the Israel of God.

How then are these seasons of early rain and latter rain divided. We can learn something about this when we go to Deuteronomy 11:16, 17:

Take heed to yourselves, that your heart be not deceived, and ye turn aside, and serve other gods, and worship them; And then the LORD'S wrath be kindled against you, and he shut up the heaven, that there be no rain, and that the land yield not her fruit; and lest ye perish quickly from off the good land which the LORD giveth you.

This is a very significant passage because it teaches there is a break between the first rain and the latter rain. This break will come if those who are commissioned and mandated by God to bring the true Gospel begin to serve other gods by bringing doctrines that do not come from the Bible.

We can further understand the early and latter rain when we recognize that the purpose of rain is to bring forth a harvest. Remember in Deuteronomy 11:14 God declared:

That I will give you the rain of your land in his due season, the first rain and the latter rain, that thou mayest gather in thy corn, and thy wine, and thine oil.

We thus must understand what the Bible has to say about harvesting. There was an early Pentecostal harvest and a harvest at the end of the year. In Exodus 23:16, God speaks of these two harvests:

And the feast of harvest, the firstfruits of thy labours, which thou hast sown in the field: and the feast of ingathering, which is in the end of the year, when thou hast gathered in thy labours out of the field.

The feast of harvest was celebrated at Pentecost. The feast of ingathering or the feast of tabernacles was celebrated in the seventh month. The feast of Pentecost, which was observed seven weeks after the Passover, was the time the firstfruits were brought in. We read in Leviticus 23:16, 17:

Even unto the morrow after the seventh sabbath shall ye number fifty days; and ye shall offer a new meat offering unto the LORD. Ye shall bring out of your habitations two wave loaves of two tenth deals: they shall be of fine flour; they shall be baken with leaven;

they are the firstfruits unto the LORD.

This offering of firstfruits was from the first or early harvest of the land. It, therefore, would relate to the first or early rain. In the New Testament this day was called Pentecost because it was fifty days after the atonement.

The feast of tabernacles was in the seventh month of the Jewish year and coincided with the completion of the harvest. We read in Deuteronomy 16:13:

Thou shalt observe the feast of tabernacles seven days, after that thou hast gathered in thy corn and thy wine.

This feast, therefore, would relate to the latter rain which we are studying in this chapter.

Three Seasons of Rain

As we assembled Biblical information that helped us understand the early and latter rain, we read in Joel 2:21-24:

Fear not, O land; be glad and rejoice: for the LORD will do great things. Be not afraid, ye beasts of the field: for the pastures of the wilderness do spring, for the tree beareth her fruit, the fig tree and the vine do yield their strength. Be glad then, ye children of Zion, and rejoice in the LORD your God: for he hath given you the former rain moderately, and he will cause to come down for you the rain, the former rain, and the latter rain in the first month. And the floors shall be full of wheat, and the vats shall overflow with wine and oil.

Because of the very helpful character of these verses, we will look at them again.

This passage is more complicated in that it declares, **"He hath given** [*should be 'gives'*] **you the former rain moderately** [*Hebrew word should be translated 'righteously'*]**, and he will cause to come down for you the rain, the former rain, and the latter rain in** [*should be 'after'*] **the first."** This passage is speaking of two seasons of rain. The first is the righteous former rain. The second is another season of rain that is divided into two parts, an early or former rain and a latter rain. The second is to come after the first righteous rain.

Remember we learned in this study that the former righteous rain was the Old Testament era that produced Jesus as the harvest. The next early or former rain identifies with Pentecost and brought as the harvest all of those who became saved during the church age.

To help us to further understand this, we should now turn to James 5:17, 18 where God declares:

> **Elias was a man subject to like passions as we are, and he prayed earnestly that it might not rain: and it rained not on the earth by the space of three years and six months. And he prayed again, and the heaven gave rain, and the earth brought forth her fruit.**

This passage immediately sends us to I Kings 17:1, where we read:

> **And Elijah the Tishbite, who was of the inhabitants of Gilead, said unto Ahab, As the LORD God of Israel liveth, before whom I stand, there shall not be dew nor rain these years, but according to my word.**

The end of the severe famine that followed came immediately after the contest on Mount Carmel. We read in I Kings 18:22-24:

> **Then said Elijah unto the people, I, even I only, remain a prophet of the LORD; but Baal's prophets are four hundred and fifty men. Let them therefore give us two bullocks; and let them choose one bullock for themselves, and cut it in pieces, and lay it on wood, and put no fire under: and I will dress the other bullock, and lay it on wood, and put no fire under: And call ye on the name of your gods, and I will call on the name of the LORD: and the God that answereth by fire, let him be God. And all the people answered and said, It is well spoken.**

Immediately following this contest, we read in I Kings 18:43-45 that there was a great rain. In other words, the famine was ended.

Mount Carmel Points Us to the Cross

When we look for the spiritual meaning of this famine and this contest on Mount Carmel, we see quite clearly that it relates to Christ's ministry, including His crucifixion and the pouring out of the Holy Spirit at

Pentecost. Elijah clearly represents Christ. James 5:17 discloses to us that the famine of Elijah's day continued for three years and six months. This is the exact time from the baptism of Jesus, when He was officially announced as the Lamb that takes away the sin of the world, until He was brought to the cross. It was at that time that the fire of God's wrath was poured out on the sacrificial animal laying on the altar, and both the animal and the altar represent Jesus who is the fulfillment of all sacrifices. The fact that the 450 prophets of Baal could not call down fire from heaven is proof that Satan could not and did not bring judgment on Christ. Only Christ as the high priest could offer the sacrificial Lamb, which was Christ Himself, which was to come under the fire of God's wrath. The fact that the 450 prophets of Baal were killed by Elijah (I Kings 18:40), represents the fact that Satan was given a death blow when Christ paid the penalty of God's wrath for our sins. Thus, before this three and a half years had come to an end, judgment had come upon Christ and judgment had come upon Satan.

> *Only Christ as the high priest could offer the sacrificial Lamb, which was Christ Himself*

Do you remember that earlier in this study we learned that there was a spiritual famine during the three years and six months that Jesus was bringing the Gospel to the land of Israel? This was so in spite of the fact that He was the perfect preacher. Did not He declare in Luke 4:43:

And he said unto them, I must preach the kingdom of God to other cities also: for therefore am I sent.

Indeed, He was the perfect preacher. He is God Himself. But preaching alone does not bring salvation. God the Holy Spirit must apply that preached Word to the hearts of those who are to be saved. We read in Matthew 13:2:

And great multitudes were gathered together unto him, so that he went into a ship, and sat; and the whole multitude stood on the shore.

When the disciples asked Him in verse 10, **"Why speakest thou unto them in parables?"** Jesus answered in verse 11:

He answered and said unto them, Because it is given unto you to

know the mysteries of the kingdom of heaven, but to them it is not given.

That is, only those to whom God gives understanding will the Gospel be understood. Those who have not been given understanding will not understand the Gospel. Jesus further declared in Matthew 13, verses 14-16:

And in them is fulfilled the prophecy of Esaias, which saith, By hearing ye shall hear, and shall not understand; and seeing ye shall see, and shall not perceive: For this people's heart is waxed gross, and their ears are dull of hearing, and their eyes they have closed; lest at any time they should see with their eyes, and hear with their ears, and should understand with their heart, and should be converted, and I should heal them. But blessed are your eyes, for they see: and your ears, for they hear.

Now we understand why after three years and six months of perfect preaching, there were only 120 in the upper room (Acts 1:15). Additionally, we read of 500 seeing Him after His resurrection (I Corinthians 15:6). Very few were being saved. For example, in John 6 we read of Jesus doing many miracles, including the miraculous feeding of the 5,000, and yet, when Christ began to teach the true nature of the Gospel, we read in John 6:66:

From that time many of his disciples went back, and walked no more with him.

Now we can understand what Jesus is teaching in Luke 10:13-15:

Woe unto thee, Chorazin! woe unto thee, Bethsaida! for if the mighty works had been done in Tyre and Sidon, which have been done in you, they had a great while ago repented, sitting in sackcloth and ashes. But it shall be more tolerable for Tyre and Sidon at the judgment, than for you. And thou, Capernaum, which art exalted to heaven, shalt be thrust down to hell.

Chorazin, Bethsaida, and Capernaum were cities near or on the Sea of Galilee. They were cities closest to where Jesus did most of His preaching, and yet this language is implying that virtually no one became saved there. This language underscores the complete unbelief of those to whom Jesus ministered. Indeed, the prophetic declaration of Amos 8:11 is clearly in evidence:

Behold, the days come, saith the Lord GOD, that I will send a famine in the land, not a famine of bread, nor a thirst for water, but of hearing the words of the LORD:

There was plenty of spiritual bread and water because Jesus was the perfect preacher. But there was a total famine of <u>hearing</u> the Word of God.

The problem was that of hearing the Word of God.

What we are understanding is that during the three years and six months that Jesus was preaching, there was not a problem of the presentation of the true Gospel. The problem was that of hearing the Word of God. In that sense, heaven was shut up and there was no rain.

We may assume that many if not most of the 120 and the 500 mentioned above were saved before Jesus began to preach. We know that the shepherds, Mary, Zacharias, Elizabeth, Joseph, Simeon, Anna, and John the Baptist are a few of those who were saved before Christ began His ministry.

Pentecost Ends the Spiritual Famine

This famine of hearing the Word of God ended with Pentecost. The Holy Spirit is now in the midst of those gathered together. The season of the church age has begun. Jesus promised in John 14:16, 17:

And I will pray the Father, and he shall give you another Comforter, that he may abide with you for ever; Even the Spirit of truth; whom the world cannot receive, because it seeth him not, neither knoweth him: but ye know him; for he dwelleth with you, and shall be in you.

The Holy Spirit who is God Himself began to apply the Word of God. Thus, even though Peter was far from being the perfect preacher that Jesus was, about 3,000 were saved in one day. Acts 2:41:

Then they that gladly received his word were baptized: and the same day there were added unto them about three thousand souls.

The three years and six months of the famine of hearing the Word of God was over when Christ arose and the former or early or first rain had begun. That is, the church age, which would continue for more than 1950 years, had begun. In principle, it began when Jesus arose from the dead for we read that He is the firstfruits (I Corinthians 15:20, 23). As long as the Holy Spirit remains in the midst of the believers who gather together as a church or congregation, the former rain continues. All who become saved are the firstfruits, that is, all who become saved during the church age are the firstfruits.

That is why in Revelation 14:4, the 144,000 are called the firstfruits. In Revelation 7, the 144,000 are identified with twelve tribes of Israel. This is so because they were typified by these twelve tribes of Israel. Remember, the nation of Israel consisted of thirteen tribes. Yet 144,000 are all the tribes of Israel even though the tribe of Dan is not mentioned. Thus, these twelve tribes who were typified by literal Israel are in fact the Israel of God which consists of all believers throughout the world.

In the Book of James, these same twelve tribes are in view as we read the salutation of James:

James, a servant of God and of the Lord Jesus Christ, to the twelve tribes which are scattered abroad, greeting.

That accords with the statement of James 1:18 where God states:

Of his own will begat he us with the word of truth, that we should be a kind of firstfruits of his creatures.

Thus, we can be assured that the Book of James is speaking particularly of the churches and congregations of the church age. The people saved during the church age are called the firstfruits both in Revelation 14 and in James 1:18. As we are learning, it is during the church age that the firstfruits of the Pentecostal harvest were brought into the kingdom of God.

The Great Tribulation Time

And then there is another break in the rain from heaven, a time when three years and six months are again featured as a time of no rain. That is, it would be a time of a famine of hearing the Word of God. The Bible records this in Revelation 11:2, where God prophesies that the temple would be trodden underfoot for a period of forty two months, and we read:

But the court which is without the temple leave out, and measure it not; for it is given unto the Gentiles: and the holy city shall they tread under foot forty and two months.

The time period of forty two months equals three years and six months. True, the three years and six months when Jesus was preaching, and when there was such a famine of hearing the Word of God, was exactly, very literally, three years and six months. On the other hand, the forty two months of Revelation 11:2 is to be understood figuratively. Literally, it is a longer period. This period identifies with the 2300 evening mornings of Daniel 8. This possibly could be an exact literal period of time. This famine which began at the completion of the church age effectively signified that the harvest of the firstfruits had been completed.

This same famine of forty two months or three years and six months is further declared in Revelation 11:9, 11 to be a period of three and a half days. Understanding the Biblical principle that a day can signify a year, the three and a half days that the bodies of the two witnesses who have been killed lie outside the gates of Jerusalem become equivalent to the three and a half years or forty two months of Revelation 11:2. As we are learning, the spiritual harvest from the latter rain period is the end of the year or the final harvest. We learn that this, too, is the same time period and the same event during which there is a famine of hearing the Word of God.

The 42 Months of Revelation 13

Remember in James 5:17, 18, we read that there was no rain for three years and six months and then, **"the heaven gave rain, and the earth brought forth her fruit."** Thus, the famine of hearing the Word during Jesus' ministry was immediately followed by the resurrection of Jesus and Pentecost, which brought into being the New Testament church age.

Likewise, the famine of hearing the Word of God signified by the 42 months or the three and a half days of Revelation 11 is immediately followed by the latter rain when the earth brings forth its fruit. As we are learning, the spiritual harvest from the latter rain period is the end of the year or the final harvest.

The Bible discloses to us the follow-up of the famine of Jesus' day. We read in Acts 2 that on that first Pentecost, about 3,000 were saved. But where does the Bible talk about much fruit being brought in after the famine of hearing the Word of God and during the time that the two witnesses lay dead? This is found in Revelation 7:9-14. Later in our study, we will look at these verses which teach that after the 144,000 were sealed, a great multitude which no man can number become saved. Revelation 7:14 assures us these are saved during the period of Great Tribulation.

Thus, we have learned from the Bible that there are two parallel events that encompass the entire New Testament era. Both begin with a time of three and a half years during which there is a famine of hearing the Word of God. Both are followed by a great program of salvation that extends into all of the world. The first event of salvation is the entire church age during which the church was commissioned to bring the Gospel to the world. The second event is the activity of those outside of the churches and congregation bringing the Gospel to the world. This is the bringing in of the final harvest of souls.

The Land Enjoys Her Sabbaths

Earlier in our study we learned that the Great Tribulation of Matthew 24:21 was typified by the terrible period of God's wrath on ancient Jerusalem and Judah. It extended from the death of the last good king, Josiah, in 609 B.C. until Babylon was conquered by the Medes and the Persians in 539 B.C. This period of seventy years symbolizes and points to the entire period of the Great Tribulation that occurs immediately before the end of the world. This is the Great Tribulation the world is now experiencing.

This seventy-year period is spoken of in II Chronicles 36:20, 21, where we read:

> **And them that had escaped from the sword carried he away to Babylon; where they were servants to him and his sons until the reign of the kingdom of Persia: To fulfil the word of the LORD by the mouth of Jeremiah, until the land had enjoyed her sabbaths: for as long as she lay desolate she kept sabbath, to fulfil threescore and ten years.**

What does it mean when the Bible teaches that during the seventy years, the land would enjoy her sabbaths? We will discover that this is a very important statement. A further reference that bears on this question is found in Leviticus 26:33-35:

> **And I will scatter you among the heathen, and will draw out a sword after you: and your land shall be desolate, and your cities waste. Then shall the land enjoy her sabbaths, as long as it lieth desolate, and ye be in your enemies' land; even then shall the land rest, and**

enjoy her sabbaths. As long as it lieth desolate it shall rest; because it did not rest in your sabbaths, when ye dwelt upon it.

We are greatly interested in this statement of Leviticus 26 because it, too, makes reference to a time of enjoying the sabbaths. II Chronicles 36:20 also relates the idea of enjoying the sabbaths to seventy years. As we have already learned, the seventy years have everything to do with God's judgment at the end of time, and it begins with God's judgment on the churches and congregations of our day.

Therefore, we will now look more closely at Leviticus 26. In doing this, we will find complete harmony with everything else that shows that God's judgment is upon the churches of our day.

In Leviticus 26:1-4, God sets forth very important commands that He expects the believers to obey. We read:

Ye shall make you no idols nor graven image, neither rear you up a standing image, neither shall ye set up any image of stone in your land, to bow down unto it: for I am the LORD your God. Ye shall keep my sabbaths, and reverence my sanctuary: I am the LORD. If ye walk in my statutes, and keep my commandments, and do them; Then I will give you rain in due season, and the land shall yield her increase, and the trees of the field shall yield their fruit.

The first emphasis is that the believer is not to worship other gods. The second is that they are to keep the sabbaths. The promise is then made that if you will do this, God will give rain in due season and the land will yield her increase. These promises are further developed in the verses that follow, ending with the promise of Leviticus 26, verses 11 and 12:

And I will set my tabernacle among you: and my soul shall not abhor you. And I will walk among you, and will be your God, and ye shall be my people.

Later, we will look at the commandment that believers are not to worship other gods. However, first, we wonder why the keeping of sabbaths is featured in this language. We are very interested in this because we are wondering about the language that the land would enjoy her sabbaths during the seventy years. Since we have learned that the seventy years identify with the Great Tribulation of our day, we want to know, if possible, the meaning of the phrase **"the land will enjoy her sabbaths."**

The Seventh-Day Sabbath

To begin to understand the phrase **"enjoy her sabbaths,"** we must go back to Exodus 31:13-15, where we read:

> **Speak thou also unto the children of Israel, saying, Verily my sabbaths ye shall keep: for it is a sign between me and you throughout your generations; that ye may know that I am the LORD that doth sanctify you. Ye shall keep the sabbath therefore; for it is holy unto you: every one that defileth it shall surely be put to death: for whosoever doeth any work therein, that soul shall be cut off from among his people. Six days may work be done; but in the seventh is the sabbath of rest, holy to the LORD: whosoever doeth any work in the sabbath day, he shall surely be put to death.**

In these verses, God is insisting that if any work of any kind was done on the seventh-day Sabbath, that person was to be put to death. God demonstrated the certainty of this law by reporting to us an incident that occurred when Israel was in the wilderness after they had left Egypt. In Numbers 15:32-36, the Bible reports:

> **And while the children of Israel were in the wilderness, they found a man that gathered sticks upon the sabbath day. And they that found him gathering sticks brought him unto Moses and Aaron, and unto all the congregation. And they put him in ward, because it was not declared what should be done to him. And the LORD said unto Moses, The man shall be surely put to death: all the congregation shall stone him with stones without the camp. And all the congregation brought him without the camp, and stoned him with stones, and he died; as the LORD commanded Moses.**

What a terrible punishment for what appears to be such a minor offense, picking up a few sticks on the Sabbath day. The solution to this puzzle, in which what appears to be such a minor offense is met with such a drastic punishment, is found in the language of Exodus 31:13. There we read that the keeping of the Sabbath was a <u>sign</u> **"that I am the LORD that doth sanctify you."**

> *A commandment that was a sign is a commandment that points to some spiritual reality.*

A commandment that was a sign is a commandment that points to some spiritual reality. The sign has no spiritual substance within it. It is a ceremonial law that is pointing to a principle that is of great spiritual substance. The spiritual substance or the spiritual reality that this sign was pointing to is the fact that Jehovah is the one who sanctifies us when we become saved. It is a parallel truth to that which is reiterated in many places in the Bible. For example, we read in Ephesians 2:8-10:

> **For by grace are ye saved through faith; and that not of yourselves: it is the gift of God: Not of works, lest any man should boast. For we are his workmanship, created in Christ Jesus unto good works, which God hath before ordained that we should walk in them.**

The work of salvation is entirely the work of Christ. God is so jealous of our understanding this that He records the incident of a man picking up a few sticks on the Sabbath day. This would be like someone believing that Christ has done all the work in saving me, but I entered into the work of becoming saved because I accepted Christ, or I was baptized in water, or the faith that God gave me and which I exercised was an instrument God used to save me.

We began looking at Leviticus 26, and remember, we read that two commands from God were especially in view. The first was that we are not to worship any other gods and the second was that we are to keep His Sabbaths.

Enjoying Its Sabbaths Equals a Gospel of Grace Alone

Now that we understand that keeping His Sabbath means that we are to be altogether certain that Christ alone has done all the work to save us, we can understand how that relates to worshipping other gods. Let us see how these commandments relate.

When we put our trust in anything, that becomes a god we are serving. The essence of serving God is that we are trusting Him for every aspect of our salvation. If we trust in our bank account, then that is our god. If we trust in an idol as Israel did in their high places, then that is our god. If we trust in any doctrine that is not firmly taken from the Bible, then we are trusting in our own minds. In that event, our minds and the individuals who designed that doctrine is our god.

Likewise, if we trust in anything that we have done as an assist or as a condition for our salvation, then that makes these works, doctrines, ceremo-

> *Likewise, if we trust in anything that we have done as an assist or as a condition for our salvation, then that makes these works, doctrines, ceremonies, or the church itself our god.*

nies, or the church itself our god. Even though we may insist we are saved by grace alone, if we hold any doctrine that teaches that anything, however small or insignificant it may appear to be, assisted in our salvation, we are worshipping another god. The account of the man picking up a few sticks should ring in our ears as it emphasizes the absolute character of salvation being entirely the work of Jesus alone.

Any time any doctrine is taught that is not altogether based upon the Bible, it is a spiritual high place, it is the worship of another god. However, in Leviticus 26, God warns that the high place of believing the teaching that even the slightest thing we have done assisted in getting ourselves saved is especially serious.

Ancient Israel fell into this sin. We read in Romans 9:31, 32:

But Israel, which followed after the law of righteousness, hath not attained to the law of righteousness. Wherefore? Because they sought it not by faith, but as it were by the works of the law. For they stumbled at that stumblingstone;

They were trusting in their faithful observance of the ceremonial laws as a condition for their salvation. However, we must sorrowfully admit that this is the problem that also exists in the churches and congregations of our day. It is embedded in prestigious confessions like the Westminster Confession and the Belgic Confession. It is loudly trumpeted by those who teach that water baptism is a condition for salvation or that we must pray a certain kind of prayer or reach out and accept Jesus in order to become saved. It is probably the basic reason that most people who are members of churches today cannot even think about the possibility of leaving their church as God commands. If they are trusting in even the slightest fashion in their water baptism, or their confession of faith, or their church membership, or their participation in the Lord's Supper as giving substantive spiritual benefit to them, they cannot countenance the idea of leaving their church. Even though they may not realize it, their trust for their salvation is based entirely on things such as water baptism and the Lord's Supper, which are ceremonial laws pointing to aspects of what salvation is.

The Land Enjoys Her Sabbaths during the Latter Rain

With this knowledge of the latter rain in hand, we can now return to an earlier question: "How is it that during the seventy years the land would enjoy her Sabbaths?" (Leviticus 26:34, II Chronicles 36:21). Remember the seventy years identify with the Great Tribulation of our day. Remember, too, that during this present period of Great Tribulation, there is bread and water. That is, the true Gospel is plentifully available, but at the same time, there is a famine of hearing the Word of God. We have learned that this famine is in the temple, the churches and congregations that have come under the judgment of God. The Holy Spirit is no longer in the midst. Satan is ruling.

However, outside the churches, the true Gospel is still going and will continue to go into all the world until Christ returns. The major character of this Gospel which identifies with the latter rain is that the high places have been removed. That is, every possible effort is made to ensure that this Gospel of the latter rain is altogether faithful to the Word of God.

> *Insistently and insidiously, doctrines are held that man*
> *must contribute some of his effort to become saved.*

Remember, too, we learned that a dominate high place that is a problem in virtually all churches and congregations is that of a works-grace gospel. Insistently and insidiously, doctrines are held that man must contribute some of his effort to become saved.

However, if one outstanding characteristic could be named concerning many who are endeavoring to faithfully bring the true Gospel outside the churches, it is that salvation is 100% by grace alone. Under no circumstance can any effort on our part, however small or unimportant we may think it is, be in any sense a contribution to our salvation. Remember, we are not to do any work of any kind to become saved. This important fact was typified by the seventh-day Sabbath when no physical work of any kind was to be done. Thus, when a Gospel is preached all over the world that emphasizes grace and grace alone, the land, the kingdom of God, will enjoy its sabbaths. It will enjoy a totally works-free Gospel.

The importance of a works-free salvation presentation cannot be stressed too strongly. When God wrote the Bible, He placed within the Scriptures some testing programs. In the Garden of Eden, He tested our first parents by planting a special tree and giving it an exotic and tempting name, **"the tree of the knowledge of good and evil."** He then commanded our first parents not to eat of the fruit of this enticing tree.

Likewise, throughout the Old Testament, God commanded that if one were to experience blessings of God, he must keep the commandments. If he disobeyed the commandments, he would be under the curse of God. Ancient Israel, therefore, tried hard to obey God by religiously keeping the commandments. But they failed to achieve the blessings of God. Why? In Romans 9:31, 32, God informs us:

> **But Israel, which followed after the law of righteousness, hath not attained to the law of righteousness. Wherefore? Because they sought it not by faith, but as it were by the works of the law. For they stumbled at that stumblingstone;**

They failed to realize that alongside these commands that they were to keep perfectly were the ceremonial laws such as burnt offerings and blood sacrifices. These observances were directing them to look for and put their trust in the Savior who would come to pay for their sins. At times, God spoke very plainly about this as He declared, for example, in Isaiah 53:4-7:

> **Surely he hath borne our griefs, and carried our sorrows: yet we did esteem him stricken, smitten of God, and afflicted. But he was wounded for our transgressions, he was bruised for our iniquities: the chastisement of our peace was upon him; and with his stripes we are healed. All we like sheep have gone astray; we have turned every one to his own way; and the LORD hath laid on him the iniquity of us all. He was oppressed, and he was afflicted, yet he opened not his mouth: he is brought as a lamb to the slaughter, and as a sheep before her shearers is dumb, so he openeth not his mouth.**

God also gave them many illustrations of the fact that only God could save them. Think, for example, of God taking them out of the land of Egypt strictly by God's efforts and bringing them through the Red Sea entirely by the work of God.

God's Judgment Will Fall

We are beginning to see that Leviticus is a very serious and important warning to us today. Fact is, Leviticus 26:14-16 warns:

> **But if ye will not hearken unto me, and will not do all these commandments; And if ye shall despise my statutes, or if your soul abhor my judgments, so that ye will not do all my commandments, but that ye break my covenant: I also will do this unto you; I will even appoint over you terror, consumption, and the burning ague, that shall consume the eyes, and cause sorrow of heart: and ye shall sow your seed in vain, for your enemies shall eat it.**

This warning of judgment upon those who violate these commandments continues for many more verses. These should be read and pondered very carefully by everyone and anyone who is concerned about his salvation. We should call special attention to verse 30, where God declares:

> **And I will destroy your high places, and cut down your images, and cast your carcases upon the carcases of your idols, and my soul shall abhor you.**

Remember, we have learned that high places have to do with the worship of false gods. That is, they have to do with any doctrine we hold that is not faithfully true to the Bible. This chapter focuses especially on the high place of violating the seventh-day Sabbath (that is, even in the slightest sense, having a works-grace gospel). Actually, however, the litany of high places is very long in our day. Think, for example, of the Biblical laws that churches have violated in teaching that there can be divorce for fornication and that there can be remarriage after divorce.

This verse is teaching that if a church has high places, those high places will be destroyed. The verses that immediately follow instruct us as to how this destruction of the high places will be accomplished. In verses 31-33, we read:

> **And I will make your cities waste, and bring your sanctuaries unto desolation, and I will not smell the savour of your sweet odours. And I will bring the land into desolation: and your enemies which dwell therein shall be astonished at it. And I will scatter you among**

the heathen, and will draw out a sword after you: and your land shall be desolate, and your cities waste.

> *God's judgment is upon them so that the Holy Spirit is no longer in their midst and Satan is ruling.*

This warning was literally carried out against the ten tribes of Israel, which were entirely destroyed by Assyria in 709 B.C. It was also literally carried out in 587 B.C., when Babylon destroyed Jerusalem. It has also been carried out in our day as the churches and congregations have become desolate. God's judgment is upon them so that the Holy Spirit is no longer in their midst and Satan is ruling.

God Is Constantly Testing

Indeed, ancient Israel was constantly under tests. Would they try to get to heaven by their efforts to obey God's commandments or would they realize that they could not be good enough? Would they therefore search out God's promises of salvation for them? As we learned from Romans 9, except for a remnant chosen by grace, they consistently failed the tests.

The very same testing condition exists for the New Testament readers of the Bible. God commands us to believe on Christ, to confess Him, to repent of our sins, to seek Him with all of our heart, etc. Most people immediately conclude, therefore, that if we do these things, we will become saved, and theologians argue that it has to be so because a good God would not command us to do something we are totally incapable of doing. They correctly admit that only Christ can pay for our sins, and this is to be understood as the grace of God. And so the Gospel is presented as the grace of God but it does require some action on our part, however small and insignificant that action might be.

These theologians and Bible teachers fail to realize that the Bible clearly teaches that we are spiritually dead. We are as dead as the dry bones in the valley of dry bones of Ezekiel 37. We are as spiritually dead as Lazarus of John 11 was physically dead so that his body stank. They fail to realize that God gave the commands to believe, to repent, etc., because we are created in the image of God. Therefore, even though we have become spiritually dead, we are still accountable to God. That is why God can righteously bring judgment on the unsaved even though they of themselves could never have pleased God. God does not look at mankind as robots or animals. He regards mankind as those who were created in the likeness of God, and therefore, completely answerable and accountable to God for the way in which they have lived.

God Commands Even Though We Cannot Obey Those Commands

God, therefore, speaks to and commands mankind to do things as if they were still capable of doing those things. He gives the commands to believe on Him, to repent, to seek Him because mankind was created to obey God. Mankind was created in the very likeness of God.

But, as we must do with any statements of Scripture, we must bring the whole Bible to bear on the verse that commands us to believe on Christ. It is then that we discover that we cannot believe, we cannot repent. We are slaves of sin. We are in bondage to Satan. Spiritually, we are dead. We are told that no one will seek after Christ. We are told that no one can come to Christ unless God the Father draws him.

> *Only God can make the choice as to whose sins were to be laid on the Lord Jesus.*

Moreover, we discover that to become saved, every one of our dirty, rotten, rebellious sins must have been laid on the Lord Jesus. This is so because He alone is capable of paying for those sins. And only God can make the choice as to whose sins were to be laid on the Lord Jesus. More than that, we discover that even after our sins have been paid for, another stupendous miracle must take place. That is, God must apply the Word of God to our life and give us a brand new resurrected soul. All of this has to happen before we are saved. And there is no part of this that we can assist. No wonder God says that it is by grace we are saved, and not of works.

When we honestly understand all that is required in order for us to be saved, we realize why our works, our efforts, could never assist in any way with our salvation. Then when we add to this the knowledge that we are a spiritual corpse, we know beyond a shadow of doubt that the only one who can save us is God Himself. We are completely at His mercy.

True, we do know that God is a merciful God. We also know that we can plead with God for His mercy. We know that it will not assist in any way in getting ourselves saved, but at least we have the assurance that God knows of our desire for salvation.

Because faith comes by the hearing of the Word of God, we can place ourselves in that environment. This will not assist us to become saved, but it does place us in an environment where God can apply His Word to our heart if it should be His good pleasure to save us.

> *Who God will save or when He will save someone is entirely God's business.*

That is the reason for the existence of an organization like Family Radio. Our only purpose for existence is to put people all over the world under the hearing of the Word of God. Who God will save or when He will save someone is entirely God's business. The one huge principle we must observe is that we are never to teach in any way that any individual can provide any kind of assistance to get himself saved.

This truth that all the work to get someone saved must be done by God can clearly be seen when God saves a baby. John the Baptist, for example, gave evidence that he had already become saved long before he was born. Obviously, the whole activity of that baby becoming saved has to do with God's activity.

Only as we bring this kind of salvation message will the land (the kingdom of God) enjoy its sabbaths.

Thus, it is a Gospel whereby the land, the kingdom of God, can enjoy its Sabbaths. Through ministries like Family Radio, through individuals and groups who fellowship together outside of the churches, the true Gospel is going into all the world. Let us pray that this activity may be continued faithfully until the last day when Christ returns.

We have learned from Revelation 7 that after the 144,000 have been sealed, a great multitude which no man can number will come to salvation. Remember, these 144,000 are the complete fullness of all those who became saved during the church age.

In Revelation 14 we find a second reference to these 144,000. Revelation 14:1 declares:

And I looked, and, lo, a Lamb stood on the mount Sion, and with him an hundred forty and four thousand, having his Father's name

written in their foreheads.

Verse 4 assures us that they are of the church age because they are spoken of as being **"the firstfruits unto God and to the Lamb."** Following these references to the 144,000, the Bible continues with verse 6, wherein God declares:

> **And I saw another angel fly in the midst of heaven, having the everlasting gospel to preach unto them that dwell on the earth, and to every nation, and kindred, and tongue, and people,**

This verse like verse 9 of Revelation 7 is speaking of another event, independent of the 144,000. We will discover that it is speaking of those who are identified with the latter rain.

Note first of all that this verse speaks of a continuing of the Gospel proclamation that is to go to every nation, kindred, tongue, and people. This language is virtually identical to that which we read in Revelation 7:9, **"of all nations, and kindred, and people, and tongues."** It is the preaching of the Gospel to the nations of the world by those outside of the churches, after the church age has come to an end.

Revelation 14:7 is of singular importance because it details the nature of the preaching that is going to all the world after the church age. We read in verse 6 that it is the everlasting Gospel that is to be preached unto them that dwell upon the earth, but verse 7 gives more detail concerning the emphasis the Gospel is to have. Verse 7 declares:

> **Saying with a loud voice, Fear God, and give glory to him; for the hour of his judgment is come: and worship him that made heaven, and earth, and the sea, and the fountains of waters.**

Preaching with a Loud Voice

This verse declares that the preaching is to be with a loud voice. We can understand this to mean that it is to be sent forth in such a way that it can be clearly heard. Surely, as we are able to send the Gospel by radio and Internet and satellite broadcasting so that it can be heard clearly in the homes of people all over the world, it is going forth with a loud voice.

Fear God

Secondly, the emphasis of the Gospel message is a warning to fear God. When we reflect for a moment on this warning to preach the fear of God, we can easily see the reason for it. Sad to say, in the church world in our day and for many decades in the past, there has been little or no evidence of the fear of God.

> *Any time they teach a doctrine that is not faithful to the Bible, effectively, they are in rebellion against God.*

Let me illustrate. The mandate that is given to every Bible teacher and preacher is to faithfully bring the whole counsel of God to those to whom they are teaching or preaching. Any time they teach a doctrine that is not faithful to the Bible, effectively, they are in rebellion against God. Effectively, they are saying that they know better than Almighty God. They are insisting that their wisdom is greater than the wisdom of God.

To illustrate this reality, think, for example, that there are preachers who preach the doctrines of the Lutheran church, others preach the doctrines of the Baptist churches, others preach the doctrines of the Methodist denomination, others, the Reformed churches, etc. Each of these denominations frequently holds their unique understanding of a particular subject, while another denomination has a different understanding of the same subject. Obviously, there can be only one understanding of the subject in question that is altogether true to the Word of God, and all of the others are teaching a false doctrine.

Therefore, with the knowledge of all of these differing views on the same subject, pastors and teachers who want to be entirely faithful to God's Word, and who tremble at the responsibility they have to bring the truth, should be constantly studying the Word of God and making correction to doctrines that they have been teaching incorrectly.

To say it another way, how many pastors today are ready to take issue with a statement or a doctrine in their church's or denomination's confession if they suspect it is not quite as faithful to God's Word as it should be? Those who have a true fear of God should constantly be studying God's Word and be ready to modify their church confession or doctrine if it is not as faithful to God's Word as it should be.

Again, for example, for hundreds of years, it was the correct Biblical position of most denominations that the there is not to be divorce for any reason and there is not to be a second marriage if the divorced spouse is still living. Today, virtually every congregation teaches that divorce for fornication is possible and remarriage after divorce is also possible. The great number of divorced people in the churches of our day and even in the ruling bodies of the churches testify to the reality of this sin.

> *How many pastors and elders or deacons wake up at night in a cold sweat because they realize their church is violating God's marriage laws?*

How many pastors and elders or deacons wake up at night in a cold sweat because they realize their church is violating God's marriage laws? In Philippians 2:13, we are told to work out our salvation with fear and trembling. If anyone should tremble before God, it is teachers and preachers of the Bible. It is with good reason that God instructs those of the latter rain that the first thing they should emphasize in their Gospel proclamation is the fear of God. And, of course, if they are to preach the fear of God, they themselves should tremble before God and make sure that they are faithful to the whole counsel of God.

Remember that the Bible teaches that God is the same yesterday, today, and forever, and that Israel in 709 B.C. and Judah in 587 B.C. were destroyed by God because of their refusal to remove the high places. These historical evidences of God's actions should cause every pastor to tremble in fear. No church today has any more protection from the wrath of God than Israel and Judah had at the time they were in the focus of God's relationship to mankind.

All Glory to God

The third aspect of the Gospel message that should be preached during the latter rain is that we are to give all glory to God.

This seems like an unnecessary command. Any time we bring the Gospel, are we not glorifying God? The fact is, if we have any kind of a works-grace gospel, we are not giving all glory to God. To some degree we are glorifying man for their part in the salvation process. If, for example, we believe that our church confessions are on a lower level of authority, and yet in practice, they are the standard by which a church measures any doctrine, then God is not being glorified. The church fathers who wrote the confessions are being glorified.

Any time a church follows any doctrine that is not firmly based on the Word of God, it is man who is glorified rather than God. In fact, today, if a church refuses to obey the abundant warnings of the Bible that it is under the judgment of God, it is not glorifying God.

God's Judgment Has Come

A fourth aspect of the Gospel that must be preached is that God's judgment has come.

Let us look closely at Revelation 14:7 where we read:

Saying with a loud voice, Fear God, and give glory to him; for the hour of his judgment is come: and worship him that made heaven, and earth, and the sea, and the fountains of waters.

We are instructed that another aspect of the Gospel message that should be preached during the latter rain is that the hour of God's judgment has come. The manner in which this sentence is written should cause all who read it to tremble with fear. The whole phrase is, **"give glory to him [*God*]; for the hour of his judgment is come."** We should immediately think of the statement of Joshua to Achan just before Achan came under the wrath of God. Achan had disobeyed God by taking for his own gold and silver that should have been destroyed. God showed Joshua that Achan had done this. As Achan stood before Joshua, Joshua said to him in Joshua 7:19:

And Joshua said unto Achan, My son, give, I pray thee, glory to the LORD God of Israel, and make confession unto him; and tell me now what thou hast done; hide it not from me.

Achan confessed his sin but it was too late. By God's command, he was stoned to death.

In parallel fashion, we must remember that God is fully aware of each and every sin of the churches and congregations. He is fully aware of the high places, the doctrines produced by the lofty thoughts of theologians rather than by humble submission to the Bible. And now, we who have the true Gospel are told to proclaim to all who claim to have an interest in the Bible, to give glory to God, for the hour of His judgment is come.

It might be noted that the proclamation that the time has come for God's judgment upon the churches and congregations is the most unhappy proclamation possible. The prophet Jeremiah had the same unhappy task in his day when he was instructed to declare to Judah that God was going to destroy Judah by the Babylonian armies. Many theologians have called him the weeping prophet, and so he was. It brought no joy to him to preach judgment to Judah.

Likewise, this is the saddest possible task assigned by God to true believers outside the church. That task is to proclaim to the churches and congregations that the time of judgment has come. The evidence that we are at that time cannot be denied.

Chapter 10.
Are We Now in the Great Tribulation?

The very solemn question every believer must face is: Has the period of Great Tribulation described in Matthew 24:21 begun? Since we believe we are living in that time of history is there clear evidence that this is so?

While a number of Scriptures detail the character of the Great Tribulation, two are especially in evidence so we need have no doubt that we have arrived at that final event.

First Evidence: Gospels of Tongues, Signs, and Wonders

In Matthew 24:24, God declares the character of the Great Tribulation. There we read:

For there shall arise false Christs, and false prophets, and shall shew great signs and wonders; insomuch that, if it were possible, they shall deceive the very elect.

Never before in all of church history has there been such an interest in signs and wonders, miracles, such as we see today. One of the most prominent signs is the phenomenon of speaking in tongues. All over the world there is an intense interest in this kind of activity. This evidence alone assures us that we are living in the period of the Great Tribulation.

God Uses Satan to Destroy using Tongues, Signs, and Wonders

The Bible discloses that right near the end of time, Satan will become the dominant ruler within the congregations. In II Thessalonians 2, God speaks of the man of sin taking his seat in the temple. It will be seen that the man of sin can be only Satan. Matthew 24:24: **"For there shall arise false Christs, and false prophets, and shall shew great signs and wonders; insomuch that, if it were possible, they shall deceive the very elect."**

In Revelation 13:7, God informs us: **"And it was given unto him to make war with the saints, and to overcome them: and power was given him over all kindreds, and tongues, and nations."** Revelation 13 speaks of the beast that comes out of the earth. This can be only Satan and his dominion, as he rules through false gospels. By this means, he is able to destroy the churches that are under the judgment of God. Thus, he is able to overcome the saints, the true believers, within the congregations.

Destruction of the New Testament church is not through political action but through the action of the church itself as it becomes apostate. Clues and guidance as to how this will materialize can be learned from God's dealings with ancient Israel, because Israel is a type, figure, or representation of the New Testament church. What happened to the nation of Israel gives insight as to what will happen to the congregations of our day.

You may recall that after the death of Solomon, God divided the twelve tribes of Israel into two nations. Ten of the tribes became a nation called Israel which had its capital in Samaria. Two of the tribes, Judah and Benjamin, became the nation of Judah which had its capital in Jerusalem. God set up a testing program for both of these nations. The testing program involved contemporary nations. During the days of the demise of the ten tribes, the testing program involved the nation of Assyria. The nation of Israel looked with longing at the beautiful horses and the beautiful apparel of the Assyrians and decided that their gods must be victorious gods. They began to play spiritual harlotry with Assyria. They began to run after the gods of the Assyrians, a nation whose language they did not understand, and God used the Assyrians to destroy Israel.

Then the nation of Judah began to play spiritual harlotry with the gods of the Babylonians and the Assyrians. They looked at the success of these nations (the beautiful horses and the beautiful apparel), and all that went along with it, and Judah began to lust after their gods. Babylon, too, was a nation whose language they did not understand. It was this nation that destroyed Judah in 587 B.C. This is the scenario that God gives to guide us into truth concerning the destruction of the New Testament church.

God's Long-Term Testing Program for the Church

The principle of a testing program is found repeatedly in the Bible. Israel, for example, was tested by God when Moses left them for forty days to receive the tables of the law on Mount Sinai. Israel failed the test by making and worshipping the golden calf. As a result, God's wrath came upon them and about 3,000 men were killed (Exodus 32).

The number forty in the Bible, or a multiple of ten of the number 40 such as 400, may be a clue that a testing program is in progress. Israel was in the wilderness forty years after coming out of Egypt. They failed the test; few of them trusted in God. The Bible records in Joshua 5:6:

For the children of Israel walked forty years in the wilderness, till all the people that were men of war, which came out of Egypt, were

consumed, because they obeyed not the voice of the LORD: unto whom the LORD sware that he would not shew them the land, which the LORD sware unto their fathers that he would give us, a land that floweth with milk and honey.

Significantly, it can be shown that there were exactly 400 years from the time when Israel came out of Egypt (1447 B.C.), and Saul became king over Israel (1047 B.C.). The latter occurred in the days of Samuel, who was the last of God's prophets to judge Israel. When Samuel was old, Israel came to him and asked for a king to rule over them. I Samuel 8:4-7:

Then all the elders of Israel gathered themselves together, and came to Samuel unto Ramah, And said unto him, Behold, thou art old, and thy sons walk not in thy ways: now make us a king to judge us like all the nations. But the thing displeased Samuel, when they said, Give us a king to judge us. And Samuel prayed unto the LORD. And the LORD said unto Samuel, Hearken unto the voice of the people in all that they say unto thee: for they have not rejected thee, but they have rejected me, that I should not reign over them.

Saul became king exactly 400 years after Israel, under the direct rule of God, came out of Egypt. They failed the test in that they did not want God to rule over them directly.

Another interesting testing program in relation to the number 40 is in the Book of Jonah. Jonah was instructed to cry against Nineveh because of their wickedness (Jonah 1:2). Jonah 3:4: "And Jonah began to enter into the city a day's journey, and he cried, and said, Yet forty days, and Nineveh shall be overthrown."

Wonderfully, the people of Nineveh were victorious in their test. Jonah 3:5 and 10 report:

So the people of Nineveh believed God, and proclaimed a fast, and put on sackcloth, from the greatest of them even to the least of them.... And God saw their works, that they turned from their evil way; and God repented of the evil, that he had said that he would do unto them; and he did it not.

Perhaps the greatest testing program of all occurred in the New Testament, when the Lord Jesus Christ took on a human nature and was tested.

We read in Luke 4:1-2:

And Jesus being full of the Holy Ghost returned from Jordan, and was led by the Spirit into the wilderness. Being forty days tempted of the devil. And in those days he did eat nothing: and when they were ended, he afterward hungered.

The first Adam was tested in the Garden of Eden, and the second Adam, Christ, was also tested. The first Adam failed the test by disobeying God and thus plunged the human race into sin, but our Lord was victorious in the test. He remained entirely obedient to God. His perfect obedience has made the incomprehensible kingdom of God a reality for all who believe on Him. Obviously, the principle that God tests the human race is firmly established in the Bible.

> *The end-time church, too, is faced with*
> *a testing program.*

The end-time church, too, is faced with a testing program. Unfortunately, the Bible reveals that the end-time church in large measure will fail its testing program, just as Adam and Eve failed in their day and as ancient Israel repeatedly did. The church will fail the test and will come under God's wrath, just as God's judgment came when Adam and Eve failed the test.

God's End-Time Testing Program

The testing program that identifies with the end-time church will be focused on a nation whose language the congregation does not understand. God gives at least two prominent clues in the Old Testament as to the nature of this end-time testing program. The first clue is in Deuteronomy 13:1-3:

If there arise among you a prophet, or a dreamer of dreams, and giveth thee a sign or a wonder, And the sign or the wonder come to pass, whereof he spake unto thee, saying, Let us go after other gods, which thou hast not known, and let us serve them; Thou shalt not hearken unto the words of that prophet, or that dreamer of dreams: for the LORD your God proveth you, to know whether ye love the LORD your God with all your heart and with all your soul.

God clearly says that He is proving, that is, testing the congregation through the activity of a false prophet within their midst. We should know about the character of this prophet and the nature of his teaching.

The introduction to Chapter 13 of Deuteronomy is the last verse of Deuteronomy 12, where God admonishes the congregation: **"What thing soever I command you, observe to do it: thou shalt not add thereto, nor diminish from it."** God says that man shall not add to nor take away from the Word of God. To recognize the Word of God as His Word and have an intense desire to be obedient to it, is, in fact, worshipping God. On the other hand, to believe that there is an additional source of divine information (to believe that a dream, vision, or tongue is from God when, indeed, it is not), that effectively is worshipping a god other than the God of the Bible.

God gives the same warning in the New Testament, in Revelation 22:18-19:

> **For I testify unto every man that heareth the words of the prophecy of this book, If any man shall add unto these things, God shall add unto him the plagues that are written in this book: And if any man shall take away from the words of the book of this prophecy, God shall take away his part out of the book of life, and out of the holy city, and from the things which are written in this book.**

"This book" can be only the Bible. The Bible alone and in its entirety is the Word of God. Any additional articulated, verbalized message supposedly from God which is delivered through a dream, vision, or by any other means, is an addition to the Bible. Because God is not adding anything to the divine revelation which is the Bible, if anyone listens to these messages and believes they are of God, he effectively is worshipping a god other than the God of the Bible. God warns in verse 18 that anyone who commits this sin is subject to the plagues written in the Bible; that is, he is subject to eternal damnation.

Deuteronomy 13 says the false prophet is a dreamer of dreams, that is, he is convinced that what he hears in his dreams is of God. If the sign or the wonder, the prophetic statement of his dream or vision, comes to pass, he believes he has received a supernatural visitation, but because the message he received was not from God, it had to be from Satan. When he teaches that the message he received in a dream or vision was from God and, therefore, is the Word of God, he is encouraging people to go after a god other than the God of the Bible. This is a deadly serious sin within the congregation. Deuteronomy 13 says that this prophet is to be put to death even if he is a loved one of someone in the congregation.

The key phrases in these verses in Deuteronomy 13 are, **"for the Lord your God proveth you"** (or tests you) and **"to know whether ye love the Lord your God with all your heart and with all your soul."** These phrases teach something about God's final testing program for the church. God clearly says that He will test the congregation by allowing those who say they declare the Word of God but who are false prophets (because their source is other than the Bible), to be within the congregation.

I Corinthians 14 Gives a Clue Concerning this End-Time Testing

The second Old Testament clue to the end-time testing program that will come against the church is that which came against ancient Israel. The signpost to this clue is in the New Testament, I Corinthians 14:21:

In the law it is written, With men of other tongues and other lips will I speak unto this people; and yet for all that will they not hear me, saith the Lord.

To understand this clue, one must know the setting in which it is found. I Corinthians 14 discusses the phenomenon of tongues, which was present in the church at Corinth. Certain individuals there received from God, as a gift of the Holy Spirit, messages in a language (a tongue), which neither they nor anyone else in the congregation could understand. In I Corinthians 14:2 God speaks of these as **"in the spirit he speaketh mysteries."**

Additionally, within that congregation God gave certain individuals the gift of interpretation. By means of this God-given gift, the message received in the tongue was made understandable to the congregation. I Corinthians 14:5 informs us that when the tongues message was interpreted, it edified the congregation.

This was a valid spiritual event in the church at Corinth. They had only that part of the Bible which is now called the Old Testament. God was still breaking the silence between the supernatural and the natural when He gave messages to Paul, John, Peter, and Agabus (Acts 11:28). Because these messages were from God, they were an addition to the Word of God. The New Testament had not yet been completed, and even with these additions, the churches of that day had an incomplete Word of God.

During the same time when it was possible for the apostles to receive direct messages from God, there were individuals in the church of Corinth who received messages from God in a tongue. The messages could have been in the form of a prayer, praise, or a revelation. Howbeit, it was a message from God, therefore, it was an addition to the written Word of that time.

In the center of the discourse on the phenomenon of tongues (I Corinthians 14:21), is a reference to the Old Testament law wherein God had written that through tongues He would speak to the people and they would not listen. God speaks about tongues in Deuteronomy 28. Moses addressed Israel when they were about to enter the promised land. He warned them that they would not be content with the Gospel he brought them, **"Because thou servedst not the LORD thy God with joyfulness, and with gladness of heart, for the abundance of all things"** (Deuteronomy 28:47). The result of their rebellion against God was punishment. This is declared in the remaining verses of Deuteronomy 28. Verses 48 and 49 summarize the warning:

> **Therefore shalt thou serve thine enemies which the LORD shall send against thee, in hunger, and in thirst, and in nakedness, and in want of all things: and he shall put a yoke of iron upon thy neck, until he have destroyed thee. The LORD shall bring a nation against thee from far, from the end of the earth, as swift as the eagle flieth; a nation whose tongue thou shalt not understand.**

This is the passage of law referred to in I Corinthians 14 in regards to the tongues phenomenon. The ten tribes of Israel were destroyed by their enemy the nation of Assyria after Israel had engaged in spiritual harlotry with the Assyrians. As a result of their spiritual rebellion, God caused the nation of Assyria, a nation whose language Israel did not understand, to destroy them. God gave a final warning of this a few years before it happened. The warning is found in Isaiah 28:11-12./

> **For with stammering lips and another tongue will he speak to this people. To whom he said, This is the rest wherewith ye may cause the weary to rest; and this is the refreshing: yet they would not hear.**

The sequel to God's judgment on Israel occurred 122 years later. The nation of Judah ran like a harlot after Babylon, a heathen nation whose language they did not understand, and Babylon is the nation that destroyed Judah in the year 587 B.C. A few years earlier they had been warned by the prophet Jeremiah. Jeremiah 5:15-17:

> Lo, I will bring a nation upon you from far, O house of Israel, saith
> the LORD; it is a mighty nation, it is an ancient nation, a nation
> whose language thou knowest not, neither understandest what they
> say. Their quiver is as an open sepulchre, they are all mighty men.
> And they shall eat up thine harvest, and thy bread, which thy sons
> and thy daughters should eat: they shall eat up thy flocks and thine
> herds: they shall eat up thy vines and thy fig trees: they shall
> impoverish thy fenced cities, wherein thou trustedst, with the sword.

God is focusing on a nation **"whose language thou knowest not."** This
passage, too, is referred to in the ominous language of I Corinthians 14:21.

Two Important Principles

Deuteronomy 13, Deuteronomy 28, I Corinthians 14, and God's
judgment are obviously tied to the end-time church when two important
principles are considered.

Ancient Israel was a picture or type
of the New Testament church.

The first principle is that ancient Israel was a picture or type of the New
Testament church. God's judgment on Israel for their spiritual adultery
sheds light on the nature of God's judgment on the New Testament church
for its spiritual rebellion.

The second principle is that God sets up testing programs for mankind.
In Deuteronomy 13 it is seen that within the church a testing program will
involve false prophets who receive supernatural messages. These false
prophets will encourage the congregations to go after other gods by
revealing their supernatural experiences, which come from a source other
than God. These two Biblical principles give us understanding as to how God
judges the end-time church.

Tongues: End-Time Testing Program

The question might be raised: Why does God write extensively in I
Corinthians 12, 13, and 14 about the phenomenon of tongues? One might be
surprised to read in the Bible about this temporary phenomenon. A few

decades after this phenomenon occurred in the church in Corinth, the visions of the Book of Revelation were received by the Apostle John on the Island of Patmos. The Book of Revelation closes with the warning that anyone who adds to its words will be subject to plagues; therefore, there can be no further revelation from God by visions, voices, tongues, or anything else. Thus, the phenomenon of tongues that occurred in the church at Corinth would also have come to an end. From that time to the present day, do not expect God to bring a message by these means or by any means other than what He has given us in the Bible.

It appears that the phenomenon of tongues from God was short-lived and confined only to the church at Corinth. It was an incidental matter even in that day; thus, the question persists: Why did God write extensively about it?

The answer lies in the realization that these three chapters of I Corinthians, which discuss the matter of tongues, are God's testing arena for the end-time church. God planted the tree of the knowledge of good and evil in the Garden of Eden, and it was the testing arena of our first parents. Satan saw his opportunity in that testing program to tempt and enslave man in sin. In the warning and testing program of Deuteronomy 13, God allows a false prophet to deceive some people within the congregation. God sets up the testing programs, but it is Satan who uses the tests as opportunities to lead people astray.

God has established the phenomenon of tongues, recorded in I Corinthians 12, 13, and 14, as a testing arena for the end-time church. God gave the true gift of tongues briefly in the church at Corinth so that the end-time churches' fidelity or infidelity to the Word of God could be discovered.

Adam and Eve were permitted to eat of every tree of the garden except one. God provided lavish blessings of fragrant and delicious fruits of the trees to satisfy the physical needs of man. Lucifer wanted man to serve Satan rather than God, and he tempted Adam and Eve into thinking they were missing something important if they did not taste the fruit of the one tree that had been placed off-limits.

Throughout the Bible, the church is reminded of the lavish blessings that attend salvation. The blessings are far more than anyone deserves; they are so wonderful that our hearts should continuously praise God. One minor, incidental blessing, briefly enjoyed by a few people in the church at Corinth (that is, being able to receive an additional message from God in an unknown language), was given before the magnificent blessings of the whole Word of God were available. God maximized His communicative blessings to mankind by giving us the entire record of His will (the New Testament and the Old Testament), and He placed off-limits the minor blessing enjoyed by the church at Corinth.

God, in His wisdom, retained the record; indeed He prominently displays the record of the phenomenon of tongues in the Bible. Its placement there makes it a testing arena for the end-time church, just as the tree of the knowledge of good and evil was the testing arena for the beginning of the human race.

Satan Uses Tongues to Destroy

Satan uses this testing arena as his final opportunity to win a decisive victory over Christ by defeating the external church. He defeated Adam and Eve by encouraging them to eat of the forbidden tree in the Garden of Eden. Likewise, he encourages the end-time church to enjoy the forbidden gift of tongues.

When God set up the testing arena in the Garden of Eden, He used language that made it easy, or at least paved the way, for Lucifer to tempt Eve. God did not give the forbidden tree a foreboding name like "forbidden" tree. God gave this tree the intriguing name "the tree of the knowledge of good and evil." Certainly, such a title would cause Adam and Eve to wonder what mysterious power the fruit of this tree possessed. This is evidenced by Eve's reaction to Satan's enticements, in Genesis 3:6:

> **And when the woman saw that the tree was good for food, and that it was pleasant to the eyes, and a tree to be desired to make one wise, she took of the fruit thereof, and did eat, and gave also unto her husband with her; and he did eat.**

Satan stimulated Eve's lustful thinking by making reference to the name God had given the tree. In Genesis 3:5 Satan declared to Eve: **"For God doth know that in the day ye eat thereof, then your eyes shall be opened, and ye shall be as gods, knowing good and evil."** Surely in giving this tree the name "the knowledge of good and evil," God gave Satan a theme that he could use to tempt our first parents into sin.

God, of course, is not the author of sin, nor is He in any way guilty of sin. God did, however, design an insistent and valid testing program, in that the fruit appeared to be especially luscious (**"the tree was good for food, and that it was pleasant to the eyes,"** verse 6), and in the name that the tree was given.

God also made the testing arena for ancient Israel quite attractive. The ten tribes of the northern kingdom, called Israel, were attracted to the Assyrians, a nation whose language they did not understand. It was a nation that apparently was blessed by God. It was the nation of Assyria; they conquered Syria (II Kings 16:9) and appeared to be the nation with all the answers. Ezekiel 23:5-6:

And Aholah played the harlot when she was mine; and she doted on her lovers, on the Assyrians her neighbours, Which were clothed with blue, captains and rulers, all of them desirable young men, horsemen riding upon horses.

"Aholah" is another name for the capital of Israel, which was in Samaria. Assyria and its political successes and worldly achievements appeared to be the nation to emulate. Similarly, Judah, the southern kingdom with its capital in Jerusalem, was enamored by the beauty, power, and successes of both the Assyrians and the Babylonians.

The beauty, power, and political successes of Assyria and Babylon were the results of God's blessings. These wicked nations were in total rebellion against God, yet God brought them to power and made them attractive to serve as testing programs for Israel and Judah.

Israel Goes to Assyria for Help

The Bible gives a vivid illustration of how God allowed a wicked nation like Assyria to appear to Israel to be a success story. During the days of Isaiah, Jerusalem was threatened by Israel and Syria. The situation was grave. II Chronicles 28 discloses the wickedness of Judah's King Ahaz and the resultant punishment God brought upon Judah by Israel and Syria. II Chronicles 28:5-6:

Wherefore the LORD his God delivered him into the hand of the king of Syria; and they smote him, and carried away a great multitude of them captives, and brought them to Damascus. And he was also delivered into the hand of the king of Israel, who smote him with a great slaughter. For Pekah the son of Remaliah slew in Judah an hundred and twenty thousand in one day, which were all valiant men; because they had forsaken the LORD God of their fathers.

The king of Judah, a wicked man named Ahaz, and all of Judah should have cried to God for help. They should have repented in sackcloth like Nineveh did when Jonah preached to them. They should have cried out to God as King Jehoshaphat did when the Moabites and the Ammonites came to destroy Judah (II Chronicles 20). Instead the Bible records that Judah went to Assyria for help. II Kings 16:7:

> **So Ahaz sent messengers to Tiglath-pileser king of Assyria, saying, I am thy servant and thy son: come up, and save me out of the hand of the king of Syria, and out of the hand of the king of Israel, which rise up against me.**

They could not have more dramatically displayed their complete lack of trust in God. God rescued sinful Judah by wicked Assyria, as II Kings 16:9 declares, **"And the king of Assyria hearkened unto him: for the king of Assyria went up against Damascus, and took it, and carried the people of it captive to Kir, and slew Rezin."**

Assyria conquered Syria. Until recent times, Syria had not been an independent nation. God used Assyria to destroy the ten tribes; they no longer existed as an independent kingdom. These two nations, Syria and the northern kingdom of Israel, therefore, were removed as a threat to Judah by the strength of the heathen nation Assyria.

> *God brought successes to Assyria to intensify the testing program that was coming against Judah.*

The point of this information is that God brought successes to Assyria to intensify the testing program that was coming against Judah. The successes of Assyria in its flower, and Babylon in its flower, suggested that their gods were more powerful and more trustworthy than Jehovah God. God, for His divine purposes, gave Assyria the victory, but Judah was convinced that the superiority of the Assyrian gods made them victorious. This spiritual mentality is seen in the citation of II Chronicles 25:14 where another king of Judah, Amaziah, worshipped the gods of an enemy called Edom or Seir. This verse declares:

> **Now it came to pass, after that Amaziah was come from the slaughter of the Edomites, that he brought the gods of the children**

of Seir, and set them up to be his gods, and bowed down himself
before them, and burned incense unto them.

II Chronicles 28:22-23 records similar action by the wicked King Ahaz:

And in the time of his distress did he trespass yet more against the
LORD: this is that king Ahaz. For he sacrificed unto the gods of
Damascus, which smote him: and he said, Because the gods of the
kings of Syria help them, therefore will I sacrifice to them, that
they may help me. But they were the ruin of him, and of all Israel.

God Intensifies the End-Time Testing Program

When God sets up a testing program, He strengthens the test by His
choice of words or by allowing the enemies of God to appear to be
successful. The same principles apply to God's end-time testing program
for the end-time church in relation to God's Word and in relation to the
successes that God allows the enemies of the Gospel to enjoy.

Three examples of words that God uses to indicate the severity of the
test for the end-time church are offered. First, God says that those who
spoke in tongues in the Corinthian church were edified as they spoke these
mysteries in the Spirit (I Corinthians 14:2-4). Surely anything that serves to
edify or build up the faith of the individual believer is to be sought after but
the context in which these words are found warns the reader to be careful.
Second, God declares in I Corinthians 14:39, **"forbid not to speak with
tongues."** Does this teach that speaking in tongues was sinful in that day? Or,
Does this teach that speaking in tongues is for today?

The third example requires more explanation. In three of the four
gospel accounts, Matthew, Mark, and John, the sin called blasphemy
against the Holy Spirit is mentioned. It is also referred to in I John 5 as a **"sin
unto death."** This sin is unusual in that those who commit it can never have
forgiveness; that is, they can never become saved. Moreover, this sin is
unusual in that God protects mankind from it to the point that it is virtually
impossible to find anyone who has ever committed this sin.

However, the scribes of Jesus' day committed this sin. Mark 3:22 says
of them: **"And the scribes which came down from Jerusalem said, He
hath Beelzebub, and by the prince of the devils casteth he out devils."**
In response to this grievous sin Jesus declares in Mark 3:28-29:

Verily I say unto you, All sins shall be forgiven unto the sons of men,

and blasphemies wherewith soever they shall blaspheme: But he that
shall blaspheme against the Holy Ghost hath never forgiveness, but
is in danger of eternal damnation.

In verse 30 He explains that the sin of blasphemy against the Holy Spirit
is to believe that Christ was under the power of Satan rather than under the
power of the Holy Spirit. The scribes who hated Jesus and desired His death
had committed this dreadful sin; they were convinced that He was of Satan.
They had no desire to look upon Him as their Messiah.

The Bible mentions only that the scribes in Mark 3 and Matthew 12
have committed this sin. The most hardened sinner today ordinarily would
not become convicted that Jesus received His power from Satan. There may
be those in the world who have committed this sin, but if they have, they will
never worry about Christ being their Savior. Anyone who has the slightest
interest in Jesus as Savior could not have committed this dreadful sin.

Why did God put an extensive record of this sin in the Bible? Its
presence in the Bible has produced much sorrow for true believers who
have been incorrectly taught that the sin of blasphemy of the Holy Spirit is
to reject Christ. Many true believers when young repeatedly rejected
Christ. They have become saved in their later years, but are haunted by the
question: Can I be saved? One reason for recording this sin in the Bible is
to increase the severity of the testing program of the end-time church.

> *Few dare to make the judgment that a*
> *"tongues gospel" is of Satan.*

A simple extension of the incorrect idea of what blasphemy of the Holy
Spirit means could be the wrong conclusion that anyone who believes that
a church is under the power of Satan has committed this terrible sin. In other
words, it might be said that if someone examines a particular gospel or
church and decides that it is of Satan, by that judgment he is in danger of
having committed blasphemy against the Holy Spirit. This conclusion is
completely erroneous but widely taught by those who believe in tongues.

Few dare to make the judgment that a "tongues gospel" is of Satan.
Almost no one dares to conclude that a gospel can be a product of Satan
when it claims that Christ is the Savior. As a result, the "tongues gospel" is
protected from criticism even by those who want to remain true to the Bible.
In fear of blaspheming the Holy Spirit, they are forced to acknowledge that

even though they disagree with many doctrines of the "tongues gospel," it must be considered an aspect of the true Gospel. This, in turn, encourages many people to follow the "tongues gospel." Thus, God has built characteristics into the tongues testing program that make it appear safe in its identification with the true Gospel.

The correct understanding of the sin of blasphemy against the Holy Spirit is to believe that Jesus, when He came as the Savior, was under the power of Satan.

The Success of the Tongues Movement

An ever-increasing number of individuals and congregations all over the world fail this end-of-time testing program. The tongues movement, also called the "charismatic movement," is sweeping through churches like wildfire. Virtually every denomination has churches that have welcomed it with open arms.

For generations, attempts have been made to unify various faiths and denominations; however, no attempt has made progress like the charismatic movement. Roman Catholics, Lutherans, Presbyterians, Methodists, Baptists, all gospels that identify with the Christian ethic, find brotherhood under the charismatic banner. To those who embrace the tongues phenomenon, it appears to be a wonderful demonstration of the power of the Holy Spirit.

The Bible guides us into truth; we can know the facts. The church has become increasingly apostate. Consequently, God is blinding people so that they believe this movement is of the Holy Spirit. They do not realize that it is of Satan. By means of this phenomenon, Satan appears to be defeating the true Gospel to a degree never before realized.

Indeed, God brought judgment on the Old Testament church (Israel and Judah), by nations whose language Israel did not understand, nations with whom Israel had engaged in spiritual harlotry. God used these nations to destroy Israel and Judah. Likewise, churches and denominations of today are engaging in grievous spiritual harlotry by blindly running after gospels that feature an unknown language called "tongues." These false gospels are being used of God as a judgment on the church. Expect to see the church destroyed by them.

Congregations will continue to exist. They may appear to be more vibrant and spiritually successful than ever. It may appear that the cause of Christ is advancing all over the world: There are crusades attended in ever-increasing numbers, churches filled to capacity, seminaries with more and more prospective preachers. Nevertheless, it must be realized that the church is under God's judgment. The abomination of desolation is standing in the holy place. The man of sin has taken his seat in the temple.

Two important characteristics always appear to be present in the tongues movement. First, acceptance of the principle that God is still speaking today. Additional revelation, it is believed, may be revealed through an unknown language called a tongue, a vision, a dream, or by hearing a voice. Invariably, where there is an interest in dreams and visions, there is an interest in tongues. Likewise, wherever there is an interest in tongues, there is an interest in dreams and visions. The true Gospel is circumscribed by the authority of the Bible alone and in its entirety. The "tongues gospel" has as its authority the Bible plus the messages that supposedly come from God in a tongue, dream, vision, or voice. It is easy to know that it is not the true Gospel, and if it is not the true Gospel, it is a false gospel.

Signs and Wonders

The second characteristic of the tongues movement is an interest in signs and wonders. There is a conviction that God is performing miracles today, as our Lord and the twelve apostles did signs and wonders. Miraculous healing is most commonly expected. The sign of people falling backward (being "slain in the spirit" as some call it), is evidence of a supernatural event. While so-called miraculous healing can be explained in earthly, physical terms, falling backwards appears to be unexplainable from an earthly, physical vantage point.

The phenomenon of someone appearing to receive a message from God in a tongue or vision, etc., may actually have a physical explanation. It could be an hallucination or it could be related to the individual's subconscious mind. Also, however, it could be supernatural activity induced by Satan; he captivates the hearts of those who are not content with the true Gospel. When it is a supernatural activity, it should be called a sign or a wonder because God calls the activity of speaking in tongues a sign in I Corinthians 14:22.

Significantly, the Bible makes reference to "signs and wonders" in connection with the end of time. The fact that these references have nothing to do with the true church is of great importance. Every reference relates to satanic activity. For example, in Matthew 24:24: **"For there shall arise false Christs, and false prophets, and shall shew great signs and wonders; insomuch that, if it were possible, they shall deceive the very elect."** This verse indicates that false prophets will come with a gospel that is so much like the true Gospel that even the elect would be deceived, if that were possible. The elect are the true believers; they were chosen by God to salvation. They cannot be deceived because God will hold them fast. False prophets can be recognized by their signs and wonders. In II Thessalonians 2:9 God warns of the man of sin who will take his seat in the temple: **"Even him, whose coming is after the working of Satan with all power and signs and lying wonders."**

In Revelation 13, in reference to Satan coming as a false prophet, God warns in verses 13-14:

And he doeth great wonders, so that he maketh fire come down from heaven on the earth in the sight of men, And deceiveth them that dwell on the earth by the means of those miracles which he had power to do in the sight of the beast; saying to them that dwell on the earth, that they should make an image to the beast, which had the wound by a sword, and did live.

In Revelation 16:14, God speaks of satanic activity just before Judgment Day:

For they are the spirits of devils, working miracles, which go forth unto the kings of the earth and of the whole world, to gather them to the battle of that great day of God Almighty.

God shows in these references that He will bring His judgment on the end-time church through false gospels that feature miracles. Do not be surprised that signs and wonders are prominent in churches with false gospels. When Christ came with the true Gospel, He attested to its genuineness by performing miracles. John 20:30-31:

And many other signs truly did Jesus in the presence of his disciples, which are not written in this book: But these are written, that ye might believe that Jesus is the Christ, the Son of God; and that believing ye might have life through his name.

As Satan comes at the end of time with his false gospels that feature tongues, he, too, attempts to attest to their genuineness with signs and wonders. Only two miracles are credited to him in the Bible: First, his ability to break the silence between the supernatural and the natural with messages in tongues and visions; and second, he can supernaturally cause people to fall backward. To add further credence to these gospels, Satan comes with lying signs and wonders, that is, his adherents will claim to do miracles and believe miracles have been done, when there has been no miracle.

> *Right before our eyes, church after church capitulates to gospels that do not consider the Bible alone and in its entirety to be the true Gospel.*

Modern means of communication such as television enhance the spread of these false gospels. People who worship in churches that are reasonably faithful to the true Gospel may become familiar with the blandishments and enticements of false gospels in the privacy of their homes. With no one knowing, they drink deeply of the poisoned water, and as the plague enters their churches, they are prepared to accept it as an aspect of the true Gospel. Right before our eyes, church after church capitulates to gospels that do not consider the Bible alone and in its entirety to be the true Gospel.

The destruction of the church, to a high degree, is accomplished through the testing program of tongues. In blindness, a church will fail the test as Satan deceives the congregation into accepting the false gospels of tongues and signs and wonders. Thus, congregations will continue to exist during the final tribulation period, but they will be increasingly false. True believers will either voluntarily leave or they will be asked to leave when the congregation begins to follow a false gospel. Those who remain within the congregations in reality will be serving Satan even though they think they are serving Christ.

Does Baptism in the Holy Spirit Relate to Speaking in Tongues?

We might wonder if there is a relationship between baptism in the Holy Spirit and the phenomenon of speaking in tongues that occurred in the church of Corinth before the Bible was completed. The Bible is very clear that there is no relationship between baptism in the Holy Spirit and speaking in tongues. Let's first consider baptism in the Holy Spirit and let's start in the Old Testament, where four signs pointed to salvation.

First, there was circumcision, to indicate that we must have the foreskin of our hearts cut off. We must be cut away from our flesh and its sinful lusts. Jeremiah 4:4:

Circumcise yourselves to the LORD, and take away the foreskins of your heart, ye men of Judah and inhabitants of Jerusalem: lest my fury come forth like fire, and burn that none can quench it, because of the evil of your doings.

Second, there was the burnt offering. Meal offerings and animal sacrifices as burnt offerings pointed to Christ, who became our burnt offering. Hebrews 10:5-7:

Wherefore when he cometh into the world, he saith, Sacrifice and offering thou wouldest not, but a body hast thou prepared me: In burnt offerings and sacrifices for sin thou hast had no pleasure. Then said I, Lo, I come (in the volume of the book it is written of me,) to do thy will, O God.

Third, there was the shedding of blood, for instance a lamb or an ox, which pointed to the shed blood of the Lord Jesus Christ who endured the wrath of God for our sins. Hebrews 9:22:

And almost all things are by the law purged with blood; and without shedding of blood is no remission.

The fourth sign used in the Old Testament was water ablution, which ceremonially indicated that a person had been cleansed of his sins. For example, Aaron and his sons were washed when they were consecrated as priests (Leviticus 8:6). The sign or symbol of water ablution or washing in water is used also in the New Testament.

From the beginning of the entrance of sin into the world, to be saved, a man, woman, or child must have his sins washed away, be born again, become a new creature in Christ. The Holy Spirit, who is eternal God, is given to the person who becomes saved.

Beginning with Pentecost, God began His work to evangelize the world through believers who were qualified by God to be witnesses, to proclaim His Word and share the Gospel. God utilized different terminology in talking about salvation. Christ talked about being baptized in the Holy Spirit. Believers in the New Testament are saved the same way believers were saved in the Old Testament; the difference in the New Testament is that every believer is qualified to share the Gospel.

We read of this in the Gospels of Matthew, Luke, and John. Acts 1:5, which reads, **"For John truly baptized with water; but ye shall be** baptized with the Holy Ghost not many days hence," speaks of an Old Testament sign because John the Baptist was a prophet on the Old Testament side of the cross. They were told that before many days, they would be filled with the Holy Spirit and become qualified to be witnesses in the New Testament program of evangelism.

When we are saved, we are baptized in the Holy Spirit. The word "baptize" means to wash, cleanse, or purify. Therefore, it denotes the fact that our sins have been washed away. Baptism of the Holy Spirit has nothing to do with miracles, signs, or wonders. Jesus says in Acts 1:8: "**But ye shall receive power, after that the Holy Ghost is come upon you: and ye shall be witnesses unto me both in Jerusalem, and in all Judaea, and in Samaria, and unto the uttermost part of the earth.**"

In the Book of Acts we find illustrations in each of these places of a special miracle to indicate that the Word of God was to be sent out to evangelize the world. (See Acts 2, Acts 8, Acts 10, and Acts 19.) After these illustrations in Acts, no outward miracle is recorded in the Bible that occurred when a person was saved.

In the first letter of Paul to the church at Corinth, Chapters 12, 13, and 14, however, we learn that in that church there was a phenomenon known as tongues or speaking in an unknown language. This was a gift that was given to a few individuals in that church, including Paul, whereby they received information from God in an unknown language. The phenomenon bears no relationship to baptism in the Holy Spirit; this gift was not bestowed upon them when they were saved.

The believers at Corinth who were given this gift were instructed to pray that they might interpret. The purpose of interpretation was to share with the congregation what God had revealed to them, for the edification of the congregation. This was possible because in that day, God had not completed the Bible.

Around A.D. 95, God completed the Bible with the writing of the Revelation of John. God is the author of the Bible, and in the last chapter of the Bible, He declares, in Revelation 22:18-19:

> **For I testify unto every man that heareth the words of the prophecy of this book, If any man shall add unto these things, God shall add unto him the plagues that are written in this book: And if any man shall take away from the words of the book of this prophecy, God shall take away his part out of the book of life, and out of the holy city, and from the things which are written in this book.**

With this statement, God ended the possibility of any further information coming from God. From that point on, we cannot expect anyone to receive a vision, tongue, or voice from God because God will not violate His own rules. God said that He has given us His Word, the revelation of His will. We are to study it, be obedient to it, and not expect any phenomena of tongues or visions such as occurred before the Bible was complete.

Since A.D. 95, various people in the New Testament period have claimed to have received a vision or a message in a tongue, which might seem very glorious. Based on the Bible, however, these activities cannot be from God. It might be from their own minds. It might be from an evil source. It might be hallucinatory. Our minds are very tricky.

Today everyone who becomes saved is baptized in the Holy Spirit. Being baptized in the Holy Spirit comes with salvation; it is not a separate gift, but rather it happens to everyone who is truly saved. The true believer is one who has come to recognize that he is a sinner under the wrath of God and he knows that his salvation is entirely the work of God. He is one who has come to trust the Bible concerning the Lord Jesus Christ, who is the only Savior given to mankind. When he is saved, that is, born again, he is baptized in the Holy Spirit. His sins are washed away, and the Holy Spirit takes up His abode with him.

Does the Bible Say that Tongues would Continue until the End?

Another important question we should address is whether the gift of tongues would continue throughout the church season.

Let us consider what God says in I Corinthians 13:8-12. There we read:

Charity never faileth: but whether there be prophecies, they shall fail; whether there be tongues, they shall cease; whether there be knowledge, it shall vanish away. For we know in part, and we prophesy in part. But when that which is perfect is come, then that which is in part shall be done away. When I was a child, I spake as a child, I understood as a child, I thought as a child: but when I became a man, I put away childish things. For now we see through a glass, darkly; but then face to face: now I know in part; but then shall I know even as also I am known.

Let us look at this passage carefully. In I Corinthians 13, God is simply saying that tongues shall cease, but He is not telling when they shall cease.

God says that prophecy and knowledge will pass away, and in verses 9-12, He says that they will pass away when we see Him face to face, that is, when we get to heaven. Notice that verses 9-12 are speaking only of knowledge and prophecy. They are not speaking about tongues. This passage does not tell us when tongues will cease.

God teaches in Revelation 22:18 that if you look for divine truth from sources other than the Bible, it indicates that you are still subject to the plagues written herein, that is, you are unsaved and subject to hell. Therefore, Revelation 22:18 gives the answer as to when tongues will cease, and that is when the Bible was completed.

It is true that the Bible speaks of signs and wonders that will still come to pass. The Bible speaks about signs and wonders in a number of places, and speaking in tongues is a sign. We read about this in I Corinthians 14. The Greek word for sign is *simeon*, which also can be translated "miracle." The Bible speaks of signs and wonders, particularly in relation to the end-time church, ominously, and unfortunately, all references to signs and wonders near the end of time are satanically related. God declares in Matthew 24:24:

For there shall arise false Christs, and false prophets, and shall shew great signs and wonders; insomuch that, if it were possible, they shall deceive the very elect.

We read in II Thessalonians 2:3-4:

Let no man deceive you by any means: for that day shall not come, except there come a falling away first, and that man of sin be revealed, the son of perdition; Who opposeth and exalteth himself above all that is called God, or that is worshipped; so that he as God sitteth in the temple of God, shewing himself that he is God.

> *The man of sin taking his seat in the temple represents or is a picture of Satan ruling in the church.*

The man of sin taking his seat in the temple represents or is a picture of Satan ruling in the church. Satan will come with signs and wonders of falsehood. God will make the followers of Satan believe a lie, so they will be prepared for judgment.

Revelation 13 speaks about the beast that comes out of the earth and a second beast. The second beast makes an image, and he gives life to that image and brings signs. These are gospels that Satan has designed so he can enslave the nations of the world to a higher degree than ever before. He will come as an angel of light and attest to the genuineness of his gospels with signs and wonders. Satan is the big deceiver. Revelation 16:13-14:

> **And I saw three unclean spirits like frogs come out of the mouth of the dragon, and out of the mouth of the beast, and out of the mouth of the false prophet. For they are the spirits of devils, working miracles, which go forth unto the kings of the earth and of the whole world, to gather them to the battle of that great day of God Almighty.**

These verses speak of the beast and the false prophet coming with signs and miracles to deceive. Every reference to signs and wonders near the end of time relates to satanic activity. This is very ominous; it indicates that we have to be extremely careful today because we are so near the end of time. We must make absolutely certain that we look only to the Bible for divine truth. The Bible alone and in its entirety is the divine Word of God.

Satan can speak in a lot of ways; he comes with all kinds of occult activities. Apart from the church, he comes through witchcraft, Ouija boards, tarot cards, and so on. In the church, he also comes with occult activity. The Bible says he does. II Corinthians 11:14: **"And no marvel; for Satan himself is transformed into an angel of light."** We must be on guard and make sure that the only place we look for divine truth is the Bible.

Could Tongues be Used to Reiterate the Teaching of the Bible?

We might wonder if it would be possible that God could speak in a tongue today just to reiterate something in the Bible or to put emphasis on a particular passage in the Bible. However, we know that this is not possible because God will not violate His own program. His program is that He has given us all of the information that He wants us to have in the Bible.

For example, there is some repeating of information in the Bible. Four times in John 6 God says concerning the believer that, **"I will raise him up at the last day."** We read this in verses 39, 40, 44, and 54. It seems unnecessary to repeat this four times, but we would not dare think of removing one of these phrases, to reduce it down to three times. We would be removing from the Word of God. In the same way, if God did it, repeated this phrase, to give it to us a fifth time, then that would be a valid addition to the Word of God.

We must keep in mind that God told us in Revelation 22:18-19 that the Bible is the complete message from God. If we want to grow stronger in the Word, we are to read the Bible. Psalm 119:11 tells us: **"Thy word have I hid in mine heart, that I might not sin against thee."** God gave us four Gospel accounts so that we have plenty of information concerning who the Lord Jesus Christ is. We are to go to the Word of God to seek the voice of God. If we say, "Well, the Word of God in not sufficient," then we are violating the Word of God.

Does the Bible Command that We Are Not to Forbid Speaking in Tongues?

We read the command not to forbid speaking in tongues in I Corinthians 14:39. We learn from a careful study of I Corinthians 14 that in the church at Corinth, the tongues were somewhat of a problem. So, they were given the mandate not to forbid speaking in tongues. However, we have to look at these chapters of I Corinthians in the light of the whole Bible.

In the Old Testament, for example, the law was that males were to go to Jerusalem three times a year to offer sacrifices. Now, we don't go to Jerusalem any more to offer sacrifices. Why don't we? It's in the Bible! It's a command of God! Why don't we do that?

The reason we don't do that is because we read that command in the light of everything else the Bible offers, and we discover in the New Testament that God says these ceremonial laws have been completed in Christ. So, we are not to be obedient to them any more. In fact, it would be wrong to offer sacrifices.

By the same token, in I Corinthians 12-14, God laid down rules insofar as tongues is concerned. But in Revelation 22:18, He has more to say about His Word. We have to read I Corinthians 12-14 in the light of Revelation 22:18, and Deuteronomy 13:1-10, and Deuteronomy 28, and other passages that speak on this matter. When doing this, we learn that God ceased to give messages in tongues once the Bible was completed.

When we realize that the Bible alone is the Word of God and we know that Satan comes as an angel of light, then we can try to put ourselves in the shoes of Satan. This is not too difficult because all of us have a sinful nature. Satan thinks, "I'm going to try to snare someone who is a very religious person. I'm certainly not going to come to that person with horns and with a forked tail. I'm going to come as an angel of light. I'm going to <u>look</u> like a legitimate emissary of the Lord Jesus Christ. The first thing I'm going to do is encourage that person to be drawn away from the Word of God, and convince him that the Bible is not the only authority. Then I can get him to begin to understand the Bible in the light of other authorities, and he will no longer attempt to get truth from the Bible only."

Satan is very careful to come with gospels that sound like the true Gospel. He quotes the Bible, but he is very deceitful. In this way, the person is completely disarmed. That person will become accustomed to listening for the Word of God from sources outside the Bible.

Satan is the father of lies. For a while, he might come with just the Word of God, then slowly, he adds a statement or a little something that is contrary to the Word of God. Satan is the great deceiver. The person listening might not know that he has begun to accept ideas that are contrary to the Word of God, ideas that are half-truths. That person might think only that he has had a happy experience, a good experience with a vision, and it seemed so holy, and he trusts that source of information. That person might not even know what happened to him.

It is so wonderful that we have the Word of God, the Bible, and we can be absolutely certain that it is the Word of God. It will always be the Word of God. We do not have to wonder or fear that perhaps Satan had something to do with this or that statement in the Bible.

The Bible is the Complete Message from God

We wonder if the "book" of Revelation 22:18-19 is speaking of just Revelation or of the whole Bible. As we consider this question, we must understand that the Book of Revelation is an integral and cohesive part of the whole Bible. Therefore, if we add a chapter to the Book of Revelation, then we have added it to the whole Bible. Whether we tried to add it sometime during the first five years after it was written or tried to add it 1,500 years after it was written, we have still attempted to add to the whole Bible. Once the last words of Revelation were penned, about A.D. 95, then the Bible was completed, and God gathered all of the separate books together into the one whole Bible that we have today.

In other words, anything that was written after the Book of Revelation was completed could not possibly be part of the holy canon. The ending verses of the Book of Revelation set the limit as to the Word of God. It does not take long to review all of the writings that came forth during the period prior to this date to see why this is the Bible that we have and not something else. There is an internal cohesiveness in the Bible.

One problem people have in accepting the fact that the Bible is the only message from God is that they read a verse like Revelation 22:18 from the vantage point of having accepted the premise that God does speak in visions or voices or tongues today, and as a result, they will not understand a verse like Revelation 22:18 in the same way that someone who is determined to let the Bible alone be his guide and his authority will understand it. This is because they have additional information that they are putting into the equation, and they are bound to come up with a different answer. Therefore, it is not surprising when so many people believe in tongues or visions or voices. This is the conclusion that people come to when they allow information outside of the Bible to be used in their understanding of what the Bible says. As a matter of fact, they reach conclusions in regards to many Biblical passages that are different from the conclusions reached by those who limit themselves to the Word of God.

The minute one tries to add to the Bible, from this vision or that tongue, or whatever, and one person adds this, and another one adds that, and someone else adds something else, and then attempt to interpret the Bible in the light of all this new information, they end up with a gospel that will take them almost anywhere. This is exactly what is happening today. The false gospels are going off in all directions.

> *The true Gospel, the Gospel of the Lord Jesus Christ,*
> *is circumscribed by the Bible alone and in its entirety.*

The true Gospel, the Gospel of the Lord Jesus Christ, is circumscribed by the Bible alone and in its entirety. Only in the Bible, the whole Bible, can truth be found.

Therefore, as we look at the church world today with abundance of tongues, signs and wonders, it is no doubt that Matthew 24:24 has been fulfilled. We have our first and most striking evidence that we have come to the time of the Great Tribulation.

Second Evidence: Calling Down Fire from Heaven

A second evidence that we are in the Great Tribulation time spoken of in Matthew 24 is the worldwide evidence of people falling backward. The churches that practice this miracle call it "being slain in the Spirit."

This miracle was foretold in Revelation 13. The whole chapter is describing the Great Tribulation period. In verse 13, we read:

> **And he doeth great wonders, so that he maketh fire come down from heaven on the earth in the sight of men.**

Falling Backward Equals Fire from Heaven

As we learned earlier, causing someone to fall backward is equivalent to calling down fire from heaven. Thus, this miracle of people falling backward to the ground, which is occurring all over the world, is clear evidence that we are now in the Great Tribulation period of Revelation 13 and Matthew 24.

Third Evidence: The Latter Rain

The third evidence that we are in the Great Tribulation time of Matthew 24 is that we are experiencing the "latter rain." As we have been learning, the latter rain is the time when God is sending out the Gospel worldwide outside of the churches and congregations, and it is a time when God is making sure that the Gospel that is sent out is very faithful to the Bible. The high places of the church age are no longer acceptable. The kingdom of God is now keeping it's sabbaths. As we will see, the latter rain is during the second half of the Great Tribulation, showing that we are now well into the tribulation time. Therefore, since we are experiencing the latter rain right now, we can know that we are well into the Great Tribulation time.

Let us begin by looking at some verses that tie the church age, the Great Tribulation, and the latter rain together.

The Great Tribulation Cannot Begin Until the Church Age Is Finished

There is another evidence that shows us that we are in the second part of the Great Tribulation. Remember Matthew 24:22 declares:

> **And except those days should be shortened, there should no flesh be saved: but for the elect's sake those days shall be shortened.**

In Revelation 7, the Bible teaches that after the 144,000 from twelve tribes of Israel have been sealed on their foreheads, a great multitude that no man can number would come out of Great Tribulation into salvation.

Who are these 144,000? We read in Revelation 7:1-4:

And after these things I saw four angels standing on the four corners of the earth, holding the four winds of the earth, that the wind should not blow on the earth, nor on the sea, nor on any tree. And I saw another angel ascending from the east, having the seal of the living God: and he cried with a loud voice to the four angels, to whom it was given to hurt the earth and the sea, Saying, Hurt not the earth, neither the sea, nor the trees, till we have sealed the servants of our God in their foreheads. And I heard the number of them which were sealed: and there were sealed an hundred and forty and four thousand of all the tribes of the children of Israel.

In this very revealing passage, God is speaking of a time when four angels would hurt the earth and the sea. But they could not bring their hurtful activity until the servants of God were sealed. These servants numbered 144,000 and were from all of the tribes of Israel.

144,000: The Complete Fullness of Those Saved During the Church Age

As we try to understand this, we know that to be sealed means to be saved. We read in Ephesians 1:13, 14:

In whom ye also trusted, after that ye heard the word of truth, the gospel of your salvation: in whom also after that ye believed, ye were sealed with that holy Spirit of promise, Which is the earnest of our inheritance until the redemption of the purchased possession, unto the praise of his glory.

Thus, we can know that these 144,000 have been saved.

Secondly, we must realize that the number 144,000 is a symbolical number. It is made up of 12,000 from each of twelve tribes of Israel. Especially in the Book of Revelation, the number twelve signifies the fullness of whatever is in view and the number ten or 100 or 1,000 signifies the completeness of whatever is in view. For example, the holy city, the new Jerusalem, is 12,000 stadia by 12,000 stadia by 12,000 stadia. It has a wall that is 144 (12 x 12) cubits. These numbers signify the fullness or the complete fullness of all believers who make up the eternal Jerusalem.

Likewise, the 144,000 of Revelation 7 are also the complete fulness of all those who would have become saved prior to the loosing of the four angels who will hurt the land and the sea.

The four angels are mentioned again in Revelation 9:14-16:

Saying to the sixth angel which had the trumpet, Loose the four angels which are bound in the great river Euphrates. And the four angels were loosed, which were prepared for an hour, and a day, and a month, and a year, for to slay the third part of men. And the number of the army of the horsemen were two hundred thousand thousand: and I heard the number of them.

In this passage, we read that the loosing of them, which must come at an hour, a day, and a month of the year, would cause the third part of men to perish. Later in our study, we will learn that the third part is a reference to the true believers who will be killed in the sense that they will be driven from the churches during the Great Tribulation. The term "third part" comes from the language of Zechariah 13:8, 9:

And it shall come to pass, that in all the land, saith the LORD, two parts therein shall be cut off and die; but the third shall be left therein. And I will bring the third part through the fire, and will refine them as silver is refined, and will try them as gold is tried: they shall call on my name, and I will hear them: I will say, It is my people: and they shall say, The LORD is my God.

The third part are the true believers who have been purged of their sins because Christ as their substitute has endured the fire of hell on their behalf. They have been driven from the churches because God's judgment has come upon the churches. It is the church that drives them out as evidenced by Revelation 9:16, which indicates the army that does the killing consists of 2,000,000 men. The number 1,000,000 symbolizes completeness and the number 2 symbolizes the church. Thus, the number 2,000,000 symbolizes that the complete number of churches will engage in this activity of driving out the true believers, symbolized by the one-third who are killed. We might recall that John 16:2 equates killing with banishment from the churches. There we read:

They shall put you out of the synagogues: yea, the time cometh, that whosoever killeth you will think that he doeth God service.

This truth is identical to that which we read in Revelation 11 wherein the Bible describes the killing of the two witnesses. The two witnesses also represent the true believers who have been driven from the churches. The horrible nature of this action is further dramatized by the lurid language of

Revelation 8 which describes a third part of the trees, of the sea, of the ships, of the rivers, of the waters, of the sun, of the moon, of the stars being destroyed or smitten. Clearly, God is giving us language that indicates the end of the church age, which is altogether in view, is super catastrophic. This is so because it is also the time that Judgment Day is about to fall on the whole world. It begins with judgment on the house of God which is the churches and congregations that God has used for over 1900 years to evangelize the world.

Thus, the language that speaks of the loosing of the four angels who will hurt the earth and the sea is speaking of the same event as the killing of the two witnesses of Revelation 11. It is the same event that is spoken of in Matthew 24:21, **"For then shall be great tribulation."** It is the same event as that spoken of in Revelation 9 where God describes the star that falls from heaven and has the key that opens the pit from which locusts and all kinds of devastation come. It is the same event as Revelation 13 which speaks of a beast that comes out of the sea and of a beast that comes out of the earth. It is the same event that Daniel 7:23 describes as the fourth beast that shall devour the whole earth. It is the same event as is given in the account of Daniel 8 where God describes the little horn that will magnify himself even to the prince of the host and cause the sanctuary to be trodden under foot for 2300 days. It is the same event as that described in Matthew 24:15 concerning the abomination of desolation that stands in the holy place. It is the same event spoken of in Luke 21:20 which describes Jerusalem being surrounded by armies.

It is the same event spoken of in Matthew 24:2, in Mark 13:2, and in Luke 21:6 where God indicates all the stones in the temple will be thrown down so that there will not be left one upon another. It is the same event spoken of in II Thessalonians 2:3-11 wherein God describes that He that restrains (restrains Satan), will be taken out of the midst and Satan will rule in the temple (the churches and congregations). It is the same truth as that which is in view as God describes the destruction of the ships of Tarshish in Isaiah 23 and the destruction of Tyrus and Zidon in Ezekiel 27 and 28. It is the same event that was anticipated by the trauma Jacob endured when he went to Egypt to escape the famine. It is the same truth anticipated by the destruction of Judah that began in 609 B.C. when the last good king, Josiah, was killed. It is the same truth that is pictured by the destruction of the ship from which 276 were saved, as recorded in Acts 27.

All of these accounts together with many others are vividly recorded in the Bible. It is amazing how much language of the Bible is employed by God to illustrate what will happen when the 144,000 have been sealed. We can be sure that God is making certain that we do not miss the significance, the importance, the reality of this tremendous event.

Because this information has been sealed until the time of the end, believers heretofore had not been made aware of this tremendous event. Remember God wrote in Daniel 12:9:

And he said, Go thy way, Daniel: for the words are closed up and sealed till the time of the end.

Therefore, before the present time, the Holy Spirit gave no believers an understanding of these verses. But now that we are in that time of Great Tribulation, it signals that the end of the world has come very close. God is opening our understanding so that we become completely aware of this tremendous change in God's plan of evangelizing the world.

Returning to the 144,000 we must notice that they were from all of the tribes of Israel but the tribe of Dan is not mentioned. The reason is that if national Israel were in view, thirteen tribes would be named, including the tribe of Dan. But the Israel that God has in view in Revelation 7 is all the churches and congregations located throughout the world. They were typified by the tribes of Israel.

In this connection, it is interesting and significant to note that James 1:1 is addressed to the twelve tribes scattered abroad. We read there:

James, a servant of God and of the Lord Jesus Christ, to the twelve tribes which are scattered abroad, greeting.

Here also the phrase is speaking of the churches and congregations which were typified by twelve tribes of Israel. Significantly, in James 1:18, they are called the firstfruits of His creatures. Earlier in this study, we learned that firstfruits identify with Pentecost. We also learned that firstfruits and Pentecost have intimate identification with the church age.

We might also note that James 4:4 uses language of Revelation 17 and 18 as God speaks of the harlot Babylon. Later, we will learn that this harlot is the churches during the Great Tribulation. But already in James 4:4, God declares:

Ye adulterers and adulteresses, know ye not that the friendship of the world is enmity with God? whosoever therefore will be a friend of the world is the enemy of God.

Summarizing what we know of the 144,000 is that they are the complete fulness of all who become saved during the church age. After they were sealed, that is, after their salvation had been accomplished, the Great

Tribulation began as typified by the four angels being loosed to hurt the earth and the sea.

We are certain that the 144,000 are the complete fullness of all those would become saved by the activity of the churches during the New Testament era. As we learned from Revelation 11 and II Corinthians 10 there would come a time when the work of the churches was finished. As we have seen, this coincides with the beginning of the Great Tribulation. It also coincides with the end of the season of the early Pentecostal rain at which time all of the harvest of the firstfruits has been brought in. This is not the end of the evangelization of the world. In Chapter 9, we learned about the season of the latter rain when a great multitude which no man can number will be harvested.

Latter Rain Comes after the Church Age

Back to Revelation 7. The sealing of the 144,000 is completed in verse 8. This is the symbolic number to represent all those saved during the church age. Notice what the next verse, Revelation 7:9 says:

> **After this I beheld, and, lo, a great multitude, which no man could number, of all nations, and kindreds, and people, and tongues, stood before the throne, and before the Lamb, clothed with white robes, and palms in their hands;**

Notice that God says; "**After this.**" We can understand this now. God is speaking of another group. Notice that God is emphasizing that it is from all peoples of the world and no man can know the number of them. In Revelation 7:14, God gives more information about those in verse 9. He says there:

> **And I said unto him, Sir, thou knowest. And he said to me, These are they which came out of great tribulation, and have washed their robes, and made them white in the blood of the Lamb.**

God explains that those in Revelation 7:14 are the those that came out of Great Tribulation. That ties them back to the Great Tribulation time that we are in, the Great Tribulation of Matthew 24. They were saved after the 144,000 were already saved which represents all those saved during the church age. Once the Great Tribulation began, the Holy Spirit was taken out of the midst of the churches, meaning that God was no longer saving in the churches. Therefore, they had to   saved outside the churches. Those in Revelation 7:9 are saved during the latter rain, which begins in the second part of the Great Tribulation.

Since we can see evidence of the latter rain today, we can know that we are in the second part of the Great Tribulation.

Chapter 11.
The Third Time. Judgment Day

At the beginning of this study, we learned that God's plan for the Gospel to this world included three seasons and three times. All three seasons were periods of spiritual rain that brought a spiritual harvest. We might recall that the first early righteous rain encompassed God's Gospel plan for the Old Testament. The harvest it brought forth was none other than Jesus Christ our Messiah. He was the first of the firstfruits.

The second rain was the early Pentecostal rain that brought the firstfruits harvest of believers who became saved during the church age. They are typified by the number 144,000 that we read about in Revelation 7 and Revelation 14.

The third rain which fell, during the third season, was the latter rain which is bringing in a great multitude which no man can number during the Great Tribulation. We are now experiencing this final harvest of souls as we are nearing the end of the world.

Between the first and second seasons, there was the three and a half year time when Jesus was ministering here on earth. It was a time of spiritual famine of hearing the Word of God. It was also a time of judgment. During this time, Satan was given a death blow and cast out of heaven. He was spiritually cast into hell in that he came altogether under the wrath of God. During this time, Jesus also was judged and experienced the punishment of damnation on behalf of all those He came to save.

Between the second and the third seasons there was the time of God's judgment on the churches and congregations. It, too, was a time of spiritual famine of hearing the Word of God. It, too, was a time that identified with three and a half years. This three and a half year time was a symbolic rather than a literal time. This second time identifies with the first part of the Great Tribulation during which God's judgment came on the churches all over the world. The Holy Spirit withdrew from the midst of the congregations and Satan became the ruler in them. He is the abomination of desolation that is standing in the holy place. The true believers are either driven from the churches or are commanded by God to come out of them.

The third season, which identifies with the last part of the Great Tribulation during which, outside of the churches, a great multitude which no man can number are saved, is followed by the third time which coincides with the last day of the world's existence. It is Judgment Day.

Why Speak about Judgment Day?

The subject of God's judgment first on the church and finally on the whole world is surely the most unpleasant subject of the Bible. But it is a subject that cannot be avoided because God has written so extensively about it in the Bible. The whole Bible is the Gospel. We cannot proclaim the Gospel without proclaiming Judgment Day. God set forth this principle in II Corinthians 5:10:

For we must all appear before the judgment seat of Christ; that every one may receive the things done in his body, according to that he hath done, whether it be good or bad.

Each and every human being has to give an account to God because we are created in the image of God. Wonderfully, if we have become saved, we have already stood before the judgment throne of God to answer for our sins. No, we were not personally there. We had a substitute, a stand-in, who stood there on our behalf. That substitute was the Lord Jesus who became laden with all of the miserable, rotten, awful sins of each one of God's elect. He was found guilty, of course, and the consequence for Him was that He had to bear the awful wrath of God as payment for our sins. His punishment was equal to that which should have been endured by each and every one of God's elect spending an eternity in hell. This is what the cross was all about. Therefore, these humans, whose sins have already been paid for because Christ endured the wrath of God for them can be forgiven and become children of God. Therefore, these individuals have already stood before the judgment throne of God and will never stand there again. In fact, when Christ comes as the judge, these saved individuals will immediately be caught up to be with Him in the air and shall always be with Him.

However, which humans are God's elect is not known to any man. Only if we have been saved do we know obviously, we are saved because we are one of God's elect. Amongst the teeming multitudes of the world, many are of God's elect, but we do not have the slightest idea who they might be. Therefore, we send the Gospel into the whole world knowing that through it, Christ will seek out and find the elect and save them.

We Are Commanded to Warn the Wicked

As we began to indicate, Judgment Day is an integral part of the Gospel. The true believers are, therefore, commanded to warn the peoples of the world that this terrible day is coming. In Ezekiel 33, God speaks of the believers as watchmen. They are to sound the alarm when the enemy approaches so that the city can be ready when the enemy arrives. We read in Ezekiel 33:7-9:

> **So thou, O son of man, I have set thee a watchman unto the house of Israel; therefore thou shalt hear the word at my mouth, and warn them from me. When I say unto the wicked, O wicked man, thou shalt surely die; if thou dost not speak to warn the wicked from his way, that wicked man shall die in his iniquity; but his blood will I require at thine hand. Nevertheless, if thou warn the wicked of his way to turn from it; if he do not turn from his way, he shall die in his iniquity; but thou hast delivered thy soul.**

We learn from this passage that if we do not warn the wicked that they will die because of their sins (they will experience Judgment Day), we ourselves will come into judgment. We have disobeyed God's commands to warn of impending judgment and that disobedience will prove that we ourselves have not become saved.

Therefore, the nature of this study to a high degree has been a warning that Judgment Day is not only coming but is already here because it begins with God's judgments on the churches and congregations.

Remember, we read in Revelation 14:7 that the believers are to publish with a loud voice that the hour of God's judgment is come. In Jeremiah 50 and Jeremiah 51, God is warning of the judgment that will come upon Babylon. Later in this study, we will learn that God speaks of the churches as Babylon during the Great Tribulation.

In Jeremiah 50:2, God commands:

> **Declare ye among the nations, and publish, and set up a standard; publish, and conceal not: say, Babylon is taken, Bel is confounded, Merodach is broken in pieces; her idols are confounded, her images are broken in pieces.**

In other words, we have no options. As true believers we are watchmen who are to warn the world of impending judgment. We are to warn the churches and congregations that they are already under the judgment of God.

Judgment Begins Earlier than Judgment Day

When we speak about Judgment Day, we are speaking about the end of the world when Christ comes on the clouds of glory as the judge of all the earth. At that time, all the saved are raptured to be with Him forevermore, and the unsaved, one by one, must appear before the judgment throne. There they will be found guilty of their sins and they will be sentenced to eternal damnation to pay for their sins.

What we do not normally recognize is that the time of judgment really begins some years earlier than the time of the end of the world. Fact is, it actually begins at the beginning of the Great Tribulation. It begins not with judgment upon the wicked of the world, instead, it begins upon the churches and congregations that exist all over the world. We can know this is the situation when we carefully examine a few Scriptures. Earlier in our study, we looked at I Peter 4:17. Because of its clear teaching, we should examine it once more. We read:

For the time is come that judgment must begin at the house of God: and if it first begin at us, what shall the end be of them that obey not the gospel of God?

A careful analysis of the original Greek language reveals that the first part of this verse would be better translated, "for the time that judgment to have begun (is) from the house of God and if first from us, what the end of them that obey not the gospel of God?" There are two entities in view in this verse, the house of God, on the one hand, and those who obey not the Gospel, on the other hand.

Throughout the church age, the house of God was the local churches as they were spread throughout the world. They were the location of the holy place because wherever there were true believers, they were normally identified with a local congregation.

On the other hand, outside of the churches were all the peoples of the world who had no interest in the Bible and no identification with the churches. They are in view in this verse as **"them that obey not the gospel of God."**

Judgment Begins with the Local Church

Thus, in this verse God is setting forth the principle that when judgment begins it will begin in the house of God which identifies with all the churches. From there it will become a worldwide judgment upon all the nations of the world. We can be sure that when it has encompassed all the nations of the world, it will be the last day, the end of the world.

This analysis of this verse is very parallel to a few verses in Jeremiah 25. Remember, earlier in our study we learned that Jeremiah 25 is focused on the judgment at the end of the world. This is seen in verses 26 and 27, which warn:

> **And all the kings of the north, far and near, one with another, and all the kingdoms of the world, which are upon the face of the earth: and the king of Sheshach shall drink after them. Therefore thou shalt say unto them, Thus saith the LORD of hosts, the God of Israel; Drink ye, and be drunken, and spue, and fall, and rise no more, because of the sword which I will send among you.**

In this verse, the king of Sheshach is the king of Babylon. Spiritually, the king of Babylon is Satan who rules the nations of the world. In Jeremiah 25, God lists a great many nations of the world which are representative of all the nations of the world which will experience the judgment of the last day. Significantly, the first peoples named are Jerusalem and Judah. We read in verses 17 and 18:

> **Then took I the cup at the LORD'S hand, and made all the nations to drink, unto whom the LORD had sent me: To wit, Jerusalem, and the cities of Judah, and the kings thereof, and the princes thereof, to make them a desolation, an astonishment, an hissing, and a curse; as it is this day;**

As we have learned throughout this study, the only entity that can identify with Jerusalem and Judah are the churches and congregations.

Then in Jeremiah 25, verses 28 and 29, God makes this declaration:

> **And it shall be, if they refuse to take the cup at thine hand to drink, then shalt thou say unto them, Thus saith the LORD of hosts; Ye shall certainly drink. For, lo, I begin to bring evil on the city which is called by my name, and should ye be utterly unpunished? Ye shall not be unpunished: for I will call for a sword upon all the inhabitants of the earth, saith the LORD of hosts.**

In these verses we find parallel language to that of I Peter 4:17. On the one hand is the city called by God's name, where the evil of God's judgment begins. That is the house of God of I Peter 4:17 where the time of judgment has begun.

On the other hand, there are all the nations of the world that must drink of the cup of God's wrath, that is, they must experience the final judgment. They are spoken of in I Peter 4:17 as those who have not obeyed the Gospel of God.

In these two parallel passages, God is teaching that when the judgment of the last day is ready to come, God begins with judgment falling on the churches and congregations. Surely, this emphasizes the perfection of God's justice. Those who have lived in the favored environment of the church, who were once enlightened, who have tasted the heavenly gifts, who were made partakers of the Holy Spirit (Hebrews 6:4-6), will first experience the wrath of God if they have not become saved. As God brings judgment on the churches where these unsaved are ordinarily to be found, it is a testimony to the nations of the world, indicating the perfect integrity of God as He follows the beginning of judgment with the judgment of the last day.

This knowledge helps us to understand
the purpose of the Great Tribulation.

This knowledge helps us to understand the purpose of the Great Tribulation. It is the time when the end-of-the-world judgment has already begun. Every church, every congregation in the world is, therefore, already under the judgment of God. It is a judgment that cannot be changed. It will transition into the judgment of the last day.

How Will Judgment Be Seen in the Local Church?

How is this judgment on the churches to be? What form will it have? We know that the judgment of the last day will be very similar to any courtroom scene. The judge will be Christ who is seated on the judgment throne (Revelation 20:11). He will be assisted in some way by the true believers (I Corinthians 6:2). The accuser will be the Word of God. The accused will be each and every unsaved person. The result of this trial will be that the accused are found guilty of sin. The sentence is that they will be in hell (also called the lake of fire) forevermore.

But if judgment begins with the house of God (I Peter 4:17), which is also called **"the city which is called by my name"** (Jeremiah 25:29), what will be the nature of that judgment? It surely will not be a trial like the judgment of the last day.

When we examine the Bible to get help with this question we can begin to understand this judgment. First of all, we have learned that the Holy Spirit is not operating within the churches to give wisdom and direction to the church overseers, and He is not applying the Word of God to the lives of the unsaved within the congregation. That already is a very severe judgment on the church because what is a church without the presence of God within it.

Secondly, Satan himself posing as an angel of light will reign in the churches. That means that those within the churches will think they are serving Christ when in actuality, they are serving Satan.

Thirdly, those within the churches will receive the mark of the beast (Satan). This means that for certain they are to be judged on the last day because the Holy Spirit is no longer in the midst of the congregation and these unsaved individuals will have no possibility of becoming saved.

Is Everyone Presently In A Church Doomed?

The question can logically be asked: Since we are now in the time of Great Tribulation, does this mean that all of those who are presently in the churches have the mark of the beast and therefore are guaranteed to end up under eternal damnation?

This is a most fearful question. But only God can answer that question. Certainly, if a person is elect of God, he absolutely will become saved if he is not already saved. However, the nature of the saved person is to do the will of God. This is true because a saved person has been given a new resurrected soul in which he only wants to do the will of God. Furthermore, God will work in him to will and to do of God's good pleasure (Philippians 2:13). Therefore, If he is a true believer, he will want to be obedient to all that God commands, even if obedience is difficult or does not seem reasonable. As we continue in this study, we will see that God has specific commands for the believers in our day.

God has specific commands for the believers in our day.

On the other hand, if he persists in disobeying God's command, he better carefully examine himself to discover whether he is indeed a child of God. If he persists in disobeying God's commands to depart out of the local church, it may be evidence that he has the mark of the beast. How terrible!

The language of the Bible concerning these questions is most ominous. But it better be listened to because the words of the Bible are God's words. Revelation 13:16 and Revelation 14:9, 10 warn:

And he causeth all, both small and great, rich and poor, free and bond, to receive a mark in their right hand, or in their foreheads:

And the third angel followed them, saying with a loud voice, If any man worship the beast and his image, and receive his mark in his forehead, or in his hand, The same shall drink of the wine of the wrath of God, which is poured out without mixture into the cup of his indignation; and he shall be tormented with fire and brimstone in the presence of the holy angels, and in the presence of the Lamb:

In Jeremiah 7:12-16, we read:

But go ye now unto my place which was in Shiloh, where I set my name at the first, and see what I did to it for the wickedness of my people Israel. And now, because ye have done all these works, saith the LORD, and I spake unto you, rising up early and speaking, but ye heard not; and I called you, but ye answered not; Therefore will I do unto this house, which is called by my name, wherein ye trust, and unto the place which I gave to you and to your fathers, as I have done to Shiloh. And I will cast you out of my sight, as I have cast out all your brethren, even the whole seed of Ephraim. Therefore pray not thou for this people, neither lift up cry nor prayer for them, neither make intercession to me: for I will not hear thee.

What happened at Shiloh? It was the place the ark, which was to be kept in the holy of holies of the tabernacle, was brought after Israel came into the land of Canaan. For over than 300 years, it was there. Remember, the ark represented the presence of God with Israel. But then in the year 1068 B.C., in the days of Samuel, the Philistines threatened Israel. The Israelites wickedly took the ark out of the holy of holies and brought it to the front line of battle. We read of the sad consequence of this action in I Samuel 4:10, 11:

And the Philistines fought, and Israel was smitten, and they fled every man into his tent: and there was a very great slaughter; for there fell of Israel thirty thousand footmen. And the ark of God was taken; and the two sons of Eli, Hophni and Phinehas, were slain.

This terrible event means that Shiloh had been utterly forsaken by God. Never again did the ark come to Shiloh. In Jeremiah 7:15 God declares that Judah (the churches of our day) will be cast out, and Jeremiah 7:14 tells us, **"this house, which is called by my name, wherein ye trust,"** will be cast out. Then comes the even more ominous declaration in verse 16:

Therefore pray not thou for this people, neither lift up cry nor prayer for them, neither make intercession to me: for I will not hear thee.

How awful! Here, God is commanding Jeremiah not to pray for the nation of Israel, the church of his day. In our day, we are now in the place of Jeremiah, so the application is that God is commanding us not to even pray for the churches. There is no hope of any kind for the local churches. We are not even to pray for them. They are in a most dangerous place.

A Warning from Ezekiel

The awesome character of God's judgment on the churches is vividly portrayed in Ezekiel 9. In this chapter God paints a picture of six men who have been given the task of destroying all the unbelievers in Jerusalem, beginning in the sanctuary. Seven men are chosen. Six of them carry a slaughter weapon. Amongst them there is a seventh man who is commissioned to **"set a mark upon the foreheads of the men that sigh and that cry for all the abominations that be done in the midst thereof"** (verse 4). Then the six men are told in verses 5-7:

And to the others he said in mine hearing, Go ye after him through the city, and smite: let not your eye spare, neither have ye pity: Slay utterly old and young, both maids, and little children, and women: but come not near any man upon whom is the mark; and begin at my sanctuary. Then they began at the ancient men which were before the house. And he said unto them, Defile the house, and fill the courts with the slain: go ye forth. And they went forth, and slew in the city.

In this ugly passage, God is emphasizing His purpose for the churches and congregations. They are typified by the sanctuary and the city. This prophecy can relate only to the judgment on the churches during the Great Tribulation. It surely indicates how serious God is about bringing His judgment. It surely indicates that there is no debating or arguing with God.

In Ezekiel 9, verses 8-10, the Bible says:

And it came to pass, while they were slaying them, and I was left, that I fell upon my face, and cried, and said, Ah Lord GOD! wilt thou destroy all the residue of Israel in thy pouring out of thy fury upon Jerusalem? Then said he unto me, The iniquity of the house of Israel and Judah is exceeding great, and the land is full of blood, and the city full of perverseness: for they say, The LORD hath forsaken the earth, and the LORD seeth not. And as for me also, mine eye shall not spare, neither will I have pity, but I will recompense their way upon their head.

These verses disclose God's conclusion concerning the condition of the churches. We can argue with God that our church is not that bad, that our minister is sincere and faithful, that we cannot see how God can bring His judgment of our church, and that we need more time to think this out, but God is teaching that His judgment will fall.

Look at the picture God has given. The city and the sanctuary are filled with those who have been slain. Verse 7 records:

And he said unto them, Defile the house, and fill the courts with the slain: go ye forth. And they went forth, and slew in the city.

Can the remnant remain in the city? We have learned from many passages that the true believers are to depart out. The city has become a house of the dead.

> *If the Holy Spirit is no longer in the midst of that church, those present have been lured into a death trap.*

A significant phrase is emphasized in these verses. In verse 9, God declares, **"The iniquity of the house of Israel and Judah is exceeding great, and the land is full of blood."**

What does it mean that the land is full of blood? Do we realize that when a church is holding its members by insisting that it remains faithful and God is still saving, effectively, they are calling for spiritual death upon those in attendance. If the Holy Spirit is no longer in the midst of that church, those present have been lured into a death trap. God is no longer saving there and yet their trust is that by being there, God might save them. What a horrible situation.

And the longer they remain in the church, the greater the reality that **"for this cause God shall send them strong delusion, that they should believe a lie"** (II Thessalonians 2:11).

Then suddenly, it is the last day. Once we get to the last day, it is too late for salvation. There is no hope for those remaining unsaved. This will be a sad day for those who remained in the churches, hoping that God would save them. But salvation is not possible in the churches today because the Holy Spirit has been taken out. Judgment Day is the day that identifies with John 5:28-29:

> **Marvel not at this: for the hour is coming, in the which all that are in the graves shall hear his voice, And shall come forth; they that have done good, unto the resurrection of life; and they that have done evil, unto the resurrection of damnation.**

It identifies with John 12:48:

> **He that rejecteth me, and receiveth not my words, hath one that judgeth him: the word that I have spoken, the same shall judge him in the last day.**

It is the event spoken about in Revelation 20:10-14:

> **And the devil that deceived them was cast into the lake of fire and brimstone, where the beast and the false prophet are, and shall be tormented day and night for ever and ever. And I saw a great white throne, and him that sat on it, from whose face the earth and the heaven fled away; and there was found no place for them. And I saw the dead, small and great, stand before God; and the books were opened: and another book was opened, which is the book of life: and the dead were judged out of those things which were written in the books, according to their works. And the sea gave up the dead which were in it; and death and hell delivered up the dead which were in them: and they were judged every man according to their works. And death and hell were cast into the lake of fire. This is the second death.**

In Revelation 19:11-15, God speaks of it using language of a final victory over the enemy:

And I saw heaven opened, and behold a white horse; and he that sat upon him was called Faithful and True, and in righteousness he doth judge and make war. His eyes were as a flame of fire, and on his head were many crowns; and he had a name written, that no man knew, but he himself. And he was clothed with a vesture dipped in blood: and his name is called The Word of God. And the armies which were in heaven followed him upon white horses, clothed in fine linen, white and clean. And out of his mouth goeth a sharp sword, that with it he should smite the nations: and he shall rule them with a rod of iron: and he treadeth the winepress of the fierceness and wrath of Almighty God.

In Revelation 16:16, it is spoken of as the battle of Armageddon:

And he gathered them together into a place called in the Hebrew tongue Armageddon.

Immediately After the Great Tribulation

The timing of this terrible and grand event is known by its relationship to the timing of the end of the Great Tribulation.

In Matthew 24, God gives us a very careful chronology that covers the relationship of the final tribulation to the return of Christ. In Matthew 24:29-30 God declares:

Immediately after the tribulation of those days shall the sun be darkened, and the moon shall not give her light, and the stars shall fall from heaven, and the powers of the heavens shall be shaken: And then shall appear the sign of the Son of man in heaven: and then shall all the tribes of the earth mourn, and they shall see the Son of man coming in the clouds of heaven with power and great glory.

This tells us emphatically that the last event before the return of Christ is the tribulation spoken of in Matthew 24:21-22. The words "immediately after" do not allow for any passage of time between the tribulation and the events spoken of in verses 29-31.

The events that immediately follow the tribulation, i.e., the sun is darkened and the moon does not give its light, indicate that it is the end of time.

The sun and the moon regulate the passage of time. When time is no more, Christ has returned. It is the last day of this world's existence. Then we read that the stars begin to fall from heaven. This is language of Judgment Day and the destruction of the universe. God gives us further amplification of this event in Revelation 6:12-17, where He declares:

And I beheld when he had opened the sixth seal, and, lo, there was a great earthquake; and the sun became black as sackcloth of hair, and the moon became as blood; And the stars of heaven fell unto the earth, even as a fig tree casteth her untimely figs, when she is shaken of a mighty wind. And the heaven departed as a scroll when it is rolled together; and every mountain and island were moved out of their places. And the kings of the earth, and the great men, and the rich men, and the chief captains, and the mighty men, and every bondman, and every free man, hid themselves in the dens and in the rocks of the mountains; And said to the mountains and rocks, Fall on us, and hide us from the face of him that sitteth on the throne, and from the wrath of the Lamb: For the great day of his wrath is come; and who shall be able to stand?

This can be language of Judgment Day only. We are not surprised to read of the collapse of the universe. In II Peter 3:10-13 we read:

But the day of the Lord will come as a thief in the night; in the which the heavens shall pass away with a great noise, and the elements shall melt with fervent heat, the earth also and the works that are therein shall be burned up. Seeing then that all these things shall be dissolved, what manner of persons ought ye to be in all holy conversation and godliness, Looking for and hasting unto the coming of the day of God, wherein the heavens being on fire shall be dissolved, and the elements shall melt with fervent heat? Nevertheless we, according to his promise, look for new heavens and a new earth, wherein dwelleth righteousness.

> *This universe will be destroyed when*
> *Christ comes again.*

We see that one fact stands out. This universe will be destroyed when Christ comes again. It must be destroyed because it is under the curse of sin.

Viruses, earthquakes, tornadoes, and famines are present because mankind has rebelled against God. Therefore, not only was man cursed but the universe over which man ruled was also cursed. We read in Romans 8:20-22:

> **For the creature was made subject to vanity, not willingly, but by reason of him who hath subjected the same in hope, Because the creature itself also shall be delivered from the bondage of corruption into the glorious liberty of the children of God. For we know that the whole creation groaneth and travaileth in pain together until now.**

The creation looks with eager longing at the revealing of the sons of glory (the believers), because it is at that time that the universe will be made free from the curse. Immediately after the unsaved are judged and removed into hell, the redemption of the earth, its destruction and re creation as a new earth, along with the new heavens, must take place.

Therefore, we are not surprised to read that the stars will fall from heaven and the heavens will be rolled up when Christ returns. From Matthew 24:29 we know that this is immediately after the tribulation.

Any system of teaching that suggests that following the tribulation Christ will return to this sin-cursed earth to set up an earthly throne, offers an impossible suggestion. The return of Christ immediately following the tribulation signals the end of the present universe.

We might note the conduct of the unsaved immediately after the tribulation, when the universe is collapsing and Christ comes in power and great glory. In Matthew 24:30 we read that all the tribes of the earth mourn. In Revelation 6:15-16 we read that all the peoples are in abject terror and call upon the mountains to hide them and the hills to fall on them. No wonder they are in great terror. It is the great day of the wrath of the Lamb! It is Judgment Day, when they must give an account of their sins and receive the righteous condemnation of God as payment for their sins.

The Elect Are Gathered

Now let us look more carefully at Matthew 24:31, for there God reveals the first thing that Christ will do when He comes in great power and glory. Note how parallel the language in this verse is to I Thessalonians 4:16-17; both passages speak of the rapture. We read in the Matthew account that Christ will send His angels. I Thessalonians 4:16 speaks of the sound of the trumpet.

Christ speaks in Matthew 24 of gathering the elect from the four winds, from one end of heaven to the other. I Thessalonians 4:17 speaks of those who are alive being caught up to be with Christ. As we saw earlier, the elect are the believers who are being raptured from all over the earth. These are the believers living on earth, whose commonwealth is heaven (Philippians 3:20).

So, we see that there is parallel language in Matthew 24:31 and I Thessalonians 4:16-17 concerning angel activity, the sound of the trumpet at Christ's return, the rapture of the believers, and the end of time, when Christ returns to judge the nations.

The Bible speaks repeatedly of Christ coming as a thief or as a thief in the night. Jesus says in Matthew 24:43 (the context concerns His return):

But know this, that if the goodman of the house had known in what watch the thief would come, he would have watched, and would not have suffered his house to be broken up.

God declares in II Peter 3:10, regarding the destruction of the universe at the end of time:

But the day of the Lord will come as a thief in the night; in the which the heavens shall pass away with a great noise, and the elements shall melt with fervent heat, the earth also and the works that are therein shall be burned up.

In Revelation 3:3 we read this warning:

Remember therefore how thou hast received and heard, and hold fast, and repent. If therefore thou shalt not watch, I will come on thee as a thief, and thou shalt not know what hour I will come upon thee.

In Revelation 16:15, God speaks of the end of the world, and He says:

Behold, I come as a thief. Blessed is he that watcheth, and keepeth his garments, lest he walk naked, and they see his shame.

Will Christ Come Silently?

On the basis of these verses, various doctrines have come forth, amongst them is the suggestion that Christ will come silently: Suddenly and quietly the Christians will be removed from the earth. This idea certainly appears to be valid in the light of the language of Christ coming as a thief in the night.

But is this really so? I Thessalonians 4:16, which speaks of the rapture of the believers, does not suggest that He will come silently as a thief. There God speaks of the shout of command and the trumpet of God. This is anything but a silent coming.

Wonderfully, the Bible is its own commentary. If we follow the Biblical rule of letting the Bible explain or interpret the Bible, an understanding of the phrase "thief in the night" can be found. We shall discover that the Biblical references that use this phrase are not at all suggesting a silent coming of Christ. Moreover, we shall discover additional support for the clear teaching of the Bible that the rapture will occur simultaneously with Judgment Day.

In I Thessalonians 5:1-9 we read:

But of the times and the seasons, brethren, ye have no need that I write unto you. For yourselves know perfectly that the day of the Lord so cometh as a thief in the night. For when they shall say, Peace and safety; then sudden destruction cometh upon them, as travail upon a woman with child; and they shall not escape. But ye, brethren, are not in darkness, that that day should overtake you as a thief. Ye are all the children of light, and the children of the day: we are not of the night, nor of darkness. Therefore let us not sleep, as do others; but let us watch and be sober. For they that sleep sleep in the night; and they that be drunken are drunken in the night. But let us, who are of the day, be sober, putting on the breastplate of faith and love; and for an helmet, the hope of salvation. For God hath not appointed us to wrath, but to obtain salvation by our Lord Jesus Christ,

In this passage, we find a clear reference to the day of the Lord coming as a thief in the night. The day of the Lord is the day when our Lord Jesus Christ will come on the clouds with power and great glory. It is the day when He comes as King of kings and Lord of lords.

As a Thief in the Night

In these verses God teaches that that day will come as a thief in the night. Is He then teaching that He will come when no one expects Him? Certainly, this is to be true for the unsaved. Verse 3 records:

For when they shall say, Peace and safety; then sudden destruction cometh upon them, as travail upon a woman with child; and they shall not escape.

The unsaved are not looking for Christ to come in judgment. They may not be looking for His return at all. They may believe, in their evolution-theory blinded minds, that mankind is finding answers to living in this world. These answers may assure them that by exercising careful diligence, mankind can continue a million years or more on this earth. Certainly they are convinced that insofar as Judgment Day is concerned, if it happens at all, it is probably millions of years away. In their own minds they have concluded that they need not reckon with God; they think they are secure and may safely pursue their lustful pleasures.

If they relate to the Bible but are unsaved because they follow a gospel other than the true Gospel, they, too, will be quite sure that Judgment Day is of no real concern. After all, God is a loving God. He does not wish that any should perish. Somehow God has a marvelous plan for this earth and its inhabitants that will ensure maximum love for all. In their blindness, by their false gospels, which seem so successful and God ordained, they will be certain that there is still hope for a utopia on this present earth. Again, as in the case of those who wish to deny God altogether, they will feel that all is secure.

So, for the unsaved, Christ comes unexpectedly. As a matter of fact, His coming will be a horrible surprise, for then those who are not saved will discover they are to stand for judgment. They will discover that, while perhaps they thought all was well between them and the Lord, they actually had been following a salvation plan designed to their own liking rather than the salvation designed by the Bible. Christ's coming will be a moment of truth. They will realize that they had never served Him as Lord. They had been obeying the Bible only when it was convenient. They had never trusted Christ as the only one who could save them. Rather, they had been seeking a salvation based on the grace of God plus their own meritorious efforts. They had thought they were at peace with God and secure in Christ, but it was a false sense of security. At His coming the terrible truth will come to them that they never had been born from above.

> *At His coming the terrible truth will come to them that they never had been born from above.*

For all these people, Christ's coming will be as a thief in the night. Notice what will happen to those for whom His coming is as a thief in the night: Sudden destruction will come upon them, and there will be no escape.

This is the language of Judgment Day. Remember what happened to the people of Noah's day? Suddenly they were deluged with water and destroyed. Remember Sodom? It, too, experienced sudden destruction. Remember the language Jesus uses as He speaks of Judgment Day in Matthew 7:13:

Enter ye in at the strait gate: for wide is the gate, and broad is the way, that leadeth to destruction, and many there be which go in thereat:

In II Thessalonians 1:9 God writes:

Who shall be punished with everlasting destruction from the presence of the Lord, and from the glory of his power;

What an awful moment! What a terrible place to be! No wonder we read in Revelation 6:16 of men calling upon the rocks to fall on them and the hills to hide them. No experience of trauma that mankind has ever experienced can approach the awfulness of Judgment Day.

The Bible discloses more that relates to this momentous occasion. It indicates that there will be people present for whom our Lord's coming is not as a thief in the night: These people are the true believers. They are ready for His coming because their sins have been washed away in Christ's blood. They are the ones who are not under the dominion of darkness. They are the children of the day (a synonym for Christ Himself). They are the children of the light. Jesus is the light. They belong to the Lord. We read in these verses that the day of the Lord will not overtake them as a thief, for they have anticipated His coming and are ready for it.

We thus see that when Christ returns in judgment, believers will still be here. Therefore, these believers could not have been raptured earlier. Since Judgment Day is the end of time, we know that the believers will now be raptured. They in no sense are to experience judgment, as I Thessalonians 5:9 declares, **"For God hath not appointed us to wrath, but to obtain salvation by our Lord Jesus Christ."**

We know that believers will go through the Great Tribulation period. That period is not the wrath of God that must be visited upon unbelievers as payment for their sins. The wrath of God is the punishment the unsaved are to experience eternally as a result of their sins. The true believers in no way are to experience this for Christ has covered all their sins by His blood.

Revelation 6:15-17 speaks eloquently of the wrath of God:

> **And the kings of the earth, and the great men, and the rich men, and the chief captains, and the mighty men, and every bondman, and every free man, hid themselves in the dens and in the rocks of the mountains; And said to the mountains and rocks, Fall on us, and hide us from the face of him that sitteth on the throne, and from the wrath of the Lamb: For the great day of his wrath is come; and who shall be able to stand?**

This is the wrath from which the saved are free. Praise God for such a wonderful salvation!

In summary, then, we see that the verses of I Thessalonians 5 can be understood very readily when we recognize that there is a simultaneous occurrence of the rapture and Judgment Day. While Christ comes as a thief in the night to bring judgment upon the unbelievers, the believers are ready for His coming. For believers He does not come as a thief in the night. For them it is the marvelous moment when their salvation is completed: They are raptured to be forever with Christ.

Before we finish our study, we should spend a little time with the subject: when is the rapture? A careful look at this question is very appropriate given the fact that it occurs immediately after the time of the Great Tribulation and immediately after the third season of the latter rain. We will examine this subject in Appendix C.

Chapter 12.
God's Command to the Believer. The Final Test

Thus far in this study we have learned a lot about the "times and seasons" of God's salvation plan. We have seen that God has three seasons of the Gospel, in which fruit can be seen. We saw the early "righteous" rain of the Old Testament, which produced the first of the firstfruits, which was our Lord Jesus Christ. We have seen the season of the firstfruits, which was the church age, and finally, we saw that we are in the final season, the latter rain, in which God is gathering that final harvest before Judgment Day. We are so thankful to know that God is still saving in these days of spiritual darkness in the churches. He is saving a great multitude that no man can number, but this salvation is outside of the churches. This is the latter rain.

We also learned that these three seasons are separated by times of spiritual famine. In the days of Jesus, almost no one became saved despite the perfect preaching of the Lord Jesus for three and a half years. We also learned that the Great Tribulation, which we are well into now, began with another spiritual famine in which God pinched off the Gospel. But, our encouragement is that in the second part of the Great Tribulation, God began the latter rain in which He is saving a great multitude throughout the world, outside of the churches and congregations. We also learned that this Great Tribulation began with the end of the church age, in which God is finished with His use of the churches to evangelize the world. In fact, the churches are now under the judgment of God, as judgment begins in the house of God (I Peter 4:17).

Since we have learned all of this, we must now search the Bible to see what God has commanded regarding our relationship with the local church. Does God have instructions for us concerning our relationship with the churches and congregations? What if I attend a reasonably faithful church, maybe it is the most faithful church in my village or town, and our church does not teach many of the wrong doctrines mentioned in this study. Does God have any commandment for me? Especially since we have seen how the churches are now under the judgment of God? Surely, this cannot include my faithful church, or can it?

Believers Must Depart Out of Their Churches

We are going to see that God does have a specific commandment for all believers, and that commandment is that they must depart out of their churches. To repeat, we will see that God has commanded that the believers must depart out of their churches. No matter how faithful their church appears, God has commanded His people to leave the church. We will see five specific passages that give this commandment to believers today. Actually, God only had to tell us once. As faithful servants, we should only have to be told once. However, God in his wonderful mercy has told us in many different ways. We will see that God has given no exceptions to this command. He has commanded each and every believer to leave the church. Along the way, we will see many other parallel passages that support this command and show how God has given similar commands in the past. As we study these passages let us pray that God would give us obedience to His Word alone.

> *God has commanded that the believers*
> *must depart out of their churches.*

First Passage

Let us look again at Matthew 24:15-16:

When ye therefore shall see the abomination of desolation, spoken of by Daniel the prophet, stand in the holy place, (whoso readeth, let him understand:) Then let them which be in Judaea flee into the mountains:

As we have learned, the abomination of desolation is Satan. This verse speaks of a time when we will see Satan stand in the holy place. We have learned that the holy place is where the Gospel is. Throughout the church age that place could be only the local churches that had been given the command to send the Gospel into all the world. The abomination of desolation standing in the holy place identifies, as we have repeatedly seen, with the Great Tribulation. We read in Matthew 24, verse 21:

For then shall be great tribulation, such as was not since the beginning of the world to this time, no, nor ever shall be.

We are assured that this terrible time will be just before the end of the world. Matthew 24:29 declares:

Immediately after the tribulation of those days shall the sun be darkened, and the moon shall not give her light, and the stars shall fall from heaven, and the powers of the heavens shall be shaken:

Verse 21 tells us the setting of Matthew 24, that it is speaking of our day, the time of the Great Tribulation. Verse 29 tells us what comes immediately after the Great Tribulation, namely, the end of the world and Judgment Day. So, we can see from this and our study thus far, that the setting of verses 15 and 16 is our day. We have also seen that the "holy place" that God has in mind are the churches and congregations throughout the world. These are the places that God had set apart for His work during the past 1900 years of the church age. But, we see the command in verses 15 and 16. When we see Satan, who is the abomination of desolation, standing in the churches (the holy place), then God has given the commandment that the believers must flee.

Notice that in verse 15 God used the phrase **"when you see the abomination of desolation."** He did not say when you "experience." As we have seen before, we can see again how Satan is now ruling in the churches and congregations. We can see both from our own experience and from the Bible that He is ruling. This is evidence that Satan has taken his seat in the temple, and therefore, the time has come that Matthew 24:15 is fulfilled, and so the believers must flee Judea.

Notice that the test God gave to the believers was not when they see Satan obviously ruling in their own local church, but when they see him ruling in the "holy place." The holy place is the temple, and the temple includes all of the churches and congregations throughout the world. In this study, we have seen that he is now ruling in congregations throughout the world, so the test of Matthew 24:15 is fulfilled without any question. Therefore, Christ has commanded that we leave the church.

The land of "Judea" included Jerusalem and the area around about. This word "Judea" in the Greek New Testament is very close to the word "Jew," so spiritually, it identifies with the word "Jew." The "Jews" that God has in mind are those of Romans 2:28-29, the true believers. So, when God says to depart from "Judea," He is telling the believers they must depart from the land of the believers, the corporate expression of the kingdom of God. They cannot leave the eternal kingdom of God, but they can leave the external body, the churches and congregations. They are the holy place, they are the Judea that exists today. The believers must leave the churches because the Holy Spirit has left the churches and given the rulership to Satan.

Therefore, Matthew 24:15-16 is telling the believers they must leave the visible kingdom of God, the churches and congregations. We are to flee to the "mountains," which represent God Himself (Psalm 121:1).

So, we can see that God has given the command that when we reach the times we are now in, with Satan ruling in the congregations, we must leave.

Second Passage

Let us look at a parallel passage, Luke 21:20-21:

And when ye shall see Jerusalem compassed with armies, then know that the desolation thereof is nigh. Then let them which are in Judaea flee to the mountains; and let them which are in the midst of it depart out; and let not them that are in the countries enter thereinto.

Verse 21 is very similar to Matthew 24:15-16. From our earlier studies, we have seen that these verses can be speaking only about the Great Tribulation just before Christ returns. The Jerusalem in view must be the churches and congregations. We learned that Galatians 4:25-26 tells us that the churches are made up of "Jerusalem above," which are the true believers, and the Jerusalem below, which are the unsaved in the churches who think they are saved. In Luke 21:20-21, God uses the language of "Jerusalem compassed with armies." This language is very similar to Revelation 20:7-9:

And when the thousand years are expired, Satan shall be loosed out of his prison, And shall go out to deceive the nations which are in the four quarters of the earth, Gog and Magog, to gather them together to battle: the number of whom *is* as the sand of the sea. And they went up on the breadth of the earth, and compassed the camp of the saints about, and the beloved city: and fire came down from God out of heaven, and devoured them.

> *This is another direct command to us today,*
> *that we must leave the church.*

In this passage, God uses the language, "camp of the saints," whereas in Luke 21, we see "Jerusalem." Both passages are speaking of the same time.

This is the time when the "armies" of Satan have compassed the corporate kingdom of God. Throughout this study, we have seen how we have arrived at that time when God has sent Satan with his armies to compass and destroy the churches. We can see that this criteria has been fulfilled. In Luke 21:20-21, we have the same command that is in Matthew 24. God repeats His command, that the believers, those in Judaea, must depart out. This is another direct command to us today, that we must leave the church.

Third Passage

We see similar language in Mark 13:14, which says:

But when ye shall see the abomination of desolation, spoken of by Daniel the prophet, standing where it ought not, (let him that readeth understand,) then let them that be in Judaea flee to the mountains:

One may wonder why we would mention this passage, also. It is important because God has given it. Many things Jesus said or did were mentioned only once in the Gospels, but this important time, this time in which we are seeing God's judgment upon the churches (I Peter 4:17), is mentioned in these three Gospels. This verse is very similar to Matthew 24:15, but God changes the language a little. In Matthew 24, God says that Satan will be standing in the "holy place," in Mark 13, God says he is standing "where it ought not."

The churches and congregations are a place that Satan should not be. He does not belong there. When we consider passages like I Timothy 3, which gives the rules God established for the leadership of the churches, we see just one example of the protection that God provided for the church throughout the New Testament era. This particular protection was the careful rules that must be followed in the selection of elders and deacons. But the churches have set aside these rules, and many other rules, and have rejected the protection that God has provided.

If we ook carefully at the vineyard of Isaiah 5:1-7 and the Jerusalem of Ezekiel 16, we will see that they are speaking of the New Testament churches and congregations. In these passages we see examples of God's great care for the corporate church. With such care, we can see why God says that the churches are a place that Satan **"ought not"** to be. God has provided such careful protection that Satan should never have been able to rule in the churches.

However, as we have seen in this study, the churches have rejected the rules of God; they have rejected the rules God gave for leadership in I Timothy 3. They have rejected the Bible as the authority and established their own authority. The result is that Satan has been appointed by God to have rulership where he "**ought not**" to be.

Fourth Passage

For our next proof text that God has commanded the believers to depart from the churches, we will look at Luke 21:5-6, which says:

> **And as some spake of the temple, how it was adorned with goodly stones and gifts, he said, *As for* these things which ye behold, the days will come, in the which there shall not be left one stone upon another, that shall not be thrown down.**

Which Temple was Christ Talking About?

When many people look at this passage, they quickly come to the conclusion that Jesus is speaking of the destruction of the physical temple in Jerusalem in A.D. 70 by the Romans. Even many people who recognize the fact that Matthew 24, Luke 21, and Mark 13 are mostly speaking about the end of the world, they still hold to the idea that this verse and its companion in Matthew 24:1-2 is speaking of the event in A.D. 70. However, we must read the passage and its surrounding verses very carefully if we are to arrive at truth.

Let's look closely at the companion verses in Matthew 24. We read in verses 1 to 5:

> **1 And Jesus went out, and departed from the temple: and his disciples came to *him* for to shew him the buildings of the temple.**

> **2 And Jesus said unto them, See ye not all these things? verily I say unto you, There shall not be left here one stone upon another, that shall not be thrown down.**

> **3 And as he sat upon the mount of Olives, the disciples came unto him privately, saying, Tell us, when shall these things be? and what *shall be* the sign of thy coming, and of the end of the world?**

4 And Jesus answered and said unto them, Take heed that no man deceive you.

5 For many shall come in my name, saying, I am Christ; and shall deceive many.

You will notice in verse 3 that the disciples came and asked Jesus when these things will happen and what is the sign of His coming and the end of the world. God guided the disciples to ask a question that tells us when the time would be that **"there shall not be left one stone upon another."** The time is at the end of the world, the time of His coming.

Notice the first sign that Jesus said would indicate when one stone will not be left upon another. That sign is that men will come as false christs to deceive. They shall be effective and deceive many. We see this in verse 5. The test that Jesus gives us to determine when **"there shall not be left one stone upon another"** is that false christs will come and deceive many. This ties into Matthew 24:24, which says:

For there shall arise false Christs, and false prophets, and shall shew great signs and wonders; insomuch that, if *it were* possible, they shall deceive the very elect.

Matthew 24:24 expands the explanation of verses 4 and 5, and as we have seen in this study, Matthew 24:24 is talking about today. So, we see that when Christ said **"There shall not be one stone left upon another,"** He cannot be talking about A.D. 70, but rather Christ is talking about our day.

An even stronger proof of this is found in Matthew 24:1. Notice what the Bible says Jesus saw: **"... the buildings of the temple."** Notice that the word "buildings" is plural. This means that this passage is not just speaking of the temple itself, but of all the related "buildings," which would include the Western Wailing Wall and the temple foundation because both were integral parts of that same stone structure. If God was talking only about the temple itself, then He would have used a singular phrase like "temple building." However, God very carefully put a plural word here. Also Mark 13:1-2 has the same plural word. From Galatians 3:16 we can see that God is very careful about the use of plural and singular words.

Therefore, we can know for a certainty that Luke 21:5-6 and Matthew 24:1-2 are not speaking of the destruction of the physical temple in Jerusalem in A.D. 70, but can be speaking only of the destruction of the churches and congregations in our day.

Not One Stone upon Another: No faithful churches left

Therefore, we can now understand what God is saying in Luke 21:5-6:

And as some spake of the temple, how it was adorned with goodly stones and gifts, he said, *As for* these things which ye behold, the days will come, in the which there shall not be left one stone upon another, that shall not be thrown down.

> *He is saying that there shall not remain one church that is still recognized by God as a part of the temple of God.*

Now, we can see what God is saying. He is saying that there shall not remain one church that is still recognized by God as a part of the temple of God. In I Corinthians 3, God says that every believer is gold, silver and precious stones in the temple of God. Therefore, each local congregation is a part of that temple. Each true believer in that church is a living precious stone that has been built into the spiritual temple structure. However, when Christ says that not one stone would be left upon another, He is saying that there shall not be any congregation that is still recognized by God as part of that temple. If there were still one church left that was still recognized by God, then it would be a little part of the temple, with some stones upon stones. But, Christ said there would not be any structure left. All the churches will become dead in God's sight.

What is the Conclusion for the Believer?

What is the necessary conclusion of this for the believer? If their church is no longer recognized by God, it is no longer Christ's church, then it must be under the rulership of someone else. This is exactly what II Thessalonians 2 is telling us. The Holy Spirit has been removed, and Satan has taken his seat in the temple. He is now ruling. The believers cannot stay because Satan is now the ruler. This passage is telling us that there will not be left one church recognized by God. Therefore, the believers must leave.

Remember the true believers are instructed in Luke 21:20 to depart out of Jerusalem in our day. Thus, we have learned that the time has now come when we must leave our churches and congregations even though we are to continue to gather together to fellowship with other true believers outside of the church (Hebrews 10:25).

But the question once more must be raised: If a church earnestly tries to remove all of its wrong doctrines (its spiritual high places), and if it still has true believers within it, why can't it continue as a viable God-blessed congregation? In answer to this question, we must carefully consider what God has said.

We have been learning that God has declared that there is not to be left one stone upon another. God has declared this, since it means that God is declaring that it is His intention that there is not to be even one church left to represent God's kingdom. If a church insists that it is still recognized by God, then it is still trying to have a small part in the temple of God and saying the believers (the stones) in that church are still in place in the temple of God. But that cannot be because God declares there will not be left one stone upon another. This means that God's usage of the churches and congregations has come to an end.

> *This means that God's usage of the churches*
> *and congregations has come to an end.*

The fact that the command to depart from the church is to be obeyed by every believer is underscored by the language of Luke 21:5, 6 where God declares that in the temple there would not be one stone left upon another stone that would not be thrown down. We have already learned that according to I Corinthians 3 the temple is the corporate church that God has been building for more than 1950 years. This is the temple that Luke 21:5, 6 says that it will not have one stone left upon another that would not be thrown down. Therefore, the believers must leave the church.

Fifth Passage: Who Does the Fallen Babylon Represent?

When a king of any nation has conquered a city so that the city is now ruled by the conquering king, that city becomes an integral part of the kingdom of the conquering king. Thus, we must understand, as we have learned from II Thessalonians 2:4, that Satan is ruling in the churches and congregations during the Great Tribulation period of our time, and those churches and congregations have become spiritual Babylon. They are a fallen Babylon because they are under the wrath of God.

Let us now look at Babylon in the Book of Revelation to see what God is telling us about Babylon and how the churches that are now called "Babylon."

We first read about Babylon in Revelation Chapter 14, wherein God has been discussing the worship of the beast and its image and those who receive the mark of the beast on their forehead or on their hand. Revelation 14:8 and 9 declare:

> **And there followed another angel, saying, Babylon is fallen, is fallen, that great city, because she made all nations drink of the wine of the wrath of her fornication. And the third angel followed them, saying with a loud voice, If any man worship the beast and his image, and receive his mark in his forehead, or in his hand,**

This verse emphasizes that she has fallen because she made all nations drink of the wine of the wrath of her fornication. Surely this Babylon is related to the beast and its image. We already have learned that the beast is Satan and the image of the beast are the churches and congregations wherein Satan is ruling during the Great Tribulation period.

We can now prove that the Babylon of Revelation 14:8, 9 are the churches and congregations of today by going to the last verse of Revelation 18. There we find the concluding statement concerning this Babylon, and we read:

> **And in her was found the blood of prophets, and of saints, and of all that were slain upon the earth.**

Moreover, we read in Revelation 17:6:

> **And I saw the woman drunken with the blood of the saints, and with the blood of the martyrs of Jesus: and when I saw her, I wondered with great admiration.**

Does this terrible indictment of murder apply to churches and congregations? What a terrible idea.

In fact, it does apply to the churches and congregations. Let us examine a principle Christ enunciated in Luke 13:33, 34. There we read:

> **. . . for it cannot be that a prophet perish out of Jerusalem. O Jerusalem, Jerusalem, which killest the prophets, and stonest them**

that are sent unto thee; . . .

Christ is saying that the one who murders the prophets is the church. Remember the church is the New Testament Israel, also called Jerusalem. Christ is not only saying that the church murders the prophets, but that the prophets are only murdered by the church, not by the world. At first this may seem surprising, but it is understandable when we realize that the world does not distinguish between the true Gospel and false gospels. Therefore, they desire to kill religious people, they will kill those of all gospels. So, they are effectively killing the "people." However, it is the church that does not want the true Gospel, just like Israel did not want the true Gospel.

Therefore, the church focuses its attack on those of the true Gospel. Therefore, they are the ones who kill the prophets. We might think that it is the world that murders the prophets, but as we study the Bible, we get the clear message that it is the church, the corporate body, that murders the prophets.

Even more emphatically, we read in Matthew 23:34, 35 that Jesus indicts Jerusalem with the words:

Wherefore, behold, I send unto you prophets, and wise men, and scribes: and some of them ye shall kill and crucify; and some of them shall ye scourge in your synagogues, and persecute them from city to city: That upon you may come all the righteous blood shed upon the earth, from the blood of righteous Abel unto the blood of Zacharias son of Barachias, whom ye slew between the temple and the altar.

Note the similar language of Revelation 18:24 and Matthew 23:35:

Revelation 18:24: **"of all that were slain upon the earth."**

Matthew 23:35: **"all the righteous blood shed upon the earth."**

Remember we read in John 16:2 that the believers are driven out of the synagogues (the place where believers are to gather together), and this is spoken of as the killing of the believers.

Remember also we learned that during the Great Tribulation period, Jerusalem can be only the churches and congregations. But Revelation 18:24 is teaching that this murderous organization is called Babylon.

Incidentally, we wonder why the murder of Abel is spoken of in the context of Jerusalem. From this passage, we learn that Jerusalem is where the truth of the Gospel is on display. It is where the Holy Spirit is actively saving. Abel was a true believer. Therefore, the Holy Spirit was with Abel. Therefore, in his day he could identify with the holy place. In the days before Jesus began to preach, Jerusalem would have been the place wherein the Holy Spirit was working. The presence of God was typified by the holy of holies in the temple. That helps us to understand why the churches and congregations of the church age are called Jerusalem. The Holy Spirit was working within them to save people.

That also explains statements such as Zechariah 14:2 which teaches that Jerusalem will be taken, and half the city shall go forth into captivity and the residue of the people shall not be cut off from the city. This verse is teaching that the churches and congregations are taken over by Satan. The true believers are driven from the churches because the abomination of desolation has come into the holy place (Matthew 24:15). Therefore, they must leave the city. But they are not cut off from the city. This is so because even though they were driven from the churches and congregations, the Holy Spirit is still in their midst so that spiritually, they are still identified with Jerusalem.

Another proof that Babylon is speaking of the churches and congregations during the Great Tribulation is found in Revelation 18:2, which says:

And he cried mightily with a strong voice, saying, Babylon the great is fallen, is fallen, and is become the habitation of devils, and the hold of every foul spirit, and a cage of every unclean and hateful bird.

Notice that this verse says that Babylon **"is become the habitation of devils."** If Babylon represented the world, God would not use the phrase "is become" because the world has been the habitation of devils since the fall. However, now with Satan ruling in the church, the church has become the habitation of devils in the Great Tribulation. So, this verse helps to confirm that we have properly understood that Babylon here is speaking about the churches and congregations of our day, the Great Tribulation.

Jerusalem Becomes Babylon

Returning to Revelation 18, we have learned that the churches and congregations had been called Jerusalem but now they are called Babylon. How can that be?

To answer this question we must remember that Jerusalem is where the Holy Spirit should be present. This is so even as in Jesus' day, Jerusalem was the holy city bcause the holy of holies was in the temple and the temple was located in Jerusalem.

When Jesus was hanging on the cross and the veil of the temple was rent, the holy of holies was no longer holy. Therefore, the temple was no longer holy and Jerusalem was no longer the holy city.

The real Jerusalem and its holy place as it continued to be found on earth shifted to the churches and congregations in which the Holy Spirit had been working throughout the era of the church age. That is why in Matthew 24:15 we read:

> **When ye therefore shall see the abomination of desolation, spoken of by Daniel the prophet, stand in the holy place, (whoso readeth, let him understand:)**

New Testament Churches Were the Holy Place

The New Testament churches and congregations were the holy place because God the Holy Spirit was present within them applying the preached Word of God to the hearts and lives of those whom God was saving.

But II Thessalonians 2:7 tells us that there would come a time when the Holy Spirit would be withdrawn from the midst and instead the man of sin (Satan) would be ruling in the temple (the churches and congregations). This parallels what we read in Matthew 24:15 where God declares that the abomination of desolation (Satan) would be standing in the Holy Place (the churches and congregations in which at an earlier time the Holy Spirit was working).

We must remember that Satan is spiritually the king or ruler of Babylon. If he is ruling in the churches and congregations, then effectively they have become Babylon. The local church has become the citadel or palace of Satan's' kingdom because Satan is seated (ruling) there. Now we can understand why in Chapters 17 and 18 and already in Revelation 14:8, the churches are called Babylon.

God's Command to the Believers Concerning Babylon

Now that we can see that the Babylon in the 14th, 17th, and 18th chapters of Revelation can be speaking only of the churches and congregations of our day, we can understand the command God has given us in Revelation 18:4.

In Revelation 18:4 God commands:

> **And I heard another voice from heaven, saying, Come out of her,**

my people, that ye be not partakers of her sins, and that ye receive not of her plagues.

We have seen the fifth verse that commands the believers to leave the churches and congregations. Also, this verse is very scary because God is warning that if we remain, we are subject to her plagues. The plagues that God is speaking about is to be cast into hell forever more, that is, to experience eternal damnation. What a scary verse. May God give us the wisdom to see the very serious nature of this question and the great danger of remaining in a church.

This command parallel a command that is given, for example, in Luke 21:20, 21:

And when ye shall see Jerusalem compassed with armies, then know that the desolation thereof is nigh. Then let them which are in Judaea flee to the mountains; and let them which are in the midst of it depart out; and let not them that are in the countries enter thereinto.

That is why Jesus said in Luke 21:5, 6:

And as some spake of the temple, how it was adorned with goodly stones and gifts, he said, As for these things which ye behold, the days will come, in the which there shall not be left one stone upon another, that shall not be thrown down.

If Babylon were referring to the nations of the world, then the command of Revelation 18:4 would not make sense. The believers are not to leave the world, but are to remain in the world until Christ comes or God takes them in death. When Christ comes, He will take the believers out of the world. They will not be obeying a command to come out on their own. The only way believers could obey a command to leave the world is to kill themselves, but that would be contrary to God's command to be a witness. Therefore, we have further assurance that Babylon refers to the churches and congregations of today.

Come Out of Babylon - God's Final Test

Let's examine this question a little more. One might immediately ask, "Isn't Babylon a reference to the entire kingdom of Satan? Isn't God in this command simply telling the believers to come out of the kingdom of Satan, that is, isn't this a command to become saved?" This seems like a plausible statement.

The problem is that the people of God (my people), are those whom God has already spiritually taken out of the kingdom of Satan and translated them into the kingdom of the Lord Jesus Christ (Colossians 1:13). However, having become citizens of the kingdom of God, we must still live in this world, which is the location of the kingdom of Satan. The fact is, we are to live in the Babylon of this world, and serve in this world as ambassadors of the kingdom of God. We live in the Babylon of this world as did Daniel and his three friends in their day. The only way we can come out of the Babylon of this world is to die. Surely, God is not commanding this in Revelation 18:4.

However, when the king of Babylon is ruling in the churches, then these churches have become Babylon. Then we know we who are believers are to come physically out of this spiritual Babylon. This is an action every believer must take.

> *This is not an option, this command is not to be debated, this command is not subject to our opinion. This is a command to be obeyed.*

God is certainly making sure that the true believers get the message. The command is loud and clear. When the churches and congregations are ruled over by Satan, when the Holy Spirit has come out of the midst, when the abomination of desolation is in the holy place, when Jerusalem has become surrounded by armies, when the Great Tribulation has begun, the believers must come out of the churches. This is not an option, this command is not to be debated, this command is not subject to our opinion. This is a command to be obeyed. Those who disobey will be included amongst those who begin to experience the judgment of God.

The emphasis and importance of this command to those in the churches and congregations of our day is no less imperative than the command given to the inhabitants of Judah when Babylon was assaulting Jerusalem and would finally destroy it in 587 B.C. They were commanded to come out of Jerusalem and go as captives to Babylon. But don't we have a contradiction? Judah was commanded to go as captives to Babylon. In our day, the true believers are commanded to come out of Babylon. How can we understand this?

Babylon of Revelation 17 and 18 cannot identify with any entity except the churches and congregations of our day. Some theologians would try to identify it with the whole world, and this seems possible because Satan who is represented by the king of Babylon has been given the authority to rule over the whole world.

However, we have already learned that it is Jerusalem that kills the prophets. That alone assures us that Babylon refers to churches. We must also recognize that the believers are to come out of her lest they become subject to the plagues coming upon Babylon (Revelation 18:4). We cannot come out of the world. We are not to love the world, we are not to place our trust in the things of the world, but we cannot come out of the world. Fact is, we are to be ambassadors of the kingdom of God to the world.

On the other hand, we are to come out of the churches and congregations. We have no business remaining in them for any reason. Churches are places of worship. Those who attend are worshipping the god who rules in the churches. Before the end of the church age, any church that was reasonably true to the Word of God was worshipping Christ. At least the true believers were worshipping Christ, but when the Great Tribulation began, God the Holy Spirit was no longer in the midst of the congregation. Instead, it is Satan who is ruling. Therefore, without realizing it, the congregation is worshipping Satan. The church has become Babylon. Those who are true believers have a great desire to obey God's commandments. Therefore, as they learn from the Bible that the time has come that God's judgment is upon the churches, they will leave the churches in obedience to God's command.

True, those remaining in the church can continue to ask all kinds of questions as to why they should not remain there, but the fact is, they are not obeying God's command to depart out. They are tempting God to see if God will really do what He has declared. They actually are acting like unsaved people who are arguing whether a good God would do this or would not do that. God is warning of the "plagues" of hell for those who remain, as we have read in Revelation 18:4:

And I heard another voice from heaven, saying, Come out of her, my people, that ye be not partakers of her sins, and that ye receive not of her plagues.

May we all take heed to this warning. When we combine the terrible warning of this verse with everything else we read in the Bible about this judgment, we know that the believers will and must leave the local churches.

We can look at this question from another vantage point. Do we realize that when a church is holding onto its members by insisting that it remains

> *As long as they are being convinced they should*
> *remain in that church, there is no possibility of*
> *eternal life being given to them.*

faithful and that God is still saving in the church, effectively, they are calling for spiritual death upon those in attendance? If the Holy Spirit is no longer in the midst of that church, those present have been lured into a death trap. God is no longer saving there and yet their trust is that by being there, God might save them. What a horrible situation. As long as they are being convinced they should remain in that church, there is no possibility of eternal life being given to them. Even those who believe they are saved and are being convinced to remain in that church are in a very dangerous situation. Their refusal to depart out may be evidence that they are not saved even though in their own hearts and minds, they are sure they are saved. How dangerous it is to remain in a church!

The Believers Are Ambassadors

We must remember that Babylon is the kingdom of Satan ruled over by Satan. The whole world is his kingdom because all of the unsaved of the world are slaves of Satan. However, in the world, the true believers do not worship Satan. They are in the world (Babylon, the kingdom of Satan), serving as ambassadors of the kingdom of God. They are in the world but they are not of the world. They are in the world, Satan's dominion, but they worship only Christ. They are like the people of Judah who were commanded to leave Jerusalem and go as captives to Babylon and there they were to do as we read in Jeremiah 29:4-7:

> **Thus saith the LORD of hosts, the God of Israel, unto all that are carried away captives, whom I have caused to be carried away from Jerusalem unto Babylon; Build ye houses, and dwell in them; and plant gardens, and eat the fruit of them; Take ye wives, and beget sons and daughters; and take wives for your sons, and give your daughters to husbands, that they may bear sons and daughters; that ye may be increased there, and not diminished. And seek the peace of the city whither I have caused you to be carried away captives, and pray unto the LORD for it: for in the peace thereof shall ye have peace.**

Likewise, during these days of the Great Tribulation the believers are to come out of Jerusalem (the churches and congregations) and sojourn outside of the churches in the world. There they are to seek the welfare of the peoples of the world by diligently bringing the Gospel. On the other hand, Jerusalem in 587 B.C. was the city to worship in. But it came under the rule of Babylon. Therefore, no one was to remain there lest they, under the judgment of God, would be killed. And as we learned earlier in our study, those who remained in Jerusalem eventually were killed.

Likewise, Jerusalem of our day is the churches and congregation. It is in the churches that worship is going on. Since the beginning of the Great Tribulation, Satan has been given the right to reign in the churches so that they have become Babylon from which the true believers are to flee.

Thus, there is no contradiction. We are to come out of Babylon, the churches wherein Satan is worshipped. We are to go into the world which is also under Satan's dominion, but we go as representatives, as ambassadors of the kingdom of God. In no sense are we to worship Satan as those do who remain in the churches.

Those who remain in the churches may argue, or may contend that they are worshipping God and in no way are they worshipping Satan. But they must listen to God's assessment of their situation. Remember we learned in our study of Revelation 13 that those who remain in the churches are worshipping the beast and its image. Remember the Holy Spirit is no longer active in churches applying the preached Word of God to the hearts and lives of the unsaved. Satan is reigning there as we read in II Thessalonians 2:4:

Who opposeth and exalteth himself above all that is called God, or that is worshipped; so that he as God sitteth in the temple of God, shewing himself that he is God.

Thus, we have seen five clear commands to depart from the church. God only needed to tell us once, but He has told us at least these five times. Plus, God has given us many other verses that show us that the churches are under the judgment of God, Satan is now ruling there, and the Holy Spirit has been removed and with Him, the possibility of salvation in the churches. With all of these verses, God has made it clear. If we love Him, we must leave the church. If we do not, we have failed this final test.*

*For further discussion of Mystery Babylon and the command to get out of her, please see Appendix A.

Chapter 13.
Why Obedience is Important

It is a very serious matter to leave an apparently faithful congregation. In spite of all that we have thus far learned concerning the command to leave the church, are we absolutely sure we are to leave the church? Let us face this question once more as we continue our study.

If we can still find or still are a part of a church that is reasonably true to the Bible, should we remain there? What are we to do if we could find a church where it appears that each and every doctrine they hold and teach is faithful to the Word of God?

As we consider these questions, let us re-examine God's commands to ancient Israel when Babylon had destroyed Jerusalem. In Jeremiah 29, God gave express commands that no one was to remain in Jerusalem. In verses 16-19 we read:

> **Know that thus saith the LORD of the king that sitteth upon the throne of David, and of all the people that dwelleth in this city, and of your brethren that are not gone forth with you into captivity; Thus saith the LORD of hosts; Behold, I will send upon them the sword, the famine, and the pestilence, and will make them like vile figs, that cannot be eaten, they are so evil. And I will persecute them with the sword, with the famine, and with the pestilence, and will deliver them to be removed to all the kingdoms of the earth, to be a curse, and an astonishment, and an hissing, and a reproach, among all the nations whither I have driven them: Because they have not hearkened to my words, saith the LORD, which I sent unto them by my servants the prophets, rising up early and sending them; but ye would not hear, saith the LORD.**

This passage plainly declares that God's judgment is upon all those who refused to go as captives into Babylon.

In fact, some did remain and their leaders were murdered. Following this, the remnant went into Egypt where they were under the judgment of God.

In other words, it was God's plan that no one was to remain in Jerusalem. The only way they could come under the blessing of God was to be captives under the care of Babylon, which represents the whole kingdom of Satan. But God would watch over them utilizing Babylon to give them protection. They could receive no help or guidance from Jerusalem.

Significantly, God declares in Luke 21:20-22:

And when ye shall see Jerusalem compassed with armies, then know that the desolation thereof is nigh. Then let them which are in Judaea flee to the mountains; and let them which are in the midst of it depart out; and let not them that are in the countries enter thereinto. For these be the days of vengeance, that all things which are written may be fulfilled.

Please notice that God is not saying that when we <u>experience</u> Jerusalem is surrounded by armies, but rather it is when we <u>see</u> Jerusalem surrounded by armies. Jerusalem or Judea represent all of the New Testament churches and denominations. When we see, as we do see, Satan's massive attack on churches all over the world we are to depart out.

This language identifies with the Great Tribulation. In this language God is commanding the same thing He commanded Jerusalem in Jeremiah 29. Get out of Jerusalem (the church).

No longer are we to be under the spiritual rulership of the church.

This command is given because God is finished with the era when the churches were used of God to evangelize the world.

We are to flee to the mountains even as Lot was told to flee to the mountain when God was ready to bring judgment on Sodom (Genesis 19:17). The mountain or mountains are a reference to God being our help (Psalm 121:1, Psalm 125:1).

Significantly, in Revelation 11, where God speaks of the work of the church being finished, He speaks of Jerusalem (the churches) as Sodom and Egypt (Revelation 11: 8).

Significantly, too, as He addresses the subject of the great tribulation, He says in Luke 17:32, **"Remember Lot's wife."** She refused to flee and ended up under judgment. Those who attempted to remain in Jerusalem in 587 B.C. came under the judgment of God. Remember we saw this warning in Jeremiah 29:16-19.

The message should be clear. We must remove ourselves from the church.

In the context of **"Remember Lot's wife,"** God declares in Luke 17:31:

In that day, he which shall be upon the housetop, and his stuff in the house, let him not come down to take it away: and he that is in the field, let him likewise not return back.

The housetop is identified with bringing the Gospel. In Luke 12:3 we read:

> **Therefore whatsoever ye have spoken in darkness shall be heard in the light; and that which ye have spoken in the ear in closets shall be proclaimed upon the housetops.**

The house identifies with the church. But as judgment comes on the church, the true believer is to stay outside the church and bring the Gospel to the world.

God speaks of this sad situation in the language of Isaiah 3:6-8:

> **When a man shall take hold of his brother of the house of his father, saying, Thou hast clothing, be thou our ruler, and let this ruin be under thy hand: In that day shall he swear, saying, I will not be an healer; for in my house is neither bread nor clothing: make me not a ruler of the people. For Jerusalem is ruined, and Judah is fallen: because their tongue and their doings are against the LORD, to provoke the eyes of his glory.**

The local church has ceased to be an institution or divine organism that God used to serve as His appointed representative on earth.

Because the church era has come to an end the churches have become dead as the church of Sardis long ago became dead (Revelation 3:1). The churches of today have had/their candlestick removed even as the church of Ephesus of Revelation 2 was warned that God would remove their candlestick if they did not return to their first love. The local church has ceased to be an institution or divine organism that God used to serve as His appointed representative on earth.

It is no wonder that it is almost impossible to find a church today that will modify its Confessions to make them more faithful to the Bible. Remember the Bible says that it is God who works in us to will and to do of His good pleasure. Therefore, if a church no longer has a candlestick it means God is not working in that church. The elders and deacons are being guided by their own minds rather than by the Holy Spirit.

In Luke 21:5, 6 the Bible says:

And as some spake of the temple, how it was adorned with goodly stones and gifts, he said, As for these things which ye behold, the days will come, in the which there shall not be left one stone upon another, that shall not be thrown down.

As we learned earlier in our study, these temple buildings represent the churches and congregations that God would build throughout the New Testament time. Those who come into this spiritual temple are gold, silver, and precious stones, and wood, hay, and stubble (I Corinthians 3:12). That is, there are true believers and those who appear to be true believers and actually are not. Thus, each congregation is an integral part of that great temple.

But Jesus declares that there will be a time when there will not be left one stone upon another. That is, the temple will be totally destroyed. It will no longer exist.

But suppose a congregation believes that it can remove all of the high places. It will endeavor to be as faithful to the Bible as possible.

It then is insisting that it is a tiny part of the temple that still exists.

But Christ said "there shall not be left one stone upon another." Thus, this congregation is effectively saying they are more holy than God. That congregation should realize that <u>no</u> church can still be a part of the temple.

We Must Be Obedient to God's Rules

One can argue, but God will save them if they are elect. True, but God's elective plan is God's business. We are to be obedient to God's commandments. We never want to set up our own rules. We are to be obedient to God's commands. He tells us the Holy Spirit has been taken from the temple and we are to come out of it. Therefore, if we have a concern for the salvation of our children, we should want to obey God's command to flee from the temple. Wonderfully, it is still the day of salvation, but it is God who sets up the plan through which He work to save.

> *If we have a concern for the salvation of our children, we should want to obey God's command to flee from the temple.*

Remember we read in Amos 8 that there would come a time of a famine of <u>hearing</u> the Word of God. Thus, even though the Word of God is faithfully preached, if God does not give spiritual ears to the hearers of that Word, they cannot be saved.

If true believers are hearing faithful sermons in their church, can we truly believe they are being blessed? Isn't that pastor in rebellion against God because he refuses to instruct his people that they should depart from the church? How can his preaching still have God's blessing?

This solemn truth bears repeating. Any children or adults who are not saved cannot be saved if God will not open their spiritual ears. In that church there will be a famine of <u>hearing</u> the Word of God. Likewise, the missionary that is sent out by that church will see no true fruit of his labors. No matter how faithful his preaching may be, there will be a famine of <u>hearing</u> the Word of God.

Now we can understand why God commands us to depart out of Jerusalem. It is for our own spiritual safety and the spiritual welfare of our children that we are to depart out.

Significantly, we learn the same lesson from Acts 28. In this chapter, Paul is a picture of all who have been cast out of the churches and congregations. In this chapter, as in Chapters 22-27 of the Book of Acts, the churches and congregations are typified by the Jews who do not want to hear the whole counsel of God. There was a New Testament church in Rome at the time Paul was there and its members had full knowledge of Paul. Yet in Acts 28 the church is not mentioned at all. This is so because spiritually, God is using that occasion as a portrait of the time of the Great Tribulation when the church era has ended.

In Acts 28 we read that Paul preached from morning till evening the Word of God. And no preacher had better knowledge of the whole counsel of God than Paul, the scribe God used to give us so many of the New Testaments books.

> *That is, they were making their own minds the*
> *final authority.*

Yet with all of his faithful preaching what was the result? While some believed (literally were being convinced, verse 24), the Jews who heard him agreed not amongst themselves (verse 25), and had great reasoning amongst themselves (verse 29). That is, they did not accept the teachings they were hearing as the Word of God that should be implicitly obeyed. Rather, they were testing what they heard by their own human reasoning. That is, they were making their own minds the final authority. In other words, God had not opened their spiritual ears.

That this is so is indicated by Acts 28, verses 25-27, which declare:

And when they agreed not among themselves, they departed, after that Paul had spoken one word, Well spake the Holy Ghost by Esaias the prophet unto our fathers, Saying, Go unto this people, and say, Hearing ye shall hear, and shall not understand; and seeing ye shall see, and not perceive: For the heart of this people is waxed gross, and their ears are dull of hearing, and their eyes have they closed; lest they should see with their eyes, and hear with their ears, and understand with their heart, and should be converted, and I should heal them.

The Remnant Left in Jerusalem Were Not Given Spiritual Ears

This principle, which applies during the Great Tribulation, God can give commands that are plainly declared but will not be heard because God does not give spiritual ears, is illustrated in the destruction of Jerusalem in 587 B.C. At that time, God had commanded all those left alive in Jerusalem to go as captives into Babylon. Jeremiah 38:2 records:

Thus saith the LORD, He that remaineth in this city shall die by the sword, by the famine, and by the pestilence: but he that goeth forth to the Chaldeans shall live; for he shall have his life for a prey, and shall live.

However, Babylon allowed some of the poor of the land to remain in the land of Judah (Jeremiah 39:10). But then a number of them were killed, and God had warned that this would happen if they did not go into Babylon as captives. Then those who were still living came to Jeremiah and asked him to find out from God what they should do. The context shows they did not want to go to Babylon as captives. They wanted to either remain in Judah or go to Egypt for safety.

God answered Jeremiah by declaring that they could remain in Judah but they were not to go to Egypt (Jeremiah 42:9-22). The answer of these Jews to this command of God shows that God's command made no impact whatsoever on them. God had not given them spiritual ears to hear and obey this latest command from God. Instead, they accused Jeremiah of lying (Jeremiah 43:2, 3) and deliberately disobeyed God by going into Egypt (Jeremiah 43:5-7). This is plain evidence that God can speak clearly but that does not mean that He will give ears to hear what He says.

The problem is that of a famine of the <u>hearing</u> of the Word of God.

The Warning of Acts 28

Let us consider Acts 28 again in more detail. Acts 28 has a lot to teach us in connection with this problem of a famine of the <u>hearing</u> of the Word of God. We have learned that the Jews who represented the churches and congregations did not have spiritual ears to hear.

On the other hand, we read in Acts 28 of Paul freely preaching to the Gentiles. That must be understood to indicate that even though Christ is no longer using the churches to bring in the elect, He is still saving all over the world. But it is done so with God no longer using the corporate external church to bring the Word. He is still using believers, but these believers are no longer a part of the corporate external church.

We must remember that while the corporate, visible, external church is under the judgment of God, the invisible, eternal church of which every true believer is a part cannot be harmed in any way. It continues until the end of the world and goes on into eternity. The true believer can never lose his salvation. The gates of hell can never prevail against the invisible, eternal church.

As we look more closely at Acts 28, we can see the risk of arguing with God. In this passage, God gives us a vivid illustration of the risk of arguing with God when His command does not appear to be reasonable or logical. This is so serious it bears special attention. In Acts 28, God records a meeting between Paul and a number of Jews who wanted to know about the theology that Paul was preaching. But those who listened had a bias against his teaching. We read in Acts 28:22:

But we desire to hear of thee what thou thinkest: for as concerning this sect, we know that every where it is spoken against.

This verse appears to indicate that they were prejudiced against this new teaching.

However, Paul, the finest theologian available in that day, taught them from morning to evening. At the end of the day, some were beginning to believe (Greek "were being persuaded"), but the rest were reasoning amongst themselves whether this was true. Verse 25 records:

And when they agreed not among themselves, they departed, after

that Paul had spoken one word, Well spake the Holy Ghost by Esaias the prophet unto our fathers,

Then Paul, under the inspiration of the Holy Spirit, declared in verses 25 and 26:

And when they agreed not among themselves, they departed, after that Paul had spoken one word, Well spake the Holy Ghost by Esaias the prophet unto our fathers, Saying, Go unto this people, and say, Hearing ye shall hear, and shall not understand; and seeing ye shall see, and not perceive:

> *The problem was they were applying their minds to the commands of God to determine if His commands were reasonable and logical.*

God is saying through Paul that God was not going to give these men any spiritual understanding. What was the problem. The problem was they were applying their minds to the commands of God to determine if His commands were reasonable and logical. Verse 29 emphasizes this:

And when he had said these words, the Jews departed, and had great reasoning among themselves.

To determine if these things are so, it is one thing to search the Scriptures as the Bereans did. That is what should be done. But it is altogether another thing to search our minds and intellects to discover if this command of God is rational. Is it reasonable? Does it make sense? How can God tell believers to leave a church that still appears faithful to the Word of God? Doesn't a command to leave the church place us in a position where no one has spiritual oversight of me and my family? You mean that I can't partake of the Lord's Supper any more? Are you saying that my children cannot be baptized? This command to abandon the congregation is not reasonable or logical. Can we be certain that the time to leave our congregation has now come? Has God really given us enough evidence that we are now in a time of great tribulation while at the same time the evangelization of the world is going on outside of the church?

These are the kinds of questions we have if we find in our minds that it is distasteful to contemplate leaving the corporate external church. We are repulsed by this idea and desperately want to find evidence in the Bible that we need not leave our church.

Beware! God's commands are not subject
in any way to the rationality of our minds.

Beware! God's commands are not subject in any way to the rationality of our minds. If we do make them subject to our minds, God will shut our minds from truth. We can have the reputation of being the finest theologian, but if God does not give us spiritual ears to hear, we will never come to truth.

We are reminded of Satan when he came into the Garden of Eden to tempt Eve. Remember his method? First, the question, **"Yea, hath God said, Ye shall not eat of every tree of the garden?"** (Genesis 3:1). Then the lie. The serpent said to the woman, **"Ye shall not surely die"** (Genesis 3:4). We are to search the Bible to understand, but we are never to attempt to disprove the Bible.

None of the Bible is Subject to Our Rational Thinking

The fact is, none of the Bible is subject to mankind's rational thinking. It is not reasonable that God spoke and brought this beautiful universe into existence. It is not reasonable that God would take on a human nature so that He could save a number of rebellious humans, and so on. We are never to make any teachings of the Bible subject to the rational, reasonable thinking of our minds. We are simply to obey. If we do not obey, we can be sure that we have failed this final test that God has given to mankind.

God Interrupts the Observance of Ceremonial Laws

There are those who wish to maintain that the phrase "**till he come,**" as we find it in a number of New Testament verses, proves that the corporate external church must continue to the end of the world. For example, we read concerning the Lord's Supper, **"For as often as ye eat this bread, and drink this cup, ye do shew the Lord's death till he come"** (I Corinthians 11:26). When God uses the phrase **"till he come,"** at first it appears that it was God's intention that this ordinance was to be observed until the return of Christ at the end of time. However, we must examine this question more carefully.

To understand this concept, we must look at the Old Testament where God records parallel situations. For example, in Leviticus 6:12-13, God commands:

> **And the fire upon the altar shall be burning in it; it shall not be put out: and the priest shall burn wood on it every morning, and lay the burnt offering in order upon it; and he shall burn thereon the fat of the peace offerings. The fire shall ever be burning upon the altar; it shall never go out.**

This is similar to many other commands of the Old Testament wherein God expected that the daily sacrifices and daily lamp stands were never to cease. That is, they were to continue until Christ came as the fulfillment of all of those ceremonial laws.

However, there was a time when Israel was not able to obey any of these commands. There came a time when they ceased to observe every one of them. But their violation did not occur because they wanted to stop obeying these commands. They ceased obeying these commands because God Himself interrupted the temple service by totally destroying Jerusalem and the temple in the year 587 B.C. God destroyed Jerusalem and the temple as a judgment on Judah. This judgment occurred because they had not removed the high places.

They ceased obeying these commands because God Himself interrupted the temple service.

Likewise, the New Testament commands concerned with the ceremonial laws of water baptism and the Lord's Supper which should be obeyed within the churches and congregations until He comes can no longer be obeyed because God has brought judgment upon the institution of the church. Thus, God has effectively ended the possibility of the observance of the New Testament ceremonial laws of water baptism and the Lord's Supper.

As the believers assemble themselves together as a fellowship, the ceremonial laws of water baptism and the Lord's Supper cannot be observed because there is no one in the fellowship who has been given the spiritual oversight of those gathered together. During the church age, the elders and deacons had this spiritual oversight. But in the fellowship of believers, no one is designated by the Bible to have spiritual oversight. Therefore, the ceremonial laws cannot be observed any longer. This is no different from the situation of Shadrach, Meshach, and Abendego who had gone into captivity in Babylon. They were unable to observe any of the ceremonial laws that had been under the spiritual supervision of the priests in the temple.

Water Baptism and the Lord's Supper are Ceremonial Laws

Incidentally, please note that circumcision in the Old Testament was a ceremonial law pointing to our need to have our sins cut away. So, too, water baptism is a ceremonial law pointing to the need to have our sins washed away. Likewise, the Passover, the burnt offerings, and the blood sacrifices were all Old Testament ceremonial commands pointing to Jesus who was the Lamb of God who was sacrificed. Likewise, the Lord's Supper was a ceremonial law pointing to the death of Christ, by which we receive eternal life, and pointing to the marriage feast of the bride and the Lamb which signifies the completion of our salvation. The church made a high place of these observances by calling them "sacraments." The word "sacrament" implies that some spiritual work is being performed in the life of the one observing the physical act. Thus, it actually makes the Gospel a works-grace gospel. This is altogether contrary to the true Gospel. The word "sacrament" is not even found in the Bible.

Isn't it wonderful how harmonious the Bible is. When the Holy Spirit has opened our eyes to truth, we are greatly encouraged as we discover the harmony that exists all through the Scriptures concerning that truth.

God Interrupts His Divine Plan in Order to Bring Judgment

We must learn the lesson that God has every right to interrupt a divine plan He has put into action. God's plan for Abraham and his seed was that they were to inherit the promised land, the land of Canaan, forever. That is, the land of Canaan was the representation of the everlasting kingdom of God until Christ would come to establish that kingdom. But in the year 1879 B.C., God brought an enormous famine in the land that could destroy all of Abraham's descendants who lived in the land of Canaan. However, God made provision for the safekeeping of His people. Two years later, in the year 1877 B.C., He caused them to enter into Egypt, a land that typified the world of that day. Thus, God interrupted His plan for Israel to occupy the land of Canaan which was a representation of the kingdom of God.

Likewise, when Israel became a nation, God promised to give the nation of Israel the land of Canaan as a possession until Christ would come to be the spiritual fulfillment of that promise.

But in 587 B.C., God again interrupted that promise of the land of Canaan to Israel by bringing the Babylonian armies to destroy Jerusalem and the temple. In this situation it was a result of Judah's refusal to remove the high places.

Likewise, in the New Testament era, God gave instruction to the corporate external churches and congregations to evangelize the world until Christ would come again. There are many references in the New Testament that the churches and congregation were to exist and be used of Christ until He comes on the last day. However, in the era of this New Testament Israel, the churches have been interrupted by God. He has loosed Satan and sent him to destroy the churches because they have not removed the high places. That is, they have not corrected their doctrines that do not agree with the Bible. Thus, the situation today is precisely parallel to that of 587 B.C. when God interrupted the temple worship because Judah had not removed the high places.

This principle of God interrupting His promises is clearly set forth in the language of Jeremiah 18:6-10:

O house of Israel, cannot I do with you as this potter? saith the LORD. Behold, as the clay is in the potter's hand, so are ye in mine hand, O house of Israel. At what instant I shall speak concerning a nation, and concerning a kingdom, to pluck up, and to pull down, and to destroy it; If that nation, against whom I have pronounced, turn from their evil, I will repent of the evil that I thought to do unto them. And at what instant I shall speak concerning a nation, and concerning a kingdom, to build and to plant it; If it do evil in my sight, that it obey not my voice, then I will repent of the good, wherewith I said I would benefit them.

Everyone - No Exceptions - Is to Leave Jerusalem

A second principle we learn by examining all three great tribulation periods is that when God commanded Israel or the believers to leave Jerusalem, He means that everyone is to leave. None are to remain behind.

When Jacob went into Egypt, no Israelites remained in the land of Canaan. When Judah went into Babylon as captives, it was God's plan that none should remain in Judea. We learned earlier that there were some who wanted to remain but either they were killed there or in rebellion they decided to go into Egypt where they were killed.

> *It is God's plan that <u>all</u> the true believers*
> *are to leave the churches and congregations.*

Likewise, in the present Great Tribulation, it is God's plan that <u>all</u> the true believers are to leave the churches and congregations. God emphasizes this by indicating that the Holy Spirit is taken out of the midst of the churches so that there is no longer any possibility of anyone becoming saved within the churches. He emphasized this truth by declaring there would not be left one stone upon another in the temple, the temple being a representation of the corporate external body of believers.

Everyone is to Leave Because God Commands Them to Leave

A third principle we can better understand as we view the historical examples of the present Great Tribulation is that God commanded to the believers to leave their land.

Joseph, under the inspiration of the Holy Spirit, told his father Jacob in Genesis 45:9:

Haste ye, and go up to my father, and say unto him, Thus saith thy son Joseph, God hath made me lord of all Egypt: come down unto me, tarry not:

God Himself encouraged Jacob by telling him in Genesis 46:3:

And he said, I am God, the God of thy father: fear not to go down into Egypt; for I will there make of thee a great nation:

Likewise, the citizens of Judah and Jerusalem were commanded to go into Babylon. In Jeremiah 21:9 we read:

He that abideth in this city shall die by the sword, and by the famine, and by the pestilence: but he that goeth out, and falleth to the Chaldeans that besiege you, he shall live, and his life shall be unto him for a prey.

This is reiterated in Jeremiah 24:5:

Thus saith the LORD, the God of Israel; Like these good figs, so will I acknowledge them that are carried away captive of Judah, whom I have sent out of this place into the land of the Chaldeans for their good.

Furthermore, God declared in Jeremiah 29:16-18:

Know that thus saith the LORD of the king that sitteth upon the throne of David, and of all the people that dwelleth in this city, and of your brethren that are not gone forth with you into captivity; Thus saith the LORD of hosts; Behold, I will send upon them the sword, the famine, and the pestilence, and will make them like vile figs, that cannot be eaten, they are so evil. And I will persecute them with the sword, with the famine, and with the pestilence, and will deliver them to be removed to all the kingdoms of the earth, to be a curse, and an astonishment, and an hissing, and a reproach, among all the nations whither I have driven them.

Again in Jeremiah 38:2 we read:

Thus saith the LORD, He that remaineth in this city shall die by the sword, by the famine, and by the pestilence: but he that goeth forth to the Chaldeans shall live; for he shall have his life for a prey, and shall live.

In similar fashion, God has given commandment to those who are in the churches and congregations of our day. Matthew 24:15, 16 declares:

When ye therefore shall see the abomination of desolation, spoken of by Daniel the prophet, stand in the holy place, (whoso readeth, let him understand:) Then let them which be in Judaea flee into the mountains:

Luke 21:20, 21 gives the same warning:

And when ye shall see Jerusalem compassed with armies, then know that the desolation thereof is nigh. Then let them which are in Judaea flee to the mountains; and let them which are in the midst of

it depart out; and let not them that are in the countries enter thereinto.

In Revelation 17 and 18 the Bible speaks of the harlot, Babylon the Great, indicating that she has fallen. Later in our study we will learn that this harlot is none other than the corporate external church which is under the judgment of God during the Great Tribulation period. In this context God warns in Revelation 18:4:

And I heard another voice from heaven, saying, Come out of her, my people, that ye be not partakers of her sins, and that ye receive not of her plagues.

Understanding what happened to those who did not heed and obey this warning when Jerusalem was destroyed in 587 B.C. should cause every believer to tremble.

There is Not to be Debate Concerning God's Command

A fourth principle we can learn from these Old Testament great tribulation examples is that there is not to be debate concerning the command of God to leave the security of the situation that appears to identify with God's promises.

When Jacob was commanded to leave the promised land Canaan and go to the world of Egypt, we do not read that he argued with the command. Just think, for 215 years, Abraham, Isaac, and Jacob had lived in the land of Canaan which was given to them as their possession.

To leave the land to go to Egypt would mean they were abandoning their God-given possession, allowing the wicked of the world to possess it. Moreover, at an earlier time when there was famine, Isaac had been expressly forbidden by God to go into the land of Egypt (Genesis 26:2).

Therefore, it would have been completely reasonable for Jacob to argue with his son, "Joseph, do you realize what the land of Canaan represents? How can I leave this promised land. Remember father Isaac had been commanded by God not to go to Egypt to escape a famine (Genesis 26:2). Surely, Joseph, my son, since you are in such a high authority in Egypt you certainly could send a few wagon loads of grain to our family. You sent grain to us for the first two years of the famine and we survived. Joseph, my son, that is a reasonable and logical solution that will allow us to remain in this blessed land the Lord has given us."

But what do we read in the Bible. No arguments. No debating the command. Just obedience.

When we look at the account of the tribulation of 587 B.C., we see that there were those who argued with God. They had been given permission by the Babylonian commander to remain. There were vineyards and fields that required cultivation. Why wasn't it altogether reasonable to remain in Jerusalem.

The Bible records the sad outcome of their response to the command that they were to go as captives into the land of Babylon. Many were killed. The rest had hearts of rebellion against God so that they finally went to Egypt where they were destroyed.

Thus, we learn that the command to leave Jerusalem (the corporate external church), is not to be debated. It is to be obeyed. This command is not subject to analysis by the brilliant intellectual minds of theologians or anyone else. It is to be obeyed.

Can Anyone Remain in Jerusalem

One passage that is sometimes used as Biblical evidence that when Christ returns, true believers will still be found in the churches is Jeremiah 39:10:

But Nebuzaradan the captain of the guard left of the poor of the people, which had nothing, in the land of Judah, and gave them vineyards and fields at the same time.

To be sure that we do not miss this truth, it is essentially repeated in II Kings 25:12 and in Jeremiah 52:16. Don't the poor of these verses identify with true believers? And are they not given authority to remain in Jerusalem? Doesn't this indicate that in spite of God's repeated command to flee from Jerusalem, it is possible that some true believers will remain in the local churches and still be under the blessing of God?

To answer these questions, let us see what happened to these poor individuals who remained in Jerusalem even though God had repeatedly told them they must not remain.

In Jeremiah 40:7, we read that the king of Babylon made Gedaliah, the son of Ahikam, governor to rule over those who remained in Jerusalem. In Jeremiah 40:11-13, we read:

Likewise when all the Jews that were in Moab, and among the

Ammonites, and in Edom, and that were in all the countries, heard that the king of Babylon had left a remnant of Judah, and that he had set over them Gedaliah the son of Ahikam the son of Shaphan; Even all the Jews returned out of all places whither they were driven, and came to the land of Judah, to Gedaliah, unto Mizpah, and gathered wine and summer fruits very much. Moreover Johanan the son of Kareah, and all the captains of the forces that were in the fields, came to Gedaliah to Mizpah,

In Jeremiah 41:2, 3, we read:

Then arose Ishmael the son of Nethaniah, and the ten men that were with him, and smote Gedaliah the son of Ahikam the son of Shaphan with the sword, and slew him, whom the king of Babylon had made governor over the land. Ishmael also slew all the Jews that were with him, even with Gedaliah, at Mizpah, and the Chaldeans that were found there, and the men of war.

Already God's warning to the Jews that they were to depart out of Jerusalem lest they be destroyed had become a reality. But there still remained in Jerusalem some of these poor who were now under the leadership of a man named Johanan the son of Kareah.

Those who remained now came to Jeremiah with a very serious question. (Incidentally, God had left Jeremiah with them as a representative of the Word of God even as the churches of our day are being warned by the Word of God.) We read in Jeremiah 42:1-3:

Then all the captains of the forces, and Johanan the son of Kareah, and Jezaniah the son of Hoshaiah, and all the people from the least even unto the greatest, came near, And said unto Jeremiah the prophet, Let, we beseech thee, our supplication be accepted before thee, and pray for us unto the LORD thy God, even for all this remnant; (for we are left but a few of many, as thine eyes do behold us:) That the LORD thy God may shew us the way wherein we may walk, and the thing that we may do.

In accordance with their request, Jeremiah agreed to once more ask God concerning His command that all the Jews were to leave Jerusalem. Verse 4 of Jeremiah 42 records:

Then Jeremiah the prophet said unto them, I have heard you; behold, I will pray unto the LORD your God according to your words; and it shall come to pass, that whatsoever thing the LORD shall answer you, I will declare it unto you; I will keep nothing back from you.

After ten days, Jeremiah brought God's answer to their request. We read in Jeremiah 42:10-12:

If ye will still abide in this land, then will I build you, and not pull you down, and I will plant you, and not pluck you up: for I repent me of the evil that I have done unto you. Be not afraid of the king of Babylon, of whom ye are afraid; be not afraid of him, saith the LORD: for I am with you to save you, and to deliver you from his hand. And I will shew mercies unto you, that he may have mercy upon you, and cause you to return to your own land.

> *It appears that God is giving them*
> *permission to remain in Jerusalem.*

As we casually read those verses, it appears that God is giving them permission to remain in Jerusalem. If this is a true understanding of these verses, why is it that as we follow the experience of these remaining poor who had not been murdered by Ishmael the son of Nethaniah (Jeremiah 41:2-10), we find that they all came to disaster. After Jeremiah's report, they answered him in Jeremiah 43:1, 2:

And it came to pass, that when Jeremiah had made an end of speaking unto all the people all the words of the LORD their God, for which the LORD their God had sent him to them, even all these words, Then spake Azariah the son of Hoshaiah, and Johanan the son of Kareah, and all the proud men, saying unto Jeremiah, Thou speakest falsely: the LORD our God hath not sent thee to say, Go not into Egypt to sojourn there:

Following this, they took action. God had expressly commanded them <u>not</u> to go into Egypt. But we read in Jeremiah 43:5-7:

But Johanan the son of Kareah, and all the captains of the forces, took all the remnant of Judah, that were returned from all nations, whither they had been driven, to dwell in the land of Judah; Even men, and women, and children, and the king's daughters, and every person that Nebuzaradan the captain of the guard had left with Gedaliah the son of Ahikam the son of Shaphan, and Jeremiah the prophet, and Baruch the son of Neriah. So they came into the land of Egypt: for they obeyed not the voice of the LORD: thus came they even to Tahpanhes.

Throughout the remainder of Jeremiah 43 and Jeremiah 44, God warns that they will be utterly destroyed in Egypt. We read in Jeremiah 44:12:

And I will take the remnant of Judah, that have set their faces to go into the land of Egypt to sojourn there, and they shall all be consumed, and fall in the land of Egypt; they shall even be consumed by the sword and by the famine: they shall die, from the least even unto the greatest, by the sword and by the famine: and they shall be an execration, and an astonishment, and a curse, and a reproach.

Thus, the consequence of disobeying God by remaining in Judea because they had permission from the king of Babylon was precisely as God had warned them. God had repeatedly warned them that if they remained in Jerusalem they would be destroyed. And even though Jeremiah 42:10-12 might be understood to mean that God had changed His mind and allowed them to remain in Jerusalem, it is obvious that they were still under the wrath of God.

We are reminded of the experience of Balaam who was employed by the king of Moab to curse Israel. God told him in Numbers 22:12:

And God said unto Balaam, Thou shalt not go with them; thou shalt not curse the people: for they are blessed.

But Balak the king of Moab insisted that Balaam again ask God whether he could go with Balak to curse Israel. Therefore, we read in Numbers 22:19, 20:

Now therefore, I pray you, tarry ye also here this night, that I may know what the LORD will say unto me more. And God came unto Balaam at night, and said unto him, If the men come to call thee, rise

up, and go with them; but yet the word which I shall say unto thee, that shalt thou do.

Surely God has now given Balaam the green light to go with Balak. But then we read in Numbers 22:21, 22:

And Balaam rose up in the morning, and saddled his ass, and went with the princes of Moab. And God's anger was kindled because he went: and the angel of the LORD stood in the way for an adversary against him. Now he was riding upon his ass, and his two servants were with him.

> *God is disclosing to us that if we persist in wanting our will to be done, God may give us our way.*

God is disclosing to us that if we persist in wanting our will to be done, God may give us our way. If our way is contrary to God's clear command, it may look like God has changed His command so that He is agreeing with our desires. However, the fact is, we are still under the fierce anger of God because we are arguing with God so that somehow we can have our own way.

Returning to Jeremiah, we know that God repeatedly told Israel to leave Jerusalem and Judah. However, the poor who were left by the Babylonians to care for the vineyards are effectively asking for God's approval to allow them to stay. Even as God gave Balaam his wish, so, too, God apparently gave the poor Jews permission to remain in Jerusalem. But it is obvious that His anger waxed hot against them. If God loved them, He would have worked in them to will and to do of God's good pleasure. What we see, however, is complete rebellion against God. It was a rebellion that ended in total disaster for all who dared to remain in Judah.

Actually No Permission was Given to Remain

In actuality, if we read Jeremiah 42:10-12 more carefully, we learn that God is not giving these poor Jews permission to remain in Jerusalem. Let us look at these verses once again. We will discover that God is answering them that God will repent of His wrath on them <u>after they return</u> to Judah. That is, after they have obeyed God's command to leave Judah, the time would come when they could return to the land of Judah and then be altogether under the blessing of God. Please take note of the opening statement of verse 10, "**If ye will still abide in this land, ...**" The word "abide" in the original Hebrew is the word *shuv* that is found hundreds of times in the Bible and is normally translated "return." Therefore, the opening phrase of verse 10 should read, "in turning back" or "in returning" you will dwell or "abide in this land." But to return means they must first go away, and God had repeatedly commanded them to go away as captives of Babylon. God had also promised that at a future time, they would return to the land of Judah to be under the loving care of God.

This statement of returning is also emphasized by the language of Jeremiah 42:12, which declares:

> **And I will shew mercies unto you, that he may have mercy upon you, and cause you to return to your own land.**

> *No one can find any kind of excuse*
> *to remain in the local congregation.*

Thus, we learn that <u>no one</u> is to remain in Jerusalem or Judea when Babylon rules over this land. That is, no one can find any kind of excuse to remain in the local congregation. No wonder God tells us to come out of Babylon lest we receive God's plagues. These historical truths reported in Jeremiah should be listened to exceedingly carefully. It is pure folly to insist to God that we have a better plan than God's plan.

Those Days Will Be Shortened

In Matthew 24:21 God speaks very succinctly about this time of Great Tribulation:

> **For then shall be great tribulation, such as was not since the beginning of the world to this time, no, nor ever shall be.**

We have understood this quite well. However, in the next verse the Bible adds words that are not immediately easy to understand. There we read:

> **And except those days should be shortened, there should no flesh be saved: but for the elect's sake those days shall be shortened.**

What can this mean? To understand this verse, we must first summarize who experiences the Great Tribulation spoken of in verse 21. There are actually three entities that are shocked by the Great Tribulation. These are:

1. The true believers in the church.
2. The members of the church who are not saved.
3. The world outside of the church.

The true believers are the Jerusalem above as spoken of in Galatians 4:26. They are the gold, silver, and precious stones of I Corinthians 3:12. They are the two witnesses of Revelation 11 who are killed. They are in great tribulation because they are driven out and/or are commanded to come out of the local church where they had faithfully served the Lord. They fully recognize the fact that their salvation is secure in Christ and not in anything the church can offer.

The second group is the unsaved who are members of the local church. They are the Jerusalem which is now as spoken of in Galatians 4:25. They are the wood, hay and stubble of I Corinthians 3:12. Their trust and spiritual security is in the local church. They believe the local congregations will continue as bodies of true believers all the way to Christ's return. They do not at all recognize that the church they continue to trust has been abandoned by God so that the Holy Spirit is no longer saving people within it, and in fact, Satan is now ruling in their local church.

The third group is the peoples of the world. Amongst them are many who are God's elect but who have not yet become saved. Throughout the more than 1950 years of the church age, during which God used the churches to evangelize the world, the possibility of salvation existed in the churches. It existed because each local church was effectively commanded to be a witness to the world. But when the spiritual famine of the first part of the Great Tribulation began, there was no possibility for their salvation by means of the churches sending the Gospel into the world. This was so because the churches and congregations no longer had a commission to bring the Gospel. Not only were the churches in great tribulation but so was the world. How awful.

When Satan was loosed at the beginning of the Great Tribulation virtually no one could become saved within the local church or anywhere out in the world. It was the time spoken of in Revelation 8:1 where God speaks of a half hour of silence from heaven. This half hour must be understood to be the first part of the Great Tribulation during which God is not saving people by means of the Gospel going forth from the churches. It was the time that identifies with the 2300 evening mornings of Daniel 8. It is the three and a half days spoken of in Revelation 11 when the two witnesses lie dead in the streets.

But there is hope. That hope is not for the second group, the unsaved members of churches who insist on remaining in their local church. They insist on remaining in the local church, unwilling to recognize that Satan is ruling in their church. Their local church will continue in Great Tribulation all the way to Christ's return. The longer they insist on remaining in their church the more blinded they will become. Remember God warns in II Thessalonians 2 of a strong delusion God will place on them.

On the other hand, for group number 1, the true believers, the initial horror of being driven out and/or commanded to leave the local congregation will be tempered by the knowledge that during the last part of the Great Tribulation, a great multitude which no man can number is being saved. This will occur at the end of the 2300 evening mornings of Daniel 8 when the sanctuary (holy place) is cleansed (is made righteous). The holy place is where God the Holy Spirit is saving. During the last part of the tribulation, when the two witnesses have stood on their feet and the latter rain has begun, the Holy Spirit will be active all over the world saving people in the environment outside of the churches.

Therefore, the horror that descended upon the whole world during the first part of the Great Tribulation will come to an end. It will be replaced by the wonderful fact of the latter rain. Thus, we can understand why Matthew 24:22 declares that for the sake of the elect those days will be shortened. The time of the Great Tribulation is not shortened insofar as the local congregations and the unsaved members within them are concerned. But, they are shortened insofar as the true believers who have come out of the churches are concerned.

Also, they are especially shortened insofar as the world outside of the church is concerned. For the sake of the elect who still must be saved, there is no hindrance to the true Gospel outside of the local church, the true Gospel is being sent forth and blessed with the salvation of all the elect who must be saved before the end of the world. Matthew 24:22, therefore in a real sense introduces us to the third season, the latter rain.

God's Timetable for the Great Tribulation

Another principle that we learn from reviewing these tribulation periods of the Old Testament is that, even as we learned earlier, the tribulation comes to a climax at a definite year in history.

The famine in Jacob's time began two years before he was actually commanded to go to Egypt (Genesis 45:6). The beginning of the famine was in the year 1879 B.C. Thus, the year 1879 marked the beginning of this great tribulation. However, it was in the year 1877 that the tribulation reached a climax when Jacob was commanded to leave the promised land, Canaan, and to go Egypt.

The tribulation that climaxed in 587 B.C. with the total destruction of Jerusalem actually began 22 years earlier (23 years inclusive) in 609 B.C. It was in 609 B.C. that the last good king who ruled over Judah was unexpectedly killed in battle. From that time on, God's judgment began to fall on Judah until finally, in 587 B.C., Jerusalem and the temple were destroyed. This year became the official year ending Israel's occupation of the land of Canaan.

Likewise, the Great Tribulation of our day had a beginning some years earlier. But as we have learned, the year 1994 marks the official year in which the church age ended and the season of the latter rain began. It coincides with the end of the 2300 evening mornings of Daniel 9. It also coincides with the end of the forty two months of Revelation 11 and the end of the three and a half days of Revelation 11. It also coincides with the beginning of the latter rain. That is, it coincides with the beginning of the season of the latter rain that brings in the end-of-the-year harvest. Later, we shall learn that this final season is occurring at the same time the Great Tribulation continues insofar as the churches and congregations are concerned.

The Great Tribulation period is divided into two parts just as the seventy year tribulation of Jeremiah was divided into two parts. As we have seen, the first part of the seventy years was from the death of King Josiah in 609 B.C. and ended in 587 B.C. when Jerusalem and the temple were destroyed. The second part was the forty eight years from 587 B.C. until 539 B.C. when Babylon was conquered by the Medes and the Persians. It can be shown that the conquering of Babylon by the Medes and the Persians is a picture of Judgment Day at the end of the world.

As we have also seen, the great tribulation of Jacob's day was divided into two parts. The first was two years in duration and the second was five years in duration. In another sense, the second part was 430 years in that Israel remained in Egypt until 1447 B.C.

How long then is the second part of the present tribulation that will end with the return of Christ? That is a question we will not attempt to answer in this study.

While we are examining the tribulation periods of history it is important to note that the 70 year tribulation period which occurred when Judah was under judgment is so closely identified with the Great Tribulation of today that

God actually uses it as a representation of the tribulation period that is taking place in our day.

The Time Is Now

We should briefly review the evidence that clearly shows that this is the time that God's judgment has begun at the house of God.

Remember we learned that the Bible teaches that there was to come a time of Great Tribulation during which the abomination of desolation would be in the holy place. The evidence of that event would be the fact that false prophets would arise with signs and wonders to lead astray if possible even the elect.

The present evidence of the intense interest in signs and wonders all over the world makes it clear that the time is now. Never before has it been like it is today. This in itself should be conclusive evidence that the time has arrived and the churches are under the judgment of God. Therefore, all who are ready to obey God's commands can know it is time to flee from the churches and congregations.

However, God in His mercy gives a second dramatic sign that the time of God's judgment on the churches has arrived. Remember we learned earlier that when Satan rules in the temple, he would call down fire from heaven. Remember we also learned that Satan cannot literally call down fire from heaven, but he can perform the supernatural "sign" of calling down fire from heaven and that sign is causing people to fall backward to the ground.

Is it possible that I want my will
to be done rather than God's will?

Because the phenomenon of people falling backward is now seen all over the world, we have tremendous added proof that the time of God's judgment on the churches is right now. The time is here. Anyone who hesitates to flee from his church should ask himself, "Why do I hesitate to obey God? Is it possible that I want my will to be done rather than God's will? If this is so, I wonder what my relationship to God truly is. Is this the way a true believer should act?"

So that we might know super conclusively that the time of the judgment of God upon the churches has arrived, God gives us additional evidence. While we see the church world falling into decay all over the world, at the same time, we see ministries like Family Radio flourishing as they send the true Gospel all over the world. This activity by ministries such as Family Radio cannot be explained in any other way but that it is the evidence of the latter rain. Certainly, it fits perfectly the language of Revelation 7:9 that a great multitude which no man can number is being saved.

Indeed, the evidence of these three signs is overwhelming proof that the time is now. Anyone who hesitates to leave his church must ask himself, "After all, who am I worshiping? Is it really God or could it be someone else?"

We have learned that the destruction of Jerusalem by Babylon in 587 B.C. was a picture or representation of the end of the church age in A.D. 1994. In fact, by looking carefully at the Great Tribulation that occurred when Jacob and his family left the land of Canaan to escape the famine, and also by carefully examining the terrible destruction of Jerusalem in 587 B.C., we have learned many valuable lessons concerning the character of the present end-time Great Tribulation, and its impact upon our lives we are now experiencing.

The Book of Jeremiah has been particularly helpful in teaching us many things about the Great Tribulation of our day. There the Bible discloses to us that there are two parts to the Great Tribulation period. In the instance of the destruction of Jerusalem, the judgment of God on Jerusalem began in the year 609 B.C., when the last God-fearing king, Josiah, was killed in battle with Egypt. This occurred in the year 609 B.C. God's judgment came on Judah because they persisted in worshiping false gods at the high places. For the next twenty three years inclusive, they were in subjugation, first to Egypt and then to Babylon. Finally, in 587 B.C., Babylon destroyed Jerusalem and the temple, and most of the people were killed. The remnant was commanded to go as captives to Babylon.

Those who went to Babylon were commanded to live fruitful lives, seeking the welfare of Babylon. Jeremiah 29:4-7 records:

> **Thus saith the LORD of hosts, the God of Israel, unto all that are carried away captives, whom I have caused to be carried away from Jerusalem unto Babylon; Build ye houses, and dwell in them; and plant gardens, and eat the fruit of them; Take ye wives, and beget sons and daughters; and take wives for your sons, and give your daughters to husbands, that they may bear sons and daughters; that ye may be increased there, and not diminished. And seek the peace of the city whither I have caused you to be carried away captives, and pray unto the LORD for it: for in the**

peace thereof shall ye have peace.

This captivity came to an end in 539 B.C., seventy years after 609 B.C., when the horror story began. In the year 539 B.C., Babylon was destroyed by the Medes and Persians. This seventy-year period is a picture or representation of the Great Tribulation of our day. The forty eight years (587 B.C. to 539 B.C.), that Judah was in captivity, during which time they were to pray for Babylon and seek God's peace for Babylon, typifies the period of the latter rain. We have learned that the latter rain period is the time during which there will be a great multitude which no man can number becoming saved as the Gospel goes into all the world after the church age has ended.

Is the Corporate External Church the Judah or Jerusalem of Bible Prophecy?

Earlier in this study, we learned that Jerusalem and Judea refer to the churches throughout the church age. Because of the importance of this question, let us look at it once more.

Who or what does Jerusalem and Judah refer to as people are told to flee from them in Matthew, Mark, and Luke? In Luke 21:20, 21 God declares:

And when ye shall see Jerusalem compassed with armies, then know that the desolation thereof is nigh. Then let them which are in Judaea flee to the mountains; and let them which are in the midst of it depart out; and let not them that are in the countries enter thereinto.

Who does God have in mind as He sets forth this command to flee to the mountains and to depart out and to not enter in.

When we carefully examine the Biblical language, we will discover that the Jerusalem or Judea God has in view can be none other than the corporate external church.

The churches and congregations are made up of true believers, who are eternally secure in Christ, together with many who are not saved. These latter individuals believe they are saved but they are like the wood, hay, and stubble who have a place in the temple of God, but Judgment Day will reveal they were never saved.

Thus, the corporate church, made up of local congregations all over the world, is parallel to ancient Judah and ancient Israel which had both saved and unsaved people within it. For this reason God speaks of those who are saved as being Jews. In Romans 2:28 and 29, we read:

For he is not a Jew, which is one outwardly; neither is that circumcision, which is outward in the flesh: But he is a Jew, which is one inwardly; and circumcision is that of the heart, in the spirit, and not in the letter; whose praise is not of men, but of God.

This is further declared in Galatians 3:29:

And if ye be Christ's, then are ye Abraham's seed, and heirs according to the promise.

The physical nation of Israel is physically the seed of Abraham. Spiritually, however, it is the true believers in Christ who are the seed of Abraham. They are the Israel of God (Galatians 6:16).

In Galatians 4 God further directs our thinking on this matter by speaking of the believers as belonging to one of two Jerusalems. We read in Galatians 4:26:

But Jerusalem which is above is free, which is the mother of us all.

This Jerusalem is above. That is, it consists of those who spiritually are seated with Christ in the heavenlies (Ephesians 2:6). These are the true believers. From the moment of salvation, we eternally belong to the Jerusalem above. This is the Jerusalem from which the saved person can never be separated. It will finally come as the new Jerusalem, the bride of Christ, to occupy the new heavens and new earth which God will create. Throughout the church age, they were the gold, silver, and precious stones in the temple which is the corporate external church.

But Galatians 4 also speaks of another Jerusalem. It represents those who have not become saved. They are the Jerusalem that now is (Galatians 4:25). They have not experienced the grace of God. Their chief problem is the same as that which existed in Old Testament Israel, they are trusting in some of their own efforts to assist in their salvation. They are also called Jerusalem even as the unbelievers in physical Israel were called Israelites. They are the wood, hay, and stubble in the temple which during the church age was the corporate external church.

Thus, we must understand that the corporate external church was made up of those who are part of the Jerusalem which is above and those who are part of the Jerusalem which now is. Therefore, the Jerusalem God speaks about in passages such as Luke 21 must be understood to be the corporate external church in which both of the Jerusalems exist here on this earth.

What is the context in which the Bible warns that those in Jerusalem and Judea are to flee and depart out? (Luke 21:20, 21). The setting is a time very near the end of the world. Luke 21:24 indicates that Jerusalem will be trodden down until the times of the Gentiles (nations) are fulfilled. Verse 27 says that it is just before they see the Son of man (Christ) coming in a cloud.

It is obviously speaking of events very near the end of time.

At this time in history, we are near the end of time. We have learned that there is ample evidence that we are already in that period of time that is called Great Tribulation. It is true that at this time in history there does exist a literal, physical Jerusalem. It is in serious political tension with the Palestinians. Is this the city from which the believers are to flee? Is this a city that is trodden down of the nations?

There is no Biblical evidence that this literal Jerusalem is in view. The literal city of Jerusalem that exists today is occupied by very few believers in Christ. As a physical city it could never relate to the worldwide events related to the Great Tribulation.

The only other Jerusalem that could possibly be in view is the spiritual Jerusalem. And the spiritual is divided into the Jerusalem above and the Jerusalem which now is. The Jerusalem above consists of only true believers and is eternal in character. If we are a citizen of the Jerusalem above we cannot flee from it even if we tried. This is so because it is an eternal city made up of all the elect.

Therefore, there is only one Jerusalem that can be in view when the Bible speaks of Jerusalem being surrounded by armies. It is the Jerusalem that consists of all the congregations and churches located throughout the world. This is the corporate external body from which we are to depart. This is the Jerusalem we are not to enter into. This is the holy place that Matthew 24:15 speaks of and God commands us to flee from it. It is called the holy place because throughout the church age, this is the place where the true believers were ordinarily found. It is the place where throughout the church age, the Holy Spirit was present within it to apply the Word of God to the hearts of those God was saving. It is the holy place because Christ was reigning there.

We have learned that we are to depart from it because its candlestick has been removed. That is, the Holy Spirit has been taken out of its midst. Therefore, it is no longer possible for people to become saved within those churches, regardless of how faithfully a congregation may try to remain true to the Bible.

The Two Jerusalems of Zechariah 14

Once we understand this, we can begin to understand the perplexing language of Zechariah 14:2, which declares:

For I will gather all nations against Jerusalem to battle; and the city shall be taken, and the houses rifled, and the women ravished; and half of the city shall go forth into captivity, and the residue of the people shall not be cut off from the city.

How can the city be taken (that is, destroyed), and yet half the city goes forth into captivity while the residue is not cut off from the city?

This can be understood if we remember that those who go into captivity are like those who went into Babylon when Jerusalem was destroyed in 587 B.C. They represent the true believers who are saved from the judgment of God as He brings judgment upon the churches and denominations during the time of the Great Tribulation.

But these same believers cannot be cut off from Jerusalem. The Jerusalem from which they cannot be cut off is the Jerusalem that is above. Remember the Jerusalem that is above is the eternal Jerusalem whose citizens are the true believers.

Thus, in these verses we must understand that those who go into captivity are the same individuals as those who are not cut off from the city.

Isaiah Presents the Same Truth

There is a significant passage in Isaiah that emphasizes this same truth. In Isaiah 4:1-3, we read:

And in that day seven women shall take hold of one man, saying, We will eat our own bread, and wear our own apparel: only let us be called by thy name, to take away our reproach. In that day shall the branch of the LORD be beautiful and glorious, and the fruit of the earth shall be excellent and comely for them that are escaped of Israel. And it shall come to pass, that he that is left in Zion, and he that remaineth in Jerusalem, shall be called holy, even every one that is written among the living in Jerusalem.

The seven women mentioned in verse 1 identify with the seven churches of Revelation 2 and 3. These seven churches represent all of the churches and congregations that have come into existence throughout the New Testament era. The churches are called women because within them are the true believers who are the bride of Christ.

In Isaiah 4:1, they are presented as those who take hold of one man. That is, they want the Son of man, Christ, to be their Savior and King. But they don't want Him to be their spiritual bread, and they don't want to be clothed with His robe of righteousness. They want their own bread and their own clothing. That is, they want the name of Christ, they want to identify with Christ, but they want their own salvation program. In other words, they want to be the final authority as to truth. They are not concerned about the truth of the Bible.

This, therefore, is an indictment against the churches of our day. They are not about to give up the doctrines of their church or denomination even though careful study reveals that many of their teachings are contrary to the Bible.

However, verse 2 of Isaiah 4 reveals that in that day, the day when this sorrowful condition exists in the churches, the branch of the Lord (Christ) shall be beautiful and the fruit of the earth (those who are becoming saved) will be excellent. They are being saved because the believers who have escaped from the church or congregation continue to bring the true Gospel outside of the church.

But verse 3 says those who remain in Jerusalem are to be called holy. Those who have escaped and are bringing the Gospel outside of the church are still an integral part of the eternal invisible Jerusalem that identifies with the church that is above. They, therefore, are holy. This Israel from which they have escaped can only be the corporate external Israel, which identifies with the churches and congregations during the time of Great Tribulation. But those who have escaped remain in the eternal Jerusalem.

These who have escaped, that is, have gone out of the churches and congregations have not left Zion, have not left the eternal spiritual Jerusalem. They are eternally secure in the Jerusalem that is above. Their names have been written in the Lamb's book of life.

We Still Assemble Together

What does one do if there are no others with whom to assemble. For example, some individuals in China or India hear the true Gospel and God saves them. They know nothing about a local church and if they did, God now commands they are not to be a part of a local congregation. How can they obey the command of Hebrews 10:25, which states:

Not forsaking the assembling of ourselves together, as the manner of some is; but exhorting one another: and so much the more, as ye see the day approaching.

The phrase "**as ye see the day approaching**" clearly shows that this command has to do with believers all the way to the end of time, all the way to the Judgment Day at the end of the world. But how are they to obey this command if they are not to assemble with the congregation of the local church?

First of all, the Greek word translated "assembling" in this verse is found in only one other place, and that is II Thessalonians 2:1, where it is "gathering together." But this gathering together consists only of true believers because it is a "gathering together unto him," as Christ comes on the last day. Thus, it is a word that identifies only with true believers. As the end of the world approaches, few true believers are found inside the churches because the era of the church as an institution used of God has come to an end. Even these few believers are commanded to leave their church and because they are true believers, they have a great desire to obey all of God's commandments. Therefore, very quickly, they, too, will leave their local church.

Significantly, God has given us the day of the week when this command is particularly to be obeyed. That day is Sunday. It is the Lord's Day on which we are not to do our own pleasure. Rather we are to "**call the sabbath a delight, the holy of the Lord, honorable; and shall honour Him, not doing thine own ways, nor finding thine own pleasure, not speaking thine own words**" (Isaiah 58:13). This day is given to us each Sunday as a day in which we can forget the cares of this world and concentrate on our relationship with our Savior. God has given us this whole day during which we are free to serve Him.

Even though we may not know others of like mind with whom we can fellowship, we can begin by spending much time reading the Bible. Immediately then we are fellowshipping with God. Moreover we are fellowshipping with all of those we read about in the Bible. They are the great cloud of witnesses we read about in Hebrews 12:1, which says:

Wherefore seeing we also are compassed about with so great a cloud of witnesses, let us lay aside every weight, and the sin which doth so easily beset us, and let us run with patience the race that is set before us,

In a real sense, a single individual can fellowship with God Himself as well as with any and all of the cloud of witnesses the Bible brings to our attention.

Of course, if and when he finds others of like faith, the assembling together can expand with fellow believers.

The glad and wonderful news is that in this time, when the Great Tribulation is being experienced in the churches, a great and wonderful thing is happening outside of the churches.

We have ample time to pray to our Lord. As I read the Bible, God is speaking to me. As I pray, I am talking to God. Thus, in this manner we can have intense fellowship with God.

Our fellowship can be expanded by using this day to share the Gospel with others. In most countries of the world, a believer can pass out tracts at the local market or other places where many people are present. Family Radio can supply those tracts free of charge. They are available in many languages.

Then, too, Sunday is a day when the aged, the feeble, the sick can be visited and encouraged. If a jail is nearby it may be possible to visit there. It is a day to write to friends to encourage them. In other words, Sunday is a beautiful day God has given us during which we can focus on our relationship with our Lord, we can commune with our Lord, and we can share the Gospel with others.

If a person has a family, these things can be done with his children. Later, perhaps we might meet another person of like spiritual mind. Then the fellowship would be a little larger. The important truth is that no one is in a situation where he cannot obey the command to not neglect the assembling of ourselves as we see the day approaching.

Obedience to the Command to Depart

Now the big question. What are we to do now that we have this information concerning the church?

If the church age has come to an end, what are the believers to do who are members of churches?

Obedience to the command of Luke 21:20-24 can be accomplished in various ways. If a person or family is a member of a church, they can withdraw their membership and fellowship on Sundays with whomever there may be who are of like mind. Such withdrawal may initiate a move by the church to excommunicate. For that individual, this is not a trauma because he has become convinced that the church era has come to an end and the church no longer has any divine authority.

If the individual or family are simply attending a church and are not members, they can stop attending that church but continue to fellowship outside of the church with individuals of like mind.

If a congregation decides to be obedient to this command, they can reorganize their congregation from a church congregation to a fellowship of believers. The elders will no longer be elders. The deacons will no longer be deacons. The pastor will no longer be pastor. In other words, no individuals will have spiritual rule over the congregation. Those members of the congregation who disagree with this decision to disband would have to find membership in another congregation.

Reflecting on the Conditions in Our Day

Certainly, something strange is happening. On the one hand, we see churches everywhere becoming more and more apostate. Yet on the other hand, we see a ministry like Family Radio becoming more and more useful to the Lord in sending the true Gospel into the world.

Virtually every one of us, as we look at the church we attend, and as we look at the other churches in our day, deplore what we are seeing. The worship service has become increasingly a time of entertainment. The preaching seldom, if ever, warns of the imminence of judgment day. Church after church features signs and wonders. Little or no money is available for mission work because of increasing obligations to pay for newer and finer buildings and greater and greater pastors' salaries.

Perhaps one of the most shocking experiences of the true believer within these churches is the rejection he will experience if he contends too strongly for greater purity in doctrine. Indeed, any spiritually-minded believer must admit something drastic has happened and is happening in even the most conservative of the churches.

How can it be then that a ministry like Family Radio appears to be increasingly blessed as it is able to share the true Gospel with an increasingly large percentage of the world's population. We do know that there are many prophecies in the Bible that indicate that as the history of the world draws to a close, the congregations and denominations will be increasingly apostate. For example, we have learned in this study that Revelation 13 speaks of a time when Satan, called the beast that comes out of the sea, will rule in the churches through false gospels. In this chapter these churches are called a false prophet that comes out of the earth. These churches have become altogether apostate. Fact is, verse 7 ominously warns:

And it was given unto him [*the beast*] to make war with the saints, and to overcome them: . . . .

Likewise, we have learned that in II Thessalonians 2:1-10, God speaks of the man of sin who can be only Satan, taking his seat in the temple, that is, he will rule in the churches that have become apostate.

In Daniel 8:10-14, God speaks of a time when the sanctuary and the host will be trodden underfoot for a period of 2300 days, and the saints of the most high shall be given into his hand. We are all familiar with the prophecy of Matthew 24:24 which teaches that false christs and false prophets coming with signs and wonders will arise to deceive the very elect, if possible.

Indeed, these are a sampling of many such prophecies in the Bible that we have been examining in this study. We who love our church because it has been such a comfort to us in the past and even to some degree in the present are not a bit happy to contemplate these dire predictions. They shock us to the core of our being. As we look at the congregation we presently attend, we would like to believe that these prophecies must be for another time. Surely the present situation cannot be as bad as these prophecies intimate.

However, if we are truly honest with ourselves, and with the Word of God, we know that something dreadful is happening in the churches and congregations of our day. No one can honestly say that all is well in today's congregations.

However, there appears to be a major contradiction between the Biblical prediction of the expectation of an increasingly dead church and the actuality of a robust healthy presentation of the Gospel by means of an organization like Family Radio.

How can we explain this anomaly that plainly is in evidence?

To make the question even more complicated, we are aware that in these days, the population of the world is mushrooming. The population statistics indicate that about 375,000 babies are born each day.

Even though approximately 145,000 people die each day, the world's population is still growing at the rate of about 230,000 individuals each and every twenty four hour period.

This tremendous increase in population has resulted in a world today of more than seven billion in population. Must these seven billion hear the Gospel call? Did not Jesus declare in Matthew 24:14:

And this gospel of the kingdom shall be preached in all the world for a witness unto all nations; and then shall the end come.

True, for more than 1950 years, God has used the churches and congregations as His means to accomplish this goal. In spite of the spiritual weaknesses and shortcomings of the church, it has been the divine organism employed by God to represent and extend the kingdom of God on this earth. Indeed, there are many glorious chapters in the history of the churches as they were more or less faithful to the great commission, go ye into all the world with the Gospel.

But what of today. How can the churches in their spiritual decline minister the true Gospel. And even if all of the churches were vibrant with the true Gospel, how can they physically minister to a world that each hour is 10,000 souls greater in population?

Indeed, we must realistically admit that the churches of today cannot by any means fulfill Christ's command to go into all the world with the Gospel. Fact is, when we honestly evaluate the totality of the mission effort that is based on a true representation of the whole counsel of God, we must admit the situation is hopeless.

But it is not hopeless. About 200 years ago, anticipating the present situation, God began to make some drastic changes in the world.

After almost 13,000 years of history, mankind has discovered and begun to use radio waves and other electronics. Are people more intelligent today than they were a thousand or ten thousand years ago? We know that cannot be. Rather, it is obvious that God prevented these discoveries from being made until it was God's good pleasure to make them available to accomplish His purposes. And once He allowed mankind to discover electromagnetic waves, etc., it seems that God is allowing mankind to understand and use more and more of these wonderful ingredients that He has built into the creation of the world.

Thus, we wonder: Does a correlation exist between all of these major subjects we have been discussing? Let us review.

1. Tremendous apostasy in the congregations and denominations.

2. Exploding population.

3. Exploding electronic knowledge, resulting in enormous advances in mass communication.

4. Increasing blessing, coming to a ministry such as Family Radio as it ministers globally with the true Gospel.

The fact is, the Bible does provide a marvelous synthesis of these things. Once we understand the Bible's teaching on these subjects, we should understand how harmonious all of these phenomena are.

Go to the Ant

One could ask the question: How will that work if during the latter rain there is no spiritual oversight over those who claim to have become saved? Is this truly a workable plan?

God gives us a very interesting and significant answer to this question in Proverbs 6. In verses 6-8, God commands:

Go to the ant, thou sluggard; consider her ways, and be wise: Which having no guide, overseer, or ruler, Provideth her meat in the summer, and gathereth her food in the harvest.

Since God can rule over the lowly ant which has neither guide, overseer, or ruler, surely He can rule over His children who at the moment of salvation had been given a new resurrected soul in which they never want to sin again and who are indwelt by the Holy Spirit.

Just because God utilized fellow humans (pastors, elders, deacons), to have spiritual oversight during the church age, that does not mean that God cannot rule directly without such spiritual oversight.

Moreover, we must remember that throughout history, most of the peoples of the world were illiterate, and Bibles were relatively scarce. Therefore, a very practical purpose was served by the spiritual rulers in the congregation who should have been literate and should have had access to a Bible.

Today, the Bible is increasingly available in printed form. Additionally, its message can be heard worldwide by radio, the Internet, satellite, etc.

In any case, we are to remember the principle set forth in Philippians 2:13, **"For it is God which worketh in you [*the true believers*] both to will and to do of his good pleasure."**

Chapter 14.
Why the Shock to the Congregation

Why are so many pastors and church members reluctant to consider the idea that the church age has come to an end? We know that churches that came out of the Reformation, such as Reformed, Lutheran, and Presbyterian, hold the Roman Catholic teaching that the churches will continue until Christ returns. On the other hand, churches more Arminian in nature do not have a legacy from the Roman Catholic church but they also must face this problem.

There are at least four verses that greatly contribute to this problem. These four verses have been interpreted by a great many churches in such a way that the pastors and therefore the local congregations, perhaps without even realizing this, have taken upon themselves an enormous spiritual authority. It is an authority of such consequence that it is almost equal to the authority of God Himself. We will examine hese four verses and indicate how they are most frequently understood. Then we will show how they should be understood.

The first verse we will examine is I Timothy 3:15:

But if I tarry long, that thou mayest know how thou oughtest to behave thyself in the house of God, which is the church of the living God, the pillar and ground of the truth.

The important question concerning this verse is whether the phrase **"the pillar and ground of the truth"** is modifying the word "church" or the word "God." Usually, it is taught that it modifies the word "church." It is understood, therefore, that the local church is the pillar and ground of truth. This teaching can give the church the idea that it has great authority.

This would be true if indeed the local church had become the foundation of truth. This understanding supports and is supported by the usual understanding of the second verse we will discuss, Matthew 16:19, wherein Christ declared to Peter as a representative of all the apostles and subsequently of all pastors, that he has been given the keys of the kingdom of God. Matthew 16:17 states:

And I will give unto thee the keys of the kingdom of heaven: and whatsoever thou shalt bind on earth shall be bound in heaven: and whatsoever thou shalt loose on earth shall be loosed in heaven.

Usually, the keys that were given are understood to be first the key of knowledge (Luke 11:52), which is the Bible by which the door is opened to salvation. There is also a second key which is the key to excommunicate, that is, to shut the door to heaven. By means of these keys, the rulers of the church are supposed to be able to open up the kingdom of God to those they believe have become saved, and to shut the kingdom to those who give clear evidence they are not saved. It is understood that the consequence of these actions of the church is that God supports and sanctions the action of the church. Whatsoever is bound or loosed on earth shall be bound or loosed in heaven. This understanding of this verse is entirely compatible with the understanding that the church is the pillar and ground of truth.

The third verse that helps to develop the concept that the local church has great spiritual authority is Ephesians 2:20:

And are built upon the foundation of the apostles and prophets, Jesus Christ himself being the chief corner stone;

This verse is usually understood to mean that the rulers of the churches beginning with the apostles and prophets are the spiritual foundation of the local church. This verse, too, therefore, seems to be altogether in agreement with the previous concept that the church is the pillar and ground of truth and that the church rulers have been given the keys of the kingdom so that they open or shut the door into the kingdom of God and the local church is built on the foundation of the apostles and prophets.

The fourth verse that is important in this matter of church authority is Matthew 16:18 wherein Jesus declared:

And I say also unto thee, That thou art Peter, and upon this rock I will build my church; and the gates of hell shall not prevail against it.

The usual understanding of this verse is that the gates of hell relate to Satan's kingdom. Thus, it is understood that the local church can never be overthrown by the action of Satan. Thus, without question, it is believed the churches under the protection of Christ will continue all the way to the end of the world.

These four verses, when understood in the way we have just looked at them, give the local pastors, elders, and deacons great spiritual authority. True, God has given some rules to follow. There was to be water baptism, there was to be obedience to all the doctrines and practices held by the church, there was to be a profession of faith. If these rules were faithfully followed by any church member, the assumption is that there can be no doubt that the individual is eternally in the kingdom of God. Thus, the local church which is the external, visible representation of the kingdom of God is understood to be essentially identical to the eternal, invisible church. This would be true if indeed all of the members were truly saved.

Likewise, the local congregation may be considered to be the bride of Christ inasmuch as it is believed that virtually all of the members are true believers. Therefore, little or no distinction is made between the eternal, invisible church and the external corporate church. In actuality, they are considered identical because all members of the local congregation are assumed to be saved.

Thus, too, the Confessions or other doctrines held by the church must be considered by its members to be faithful to God's desires. After all, isn't the church the pillar and ground of truth.

As long as they faithfully follow the rules of the local church, they are assured by the rulers of these churches that they belong to Christ.

By means of this kind of understanding of these verses, the members of these churches are given vast assurance that they are safe and secure in the kingdom of God. As long as they faithfully follow the rules of the local church, they are assured by the rulers of these churches that they belong to Christ.

With this understanding of these verses, it is completely understandable that the churches of our day recoil in horror at the idea that the church age has come to an end and the true believers are to depart out of the churches. To them it would be the equivalent of committing spiritual suicide. Moreover, what pastor is ready to surrender this huge spiritual authority that he believes God had given him at the time his fellow pastors laid hands on him as a sign that he was ordained by God to have this authority.

Is the Church the Pillar and Ground of Truth?

We will now look at these four verses to discover what they are really teaching. The first verse we examined was I Timothy 3:15, which declares:

But if I tarry long, that thou mayest know how thou oughtest to behave thyself in the house of God, which is the church of the living God, the pillar and ground of the truth.

Is the church the pillar and ground of the truth? Or is God the pillar and ground of the truth? If the church is the pillar and ground of truth, how can it be that one church holds the doctrine that Jesus died for everyone while another church teaches that Christ died only for the elect. How can one church teach baptism by immersion and another teaches baptism by sprinkling.

Differences between church beliefs are concerned with a host of doctrines. So how can the church be the foundation of truth. Only God can be that foundation. The Bible says it very plainly in I Corinthians 3:11:

For other foundation can no man lay than that is laid, which is Jesus Christ.

Under no circumstance can the church be the pillar and ground of truth.

Under no circumstance can the church be the pillar and ground of truth. It is true that during the church age the believers were living stones in the temple (the churches). They will even be called a pillar in the eternal temple (Revelation 3:12), but they can never be the foundation of truth. Only Christ who is God can be the pillar and foundation of truth.

Suppose I am a pastor, and I suspect that a doctrine our church or denomination holds is not altogether faithful to the Bible. My church theologians assure me this doctrine, about which I am concerned, is faithful to the Bible. After all, doesn't the Bible teach in I Timothy 3:15, **"the church of the living God, the pillar and ground of the truth."** Doesn't God clearly teach in this verse that the church is the pillar and ground of truth? Isn't that a sufficient teaching of the Bible to arrest any concerns I might have regarding faithfulness to God's Word? This conclusion is widely held amongst churches. It produces the notion that if a church acts in solemn assembly concerning any doctrine, they can be sure the conclusions of this solemn assembly are altogether faithful to God's desires.

To further substantiate this notion, the council in Jerusalem, recorded in Acts 15, is frequently offered as an example of how God interacts with solemn ecclesiastical assemblies. However, these theologians fail to realize that the council recorded in Acts was meeting at a time when God was still writing the Bible. To make sure we do not misunderstand, God records in Acts 15:28:

For it seemed good to the Holy Ghost, and to us, to lay upon you no greater burden than these necessary things;

God is instructing us by this language that God the Holy Spirit was guiding this council so that what was concluded could become a part of God's Word. This is so because God used this incident as a further means of producing the Bible. Holy men in this council in Jerusalem spoke as God the Holy Spirit moved them. This does not for a moment suggest that any time there is a solemn meeting of church pastors that the conclusions arrived at in that meeting are necessarily true to the Bible. Whether they are true or not must be tested by the Bible. The principle of Romans 3:4, **"let God be true, but every man a liar,"** must always be kept in mind.

This wrong understanding of I Timothy 3:15 has set up a great many churches to neatly come out from being under the authority of the Bible. They have have set themselves up to be the authority that rules over the Bible.

The corporate external church can never be the pillar and ground of truth. The foundation upon which truth is built is Jesus Christ. I Corinthians 3:11 declares:

For other foundation can no man lay than that is laid, which is Jesus Christ.

The pillar and ground of truth cannot modify the word "church." These words must modify the word "God." The church of "<u>God</u> the pillar and ground of truth." Christ is the Word, He is the truth. His name is True. How could it be that faulty sinful men meeting in some solemn ecclesiastical meeting can be the foundation of truth?

But this audacious conclusion has served the churches so that many believe that their confessions, their particular church doctrines, are sacrosanct. Thus, as they preach, they feel secure in their faithfulness to God as long as they faithfully declare what their church doctrines and confessions teach. I am afraid that it is this kind of thinking that has fostered an intense lack of fear of God. After all, as long as we carefully follow the doctrines our church holds recognizing that the church is the pillar and ground of truth, then we know we are being faithful to all that God would have us believe. Unfortunately, and sadly, this attitude must be considered to be dreadful arrogance and pride. No wonder God's wrath has come against the churches. We could even wonder, "Why did God take so long to bring judgment on the churches."

God Is Testing the Church

Isn't it interesting the way God has designed this verse, I Timothy 3:15? Remember, God is the author of the Bible. Holy men of old spoke as the Holy Spirit moved them. God could have phrased this verse so that there would be no question at all concerning who or what is the pillar and ground of the truth. But the way it is written allows either possibility. The church is the pillar and ground of the truth or God is the pillar and ground of the truth.

We must remember that God has constantly set up testing programs. Adam and Eve were tested in the Garden of Eden. Abram was tested when he was told to sacrifice his son Isaac. Israel was tested when Moses remained on Mount Sinai for forty days. Jesus was tested for forty days immediately after He was baptized. Indeed, testing is an important aspect of God's dealings with mankind.

By this verse, the churches are being tested. Which conclusion will they adopt? If God is the pillar and ground of the truth, then the churches must remain very humble, looking only to the Bible as the authority. If the church is to be understood as the pillar and ground of truth, then the church has been given vast spiritual authority.

A similar test is introduced in the Bible by a verse in I Peter 5. In this chapter, God gives instruction to the overseers of the congregation. He instructs them to feed the flock, that is, they are to carefully teach the congregation the truths of the Bible. God further instructs in I Peter 5, verse 3:

Neither as being lords over God's heritage, but being ensamples to the flock.

But then the Bible declares in verse 4:

And when the chief Shepherd shall appear, ye shall receive a crown of glory that fadeth not away.

Is this verse teaching that those who feed the flock will receive a special crown as a glorious reward for their work of shepherding the congregation? It would surely appear that this could be the situation. Nowhere else in the

Bible does God speak of anyone receiving a crown of glory. All believers are given a crown of righteousness (II Timothy 4:8) and a crown of life (James 1:12), but this passage is particularly speaking of the elders, those who have the spiritual oversight of the congregation. Doesn't this agree with the statement of I Timothy 5:17, where we read:

Let the elders that rule well be counted worthy of double honour, especially they who labour in the word and doctrine.

Indeed, it would appear that pastors have a special relationship with God. When these verses are tied into Ephesians 2:20, for example, which appears to teach that the foundation of the house of God is the apostles and prophets, it is very easy to come to the conclusion that pastors have a great spiritual authority, even as those who contend that the church is the pillar and ground of the truth have taken on a great spiritual authority.

Furthermore, this makes the office of the pastor exciting and wonderful. Throughout eternity future, they, and only they, will wear the special crown of glory.

But there is another side to this test. Do the foregoing conclusions agree with the immediate context in which this statement of the crown of glory is found? Doesn't the previous verse teach that these shepherds are to be examples? And isn't the supreme and most trustworthy example we are to follow Christ Himself? Doesn't He say in Matthew 11:29:

Take my yoke upon you, and learn of me; for I am meek and lowly in heart: and ye shall find rest unto your souls.

Wasn't Moses a great type of Christ and don't we read of him in Numbers 12:3:

Now the man Moses was very meek, above all the men which were upon the face of the earth.

How do these statements correlate with the idea of special glory to the pastor? True, he is to be honored, that is, respected as a servant of God, but this in no sense gives him special spiritual authority. The only spiritual authority is the Bible.

Moreover, the Bible neatly puts to rest any grandiose ideas of some special glory that awaits pastors in eternity future. In Luke 17:10, God lays down this principle:

**So likewise ye, when ye shall have done all those things which are
commanded you, say, We are unprofitable servants: we have done
that which was our duty to do.**

As if that is not enough, in Luke 18:28-30, God makes sure we
understand that all future blessings are encompassed in the fact that we have
been given eternal life. We read in this passage:

**Then Peter said, Lo, we have left all, and followed thee. And he said
unto them, Verily I say unto you, There is no man that hath left
house, or parents, or brethren, or wife, or children, for the
kingdom of God's sake, Who shall not receive manifold more in
this present time, and in the world to come life everlasting.**

How interesting and significant that it is the Apostle Peter who is
concerned about this subject. If any of the apostles were singled out for
special recognition, it was Peter. Therefore, we can be certain that the
principle God is stating in these verses applies to every believer, regardless of
what their task might be.

And what is the principle that God set forth? In this life, we will receive
many blessings as we serve God in the kingdom of God, but in eternity future,
we receive eternal life.

But eternal life is given by God's grace to each and every believer.
Every blessing of salvation is included in the gift of eternal life. Therefore,
the crown of glory is included in the gift of eternal life. Thus, we can be sure
that every true believer is given a crown of glory.

Therefore, if a pastor concludes on the basis of I Peter 5:4 that he has
some spiritual authority, he has failed the test. He has failed the test just like
those who believe the church is the pillar and ground of the truth have failed
the test.

That brings us to the second passage, Ephesians 2:20, 21:

**And are built upon the foundation of the apostles and prophets,
Jesus Christ himself being the chief corner stone; In whom all the
building fitly framed together groweth unto an holy temple in the
Lord:**

The apostles and prophets cannot be the foundation of the holy temple.
The foundation of the apostles and prophets is the Word of God, Jesus
Christ being the chief corner stone. As a matter of fact, Jesus is the Word

that became flesh and dwelt among us. Thus, Christ is the foundation even as we learned from I Corinthians 3:11. We could paraphrase this verse to read, "And are built upon the Word of God which is the foundation of the apostles and prophets, Jesus Christ Himself being the chief corner stone."

It is true that we read in Revelation 21:14 about the holy city, new Jerusalem having **"twelve foundations, and in them the names of the twelve apostles of the Lamb,"** but we must understand that the foundations represent Christ. Throughout eternity future in the new heaven and new earth, the fullness of the believers represented by the twelve apostles are His body. They are forever intimately identified with Him.

This verse, too, is designed by God to be a test for the church. Unfortunately, a great many pastors and Bible teachers have failed the test.

How then are we to understand Matthew 16:19, where we read:

And I will give unto thee the keys of the kingdom of heaven: and whatsoever thou shalt bind on earth shall be bound in heaven: and whatsoever thou shalt loose on earth shall be loosed in heaven.

What are the keys that are given to the church. The keys can only be the Bible. God uses the key which is the Bible to open the gates of hell to free men from the wrath of God. God uses the key of the Bible to open the door (Christ) into the kingdom of God. That is why we read in II Corinthians 2:15, 16:

For we are unto God a sweet savour of Christ, in them that are saved, and in them that perish: To the one we are the savour of death unto death; and to the other the savour of life unto life. And who is sufficient for these things?

We are this fragrance because we as true believers are custodians of the keys, the Bible. But who opens and shuts these gigantic spiritual doors. We read in Revelations 3:7:

And to the angel of the church in Philadelphia write; These things saith he that is holy, he that is true, he that hath the key of David, he that openeth, and no man shutteth; and shutteth, and no man openeth;

This verse clearly teaches that it is Christ who opens and shuts.
Significantly, God wrote Matthew 16:19 very carefully. Unfortunately,

something of this care was lost when the Greek words were translated into English. The verse should read:

> **... whatsoever thou shalt bind on earth <u>shall having been bound in</u> heaven; and whatsoever thou shalt loose on earth <u>shall having been loosed</u> in heaven.**

By use of the past perfect tense, God is assuring us that the prior action was God's action. He has elected and saved a person because the church which was made the custodian of the keys, the Bible, had faithfully declared the Gospel.

Does Church Membership Guarantee Salvation?

There are many pastors who take comfort in these words of Matthew 16:19 as well as the words of Matthew 18:18, which reads:

> **Verily I say unto you, Whatsoever ye shall bind on earth shall be bound in heaven: and whatsoever ye shall loose on earth shall be loosed in heaven.**

They wrongly believe that when the pastor and elders or deacons conclude that a person has become saved, it is guaranteed that the person has indeed become saved. They fail to realize that the verb tenses in this verse, as was true with the verbs in Matthew 16:19, which describe salvation, are in the past perfect tense. "Whatsoever ye shall bind on earth shall having been bound in heaven," and "Whatsoever ye shall loose on earth shall having been loosed in heaven."

The action of saving is God's action. The external church functioned as God's servant to send out the Gospel. It functioned as God's servant to welcome those who appeared to have become saved into the congregation. It functioned as God's servants to teach and guide, by means of the Bible, those who appeared to have become saved.

> *But no pastor and no church can cause someone being ministered to within the congregation to become saved.*

But no pastor and no church can cause someone being ministered to within the congregation to become saved. No human has an insight as to who is elect of God. That is God's work entirely. Therefore, the best the church leaders can do is assume that some within the congregation may have become saved. On the other hand, there may be those who appear to have become saved but in actuality, they have not become saved.

Therefore, the preaching to the congregation and the guidance of the congregation during the church age always had to include warnings concerning God's judgment on the unsaved as well as the warning to the whole congregation to make sure of their salvation. This is so, as II Corinthians 13:5 admonishes:

Examine yourselves, whether ye be in the faith; prove your own selves. Know ye not your own selves, how that Jesus Christ is in you, except ye be reprobates?

Those who search their own hearts and know they are saved can know that they are a part of the bride of Christ, the eternal invisible church over which the gates of hell cannot prevail because Christ has paid for all of their sins.

On the other hand, we can know that the corporate external church known as congregations and denominations have no assurance that they are safe from the wrath of God.

Since the true believers within a congregation cannot come under God's wrath, this warning was particularly leveled against the external body, which consists of all the churches and congregations that exist today. Even as the seven churches of Revelation 2 and 3 were judged and were completely removed, so any and every congregation can come under the judgment of God. Because there has never been a perfect church at any time in the history of the world, it is a testimony to the patience and mercy of God that congregations and denominations continued to flourish in the New Testament era. In spite of their flaws and defects, God has used the churches during the last more than 1950 years to bring the Gospel to the world. These churches from many different denominations have been the vehicle, the instrument by which the Gospel of salvation has gone into virtually every country of the world.

This helps us to understand John 20:22, 23 which declares:

And when he had said this, he breathed on them, and saith unto them, Receive ye the Holy Ghost: Whose soever sins ye remit, they are remitted unto them; and whose soever sins ye retain, they are retained.

We know, of course, that only God can forgive sins (Mark 2:7). Therefore, we must understand that this verse is teaching that it is God who does the forgiving. The church acknowledges the person's forgiveness (salvation) by welcoming him into the congregation as a saved person.

Under no circumstance may the church believe that those who follow the rules of the church and become members are definitely those who were elected to salvation. Only God can know who the elect are. We must consider, for example, the Old Testament nation of Israel which was the church (Acts 7:38) until the season of the New Testament church. We read of them in Hebrews 3:17-19:

> **But with whom was he grieved forty years? was it not with them that had sinned, whose carcases fell in the wilderness? And to whom sware he that they should not enter into his rest, but to them that believed not? So we see that they could not enter in because of unbelief.**

Again in Romans 9:31, 32, God makes reference to them:

> **But Israel, which followed after the law of righteousness, hath not attained to the law of righteousness. Wherefore? Because they sought it not by faith, but as it were by the works of the law. For they stumbled at that stumblingstone;**

Indeed, these verses tell us that a church can be used of God to further His kingdom and yet have very few true believers within it. We also have the information on the church of Sardis (Revelation 3:6). It had already become a dead church (verse 1) although it still had a few names (verse 4) of true believers.

As we have looked more carefully at these three verses, we have found no indication that the pastor and church rulers have great spiritual authority. Nor do we find that the church doctrines are necessarily to be trusted as true and trustworthy. The elders are overseers who cared for the church. They ruled over the church to make sure the preached Gospel was as accurate as possible. They were to be sure that everything was done decently and in good order. They were to make sure that the elders and deacons meet the qualification set forth in I Timothy 3. But the only authority that saves people is God Himself. God is the only one who knows who the elect are. God is the only one who decides when He will apply His Word to the life of the individual He plans to save. The elders were to then welcome that person into the church membership.

Continually in Prayer and Ministering the Word

Fact is, there is a very revealing statement given in Acts 6:4:

But we will give ourselves continually to prayer, and to the ministry of the word.

The occasion is the appointment in the early church of seven men to ease the load of the apostles. In this verse, God describes how the spiritual heads of the church were to operate. They are to minister the Word, that is they were to teach and preach the Bible. To do this adequately, they had to study the Word to make sure they were teaching and preaching what God declares and not ideas that came from men's minds. They were to faithfully preach the whole counsel of God so that the unsaved hear of their need for salvation and the true believers could learn more and more about the kingdom of God, so that through God's Word, they will grow in grace.

But secondly, they were to give themselves continually in prayer. Why is this emphasized? What is prayer. Prayer is communicating with God. Why must the spiritual shepherds of the church continually communicate with God?

It is easy to understand this if we are walking very humbly before God. We will recognize that in ourselves we have no understanding, no spiritual strength, no wisdom. We know that in ourselves we will never understand the Bible. God the Holy Spirit must open our eyes. We know that we can't get anyone saved. But we can plead with God for mercy on behalf of those to whom we are ministering the Word. We should pray that our life will be a faithful example to the congregation. We are to continually pray because we are completely dependent upon God working in us to will and to do of His good pleasure in every aspect of our lives, and this is particularly true as we shepherd the congregation.

> *There is no place in their life for pride or the idea that they have great spiritual authority.*

In other words, the spiritual rulers in the congregation were to be totally dependent upon God. They must always remember they are simply His humble servants who had been given the task of shepherding the flock. There is no place in their life for pride or the idea that they have great spiritual authority. Neither is there any Biblical basis for believing that the Confessions or other doctrines held by a church are necessarily pleasing to God.

The Bible alone and in its entirety is the only authority that rules as truth. That is, every doctrine held by a church must always be subject to the authority of the Bible. In fact, in I Peter 5:2, 3, God admonishes the spiritual rulers of the church:

> **Feed the flock of God which is among you, taking the oversight thereof, not by constraint, but willingly; not for filthy lucre, but of a ready mind; Neither as being lords over God's heritage, but being ensamples to the flock.**

The pastor and the elders, as humble examples to the congregation, should have been the first to depart out of the local congregation. As spiritual rulers they are overseers who tenderly care for the flock. As we just read, they are not "lords" over the congregation.

Faithful to the Word

Actually, the problem is much greater and more serious than that which we have been describing. Let us think again of what the task of the pastor was. He has been called of God to faithfully bring forth what the Bible teaches. When he tells his congregation, "thus saith the Lord," it better be exactly what the Bible teaches. If he teaches wrongly, he cannot lay the blame on his seminary or on his fellow pastors or on the elders. He has been called to be a faithful shepherd of the flock, which is the congregation over which he has the spiritual oversight.

Therefore, he must carefully and diligently check out everything he teaches to be sure it accords altogether with the Bible. If he is trusting certain doctrines because that is what the confession teaches or that is what we Baptists or we Lutherans or we Methodists believe, then he is trusting men rather than God. He must personally check out each doctrine he teaches so that he can show from God's Word that what he is teaching is true. Unless this is done, it will simply mean that he is worshipping the men who designed these doctrines.

For example, the Bible says faith is work (I Thessalonians 1:3, II Thessalonians 1:11). It also declares our salvation is not of our work (Ephesians 2:8-9). If a pastor teaches what the theologians who wrote the confession teach, namely, that faith is an instrument through which God works to save us, the pastor is preaching a man-made gospel. Another example is that the Bible declares that what God hath joined together, let not man put asunder (Matthew 19:6), and **"the woman which hath an husband is bound by the law to her husband so long as he liveth"** (Romans 7:2, I Corinthians 7:39). If the church allows the teaching that there can be divorce for fornication, it has established its own law. It is teaching the laws of men rather than the law of God. Moreover, the Bible declares that whosoever marrieth her that is put away from her husband committeth adultery (Luke 16:18, Romans 7:3, etc.). If a church or a pastor teaches other than this, a teaching is being offered that is out of the mind of man rather than from God.

Many, many doctrines taught by pastors can be added to this brief list. The scary and sad conclusion we must come to is that there is little or no evidence that many of these pastors have a fear of God. They do not tremble at His Word. It is no wonder, then, that God's wrath is upon them and their church as God warns in Jeremiah 1:16:

> **And I will utter my judgments against them touching all their wickedness, who have forsaken me, and have burned incense unto other gods, and worshipped the works of their own hands.**

The Bible alone and in its entirety must always be considered the divine authority. No local church may in any way claim that authority.

Salvation By Grace Alone

Our understanding of the nature of salvation is second in importance only to our understanding of the authority of the Bible. It is a subject that flows from the teachings of the Bible.

The Bible insists that our salvation is by the grace of God alone. Under no circumstance is any work on our part to be regarded as even the smallest assist to our salvation. Unfortunately, while in the most faithful churches, lip service is paid to the concept of grace alone, in actuality, it is not believed or taught. The proof that it is not believed is seen in such actions and doctrines as the following.

1. Faith is an instrument through which God works His salvation plan.
2. Water baptism is a necessary act before we are saved.
3. We must accept Christ and only then will we become saved.
4. The atonement of Christ has made provision for the sins of every individual in the whole world.

5. We must believe in Christ before we can become saved.
6. We must repent of our sins before we can become saved.
7. We can become saved only if we are part of a church or congregation.
8. We must make public profession of our faith before we become saved.
9. We can pray certain prayers and thus become saved.
10. If we no longer attend church, it indicates that we were never saved.

Some of these wrong ideas are present in virtually all churches and congregations. Perhaps it is not realized, but each and every one of these ideas makes salvation conditional, that is, we can only become saved if we do something.

Does the Church Need the Lord Jesus?

Earlier in our study we learned that the Book of Jeremiah has as a primary focus the end of the church age. This means that its warnings and judgments are being leveled at the churches of our day. Thus, in Jeremiah 2:6 we read:

Neither said they, Where is the LORD that brought us up out of the land of Egypt,

In Jeremiah 2:8 we read:

The priests said not, Where is the LORD? and they that handle the law knew me not: the pastors also transgressed against me, and the prophets prophesied by Baal, and walked after things that do not profit.

The plain implication of these statements is that those who have the spiritual oversight in the churches do not need God to further God's plan of salvation. True, they pay lip service to the idea that they need God, but in reality, all that is necessary to further God's salvation plan is under the control of the church. In the church all the necessary activities are going on to guarantee the salvation of the unsaved. Whatsoever is loosed by the activity of the church will be loosed in heaven. Whatsoever is bound or excommunicated by the church has been excommunicated by the edict of the church. Those who have made confession of faith are certainly believers.

In other words, the church does not need God to get people saved. According to their incorrect understanding of the Bible, they have in place all the decisions and actions that are required by anyone who desires to become saved.

Before We Are Saved We Are Spiritually Dead

They take at face value that when God commands us to believe, to repent, to seek God, to call on Him, etc., we should and can do these things. They fail to realize that we are spiritually dead. By nature, we will never seek God, that is, seek God on His terms. They do not realize that no one can come to God unless God draws him. The do not realize that we are as spiritually dead as Lazarus of John 11 was physically dead. They do not realize that even as Christ called the physically dead Lazarus to come forth, He commands us, who are spiritually dead, to believe, to repent, etc. Lazarus obeyed the command to come forth, and he came out of that tomb. He could do so only because Christ gave him physical life and ears to hear. Likewise, before any spiritually dead person can obey God's command to believe, God must save that spiritually dead person, give him spiritual ears to hear and a new resurrected soul, so he will obey.

These two huge issues, the authority of the Bible and the nature of salvation, are far more important than the Biblical teaching that we have come to the end of the church age.

I hope the reader is beginning to see the utmost seriousness of these statements. These statements have not been made because of a crusade or vendetta against the church. They are being made as solemn facts setting forth a realistic analysis of the condition that exists in the churches of our day.

And that brings us to the fourth verse. In Matthew 16:18 Jesus declared:

I will build my church; and the gates of hell shall not prevail against it.

Do the gates of hell identify with Satan? It is true that Satan is to spend eternity in hell, but does he control who is to go through the gates into hell? This must be obvious. Only God is the judge of the earth. Only God is in charge of who is to go through the gates into hell. The sad fact is that the gates of hell will prevail against all who remain unsaved. Hell will make its claim on every unsaved person because the wages of sin must be paid.

But there are those whom hell cannot have. They are those who have become saved. The gates of hell cannot prevail against them. They have become eternal members of the invisible body of believers who are the eternal church of God. The corporate external church can have a few of these members of the eternal church (like the church of Sardis) or it can have a sizable percentage of such members. Only God know who the true believers are in any congregation.

The Gates of Hell Will Prevail Against the Unsaved in the Church

This verse cannot be teaching that the local churches will continue as the house of God all the way to the end of the world. Even as the seven churches of Revelation 2 and Revelation 3 came to an end, so can any or all churches come to an end. True, they will still physically be here all the way to the end, just as synagogues which were a part of an earlier season of God's program of the Gospel, are still here. But as we approach the end neither the synagogues nor the churches have any part in God's Gospel program. It must be clearly understood that on this earth there are two churches. The one which is called Jerusalem above (Galatians 4:26), consists of those who truly have been saved. The persons who are a part of this church may be only a small part of the members of a local congregation. The gates of hell cannot prevail against these individuals.

There also exists the Jerusalem which is now (Galatians 4:25). They are all the members of the local congregation who are not saved. The gates of hell will prevail against them.

In Matthew 16:18 God gave His wonderful promise, **"I will build my church; and the gates of hell shall not prevail against it."** As we have seen, in the minds of many people, the church against which the gates of hell cannot prevail is considered to be the corporate external church known by such names as the First Methodist Church, Redeemer Lutheran Church, or Second Reformed Church.

> *These churches and denominations have no guarantee of length of time of existence.*

It is true that these external corporate bodies (which include all of the congregations and denominations that believe the Bible is the Word of God), are holy organisms established more or less according to Biblical rules. For example, in I Timothy 3 God gives very careful rules for the selection of elders and deacons. But these churches and denominations have no guarantee of length of time of existence. For example, in Revelation 2 and Revelation 3 God speaks of seven churches that were in existence at the time the Bible was being finished. Yet a few hundred years later, all of these churches had disappeared. Indeed, afterwards for many hundreds of years there was no Christian witness of any kind in the cities wherein these churches had been located. Thus, we can be certain that the church Christ has in view in Matthew 16 is not the corporate external church which consists of local congregations that can be found throughout the world.

What church is it then that Jesus had in view when He said, **"the gates of hell shall not prevail against it."** As we have seen, the solution is that there is an eternal church which is made up of all those individuals who personally have become saved. They were given eternal life because Jesus as their Savior has paid for each and every one of their sins. Therefore, forever more they had become safe and secure, Matthew 16 very definitely has this spiritual church in view. It can never come under the wrath of God which is the essence of hell. The gates of hell can never make a claim upon those who are truly saved.

There is a corporate external church which consists of all the churches and congregations as they are found on the face of the earth. There is also an eternal invisible church that is made up of all the true believers who during the church age were normally found in the corporate external churches. But when Christ says, **"I will build my church; and the gates of hell shall not prevail against it,"** He is not speaking of the corporate external churches. The same holds true when He speaks of the church as the bride of the Lamb. Only the eternal invisible church is the bride of Christ.

When He speaks of the church as His body, He can be speaking only of the eternal invisible church. When He speaks of the church in Ephesians 3:10 as the evidence of the manifold wisdom of God, it can only be the eternal invisible church. When He declares in Colossians 1:18 that He is the head of the church, again, it can only be the eternal invisible church.

Is the Local Congregation the Bride of Christ?

Unfortunately, in a great many churches, no distinction is made between the corporate external church that consists, on the one hand, of various local congregations, and on the other hand, the eternal invisible church. Fact is, in many churches, it is assumed that those who have made profession of faith, who have been baptized in water, who have become members of the church, and who regularly partake of the Lord's Supper, are truly saved. Therefore, the idea exists that the whole congregation is saved.

Therefore, effectively, it is believed that the congregation itself is the body of Christ, the bride of Christ. The congregation then is looked upon as the eternal invisible church.

But this thinking is without Biblical justification. None of the above actions which have been performed by each church member initiates or proves salvation. A person can do all of these things and still be as unsaved as the most wicked individual in the world.

Salvation is 100% an action of God in which He makes the individual a new creation. He gives the saved one a new resurrected soul in which he never wishes to sin again. And only God knows those whom He has saved. True, the one who has become saved will know he has become saved. I John 2:3 assures us:

And hereby we do know that we know him, if we keep his commandments.

Therefore, the one who has truly become saved will be deeply concerned that all of the doctrines he holds are true to the Bible. He will realize that church doctrine and confessions may never be considered to be ultimate truth. In fact, perhaps without realizing it, he will be of the same mond as the writer of Article VII of the Belgic Confession, which places that Confession and church doctrines precisely where they ought to be. This article reads as follows.

Article VII

The Sufficiency of the Holy Scriptures to be the Only Rule of Faith

We believe that those Holy Scriptures fully contain the will of God, and that whatsoever man ought to believe unto salvation is sufficiently taught therein. For since the whole manner of worship which God requires of us is written in them at large, it is unlawful for any one, though an apostle, to teach otherwise than we are now taught in the Holy Scriptures: nay, though it were an angel from heaven, as the apostle Paul says. For it is forbidden to add unto or take away anything from the Word of God, it does thereby evidently appear that the doctrine thereof is most perfect and complete in all respects.

Neither may we consider any writings of men, however holy these men may have been, of equal value with these divine Scriptures, nor ought we to consider customs, or the great multitude, or antiquity, or succession of times and persons, or councils, decrees or statutes, as of equal value with the truths of God, since the truth is above all; for all men are of themselves liars, and more vain than vanity itself. Therefore, we reject with all our hearts whatsoever does not agree with this infallible rule, as the apostles have taught us, saying, Prove the spirits, whether they are of God. Likewise: If any one cometh unto you, and bringeth not this teaching, receive him not into your house.

Unfortunately, while this excellent statement of Article VII continues to be in the Belgic Confession of our day, there exists hardly a person anywhere who is paying attention to this Article. Had it been taken seriously, it would have meant that the churches that used the Belgic Confession would have been constantly examining this Confession to make sure that in every part it was as Biblical as possible. Had they done this, they would have discovered that many statements in the Belgic Confession are not nearly as Biblical as they should be.

For example, Article XXIV of this Confession states:

We believe that this true faith, being wrought in man by the hearing of the Word of God, and the operation of the Holy Spirit, regenerates him and makes him a new man.

This statement long ago should have been corrected. The Bible teaches that faith is a work. Therefore, this statement is effectively teaching that there is some work (faith) that we do that regenerates us. The truth is that the faith God gives the believer is always a result or product of salvation. Faith is a good work like all of the good works that become evident in the life of the one who becomes saved.

Throughout the years that followed the adoption of the various confessions, like the Belgic Confession, the Heidelberg Catechism, the Canons of Dort, the Westminster Confession, the Baptist Confession, the Augsburg Confession, churches should have continued to check the Confessions by the Word of God and made necessary corrections. True, these Confessions would never have become a perfect presentation of truth because they were not divinely inspired. But they could have become much more accurate than they are. Furthermore, as they were corrected, the emphasis would have been made more clear that the final authority is the Bible alone and its entirety.

Instead, however, the churches accepted these Confessions as they were first adopted by the churches. They were looked upon as a final authoritarian statement concerning Biblical truth. And as the years went by, they became venerated as truth, their antiquity giving credence to this concept. Thus, the incorrect teachings in these Confessions became high places. They effectively were lies in that they claimed that God had said these things when God had not said these things.

If we are truly saved, we will realize that the ultimate source of truth can only be the Bible. We will begin to realize that church teachings such as Confessions can serve as guides but can never be considered the final authority. Unfortunately, in the churches of our day, few church members see that there is a difference between what the church teaches, as it tries to remain faithful to the Confessions, and what the Bible teaches.

> *We will begin to realize that church teachings such as Confessions can serve as guides but can never be considered the final authority.*

That is why we, therefore, must clearly recognize there is a great difference between the corporate external church and the eternal invisible church. This great difference exists even though during the church age, the members of the eternal invisible church worshipped under the roof of the external visible church wherein could be found many defects.

Actually, at times, perhaps only a tiny remnant of a congregation was a part of the eternal invisible church. Certainly, at any time during the church age, it was presumptuous for a pastor to assume that virtually all of the members of his church were part of the eternal invisible church.

We have learned that a great many New Testament churches have fallen into the snare of pride. They unwittingly have developed the idea that they virtually have as much authority as God Himself.

Thou Art a Man, and Not God

Now we understand one good reason why God has written Ezekiel 28. There God speaks of the merchant city Tyre that sent out the ships of Tarshish. A careful study of this chapter would show that Tyre represents the churches as they send the Gospel into the world. By this means the gold and silver and other valuable commodities that represent the true believers are brought into the kingdom of God. The prince of Tyre represents the pastors, the elders, and the deacons who have been given the spiritual rule of the congregation God warns these rulers in verse 2:

> **Son of man, say unto the prince of Tyrus, Thus saith the Lord GOD; Because thine heart is lifted up, and thou hast said, I am a God, I sit in the seat of God, in the midst of the seas; yet thou art a man, and not God, though thou set thine heart as the heart of God:**

This verse is striking the nail on the head. God resists the proud but gives grace to the humble. When a church begins to think and act as if it has virtually the same authority as God, something is going to happen. God is long suffering. He overlooked the spiritual high places for a long time. But He finally brings that pride to an end. We presently are living at that time when God's judgment has fallen upon the churches. The church rulers are not God, they are men!

Ezekiel 28:6-10 records:

> **Therefore thus saith the Lord GOD; Because thou hast set thine heart as the heart of God; Behold, therefore I will bring strangers upon thee, the terrible of the nations: and they shall draw their swords against the beauty of thy wisdom, and they shall defile thy brightness. They shall bring thee down to the pit, and thou shalt die the deaths of them that are slain in the midst of the seas. Wilt thou yet say before him that slayeth thee, I am God? but thou shalt be a man, and no God, in the hand of him that slayeth thee. Thou shalt die the deaths of the uncircumcised by the hand of strangers: for I have spoken it, saith the Lord GOD.**

In Conclusion

We have learned that the four verses we have been considering are very frequently understood to teach that the corporate, external church which is made up of local churches, is the foundation of truth. The spiritual rulers are its foundation. They act to save people and God sanctions their actions. Thus, they need not spend much time differentiating between the eternal church and the external church. They are convinced that essentially they are one and the same because they believe virtually all members of the church are saved. This kind of thinking fostered the same kind of wrong thinking that Lucifer fell into. He wanted to be God (Isaiah 14:13-14), when in actuality, he had been created to be a ministering spirit (Hebrews 1:13). True believers always recognize we are humble servants of God. We read of Moses the servant of God (Joshua 1:1) and of Joshua the servant of the Lord (Joshua 24:29). Could it be that each of us might humbly be the servant of Christ.

Unfortunately, the conclusions of this chapter make virtually all congregations look bad. Therefore, they will greatly offend many pastors and church members. There are many church members who have complete confidence in the spiritual integrity of their pastor. They believe he is a loving faithful shepherd who is faithfully declaring the Word of God.

The real test, however, is not what is seen with our eyes, but what any pastor or denomination does with these four verses. If they believe that the church is the pillar and ground of truth, if they believe that those who have made a profession of faith and who trust that what their church teaches is faithful to God's Word, and therefore, ordinarily are always to be considered true believers, then this may be an indication that these church overseers have taken on great spiritual authority. They will have taken on a spiritual authority that is far beyond that which the Bible teaches.

To further test this situation one has only to examine the teachings of the denomination to which this church belongs. Ordinarily, a pastor will be altogether faithful to the doctrines held by his denomination. If he is not faithful to these doctrines, he would soon no longer be able to continue as a pastor in that denomination. If the denomination teaches that the local churches will endure to the end because Satan cannot prevail against them, if it teaches that the local church membership consists mostly of born-again believers, usually he will also hold those doctrines as truth. It will be clear evidence that, that church has many high places.

Ultimately, of course, we have learned in this study and we must realize that even if a local church could be found in which the pastor is the loving, humble overseer a pastor ought to be, the Holy Spirit would still not be saving people in that congregation. Even if the pastor is an exemplary example of a humble, faithful servant of Christ constantly praying for God's mercy upon those to whom he is ministering the Bible, the believers should depart out. These statements are true because the era of the church age, the season of the early rain that has brought in the Pentecostal harvest of the firstfruits, has ended. The temple has come to an end so that all the precious, living stones within it have been thrown down.

Appendix A.
Further Explanation of Revelation

Worship God The Creator

Earlier in our study, we began to examine the question of worshipping the beast (Satan). We should be worshipping God as the Creator and Savior. In Revelation 14:7, God declares, **"worship him that made heaven, and earth, and the sea, and the fountains of waters."**

What does it mean to worship someone? Worship is identified with bowing down before the one who is our master. It is to acknowledge Him as the giver of every benefit and blessing we receive. It is an acknowledgment that He is the one we will serve because our will is surrendered to Him.

But doesn't everyone in the churches recognize this? Surely, everyone knows that God who is the Creator of the universe is the only one we should worship.

Unfortunately, it is one thing to know and it is another thing to do what we know. In Revelation 14:9, God warns:

And the third angel followed them, saying with a loud voice, If any man worship the beast and his image, and receive his mark in his forehead, or in his hand,

Why should God warn that we are not to worship the beast or his image? And what is the image of the beast?

To answer these questions we must become better acquainted with Revelation 13. We will discover that the entire chapter is devoted to Satan's rule during the Great Tribulation period which we are now experiencing. Revelation 13:1, 2 declare:

And I stood upon the sand of the sea, and saw a beast rise up out of the sea, having seven heads and ten horns, and upon his horns ten crowns, and upon his heads the name of blasphemy. And the beast which I saw was like unto a leopard, and his feet were as the feet of a bear, and his mouth as the mouth of a lion: and the dragon gave him his power, and his seat, and great authority.

The picture of the beast with seven heads and ten horns typifies Satan. We first read of this beast in Revelation 12:3:

And there appeared another wonder in heaven; and behold a great red dragon, having seven heads and ten horns, and seven crowns upon his heads.

There are at least three differences in these two accounts. Revelation 12:3 calls this animal a dragon. Revelation 13:1, 2 calls it a beast. Revelation 12:3 says the heads are crowned. Revelation 13:1, 2 says the ten horns are crowned. Revelation 12:3 informs us the dragon is identified with heaven. Revelation 13:1, 2 tells us the beast comes out of the sea. The solution to these differences can be known.

The Believers Give Birth to Christ

First, we should briefly outline the truths set forth in Revelation 12. Verses 1, 2 declare:

And there appeared a great wonder in heaven; a woman clothed with the sun, and the moon under her feet, and upon her head a crown of twelve stars: And she being with child cried, travailing in birth, and pained to be delivered.

The woman is the Old Testament believers represented by Mary who gave birth to Jesus. They are clothed with the sun, that is, they are clothed with Christ who is their robe of righteousness. The moon is under her feet. The moon represents the law of God. The believers have become victorious over the law in the sense that the law of God can no longer condemn them. The crown of twelve stars signifies that the believers reign with Christ.

Verses 3 and 4 continue:

And there appeared another wonder in heaven; and behold a great red dragon, having seven heads and ten horns, and seven crowns upon his heads. And his tail drew the third part of the stars of heaven, and did cast them to the earth: and the dragon stood before the woman which was ready to be delivered, for to devour her child as soon as it was born.

The third part represents all who are believers. We in Adam were created to be perfect. But when Satan the dragon caused Eve to sin, he effectively caused all who would eventually become believers (the stars of heaven), to be cast out of heaven. This dragon (Satan) was ready to kill

Jesus as soon He was born. The seven heads are crowned, indicating Satan's rule over unsaved mankind throughout the history of the world. Verse 5 continues:

> **And she brought forth a man child, who was to rule all nations with a rod of iron: and her child was caught up unto God, and to his throne.**

The Entire New Testament Era Equals 1260 Days

The man child, Jesus, returns to heaven and the woman (the New Testament believers), continue under God's protection for 1260 days. The figure 1260 days equals three and a half years. However, to inform us that it represents a different time period from the forty two months of Revelation 11:2, God speaks of it as 1260 days. This period is the same period of time set forth in Daniel 9:27 where God emphasizes there is a half a week (½ of 7) from the cessation of sacrifice and offering (this occurred when Christ was offered as the sacrifice), until the abomination of desolation and the consummation (the end of the world). Thus, the 1260 days of Revelation 12:6 covers the entire period from the cross to the end of the world.

Verses 7 to 11 of Revelation 12 describe the victory Christ won over Satan when Christ went to the cross. We read:

> **And there was war in heaven: Michael and his angels fought against the dragon; and the dragon fought and his angels, And prevailed not; neither was their place found any more in heaven. And the great dragon was cast out, that old serpent, called the Devil, and Satan, which deceiveth the whole world: he was cast out into the earth, and his angels were cast out with him. And I heard a loud voice saying in heaven, Now is come salvation, and strength, and the kingdom of our God, and the power of his Christ: for the accuser of our brethren is cast down, which accused them before our God day and night. And they overcame him by the blood of the Lamb, and by the word of their testimony; and they loved not their lives unto the death.**

Michael is Christ who defeated Satan by the blood of the Lamb (Christ gave His life as the sacrificial Lamb). The result was that Satan was given a death blow, he was cast out of heaven. He was bound so that he could no longer deceive the nations (Revelation 20:2, 3). He was cast into hell

(Revelation 20:3 and II Peter 2:4), that is, he was placed eternally under the wrath of God so that on the last day, he will be cast into the lake of fire (Revelation 20:10).

Thus, we learn from Revelation 12 that Satan is presented as a dragon who rules over unsaved mankind throughout the history of the world. At the cross, he was defeated and became subject to hell.

As we learned earlier, Revelation 13 discusses the rulership of Satan over all of the unsaved during the Great Tribulation of our day. We can see the differences here between God's plan for the Gospel and Satan throughout time.

As we continue our study, let us look again at Revelation 14:8. We read:

And there followed another angel, saying, Babylon is fallen, is fallen, that great city, because she made all nations drink of the wine of the wrath of her fornication.

What does Babylon have to do with the verses we have been studying in these chapters? We are learning that Babylon has everything to do with Chapters 13 and 14 of Revelation. We must remember that already in Isaiah 14, God typified Satan by the king of Babylon.

Furthermore, earlier in this study when we compared the judgment on Judah in 587 B.C. with the Great Tribulation of our day, the king of Babylon whom God used to destroy Judah typifies Satan whom God has loosed so that he takes his seat (he reigns) in the temple (the churches and congregations of our day).

Seated on a Scarlet Beast

Let us look some more at Revelation 17. We see in Revelation 17:3 that the woman, Babylon, is seated on a scarlet beast having seven heads and ten horns. We know that without question this beast with seven heads and 10 horns is Satan. But why is the color scarlet used as its color? The harlot, too, is clothed with purple and scarlet.

The color scarlet is associated with salvation. In Hebrews 9:19 God speaks of scarlet wool as being associated with the ceremonial activity that pictures salvation.

It was also a royal color; the color fit for a king. Remember during the suffering of Jesus, they put a scarlet robe on Him (Matthew 27:28) and mocked Him saying, **"Hail, King of the Jews!"** (Matthew 27:29).

Thus, on the one hand, in Revelation 17 Satan is showing himself to be a counterfeit christ, an antichrist. And he is also showing himself to be a king. The woman, too, is clothed with purple and scarlet. Actually the verb tense is past perfect. Thus, it should read "has been arrayed." During the church age the church was the holy place where most of the true believers were found. The Bible says that they shall reign on earth (Revelation 5:10). They are a royal priesthood (I Peter 2:9). Therefore, the churches have been intimately identified with those who reign.

After the church age, the churches still insist that they are identified with a royal reign as seen in the citation of Revelation 18:7, wherein the fallen church declares "I sit a queen." Moreover, Revelation 17:18 declares:

And the woman which thou sawest is that great city, which reigneth over the kings of the earth.

The Bible Rules Over the Church

What does it mean that she reigns over the kings of earth. During the church age the church is the external representation of the kingdom of God on this earth. God has made the churches the custodian, the steward that is to declare the commands of the Bible to the world. In that sense the Bible rules over the whole earth.

The proof of this truth will be seen at Judgment Day. Every person on the face of the whole earth who has not obeyed the commands of the Bible will be judged and found guilty of violating those commands. According to the rules of the Bible, those found guilty will be sentenced to eternal damnation.

However, when Satan began to rule in the churches, the Holy Spirit was not in the midst. Satan has become the ruler. Because he is allowed by God to rule over all the unsaved of the world, and because he now is the ruler over the church, in that sense, the churches now rule over the whole world. Therefore, in that sense, the woman rules over all the earth. This is so because Satan has become the ruler in the churches.

Verse 4 of Revelation 17 says that the woman was decked with gold, precious stones, and pearls. Again the verb tense is in the past perfect so that it should read "has been decked."

The woman Babylon (the churches and congregations) is a harlot. Yet within her there have been true believers (gold, precious stones, and pearls). But they have been either driven out or if they are still in, they are commanded to come out of her (Revelation 18:4).

This woman also has a golden cup in her hand (vs. 4). This cup should be filled with the pure water of the Gospel which is offered to the kings of the earth to drink. But it has become filled with the filthiness of her fornication. Instead of the true Gospel, she is offering a gospel designed by men. Instead of being filled with true believers who are the pure bride of Christ and who are faithfully bringing the pure Gospel, it has become adulterated with those whom we read about in I Corinthians 3:12 as wood, hay, and stubble.

Mother of Harlots

Verse 5 of Revelation 17 describes her as the mother of harlots. Let us examine this statement. In the Old Testament, Israel is described as being married to God. We read in Isaiah 50:1:

Thus saith the LORD, Where is the bill of your mother's divorcement, whom I have put away? or which of my creditors is it to whom I have sold you? Behold, for your iniquities have ye sold yourselves, and for your transgressions is your mother put away.

In Jeremiah 3:14 we read:

Turn, O backsliding children, saith the LORD; for I am married unto you: and I will take you one of a city, and two of a family, and I will bring you to Zion:

Israel as a nation was married to God, but because of her spiritual adulteries God divorced her. That divorce became final when Christ was on the cross and the veil of the temple was rent. At that moment the holy of holies was no longer holy. Therefore, the temple was no longer the Holy Place. Jerusalem was no longer the holy city. God's spiritual relationship with national Israel came to an end.

The Bible does not indicate that God became married to the New Testament Israel, the churches and congregations that would be in existence throughout the church age. Instead, God indicates that the true believers became the bride of Christ. All of the sins, past, present, and future, of these who have become saved have been covered by the blood of Christ. Therefore, in no sense does God look upon them as adulterous even though sin is still found in them. God speaks of them as those who were not defiled with women for they are virgins (Revelation 14:4). This language assures us that from God's vantage point, the bride of Christ which consists of all true believers is pure.

However, within the churches are a great many who believe they are saved but who have not actually become saved. They are the wood, hay, stubble. They, like all unsaved mankind, are married to the law of God. We read in Romans 7:1-4:

> **Know ye not, brethren, (for I speak to them that know the law,) how that the law hath dominion over a man as long as he liveth? For the woman which hath an husband is bound by the law to her husband so long as he liveth; but if the husband be dead, she is loosed from the law of her husband. So then if, while her husband liveth, she be married to another man, she shall be called an adulteress: but if her husband be dead, she is free from that law; so that she is no adulteress, though she be married to another man. Wherefore, my brethren, ye also are become dead to the law by the body of Christ; that ye should be married to another, even to him who is raised from the dead, that we should bring forth fruit unto God.**

Verse 4 assures us that before salvation, we were married to the law of God. Therefore, each time an unsaved person sins, he is committing an act of spiritual adultery against the law of God which is the husband. Therefore, an unsaved person is a harlot because sin is very common in that person's life.

This sad condition is underscored by the language of James 4:4:

> **Ye adulterers and adulteresses, know ye not that the friendship of the world is enmity with God? whosoever therefore will be a friend of the world is the enemy of God.**

It is at the judgment throne that the husband, the law of God, will point an accusing finger at his wife, the unsaved person, because of all the sinful (adulterous) actions of this person. Christ the judge will rule that the guilt of this spiritual adultery must be punished by consigning the wife (the sinful person) to eternal damnation.

Returning to the harlot of Revelation 18, we can now understand why she is called a harlot and the mother of harlots. Most of the true believers have already been driven out as pictured by the two witnesses who were killed in Revelation 11:7. The church or congregation consists mainly of unsaved people who are adulterers and adulteresses in that they love the world more than Christ.

The church, therefore, spiritually has become a harlot. The church is also the mother of harlots in that it is caring for or mothering a congregation of harlots.

This is very ugly language. However, it is no different from the language God employs when He speaks of ancient Israel or when He speaks of the New Testament church in the Book of James. In Ezekiel 16:24-26, God declares:

> **That thou hast also built unto thee an eminent place, and hast made thee an high place in every street. Thou hast built thy high place at every head of the way, and hast made thy beauty to be abhorred, and hast opened thy feet to every one that passed by, and multiplied thy whoredoms. Thou hast also committed fornication with the Egyptians thy neighbours, great of flesh; and hast increased thy whoredoms, to provoke me to anger.**

This is only a sample of a great many verses recorded especially in Ezekiel 16 and Ezekiel 23. And we remember James 4:4, where God speaks of those in the New Testament church who want to be friends of the world as adulterers and adulteresses.

We might recall that Ezekiel prophesied during the last six years before Judah was destroyed by the Babylonians in 587 B.C. Earlier in our study, we learned that this destruction typified and anticipated the destruction of the churches and congregations during the Great Tribulation period of our day. Therefore, we must assume that the ugly language of Ezekiel 16 and Ezekiel 23 is also speaking of the churches and congregations of our day.

Mystery Babylon

It should be noted that this harlot is called "mystery, Babylon." Why is she called mystery, Babylon? When we study the word "mystery" as it is used in the Bible, we find that it is used in connection with a truth that has been hidden from mankind and can be properly understood only by true believers whose spiritual eyes have been opened by the Holy Spirit.

For example, in I Corinthians 2:7-10, we read:

> **But we speak the wisdom of God in a mystery, even the hidden wisdom, which God ordained before the world unto our glory:**

Which none of the princes of this world knew: for had they known it, they would not have crucified the Lord of glory. But as it is written, Eye hath not seen, nor ear heard, neither have entered into the heart of man, the things which God hath prepared for them that love him. But God hath revealed them unto us by his Spirit: for the Spirit searcheth all things, yea, the deep things of God.

And in Ephesians 3:4-6 God declares:

Whereby, when ye read, ye may understand my knowledge in the mystery of Christ) Which in other ages was not made known unto the sons of men, as it is now revealed unto his holy apostles and prophets by the Spirit; That the Gentiles should be fellowheirs, and of the same body, and partakers of his promise in Christ by the gospel:

In these verses and in others, we learn that the Gospel is a mystery to the unsaved. Only when God gives spiritual eyes to an individual will the truth no longer be a mystery, but only a remnant hear the Gospel with the spiritual ears that only God can give. That is why many people are under the hearing of the Gospel, but the Gospel remains a mystery to them.

True, an individual can have an intellectual understanding of the Gospel. But if that understanding is not in his heart, so that he has an intense desire to be obedient to the Bible, which this understanding calls for, the Gospel will still be a mystery to him. That is why the harlot of Revelation 17 is called mystery Babylon. There will be those who will not understand that this harlot Babylon is the corporate external church of today. There will be others who will intellectually understand this but they cannot understand why it applies to them personally. They will have no desire or conviction that they should obey the command of Revelation 18:4 wherein God calls for decisive action on the part of the true believers. This verse commands:

And I heard another voice from heaven, saying, Come out of her, my people, that ye be not partakers of her sins, and that ye receive not of her plagues.

For anyone who does not take decisive action to come out of the corporate external church, this whole subject will still be a mystery. This is true even as salvation remains a mystery to anyone who has not actually become saved.

Does the Church Rule Over Satan?

Before we continue to examine this harlot Babylon, we should look more closely at the beast upon which she is sitting. We read in Revelation 17:3 that the woman was sitting upon a scarlet colored beast.

When Jesus entered Jerusalem just before He was crucified, He sat on a pair of donkeys. Spiritually, it can be shown that these donkeys represent unsaved people that He came to save. By His sitting upon them, spiritually, it indicates that He has the rule over them.

Likewise, we can understand the fact that the woman sits on the beast, and spiritually, it indicates that she has the rule over the beast. This is the lie that Satan wants us to believe as he comes as the father of lies. It is significant today that the churches which show most clearly they are under the rule of Satan, as they come with their signs and wonders, etc., are the very churches which most stridently declare that they have conquered and are conquering Satan. This is part of the great deception that has become a part of the spiritual Babylon of our day.

Earlier, we looked at Revelation 17:18 which declares that the woman rules over the kings of the earth. However, we must keep in mind that it is Satan who is ruling over the woman (the churches and congregations), so that effectively, Satan is the ruler. Remember II Thessalonians 2:3 declares that the man of sin (Satan) sits (rules) in the temple (the churches and congregations).

Looking more closely at this beast who is a representation of Satan, we learn from Revelation 17:8 that it **"was, and is not; and shall ascend out of the bottomless pit, and go into perdition."** In the light of the Bible, we can understand this.

From the fall of man in the Garden of Eden, Satan has ruled over mankind with great freedom, and he was even allowed to be in heaven. However, at the cross he was given a death blow by Christ's victory over him. In that sense Satan "is not." He ascended out of the bottomless pit when Christ loosed him to facilitate God's plan to bring judgment on the churches during the Great Tribulation period. He shall go into perdition when Christ comes on the last day and casts him into the lake of fire.

But the Bible further explains that the seven heads are seven mountains. Mountains in the Bible frequently signify kingdoms. This is in view in this reference because verse ten refers to seven kings. These seven kingdoms or kings refer to the rule of Satan throughout the history of the world. It identifies with Revelation 12:3 which speaks of the red dragon **"having seven heads and ten horns and seven crowns on the heads."**

At the time the Book of Revelation was being written, more than five sevenths of the rule of Satan over the world had already happened. The world was about 11,000 years old. It would continue about 2000 years longer. Five sevenths of 13,000 years equals about 9300 years. That time had already passed (five are fallen). Six sevenths of 13,000 years equals 11,140 years. Therefore, at the time this was written it was close to the time of Satan's reign as the seventh king.

But during the Great Tribulation, the reign of Satan is represented by the ten horns. We read in Revelation 17:12:

And the ten horns which thou sawest are ten kings, which have received no kingdom as yet; but receive power as kings one hour with the beast.

This coincides with the language of Revelation 13:1. Remember in Revelation 13:1 the beast that came out of the sea is Satan's overall rule in the world during the Great Tribulation. That is why Revelation 17:11 speaks of the beast as the eight. That is, even though the Great Tribulation will be focused on the ten horns, it is still the reign of Satan that is occurring. This agrees with Revelation 17:13 where God declares:

These have one mind, and shall give their power and strength unto the beast.

In verse 12 we read that these ten kings or horns will reign "one hour." We will find that this phrase identifies with the duration of the Great Tribulation. We should focus our attention on this phrase.

One Day or One Hour

When we study the Bible carefully, we discover that God speaks of Judgment Day as a day or as an hour. It appears that the two words "day" and "hour" are speaking of the same event, the time that God comes to judge the world (Matthew 24:36, 42, 44, II Thessalonians 1:10, I Thessalonians 5:2, etc.).

However, the Bible uses the phrase "one day" or "one hour" in only a few places. They all appear to relate in some way to the Great Tribulation. In Revelation 17:12 we have already seen that this is the period during which the ten horns are ruling. In Revelation 18 God speaks of the destruction of Babylon. Remember we learned that Babylon represents the churches and congregations that have come under the judgment of God during the Great

Tribulation. In three verses we find this time period referred to as "one day" or "one hour." The verses are Revelation 18:8, 10, 17 wherein God declares:

> **Therefore shall her plagues come in one day, death, and mourning, and famine; and she shall be utterly burned with fire: for strong is the Lord God who judgeth her.... Standing afar off for the fear of her torment, saying, Alas, alas, that great city Babylon, that mighty city! for in one hour is thy judgment come.... For in one hour so great riches is come to nought. And every shipmaster, and all the company in ships, and sailors, and as many as trade by sea, stood afar off,**

Significantly, God uses the same phrase "one hour" in Matthew 20:12 in connection with the man who received a full days wages for one hour of work. The only other place it is found is in connection with the suffering of Jesus in Gethsemane where He asks Peter, who together with two other apostles had gone with Him into the garden, **"couldest not thou watch one hour?"** (Mark 14:37, Matthew 26:40).

What is the spiritual significance of the phrase "one hour" or "one day"? The setting of its use in Revelation 17 and 18 is that of the entire Great Tribulation period. This we can be sure of because in Revelation 17:12 the ten horns receive power for one hour. We must understand from Revelation 13 that the ten horns rule as the beast that comes out of the sea and as the beast or false prophet that comes out of the earth.

Once we understand this we receive a fresh insight concerning the laborers who received a full days wages for one hour of work in the vineyard. They are a picture of the last to become saved. They are saved during the "one hour" period, that is, they are saved during the Great Tribulation. In Matthew 20 Jesus speaks of them as the last who shall be first (Matthew 20:16).

Watch with Me One Hour

But what about the use of the phrase "one hour" in connection with the suffering of Christ in Gethsemane. In that situation, Peter is a picture of the body of believers who are not watching. He was told to **"Watch and pray, that ye enter not into temptation"** (Matthew 26:41). The occasion was Judgment Day. On this Judgment Day, the wrath of God was being poured out on Jesus. Peter representing the believers is asleep. A few hours later, he will be denying his Lord. He has not been watching.

This report is pointing to another Judgment Day, that which begins with judgment on the churches and congregations. In Gethsemane, Jesus told Peter to watch one hour. The Great Tribulation period is also one hour. Therefore we, too, are being admonished to watch.

Revelation 16:15 warns, **"I come as a thief. Blessed is he that watcheth."** Mark 13:35 warns, **"Watch ye therefore: for ye know not when the master of the house cometh."** Many other verses of a similar nature can be cited.

In one sense, we must always be ready for Christ's coming because physical death is effectively the end of the world for those who die. Since no one has a guarantee he will be alive tomorrow, we must be ready right now.

However, when we come to the time in history called "one hour" or "one day" which identifies entirely with the Great Tribulation period, then the admonition to "watch" takes on a far greater meaning.

For example, if we are young and healthy, normally we can expect to have a great many years of life ahead of us. But when we are living in the time of history that God calls "one hour," it means the last day of this earth's existence has drawn very close. Thus, no matter how young or healthy we may be, the end of the world and the return of Christ has drawn very close.

Judgment Day Is Exceedingly Close

Thus, the term "one day" or "one hour" as it is used in Revelation 17 and 18 is a further warning to this world, which is now in the time of the Great Tribulation, that we better know that the time has come exceeding close to the time the whole world must face Him, the judge of all the earth. Even more ominously, it is the time when judgment has already begun. Just as surely as Jesus was already experiencing judgment during the one hour in the Garden of Gethsemane, so, too, God's final judgment at the end of the world has already begun.

This information that indicates that the phrase "one hour" is the entire Great Tribulation period also sheds light on Revelation 8:1, where we read:

And when he had opened the seventh seal, there was silence in heaven about the space of half an hour.

Remember earlier we learned that during the New Testament era there is the former or early rain and the latter rain. Remember we learned that the early rain identifies with the church age during which the firstfruits are brought in. Then when the churches' work has been finished, the two witnesses are killed. We learned that the killing of the two witnesses coincides with the beginning of the Great Tribulation. This time coincides with the withdrawal of the Holy Spirit from the churches and the beginning of the reign of Satan (the ten horns) in the churches.

However, after three and a half days (a time also called forty two months), the two witnesses stand on their feet and continue to testify. That is, after a period of great spiritual drought, the Gospel will again go into the world. That period of spiritual drought is the "about half an hour" of Revelation 8:1. It is the first part of the Great Tribulation period that coincides with the 2300 evening mornings of Daniel 8, the three and a half days of Revelation 11, and the forty two months of Revelation 11.

Unfortunately, this terrible condition in the churches and congregations will continue to the end of the world. However, the coming of the latter rain (the bringing of the true Gospel by those outside the churches), will make certain the salvation of the elect during the "one hour" of the Great Tribulation.

Thus, we can understand Matthew 24:24, which declares:

For there shall arise false Christs, and false prophets, and shall shew great signs and wonders; insomuch that, if it were possible, they shall deceive the very elect.

The days of the Great Tribulation are shortened in the sense that during the last part of the Great Tribulation, God is sending the latter rain so that a great multitude which no man can number shall be saved.

Returning to Revelation 17:16, 17, we read:

And the ten horns which thou sawest upon the beast, these shall hate the whore, and shall make her desolate and naked, and shall eat her flesh, and burn her with fire. For God hath put in their hearts to fulfil his will, and to agree, and give their kingdom unto the beast, until the words of God shall be fulfilled.

A Strong Delusion

In these verses, God is stating His plan and methodology by which He brings judgment on the churches wherein spiritual adultery abounds. God has withdrawn His loving concern for the safety and continuing nurture of the churches. Instead, He has sent upon the members of the churches a strong delusion (II Thessalonians 2:11), that they should believe a lie. Thus, God has put in their hearts to fulfill His will and to agree and give their kingdom to the beast.

These are terrible words. They echo the truth that the Holy Spirit is no longer working in the churches. Instead, it is God's plan that the blind follow their blind leaders into greater subjection to Satan who is now ruling in the churches.

Because God has given them a strong delusion (II Thessalonians 2:11), they do not see their danger. They do not realize how seriously sinful their situation has become. Only the true believers who are watching, who are on guard, will realize the true state of affairs that exists in the churches and will depart out of the churches, even as Christ has commanded.

The ten horns (Satan) shall make the churches desolate and increasingly sinful, thus preparing the members of those churches for the judgment of the last day. The phrase **"and burn her with fire"** (vs. 16) requires a closer look.

Burning with fire is the language of bringing judgment. It is a phrase taken from Jeremiah 34:3, where we read:

> **And thou shalt not escape out of his hand, but shalt surely be taken, and delivered into his hand; and thine eyes shall behold the eyes of the king of Babylon, and he shall speak with thee mouth to mouth, and thou shalt go to Babylon.**

We must remember that the end of the churches parallels and is anticipated by the destruction of Jerusalem in 587 B.C.

However, it was not Satan who pronounced judgment upon Jerusalem or upon the churches. He, as the king of Babylon in 587 B.C., as Satan himself in our day, is the means by which God is bringing judgment. This can be seen clearly by the statement of Revelation 18:8:

> **Therefore shall her plagues come in one day, death, and mourning, and famine; and she shall be utterly burned with fire: for strong is the Lord God who judgeth her.**

By Satan becoming ruler in the churches, God is showing that it is God's judgment that is upon the churches. And judgment is identified with fire for God is a consuming fire (Hebrews 12:29). Thus, Satan's rule in the churches indicates they have come under the judgment of God.

As we continue to examine the Biblical language concerning Babylon, we read in Revelation 18:2:

And he cried mightily with a strong voice, saying, Babylon the great is fallen, is fallen, and is become the habitation of devils, and the hold of every foul spirit, and a cage of every unclean and hateful bird.

In verse 18 of Revelation 14, the woman which is Babylon is called a great city. Great city, Babylon the great, is emphasizing that this was the external representation of the great kingdom, the kingdom of God. In Revelation 21:10 God speaks of the eternal kingdom as the **"great city, the holy Jerusalem."** However, in Revelation 17 and 18, it is called the great city of Babylon. This external representation of the kingdom of God has become a harlot.

Babylon Has Fallen

We read that Babylon has fallen (Revelation 14:8, 18:2). From where and to where has she fallen? Remember that the churches during the church age represented the kingdom of God. They were the most important entities on earth that related to the God of heaven. There was nothing else in the whole world that was held in the high esteem that God had for them.

But now they are fallen. Revelation 18:2 describes how low she has fallen. She has **"become the habitation of devils, and the hold of every foul spirit, and a cage of every unclean and hateful bird."**

This language emphasizes the fact that she has become totally identified with Satan and is under the wrath of God. It is similar in meaning to Matthew 24:15, **"the abomination of desolation, spoken of by Daniel the prophet, stand in the holy place."** She has fallen from being the chosen vessel of God to bring the Gospel to the world to being identified altogether with Satan.

As we continue in Revelation 18, we come to verse 3, where the Bible records:

For all nations have drunk of the wine of the wrath of her fornication, and the kings of the earth have committed fornication with her, and the merchants of the earth are waxed rich through the abundance of her delicacies.

Satan is, of course, the bitter and angry foe of Christ. The believers are the body of Christ. Throughout the church age, ordinarily, they were found in churches and congregations. He expresses His anger by causing the unsaved in the churches to commit spiritual fornication.

We are reminded of Satan's attempt to destroy Israel just before they crossed the Jordan River into the promised land. We read in Numbers 25:1-3:

> **And Israel abode in Shittim, and the people began to commit whoredom with the daughters of Moab. And they called the people unto the sacrifices of their gods: and the people did eat, and bowed down to their gods. And Israel joined himself unto Baalpeor: and the anger of the LORD was kindled against Israel.**

As we have learned, any time a church teaches a doctrine that is not in agreement with the Bible, it is engaging in spiritual harlotry. This is the kind of action Satan rejoices in. And when the Holy Spirit is no longer functioning in the churches, the opportunity for Satan to foster these adulterous actions is greatly increased.

The Kings of the Earth

As we consider Revelation 18:3 we read of **"the kings of the earth have committed fornication with her [*the harlot*]."** We must look at the phrase "kings of the earth." When we carefully study the Bible, the word "kings" is used in four ways. The first usage of the word "kings" points to our Lord Jesus Christ. He is King of kings and Lord of lords.

The second usage points to Satan as he, for example, is described using the illustration of the ten crowned horns as ten kings (Revelation 17:12).

The third is God's use of the word "kings" as He speaks about the secular or political rulers of the world. This includes the kings who ruled in the Old Testament as well as New Testament rulers such as King Agrippa. They are in view, for example, in Revelation 6:15, where we read:

> **And the kings of the earth, and the great men, and the rich men, and the chief captains, and the mighty men, and every bondman, and every free man, hid themselves in the dens and in the rocks of the mountains;**

The fourth use of the word "kings" is in connection with the true believers, as we read in Revelation 5:10:

> **And hast made us unto our God kings and priests: and we shall reign on the earth.**

The believers are in view, for example, in Revelation 1:5, where we read:

And from Jesus Christ, who is the faithful witness, and the first begotten of the dead, and the prince of the kings of the earth. Unto him that loved us, and washed us from our sins in his own blood,

Returning now to Revelation 17 and Revelation 18, we read about kings of the earth three times in these chapters. Who are these king? Are they political rulers or are they the true believers or are they unsaved members of the church?

We do know that Revelation 17 and Revelation 18 are focused entirely on the churches and congregations which are called Babylon. However, to understand which kings are in view in each of these three passages we must examine their context very carefully. The first citation we will examine is Revelation 17:2, which declares:

With whom the kings of the earth have committed fornication, and the inhabitants of the earth have been made drunk with the wine of her fornication.

We should note in this verse that the action of committing fornication is in the past tense. Therefore, it must be speaking about true believers who in the past, while they were members of the visible church, they committed fornication. This is because they were trusting the doctrines taught to them by the church. If any of those doctrines were contrary to the Bible it made those true believers commit spiritual fornication. Of course, from God's vantage point, they still remained the pure bride of Christ because all of their sins had been covered by the blood of Christ. Once they leave the church and are no longer required to be under its authority, that spiritual fornication can come to an end. There is no possibility that this verse is speaking about the secular or political kings of the earth. This is so because their spiritual fornication continues regardless of what happens to the churches.

In the same verse, God describes others in the church (Babylon) who are guilty of spiritual drunkenness. They closely identify with those whom we read about in Isaiah 28:7:

But they also have erred through wine, and through strong drink are out of the way; the priest and the prophet have erred through strong drink, they are swallowed up of wine, they are out of the way through strong drink; they err in vision, they stumble in judgment.

The Political Kings Are Ruled Over By Satan

The second citation where we read the phrase "kings of the earth" is Revelation 17:18, which reads:

And the woman which thou sawest is that great city, which reigneth over the kings of the earth.

In this verse Babylon, which had been the spiritual Jerusalem, is called the great city that reigns over the kings of the earth. In Revelation 21:10, the eternal church is called the great city. Jerusalem is the great city because it is the city of God. On this earth, it is the external representation of the kingdom of God. There exists no kingdom that is greater than the kingdom of God. Therefore, it is a tremendous honor for the churches and congregations to represent the kingdom God. This is the city that throughout the church age had been given the spiritual oversight of the believers, who in this verse are called the kings of the earth.

It is, of course, true that the Bible is God's law book that rules over every person in the world. This is proven by the fact that on the last day, each and every individual who has not become saved must answer the accusations of the law of God. Because the visible church has been mandated by God to faithfully declare the law of God (the Bible), to the world, therefore, in that sense, it rules over all the secular and political kings of the earth.

But who are these kings that the Bible refers to in this verse? Please note that the verb **"which reigneth"** is in the present tense. That means it is a reign that continues. We know, therefore, it cannot refer to the believers who have been driven out of the churches. The kings who are the true believers are no longer under the rule of the church once they leave the church. Therefore, the kings who are in view in this citation must be the political kings.

But does Babylon which had been spiritual Jerusalem rule over the secular or political kings? Indeed, yes! Satan is the ruler in the churches that have become Babylon. But as we learned earlier in our study, he is also the spiritual ruler of all the unsaved of the world. He has been given this authority by Christ who is, of course, King of kings and Lord of lords.

The rule of Satan over all the unsaved in the whole world is emphasized by Revelation 17:15, which declares:

And he saith unto me, The waters which thou sawest, where the whore sitteth, are peoples, and multitudes, and nations, and tongues.

Only when we become saved are we translated out of the dominion of darkness (Satan's kingdom) into the Kingdom of the Lord Jesus Christ.

All the World Became Spiritual Fornicators Beginning in the Garden of Eden

The third citation of the phrase "kings of the earth" is given in Revelation 18:3, where we read:

> **For all nations have drunk of the wine of the wrath of her fornication, and the kings of the earth have committed fornication with her, and the merchants of the earth are waxed rich through the abundance of her delicacies.**

Again, the verb "have committed" is in the past tense. Therefore, the kings being referred to must be the true believers who were at one time members of churches and therefore susceptible to spiritual fornication because of wrong doctrines held by their churches.

On the other hand, this verse begins with the statement "all nations have drunk of the wine of the wrath of her fornication." The verb "have drunk" is in the perfect past tense. This indicates the action was completed in the past. Thus, we can know that this statement must refer to Satan's success in defeating mankind in the Garden of Eden. At that time, the whole human race became fornicators in that they began to disobey their husband, the law of God. Romans 7:1-4 assures us that unsaved mankind is married to the law of God.

Later in our study, we will examine the last phrase in this verse, which discusses the merchants of the earth.

Returning to the phrase "kings of the earth," we find it once more. It is recorded in Revelation 18:9. There we read:

> **And the kings of the earth, who have committed fornication and lived deliciously with her, shall bewail her, and lament for her, when they shall see the smoke of her burning,**

Once again we find that the verbs "have committed" and "lived" are in the past tense. Therefore, again, we can know that these kings represent the true believers who before they were driven from the churches or before they obeyed God's command to leave the churches had committed spiritual fornication.

To summarize the teaching of the Bible concerning the kings of the earth, we can set forth these principles.

1. The only kings present in the churches and congregations are the true believers. All other references to kings of the earth must refer to the political kings or rulers of the world.

2. When these true believers hold doctrines taught to them by their church but which are contrary to the Word of God, they are engaging in spiritual fornication.

3. They do not continue in this spiritual fornication because they are driven out or they obey God's command to leave the churches. Fact is, they may be driven out because they refuse to continue in spiritual fornication.

4. Satan who reigns in the churches during the Great Tribulation is the same one who has caused the whole human race to drink of her fornicating wine (her false gospels) at the very beginning, when the serpent tempted Eve to sin.

5. Satan who reigns in the churches also reigns over the unsaved throughout the world.

The True Believers Are Merchants

As we continue our study we should examine the last phrase of Revelation 18:3, which declares, **"and the merchants of the earth are [were] waxed rich through the abundance of her delicacies."**
First of all, the verb "are" should be in the past tense, "were." These merchants, therefore, are like the kings of the earth who had in the past committed fornication. But later they are no longer becoming rich through the abundance of her delicacies. How are we to understand this? Who do these merchants represent?
Earlier, we learned that God portrays the sending forth of the Gospel as merchandising. Christ is portrayed as a merchant in the parable of Matthew 13:45. Therefore, we immediately suspect that the merchants in Revelation 18:3 are the true believers who had been very active bringing the Gospel in the churches and congregation.
But what does it mean that they had become rich through the abundance of her delicacies. First, let us recognize that the word "rich" identifies with the

situation of true believers. For example, in II Corinthians 9:11, we read:

> **Being enriched in every thing to all bountifulness, which causeth through us thanksgiving to God.**

And Ephesians 3:8 declares:

> **Unto me, who am less than the least of all saints, is this grace given, that I should preach among the Gentiles the unsearchable riches of Christ;**

And II Corinthians 8:9 is another example:

> **For ye know the grace of our Lord Jesus Christ, that, though he was rich, yet for your sakes he became poor, that ye through his poverty might be rich.**

Obviously, when we become saved we become rich beyond our wildest imagination. Just think, we become co-heirs with the Lord Jesus Christ. We become the inheritors of the new heaven and earth, etc.

But what about the word "delicacies." It is a Greek word that signifies luxury. Indeed, the Gospel is spiritually super luxurious. Just think, the true believer has been adopted as a son of God. The payment for each and every one of his sins has been paid. He lives out his life knowing that God will never leave him or forsake him. At any moment, he can enter God's throne room to speak to his heavenly Father. He has the Bible to guide him in all of his thoughts and actions. Indeed, these are luxuries of the highest magnitude.

In the phrase we are examining, the word "abundance" should more properly be translated as "power" or "strength." All of these magnificent delicacies that the true believer enjoys give him strength and courage to continue faithfully as a merchant bringing the Gospel. These wonderful, luxurious delicacies under the working of the Holy Spirit empowered the churches and congregations to continue the task of sending the Gospel into all the world.

While we are speaking of the merchants in Revelation 18:3, we should continue to examine the other verses of Revelation 18 that address the activities of these merchants. Revelation 18:11 declares:

> **And the merchants of the earth shall weep and mourn over her; for no man buyeth their merchandise any more:**

Remember the merchants represent the true believers as they, on behalf of the churches, are sending the Gospel into the world. The churches had been given this responsibility. But at the beginning of the Great Tribulation, the churches were no longer used of God to evangelize the world. The candlestick has been removed. The two witnesses have been killed. We have learned that the killing of the two witnesses coincides with the beginning of the Great Tribulation. We will learn that this time also coincides with the language of the Old Testament that teaches that the ships of Tarshish were wrecked. Let us briefly examine these ships.

In the Old Testament, God gives pictures or portraits of New Testament truth. This includes the concept that the sending forth of the Gospel is like merchandising. Remember earlier in our study we looked at Isaiah 55 and Proverbs 31 where God speaks of sending the Gospel out like it is merchandise. Remember in Matthew 13:45, 46, Christ is spoken of as a merchant who sold everything He had to buy one pearl.

In the Old Testament, God makes reference to Tyre and Sidon. These were seaports located just outside of Israel. From these seaports, merchant ships went all over the known world to bring gold, silver, precious stone, and all manner of valuable goods to Jerusalem. The ships that carried these goods were called ships of Tarshish, possibly because Tarshish was a major seaport on the far coast of the Mediterranean Sea. From this seaport, perhaps much merchandise was loaded on the ships that brought merchandise to Tyre and Sidon for delivery to Jerusalem.

Tyre and Sidon — A Portrait of the Church

In any case, Tyre and Sidon are written about particularly in Ezekiel 26 to Ezekiel 28 as a picture of the New Testament church as it sends the Gospel into all the world. The gold and other valuable cargo that comes into Jerusalem by means of these ships are the believers who are brought into the kingdom of God.

Ezekiel 27:25 declares:

The ships of Tarshish did sing of thee in thy market: and thou wast replenished, and made very glorious in the midst of the seas.

But the next verses, Ezekiel 27:26, 27, inform us:

Thy rowers have brought thee into great waters: the east wind hath broken thee in the midst of the seas. Thy riches, and thy fairs, thy

merchandise, thy mariners, and thy pilots, thy calkers, and the occupiers of thy merchandise, and all thy men of war, that are in thee, and in all thy company which is in the midst of thee, shall fall into the midst of the seas in the day of thy ruin.

But the Bible then says in verses 29-31:

And all that handle the oar, the mariners, and all the pilots of the sea, shall come down from their ships, they shall stand upon the land; And shall cause their voice to be heard against thee, and shall cry bitterly, and shall cast up dust upon their heads, they shall wallow themselves in the ashes: And they shall make themselves utterly bald for thee, and gird them with sackcloth, and they shall weep for thee with bitterness of heart and bitter wailing.

Please note the parallel language to that which we read in Revelation 18:11, 12:

And the merchants of the earth shall weep and mourn over her; for no man buyeth their merchandise any more: The merchandise of gold, and silver, and precious stones, and of pearls, and fine linen, and purple, and silk, and scarlet, and all thyine wood, and all manner vessels of ivory, and all manner vessels of most precious wood, and of brass, and iron, and marble,

In Revelation 18:15-17, God says:

The merchants of these things, which were made rich by her, shall stand afar off for the fear of her torment, weeping and wailing, And saying, Alas, alas, that great city, that was clothed in fine linen, and purple, and scarlet, and decked with gold, and precious stones, and pearls! For in one hour so great riches is come to nought. And every shipmaster, and all the company in ships, and sailors, and as many as trade by sea, stood afar off,

These merchants are the true believers who had been active during the church age bringing the Gospel. They had become rich in spiritual blessings as they engaged in this activity in obedience to God's command to send the Gospel into all the world.

The Ships Are Wrecked

But at the beginning of the Great Tribulation, God removed the candlestick from the churches. No longer did they have a gospel that God would bless as it was preached in the churches. This was because God the Holy Spirit was no longer applying the Gospel to the hearts of people to save them. Effectively, the ships of Tarshish had been wrecked. Those true believers who had a great spiritual concern to bring the true Gospel are driven out or have left the churches in obedience to the command to come out of Babylon. Yet they weep and wail because they are witnesses of the awful fact that God has begun to pour out judgment on the churches.

Incidentally, while looking at Tyre and Sidon as a portrait of the New Testament churches, we might note a solemn statement in Ezekiel 28:2. There God declares:

Son of man, say unto the prince of Tyrus, Thus saith the Lord GOD; Because thine heart is lifted up, and thou hast said, I am a God, I sit in the seat of God, in the midst of the seas; yet thou art a man, and not God, though thou set thine heart as the heart of God:

This verse summarizes the reason the churches have come under God's judgment. The prince of Tyrus is the spiritual rulers in the churches. They are to be humble servants of God faithfully preaching only what the Bible teaches. However, any doctrine that is taught by the churches that is not in agreement with the Bible and yet is taught as Biblical truth places the preacher in the position of being God. For example, when any doctrine is tested by its faithfulness to a Confession rather that its faithfulness to the Bible, the theologians in the church are taking the place of God. Or, for example, if the church teaches there can be divorce for any reason, then the spiritual rulers of the church have taken the place of God. They are sitting (ruling) in the seat (the throne) of God.

No wonder then that God declares in Ezekiel 28, verses 6-8:

Therefore thus saith the Lord GOD; Because thou hast set thine heart as the heart of God; Behold, therefore I will bring strangers upon thee, the terrible of the nations: and they shall draw their swords against the beauty of thy wisdom, and they shall defile thy brightness. They shall bring thee down to the pit, and thou shalt die the deaths of them that are slain in the midst of the seas.

The Plagues

As we continue our examination of Revelation 18, we should look most carefully at the next verse, Revelation 18:4:

And I heard another voice from heaven, saying, Come out of her, my people, that ye be not partakers of her sins, and that ye receive not of her plagues.

One might wonder how those who remain in the churches receive her plagues. How do they come under the judgment of God if they are true believers?

First of all, we must remember that true believers were given a new resurrected soul at the time they were saved. In their new resurrected soul, they never want to sin. Therefore, they have a great desire to obey God's commandments. Therefore, the command of God to come out of Babylon will impact them very greatly.

If they insist on remaining in the churches, they better ask the fair and honest question, "Am I truly a child of God? Is it really true that Christ is my Savior and King?" A pastor who remains in the church should ask himself the serious question, "Is it possible that I carry the mark of the beast given the fact that I continue to buy and sell (bring the Gospel) in the church?"

These are not idle questions. These questions must be asked by those who insist in remaining in their church. One judgment that will come is that God will send a strong delusion upon them, that they should believe a lie (II Thessalonians 2:11). Another judgment that will come upon them is that their children and any member of their family who are not saved cannot possibly become saved as long as they remain in the church. This is because the Holy Spirit is not in their midst. They will be in a situation where there may be bread and water (the true Gospel) but there will be a famine of hearing the Word of God. They will be in a situation where God says, **"Hearing ye shall hear, and shall not understand; and seeing ye shall see, and not perceive"** (Acts 28:26).

We are learning that there are two major shifts in God's Gospel plan for the world. The first is the shift from Old Testament Israel to the New Testament church age. Ever since Israel came out of Egypt in 1447 B.C. until Christ arose from the grave in A.D. 33, the nation of Israel was the congregation with which most believers identified. The temple in Jerusalem and the synagogues located in various cities of Israel were the houses of worship in which the Bible believers gathered.

However, when Jesus was announced as the Lamb of God, it marked the beginning of intense spiritual famine of hearing the Word of God. For three and a half years, very few were saved.

Immediately after this three and a half years, God made a major shift in the focus of the Gospel. No longer was the temple to have any part of the Gospel focus. No longer were people to go to the synagogues to hear Biblical truth. They now were to go to the churches that began to spring up all over the world.

This shift met with great resistance on the part of the leaders of the synagogues. Saul of Tarsus who later became Paul is an example. He was ready to physically murder people who left the synagogues to join the Christian movement. After he became saved, he became the target of these synagogue rulers. He was stoned and left for dead. He was beaten with rods on four different occasions. He indeed experienced the anger of the synagogue leaders.

However, the shift to the church age was God's plan. It began with Pentecost in A.D. 33 and continued until A.D. 1994, which officially ended the church age. The end of the church age identifies with the early rain that brought in the harvest of the firstfruits.

Finally, God's plan included one more shift. The shift was from the church age to the season of the latter rain that would bring in the end-time harvest. The latter rain season was also preceded by a period of a famine of hearing the Word of God. Even as the famine during Christ's ministry was precisely three and a half years, so this famine at the end of the church age is symbolically indicated to be three and a half days and as forty two months. Utilizing the Bible's methodology, we can see that the three and a half days is the same period as that spoken of as three and a half years. This three and a half years or forty two months season is not an actual literal season of three and a half years as was the situation during Christ's ministry. More likely it identifies literally with the 2300 evening mornings of Daniel 8. Thus, in all likelihood the Great Tribulation began in 1988.

The church age was the time the firstfruits were brought in. It was totally identified with Pentecost. Therefore, it is possible that the last year of the church age ended the day before the day in which Pentecost was observed in 1988. That would have been May 1988. It is curious and perhaps significant that 1988 is precisely the 13,000 year anniversary of the creation of the world.

Curiously and perhaps significantly, 2300 days after the day before Pentecost was observed arrives at September 6, 1994. This also is a day that identifies with the Old Testament feast days. If they are extended into the New Testament era, it would be the first day of the seventh month which during the Old Testament was a memorial of blowing of trumpets. Leviticus 23:24 records:

> **Speak unto the children of Israel, saying, In the seventh month, in the first day of the month, shall ye have a sabbath, a memorial of blowing of trumpets, an holy convocation.**

It was an especially important new moon (first day of a Jewish month) because it was during the seventh month that the Jubilee was observed (tenth day) and the feast of ingathering identifies with the final harvest which we are discovering also identifies with the latter rain.

The shift from the synagogue and temple era to the New Testament church era was, as we have already learned, greatly resisted by the religious rulers. Already during the three and a half years of Jesus' ministry, the Pharisees, the Sadducees, and the priests wanted Jesus killed. After the church age began, Paul and the other missionaries who were active, ordinarily experienced great opposition from the synagogues. Paul was stoned and left for dead. He was beaten with rods several times.

The synagogue at Berea was the exception to the rule in that they, **"received the word with all readiness of mind, and searched the scriptures daily, whether those things be so"** (Acts 17:11-15). However, even in this synagogue, eventually resistance to the church age developed. We read in Acts 17:13:

> **But when the Jews of Thessalonica had knowledge that the word of God was preached of Paul at Berea, they came thither also, and stirred up the people.**

We also know that at least two of the Pharisees, Nicodemus and Saul of Tarsus, and an honorable counselor, Joseph of Arimathaea (Mark 15:43) became believers. We also read that a great company of priests were obedient to the faith (Acts 6:7). But outside of these references, we know of no other leaders in the temple or synagogues who became believers. We also know that all the way to the present day, the leaders in the synagogues are still very much opposed to the churches that speak of Christ as the Savior.

Likewise, we can be sure that the shift from the church age to the season of the latter rain will be greatly misunderstood and greatly opposed by the leaders in the churches and congregations. We should pray that God will bring many of these leaders to truth so that they will understand and be obedient as God shifts from the church age to the latter rain season.

Could it be that even as there were many priests who became obedient to the faith (Acts 6:7), may there be many pastors, elders, and deacons who will become obedient to God's command to come out of Babylon.

Appendix B.
More Information on the Two Witnesses

The command to go into all the world with the Gospel had been given at the beginning of the church age. The carrying out of this command was typified by the two witnesses that we read about in Revelation 11. Revelation 11:3, 4 declares:

And I will give power unto my two witnesses, and they shall prophesy a thousand two hundred and threescore days, clothed in sackcloth. These are the two olive trees, and the two candlesticks standing before the God of the earth.

These two witnesses prophesy for a period of 1260 days which equals three and a half years. This figure must come from Daniel 9:27 where God speaks of a final seven of years called one week. There we read that the last half of this last week (seven) will go from the time of the cessation of sacrifice and offering (the time of the cross) to the time of the over spreading of abominations, until the consummation (the end of time). Thus, the two witnesses are to bring the Gospel all the way to the end of the world.

The three and a half years are spoken of as 1260 days to distinguish this period of time from the forty two months (also three and a half years), during which the temple was trodden under foot. The forty-two months symbolically represent the first part of the Great Tribulation season. It is the same period indicated in Revelation 13:5 during which Satan begins to rule in the churches and congregations. It is the period that goes from the official beginning of the Great Tribulation period (probably 1988), until the official end of the church age (1994).

On the other hand, the 1260 days represent the entire period from the cross to the end of the world. It is the same period during which the woman of Revelation 12 is nourished in the wilderness. This woman is first of all the true believers (the eternal invisible church) in the churches during the church age, and finally, include also the true believers during the latter rain. This 1260-day period is also called a time, times, and half a time (thus, a total of three and a half times), in Revelation 12:14. She is nourished (by God) from the face of the serpent (Satan). Thus, during the church age as well as during the latter rain season, the true believers need have no fear of Satan.

As we saw, the two witnesses are identified in Revelation 11:4 as two olive trees and two candlesticks. The two olive trees identify with the olive tree of Romans 11:16-24. This underscores the fact that these two witnesses represent true believers.

The two witnesses also identify with the two candlesticks. This immediately identifies with the church age. Revelation 1:20 and Revelation 2:1 teach us that symbolically, each church is represented by a candlestick amongst which Christ walks. The candlestick represents the light of the Gospel as it is sent out into the world during the church age by the churches and during the latter rain by the true believers who are altogether outside of the churches.

The number two (two witnesses, two olive trees, two candlesticks), identifies with true believers who faithfully bring the Gospel. Remember Jesus sent the twelve disciples out two and two (Mark 6:7) and the seventy by two and two (Luke 10:1).

The two witnesses of Revelation 11 embrace both the church age and the latter rain season. Note the language of Revelation 11:6, **"These have power to shut heaven, that it rain not in the days of their prophecy."** The period when the heavens are shut up is that time which divides the church age from the latter rain season.

One verse we must look at in connection with these two witnesses is Revelation 11:7, which declares:

> **And when they shall have finished their testimony, the beast that ascendeth out of the bottomless pit shall make war against them, and shall overcome them, and kill them.**

The duration of the time that the two witnesses lie dead is three and a half days. Utilizing a day for a year, this period during which the witnesses lie dead is symbolically three and a half years. As we have already learned, this is the first part of the Great Tribulation which also identifies with the 2300 evening mornings of Daniel 8.

The end of the three and a half days of Revelation 11 appears to coincide with the end of the 2300 days of Daniel 8. We read in Daniel 8:13, 14:

> **Then I heard one saint speaking, and another saint said unto that certain saint which spake, How long shall be the vision concerning the daily sacrifice, and the transgression of desolation, to give both the sanctuary and the host to be trodden under foot? And he said unto me, Unto two thousand and three hundred days; then shall the sanctuary be cleansed.**

The last phrase of verse 14 more correctly should be translated, "then shall the holy place be made righteous." During the church age, the holy place was the local church. But during the latter rain, the only holy place, that is, the place wherein the Holy Spirit is saving, is outside of the churches. Outside of the churches is where we find the true Gospel that is altogether free from a works-grace gospel. The latter rain, during which the end of the year harvest is brought in, thus officially may have begun 2300 days after the end of the church age and the beginning of the Great Tribulation. It is possible that the end of the church age ended in 1988. Thus, it is also possible that the beginning of the latter rain officially began in 1994.

Returning to the two witnesses, we learn that the dead two witnesses lie in the street of **"the street of the great city, which spiritually is called Sodom and Egypt, where also our Lord was crucified"** (Revelation 11:8). Jesus was crucified in Jerusalem. We learned earlier that during the Great Tribulation, Jerusalem identifies with the churches and congregations of our day. God now is speaking of them as Sodom and Egypt. We are reminded of the language of Revelation 18:2 where God speaks of the churches as Babylon which, **"is become the habitation of devils, and the hold of every foul spirit, and a cage of every unclean and hateful bird."**

We learned earlier that to be killed means to be driven from the churches. Verse 10 of Revelation 11 tells us why they were killed (driven from the churches). There we read:

> **And they that dwell upon the earth shall rejoice over them, and make merry, and shall send gifts one to another; because these two prophets tormented them that dwelt on the earth.**

Why had these two prophets tormented those that dwell on the earth? The answer can be found if we understand that true believers want truth and wish to declare truth. But truth begins with a fact that is unacceptable to the unsaved. The fact is that before we are saved, each one of us is dead in sin. We are under the wrath of God. This means we will eventually be dammed forever in hell. And we can't do anything to save ourselves. We have to trust totally on the mercy of God. This is an unacceptable doctrine to anyone who has not truly been saved.

Moreover, doctrines we have been taught in our church that are not altogether in harmony with the Word of God must be repudiated. Thus, our water baptism, our faith, our reaching out to God have nothing to do with our becoming saved. All of these ideas are reprehensible to those who are not truly saved.

The true believers want all of these wrong ideas to be corrected. They fear God and earnestly want all of their witnessing to be altogether faithful to the Bible.

Thus, when these two believers are killed (driven from the churches), there is great happiness in the churches. Now those who remain in the churches can do whatever they think is right without receiving the criticism of true believers who always insist that the congregation should be more faithful to the Word of God.

Revelation 11:7 informs us that these two witnesses will be killed when their work is finished. It is not finished in the ultimate sense because the period of the latter rain still must come. But it is finished insofar as the churches are concerned. God has used the churches for more than 1900 years (probably exactly 1955 years), as His means to send out the Gospel into all the world. By this means, the complete fullness (the 144,000 of Revelation 7), of all those who were to become saved as the churches sent the Gospel into all the world did become saved. We must remember the 144,000 is not an actual number. It is a symbolic number that signifies complete fulness.

But at the beginning of the Great Tribulation, the work of the churches was finished. Simultaneously, the Holy Spirit was no longer operating in the midst of the church. Satan, the abomination of desolation, has become the ruler of the churches. Those who insist on remaining in the churches are given a strong delusion by God that they should believe a lie (II Thessalonians 2:11). No wonder there is such happiness in the churches when the true believers are driven out.

However, the work of the two witnesses is not finished. There is still the season of the latter rain that must follow the first part (symbolically, three and a half days or forty two months or three and a half years) of the Great Tribulation. Revelation 11:11 declares:

And after three days and an half the Spirit of life from God entered into them, and they stood upon their feet; and great fear fell upon them which saw them.

At first blush, this might appear to indicate that the rapture is in view. This cannot be for several reasons. First of all, nowhere in the Bible does God use the language **"they stood upon their feet"** in connection with the language of the rapture.

Secondly, nowhere in connection with the rapture does the Bible speak of the Spirit of life entering those who are being raptured.

Furthermore, there are at least two passages in the Bible that use language very similar to this verse to record God's command to send forth the Gospel. The first is Ezekiel 2:1-4, where we read:

And he said unto me, Son of man, stand upon thy feet, and I will speak unto thee. And the spirit entered into me when he spake unto me, and set me upon my feet, that I heard him that spake unto me. And he said unto me, Son of man, I send thee to the children of Israel, to a rebellious nation that hath rebelled against me: they and their fathers have transgressed against me, even unto this very day. For they are impudent children and stiffhearted. I do send thee unto them; and thou shalt say unto them, Thus saith the Lord GOD.

Notice before Ezekiel is to be sent to speak to Israel, he is commanded to **"stand upon thy feet"** and then **"the spirit entered into me."** Note the parallel language to that of Revelation 11:11, **"the Spirit of life from God entered into them, and they stood upon their feet."**

Similarly, in Acts 26:16, the Apostle Paul was commanded to rise and stand upon his feet at the time he was commanded to bring the Gospel to the Gentiles. Therefore, we can be very certain that when the two witnesses stand on their feet as the Spirit of life from God enters into them, they are about to continue their witnessing. This signifies the witnessing of the true believers during the latter rain season.

We next read in Revelation 11:11, **"and great fear fell upon them which saw them."** What could this mean? Remember we learned that the emphasis of the latter rain preaching is, **"Fear God, and give glory to him"** (Revelation 14:7). The characteristic of the true believer is that he fears God. He works out his salvation (the salvation God has given him), with fear and trembling (Philippians 2:13)/

Therefore, those who see the true nature of the two witnesses (the believers during the latter rain season), will experience great fear as they hear the true Gospel being proclaimed. This will be the occasion of a great multitude which no man can number being saved.

In fact, the primary work of the true believers during the latter rain season will be to bring the Gospel to the world. Jesus said, **"Occupy till I come"** (Luke 19:13). In Mark 13:15, Jesus commands:

And let him that is on the housetop not go down into the house, neither enter therein, to take any thing out of his house:

To be "on the housetop" is to be busy proclaiming the Gospel. In Matthew 10:27, we read:

What I tell you in darkness, that speak ye in light: and what ye hear in the ear, that preach ye upon the housetops.

Being "on the housetop" identifies with publishing the Gospel. According to Mark 13:15, we are not to go into the house to take anything out of the house. The house identifies with the churches from which the true believers were driven out or were commanded to leave. We are not to go into the churches again. We are to stay on the housetop, that is, we are to diligently continue with the God-assigned task of bringing the true Gospel to the world. And we know that a great multitude will become saved during the latter rain season which coincides with the last part of the Great Tribulation.

We stand in awe as we see the opportunity God gives us at this time to send the true Gospel into all the world. Never before has the population of the world been as great as it presently is. It is more than six billion individuals, and it continues to grow at a rate of about ten thousand people added each and every hour of the day and night.

But simultaneously, God has provided magnificent means of communication. By radio, by satellite, by Internet, and by massive tract distribution the people of entire continents are potentially under the hearing of the true Gospel. A very high percentage of the peoples of the world can hear the Gospel in their own language. They can hear it seven days a week. They can hear it for a minimum of a whole hour once or twice a day. In many instances, they can hear it many hours each day. It seems very obvious that God has allowed all the electronic discoveries and inventions to take place at this time so that His last season, the season of the latter rain, would be facilitated so that in the briefest time, the whole world can hear the true Gospel.

Of course, a great many have the opportunity to hear false gospels. False gospels, too, can be found on the Internet and on the airways. However, it is the true Gospel that God has made available to the world. Thus, the prophecy of Revelation 7 might be fulfilled. Indeed, we believe that there is a great multitude which no man can number who are becoming saved at this time.

Significantly, the next experience of the two witnesses is that they are raptured. Revelation 11:12 declares:

And they heard a great voice from heaven saying unto them, Come up hither. And they ascended up to heaven in a cloud; and their enemies beheld them.

This harmonizes with those verses that teach that Jesus will return only after the last of the elect have become saved. In II Peter 3, God speaks about the end of the world and declares in verse 9:

The Lord is not slack concerning his promise, as some men count slackness; but is longsuffering to us ward, not willing that any should perish, but that all should come to repentance.

In Matthew 24:14, we read:

And this gospel of the kingdom shall be preached in all the world for a witness unto all nations; and then shall the end come.

We can now understand Matthew 24:22 which declares:

And except those days should be shortened, there should no flesh be saved: but for the elect's sake those days shall be shortened.

The Great Tribulation occurs at the very time that there is an explosion of population and amongst these people are many of God's elect. But if this is happening right at the time the church age has come to an end, and if the churches had been given the command to go into all the world with the Gospel, how will the elect who are part of this end-time exploding population become saved?

God provides the answer. For the sake of the elect who still must become saved, God dramatically causes the latter rain Gospel to be sent out into the world. Thus, the terrible impact of the Great Tribulation is shortened. We must remember that the Great Tribulation brought into place a most awful situation in the world. God had given the task of evangelizing the world to the New Testament churches. Therefore, during the church age, as they were engaged in this magnificent task, great blessing came to the churches. But great blessing came to the world as God blessed the Gospel that was sent out by the churches into the world.

Therefore, when the Great Tribulation began, it was tribulation for the churches and the world. It was Great Tribulation for the churches because the Holy Spirit was no longer in the midst of the churches, applying the Word of God to the lives of those who were hearing the Gospel.

But it was also Great Tribulation because the churches were no longer being used of God as a means by which God was saving people in the world. In other words, the Gospel impact of the churches has been reduced to zero.

No one will become saved through the ministrations of the churches.

However, for the sake of the elect who still must become saved, right in the middle of this time of Great Tribulation, God began His program of the latter rain.

The latter rain did not benefit the churches in any way. They remain under the judgment of God. Satan will rule in them all the way until the end. That is why Jeremiah was told not to pray for Judah. We read in Jeremiah 7:12-16:

> **But go ye now unto my place which was in Shiloh, where I set my name at the first, and see what I did to it for the wickedness of my people Israel. And now, because ye have done all these works, saith the LORD, and I spake unto you, rising up early and speaking, but ye heard not; and I called you, but ye answered not; Therefore will I do unto this house, which is called by my name, wherein ye trust, and unto the place which I gave to you and to your fathers, as I have done to Shiloh. And I will cast you out of my sight, as I have cast out all your brethren, even the whole seed of Ephraim. Therefore pray not thou for this people, neither lift up cry nor prayer for them, neither make intercession to me: for I will not hear thee.**

The ark of the covenant was placed in Shiloh when Israel came into the land of Canaan. But when it was taken out of Shiloh (I Samuel 4:10-11), it was never returned to Shiloh, like when God left the churches at the beginning of the Great Tribulation, He will not return. Therefore, we are not to pray that somehow this terrible judgment might be removed from the churches. Surely, we can continue to pray for individuals within the churches, but we are not to pray that the church as a divine organism might repent and again be used as God's servant to send the Gospel into the world.

God speaks of Judah and Jerusalem in Jeremiah 7:17 and in that context declares in Jeremiah 7:20:

> **Therefore thus saith the Lord GOD; Behold, mine anger and my fury shall be poured out upon this place, upon man, and upon beast, and upon the trees of the field, and upon the fruit of the ground; and it shall burn, and shall not be quenched.**

Therefore, now that the Great Tribulation is being experienced by the churches all over the world, we can be certain that this will be the terrible situation within them to the very end of time.

But what about the tribulation that impacts the world at the moment God is no longer using the churches to evangelize the world. Outside of the churches, there is an exploding population in which there must be many of God's elect.

It is for their sake that God begins to pour down the latter rain in the midst of the time of Great Tribulation. Outside of the churches, the Gospel goes forth so that the tribulation's impact upon the world is shortened. Indeed, there is a great final harvest of souls being brought into the kingdom of God.

Appendix C.
When Is The Rapture?

In the preface of this study, we saw that God had given those who hold the pre-millennium position on the return of Christ a remarkable glimpse of a faint outline of the events that occur at the end of time. However, we must look carefully at one of their doctrines, namely, the idea that the church age will come to an end because the believers have been raptured. This teaching is incorrect, and we should spend some time looking at the Biblical teaching that the time of the rapture can only be on the last day of this earth's existence.

One of the events that gives great comfort to the child of God is the rapture of the believers. By the word "rapture," theologians have in mind that moment in history when the believers in Christ who have not experienced physical death will be changed into their glorified bodies. At that time, they will be caught up in the air to be with Christ, as I Thessalonians 4:17 declares:

Then we which are alive and remain shall be caught up together with them in the clouds, to meet the Lord in the air: and so shall we ever be with the Lord.

A puzzling situation has developed, however, concerning the timing of the rapture. Some people believe that it will be 1007 years before the end of the world. Others believe the Bible teaches that it will be 1003.5 years before the end, while still others suggest 1000 years. Then there are those who teach that this grand event will occur right at the end of time.

Is the Biblical teaching concerning the timing of the rapture obscure? Why is the language of the Bible on this subject difficult to understand? One would surely wish to understand the Bible more clearly on these questions and thus to know more specifically how the believers will relate to the final tribulation period of which the Bible speaks. Moreover, a clear understanding of the timing of the rapture will greatly help us to understand many other details that relate to the end of time.

Wonderfully, the Bible has much to say about the rapture. It is not an event that is rarely alluded to in the Bible. The timing of the rapture in relation to judgment day and the end of time is extremely well documented in the Scriptures. We need have no doubt whatsoever concerning the rapture's place in the sequence of events that relate to Christ's return.

In this study, we will examine several different sets of Scriptures that deal with the rapture. As we go through these Scriptures, we will find many independent paths that lead us to the same inescapable conclusion: The rapture of the believers will occur at the end of time. The rapture will take place at the same time that our Lord comes to judge the world. It will come right at the time that the world is beginning to collapse and when God prepares to destroy the world by fire.

May we be grateful to our Lord for the abundant Biblical information He has provided on this important event. Let us look at the first of these paths.

The Last Trump and the Rapture

In I Corinthians 15:51-53, we read:

> **Behold, I shew you a mystery; We shall not all sleep, but we shall all be changed, In a moment, in the twinkling of an eye, at the last trump: for the trumpet shall sound, and the dead shall be raised incorruptible, and we shall be changed. For this corruptible must put on incorruption, and this mortal must put on immortality.**

In these verses, God discusses the fact that not everyone will die. (To fall asleep is Biblical language that signifies death.) There will be those who will instantaneously receive their resurrected bodies without first falling asleep. This language is clearly concerned with the rapture because verse 53 speaks about the believers receiving their immortal bodies.

God tells us when this event will occur. He declares that it will be at the sound of the last trump. This is a time clue; God is effectively saying that when the last trumpet sounds the rapture will occur.

If we follow the Biblical principle that the Bible interprets the Bible, we must search the Bible to find language that relates to the sound of the last trump. If such references can be found, perhaps they will tell us when the last trumpet will sound.

In Revelation 11:15-18 we read:

> **And the seventh angel sounded; and there were great voices in heaven, saying, The kingdoms of this world are become the kingdoms of our Lord, and of his Christ; and he shall reign for ever and ever. And the four and twenty elders, which sat before God on their seats, fell upon their faces, and worshipped God, Saying, We give thee thanks, O Lord God Almighty, which art, and wast, and**

art to come; because thou hast taken to thee thy great power, and hast reigned. And the nations were angry, and thy wrath is come, and the time of the dead, that they should be judged, and that thou shouldest give reward unto thy servants the prophets, and to the saints, and them that fear thy name, small and great; and shouldest destroy them which destroy the earth.

In this passage, God gives us an outline of the events that will accompany the sound of the seventh and last trump. At that time, the following becomes reality:

1. The time has come for the dead to be judged.

2. The time for the rewarding of the saints has come.

3. The time for destroying the destroyers has come.

In other words, the sounding of the seventh trumpet signals that judgment day has come. It signals that the time has come for the believers to receive their reward. It is the time that the forces of evil are to be cast into hell. Therefore, the sounding of the last trumpet must be at the end of time; it is at the end of time that judgment day occurs and Satan is thrown into the lake of fire.

We will recall that God effectively declares in I Corinthians 15:51-53 that the rapture of believers is to occur at the sound of the last trumpet. Since we have seen from Revelation 11 that at the sound of the seventh trumpet judgment day occurs, we can therefore know that the rapture is an event that will occur simultaneously with judgment day.

Incidentally, we might note that the reward the believers receive is their glorified resurrected bodies in which they will reign with Christ forever.

Sodom's Destruction and the Rapture

From I Corinthians 15:51-53 we have seen that the rapture is to occur at the time Christ returns to judge the world. Let us now look at a second path that will help us to see the timing of the rapture. In Luke 17:28-37 we read:

Likewise also as it was in the days of Lot; they did eat, they drank, they bought, they sold, they planted, they builded; But the same day that Lot went out of Sodom it rained fire and brimstone from

heaven, and destroyed them all. Even thus shall it be in the day when the Son of man is revealed. In that day, he which shall be upon the housetop, and his stuff in the house, let him not come down to take it away: and he that is in the field, let him likewise not return back. Remember Lot's wife. Whosoever shall seek to save his life shall lose it; and whosoever shall lose his life shall preserve it. I tell you, in that night there shall be two men in one bed; the one shall be taken, and the other shall be left. Two women shall be grinding together; the one shall be taken, and the other left. Two men shall be in the field; the one shall be taken, and the other left. And they answered and said unto him, Where, Lord? And he said unto them, Wheresoever the body is, thither will the eagles be gathered together.

In this passage, God uses the destruction of Sodom as a figure or type of the judgment of the last day. We will see that the saving of Lot and his family is a figure of the rapture, which will occur simultaneously with judgment day.

Just before the destruction of Sodom, God sent angels to rescue the family of Lot (Genesis 19). On the heels of this rescue operation, God rained down fire and brimstone upon Sodom and the other wicked cities and utterly destroyed them.

God declares in Luke 17:30, **"Even thus shall it be in the day when the Son of man is revealed."** Thus, Christ links the destruction of Sodom to judgment day. God also links the rescue of Lot and his family to the rapture. Note that God declares in verse 34, **"I tell you, in that night there shall be two men in one bed; the one shall be taken, and the other shall be left."**

The parallelism between the destruction of Sodom and the end of the world is clearly evident. Sodom, a wicked city ripe for judgment, is populated by two kinds of people: The wicked, who are to be destroyed, and the true believers, represented by Lot and his family, which is a tiny little remnant of the population of the wicked city.

So it is today, the world is mostly populated with those who are altogether rebellious against God. Amongst the vast population of the world there are the true believers, who are only a tiny percentage of the people.

Then judgment day came for Sodom. The cup of their iniquity was full. God utterly destroyed them for their sins, but just ahead of that judgment God rescued Lot. The rescue was so close in time to the poured out judgment of God that Lot's wife was destroyed in the judgment. So it will be at the end of time. When the nations have become ripe for judgment, God will send His angels to rescue the believers. Two will be in one bed; one will be taken and the other left. The one that is taken will be caught up in the air to be with Christ as I Thessalonians 4:17 teaches. The one that is left will be left to stand for judgment as the wicked of Sodom were left for judgment.

Thus, Christ teaches that the rapture will occur simultaneously with judgment day. There is complete agreement between the account of Jesus concerning the destruction of Sodom and the I Corinthians 15 account, which speaks of the rapture coming at the sound of the last trumpet.

The Noachian Flood and the Rapture

A third path of the Bible continues to give us vast assurance that the rapture will occur simultaneously with judgment day. This is found in the language Jesus utters when He compares the Flood with its events to Judgment day with its events. In Matthew 24:3-41 we read:

> **But as the days of Noe were, so shall also the coming of the Son of man be. For as in the days that were before the flood they were eating and drinking, marrying and giving in marriage, until the day that Noe entered into the ark, And knew not until the flood came, and took them all away; so shall also the coming of the Son of man be. Then shall two be in the field; the one shall be taken, and the other left. Two women shall be grinding at the mill; the one shall be taken, and the other left.**

In this passage, God sets up parallel language that relates the Flood that destroyed the world of Noah's day to Jesus' return. This parallelism, which indicates that the destruction of the world in the Noachian Flood was a type or figure of judgment day, is also set forth in II Peter 3, verses 3-7, where we read:

> **Knowing this first, that there shall come in the last days scoffers, walking after their own lusts, And saying, Where is the promise of his coming? for since the fathers fell asleep, all things continue as they were from the beginning of the creation. For this they willingly are ignorant of, that by the word of God the heavens were of old, and the earth standing out of the water and in the water: Whereby the world that then was, being overflowed with water, perished: But the heavens and the earth, which are now, by the same word are kept in store, reserved unto fire against the day of judgment and perdition of ungodly men.**

From the Flood account given in Genesis 7, we see that seven days before the Flood, God gave Noah notice that the Flood would come in seven days. Therefore, Noah and his family were to go into the ark.

Genesis 7:1: **And the LORD said unto Noah, Come thou and all thy house into the ark; for thee have I seen righteous before me in this generation.**

Genesis 7:4: **For yet seven days, and I will cause it to rain upon the earth forty days and forty nights; and every living substance that I have made will I destroy from off the face of the earth.**

The Flood did indeed come seven days after the notice was given as we learn from Genesis 7:10, **"And it came to pass after seven days, that the waters of the flood were upon the earth."**

The Bible then records the precise date of the Flood, together with the information that Noah actually entered the ark the same day that the Flood came. We read this in Genesis 7:11-13:

In the six hundredth year of Noah's life, in the second month, the seventeenth day of the month, the same day were all the fountains of the great deep broken up, and the windows of heaven were opened. And the rain was upon the earth forty days and forty nights. In the selfsame day entered Noah, and Shem, and Ham, and Japheth, the sons of Noah, and Noah's wife, and the three wives of his sons with them, into the ark.

Christ teaches that the peoples of Noah's day continued eating and drinking until the day that Noah entered the ark and the Flood swept them away. Luke 17:27 reads:

They did eat, they drank, they married wives, they were given in marriage, until the day that Noe entered into the ark, and the flood came, and destroyed them all.

Certainly, we can see the parallelism that exists between the Flood and judgment day. Noah and his family lived in a world cursed by sin; and at judgment day, believers will exist as a tiny remnant in a world cursed by sin. When the Flood was to begin, Noah and his family entered into the ark, a haven of safety for them; and at judgment day, the believers will be raptured while the unsaved will be judged and removed into hell. **"Then shall two be in the field; the one shall be taken, and the other left"** (Matthew 24:40). The one taken is like Noah. Even as Noah went into the safety of the ark, so the believer is caught up to the safety of Christ. The one left is left for judgment, even as the people outside the ark were left for judgment. Once again, therefore, we see that the rapture occurs simultaneously with judgment day.

When Christ rose from the grave, He showed the resurrection to be a fact by many proofs (Acts 1:3). Likewise, His teaching concerning the timetable of the rapture is set forth in many places in the Bible. We shall now look at a fourth path in the Bible where this truth is taught.

The Resurrection of the Dead and the Rapture

In I Thessalonians 4:14-17 we find one of the most frequently quoted passages concerning the rapture. We shall begin with this passage in our discussion of the fourth path that shows the timing of the rapture. There we read:

For if we believe that Jesus died and rose again, even so them also which sleep in Jesus will God bring with him. For this we say unto you by the word of the Lord, that we which are alive and remain unto the coming of the Lord shall not prevent them which are asleep. For the Lord himself shall descend from heaven with a shout, with the voice of the archangel, and with the trump of God: and the dead in Christ shall rise first: Then we which are alive and remain shall be caught up together with them in the clouds, to meet the Lord in the air: and so shall we ever be with the Lord.

The first truth that we shall look at in this passage is the fact that the rapture will be on the same day as the resurrection of our bodies. God indicates that at His coming He will bring with Him those who have fallen asleep. In II Corinthians 5:8 God clearly teaches that to be absent from the body is to be present with the Lord. When Christians die, because they were given their resurrection souls at the time of their salvation, in their souls they can go to be with Christ. In this condition they live and reign with Him in heaven.

At Christ's return all those who have died, that is, who have fallen asleep, and who have been living with Christ in heaven, will come with Him, as I Thessalonians 4:14 teaches. Then the graves are to be opened and the bodies of those who have died will be resurrected. At the same time, all the believers who have not died will be given their resurrected bodies. Immediately following this, the resurrected bodies from the graves, together with the believers who have not died but who have been given their new bodies instantaneously, will be caught up in the air to be with the Lord forever. Only the unsaved will remain on the earth to face the wrath of God, which will be poured out upon them because of their sins.

We want to look more closely at the fact of these resurrected bodies. The Bible teaches the precise time when these bodies will be resurrected, and since, as we have just seen, the rapture will occur simultaneously with the resurrection of the bodies of the believers, the determination of the time of the resurrection of the bodies of the believers will give us the timetable of the rapture. In John 6 Jesus declares four times that the resurrection of believers' bodies will occur on the last day.

John 6:39: **And this is the Father's will which hath sent me, that of all which he hath given me I should lose nothing, but should raise it up again at the last day.**

John 6:40: **And this is the will of him that sent me, that every one which seeth the Son, and believeth on him, may have everlasting life: and I will raise him up at the last day.**

John 6:44: **No man can come to me, except the Father which hath sent me draw him: and I will raise him up at the last day.**

John 6:54: **Whoso eateth my flesh, and drinketh my blood, hath eternal life; and I will raise him up at the last day.**

The phrase **"the last day"** is quite significant. It is found only eight times in the Bible. Since God chooses words very carefully, we know this phrase has been selected to signify important truth.

Let us look at this phrase for a moment. As we have already seen, it is used four times in John 6. The other four references are as follows.

John 11:24: **Martha saith unto him, I know that he shall rise again in the resurrection at the last day.**

John 12:48: **He that rejecteth me, and receiveth not my words, hath one that judgeth him: the word that I have spoken, the same shall judge him in the last day.**

John 7:37: **In the last day, that great day of the feast, Jesus stood and cried, saying, If any man thirst, let him come unto me, and drink.**

Nehemiah 8:18: **Also day by day, from the first day unto the last day, he read in the book of the law of God. And they kept the feast seven days; and on the eighth day was a solemn assembly, according unto the manner.**

Quickly we see that in John 11:24 God is showing us that Martha understood the truth that is offered in the four verses of John 6. The resurrection of believers is the last day.

From John 12:48, we discover that the last day is judgment day, when God will have all the unsaved give account of their sins, and He will remove them into hell to pay for their sins. Thus, we see that the resurrection of believers, which is also to occur the last day, is simultaneous with judgment day.

Since we saw from I Thessalonians 4:14-17 that the resurrection of our bodies is the same day as the rapture, we know from these verses that the rapture occurs simultaneously with judgment day.

Before we look at the remaining two references to the "last day," let us think a bit longer on John 12:48. If judgment day is the last day, then the resurrection of the unsaved must be the last day, for Revelation 20:13 indicates that the sea gave up the dead, and death and hell gave up the dead, and all were judged and cast into the lake of fire. So, the resurrection of unbelievers is the last day. There must be one general resurrection of both the saved and the unsaved on the last day. Under no circumstances are we to understand that the believers are resurrected at one time and the wicked another time.

The Bible teaches in John 5:28-29:

The hour is coming, in the which all that are in the graves shall hear his voice, And shall come forth; they that have done good, unto the resurrection of life; and they that have done evil, unto the resurrection of damnation.

In other words, everyone will be resurrected at the moment of Christ's return. No one will be left in the grave. In I Thessalonians 4:16 we read that the believers will hear the shout of a command. John 5:28-29 shows that the unbelievers, too, will hear that shout, for there our Lord declares, **"all that are in the graves shall hear his voice."**

John 5:29 says that those who come forth from the tombs will go to one of two destinations. Those who have done good, that is, those who have had their sins covered by Christ's righteousness, will be resurrected to life. Those who have done evil, that is, the unsaved, who have not had their sins covered, will be resurrected to judgment and damnation.

We have compared the Scriptures that speak of the "last day" with I Thessalonians 4:14-17 and John 5:28-29 and discovered that the Bible clearly teaches that the rapture, the resurrection of believers, the resurrection of unbelievers, and Judgment day all occur at the end of time. Isn't it marvelous how all these verses fit together so perfectly?

We have looked at six of the eight verses in the Bible that use the phrase "last day." The two remaining are:

John 7:37: **In the last day, that great day of the feast, Jesus stood and cried, saying, If any man thirst, let him come unto me, and drink.**

Nehemiah 8:18: **Also day by day, from the first day unto the last day, he read in the book of the law of God. And they kept the feast seven days; and on the eighth day was a solemn assembly, according unto the manner.**

The Last Day of the Feast of Tabernacles

We should also look at these to make certain that we are checking everything that relates to the phrase "last day." Both of these references are related to the feast of tabernacles. The fact is, both speak of the last day of the feast of tabernacles.

What does the last day of the feast of tabernacles have to do with the rapture or judgment day? We shall see that it is intimately involved with these subjects.

Let us look at the nature of the feast of tabernacles. It was a feast commemorating two events. First, it looked back on Israel's sojourn in the wilderness, and second, it was the time of the completion of the harvest.

In Leviticus 23:42-43, we read:

Ye shall dwell in booths seven days; all that are Israelites born shall dwell in booths: That your generations may know that I made the children of Israel to dwell in booths, when I brought them out of the land of Egypt: I am the LORD your God.

It was celebrated beginning on the fifteenth day of the seventh month as we read in Leviticus 23:34:

Speak unto the children of Israel, saying, The fifteenth day of this seventh month shall be the feast of tabernacles for seven days unto the LORD.

These verses teach that it was a feast that looked back on the wilderness sojourn of Israel, and how they entered the promised land, the land of rest. So, too, believers today are living in the wilderness of this world.

When Christ comes, our rest in Him will be complete. We are strangers and pilgrims now, but when we receive our resurrected bodies we will be forever with Christ (II Thessalonians 4:17). Therefore, we can see how this feast identifies with Christ's return: It is then that we receive our resurrected bodies. It is then that our salvation is complete; it is then that our wilderness sojourn is ended.

The second reason for the feast of tabernacles was the celebration of the end of the harvest. In Exodus 23:16 we read of, **"The feast of ingathering, which is in the end of the year, when thou hast gathered in thy labours out of the field."** This is a surprising verse because it speaks of the Feast of Ingathering, which is the same as the feast of tabernacles, as the end of the year.

This is the same feast the Bible speaks of in Leviticus 23:39, 40, where we read:

Also in the fifteenth day of the seventh month, when ye have gathered in the fruit of the land, ye shall keep a feast unto the LORD seven days: on the first day shall be a sabbath, and on the eighth day shall be a sabbath. And ye shall take you on the first day the boughs of goodly trees, branches of palm trees, and the boughs of thick trees, and willows of the brook; and ye shall rejoice before the LORD your God seven days.

Clearly, it was a feast that celebrated, on the one hand, the bringing in of the end-of-the-year harvest, and on the other hand, the completion of the wilderness sojourn.

The Feast of Tabernacles was celebrated beginning on the fifteenth day of the seventh month (Leviticus 23:34). The seventh month is many months from the end of the year and yet God speaks of it as the "end" or "going out" of the year (Exodus 23:16).

When we see how intimately this feast is related to the end of time, we can see why God speaks of it as the end of the year.

Jesus speaks in Matthew 13 of His return at the harvest time (Matthew 13:30 and 39).

Matthew 13:30: **Let both grow together until the harvest: and in the time of harvest I will say to the reapers, Gather ye together first the tares, and bind them in bundles to burn them: but gather the wheat into my barn.**

Matthew 13:39: **The enemy that sowed them is the devil; the harvest is the end of the world; and the reapers are the angels.**

Since the Feast of Tabernacles celebrated the harvest and related it to the end of the year, and since Christ speaks of the end of the world as a harvest time, we can see that a beautiful relationship exists between the Feast of Tabernacles and the end of the world.

It is no wonder, then, that the phrase "last day" is found in connection with the resurrection of believers, Judgment day, and the Feast of Tabernacles.

The following chart shows these relationships.

Feast of Tabernacles	End of world
End of year	End of time
Harvest time for crops	Harvest time for mankind
End of wilderness sojourn for Israel	End of wilderness sojourn for believers
Last day (Exodus 23:16)	Last day (John 12:48, John 6:39-40)

Thus, we can see why in Nehemiah 8:18 and John 7:37 God used the phrase "last day" in connection with the Feast of Tabernacles. Before we leave the feast of tabernacles, one other important fact should be noted, which links the feast of tabernacles to the last day or the end of time. In the Old Testament, all the men of Israel were required to appear before the Lord three times during the year, as is recorded in Exodus 23:14-17:

> Three times thou shalt keep a feast unto me in the year. Thou shalt keep the feast of unleavened bread: thou shalt eat unleavened bread seven days, as I commanded thee, in the time appointed of the month Abib; for in it thou camest out from Egypt: and none shall appear before me empty: And the feast of harvest, the firstfruits of thy labours, which thou hast sown in the field: and the feast of ingathering, which is in the end of the year, when thou hast gathered in thy labours out of the field. Three times in the year all thy males shall appear before the Lord GOD.

The first feast was the feast of unleavened bread that began with and was identified with the Passover. This feast began in the evening of the fourteenth day of the first month (Leviticus 23:5) and continued for seven days after the fifteenth day (Leviticus 23:6, Deuteronomy 16:1 3). It was the day that anticipated the shedding of Christ's blood as the Passover Lamb to take away the sins of the world. It brought in the first of the firstfruits, the Lord Jesus.

The second feast was the feast of harvest or the "firstfruits" or "feast of weeks." This feast was observed seven full weeks from the morrow after the Sabbath, that is, the Sabbath that occurred during the Passover week (Leviticus 23:15 16 and Deuteronomy 16:9). Because this feast was fifty days after the Passover, it was also called Pentecost (penta is groups of five). It was a day that anticipated the spiritual harvest that would begin as a result of Christ going to the cross. It brought in all those who would become saved throughout the church age. They are the Pentecostal firstfruits harvest.

The third feast at which the males had to appear before the Lord was the feast of tabernacles, which was preceded by the day of atonement (the tenth day of the seventh month). The feast of tabernacles continued for eight days from the fifteenth day of the seventh month (Leviticus 23:27, 34, 39). It was a feast day, as we shall see, that anticipated the completion of the spiritual harvest that would result from the salvation God provided through the Lord Jesus Christ.

The awe-inspiring fact that now faces us is that while these feast days anticipated and pointed to the historical accomplishments of the atonement, on the very same days that the nation of Israel was celebrating these feasts, God brought to pass the spiritual reality to which these days pointed. On the Passover in A.D. 33, while the Jews were keeping the Passover, Jesus hung on the cross as the Passover Lamb. On the Jewish Feast of Pentecost, the Old Testament Feast of Weeks, the Holy Spirit was poured out and the harvest of souls began. It was at that time that the firstfruits of the harvest were seen: 3,000 from eighteen nations were saved (Acts 2:41).

So we see that two of the three most important feasts, those specifically emphasized as times when Jewish men journeyed to Jerusalem, were the literal times when God's program of redemption was carried out. The Jewish Passover was celebrated the very day that Christ, the Passover Lamb, was slain. The Jewish feast of the firstfruits, Pentecost, was observed the very day that God poured out His Holy Spirit, and the firstfruits of the spiritual harvest were seen.

The one remaining feast day is the Feast of Tabernacles or the Feast of Ingathering. We can speculate that the Bible is suggesting that it is possible that Christ may return in literal fulfillment of this feast, even as there was literal identification with the other two important feasts!

It is no wonder, then, that God uses the phrase "last day" in connection with the feast of tabernacles. The feast of tabernacles is identified with Christ's return, just as the resurrection of our bodies and Judgment day are identified with Christ's return.

We see, therefore, that in all eight places where the phrase "last day" is found in the Bible, it points to the end of time. It points to the end of the earth's existence, when Christ will return in judgment.

Returning now to I Thessalonians 4:14-17, we have seen that the rapture will occur simultaneously with the resurrection of believers. From John 6 we have seen that the resurrection of believers is the last day. From John 12 and from the "last day" references to the Feast of Tabernacles, we have seen that the last day is judgment day. Moreover, we have seen that these truths agree precisely with the statement of John 5:28-29, which speaks of one general resurrection at Christ's return.

We have seen that I Thessalonians 4, when looked at in the light of John 6 and the other passages that tell us when the resurrection of believers will occur, ties the rapture to the same day as judgment day and the end of time.

Thus, this fourth path we have followed agrees precisely with the three we examined earlier.

The Tribulation and the Rapture

Thus far we have seen from four separate and distinct Biblical paths that the rapture must be on the last day of this earth's existence. It must be simultaneous with the resurrection of all humanity and with judgment day. But the Bible has more to say about this. Let us look at this question from another viewpoint.

In Matthew 24, Christ gives us an outline of the signs or events that will take place just before the end of the world. He declares in Matthew 24:21-31:

For then shall be great tribulation, such as was not since the beginning of the world to this time, no, nor ever shall be. And except those days should be shortened, there should no flesh be saved: but for the elect's sake those days shall be shortened. Then if any man shall say unto you, Lo, here is Christ, or there; believe it not. For there shall arise false Christs, and false prophets, and shall shew great signs and wonders; insomuch that, if it were possible, they shall deceive the very elect. Behold, I have told you before. Wherefore if they shall say unto you, Behold, he is in the desert; go not forth: behold, he is in the secret chambers; believe it not. For as the lightning cometh out of the east, and shineth even unto the west; so shall also the coming of the Son of man be. For wheresoever the carcase is, there will the eagles be gathered together. Immediately after the tribulation of those days shall the sun be darkened, and the moon shall not give her light, and the stars shall fall from heaven, and the powers of the heavens shall be shaken: And then shall appear the sign of the Son of man in heaven: and then shall all the tribes of the earth mourn, and they shall see the Son of man coming in the clouds of heaven with power and great glory. And he shall send his angels with a great sound of a trumpet, and they shall gather together his elect from the four winds, from one end of heaven to the other.

When we examine these verses, we shall see that the rapture not only immediately follows the final tribulation, which believers must endure, but that it will occur simultaneously with the end of the world. Thus, it must occur simultaneously with judgment day.

In verses 21 and 22, God speaks of the increasingly great tribulation that will come upon the earth. For the sake of the elect, this tribulation will be shortened. Earlier in this study, we discovered the implication of this tribulation.

Who Are the Elect?

We should ascertain who **"the elect"** are who are spoken of in verse 22. God uses the word **"elect"**, which is the Greek *eklektos*, some twenty three times in the New Testament.

Some teach that the "elect" refers only to believing Jews on the grounds that Matthew 24 relates only to the nation of Israel and not to the Gentiles. If we were to follow this line of thought, and declare Matthew 24 is only for the Jews inasmuch as Jesus was speaking to the disciples who were Jews, then we could logically argue that John 3 has no reference to Gentiles because Christ was speaking to Nicodemus, who was a Jew. On that basis, only Jews must be born again to enter the kingdom of heaven. Likewise, the Book of Romans has no import for us today because it was addressed to the church at Rome. And Isaiah and Jeremiah have no interest for Gentiles because these prophets were sent primarily to Israel. On this basis, only certain books of the Bible would be considered pertinent and authoritative for the New Testament believers.

We immediately sense the error of this line of Biblical interpretation. The Bible says in II Timothy 3:16 that all Scripture is profitable for doctrine, for reproof, for teaching, etc. All the Bible is to be studied and obeyed. Matthew 24 is to be read and studied by Gentiles and Jews as carefully as John 3 or any other part of the Bible.

The fact is, when we read Matthew 24 carefully, we see that God is discussing the whole world. In verse 24 He speaks of the Gospel going to every nation. In verses 28 to 31 He speaks of His return in power and great glory. He will not return to the Jews only. He will return to the whole world. Therefore, the warnings of Matthew 24 are to the whole world. The statement of Matthew 24 is as important to Gentiles as I Thessalonians 4:14 or any other passage of the Bible.

Returning to the Greek word for "elect," as found in Matthew 24:22, we find that in the King James Bible it is translated as "chosen" or as "elect." Examining the twenty three places where *eklektos* is used, we see very quickly that the Bible is speaking of those who are elected of God to be believers. This can be seen in such passages such as:

Matthew 20:16: **So the last shall be first, and the first last: for many be called, but few chosen.**

Revelation 17:14: **These shall make war with the Lamb, and the Lamb shall overcome them: for he is Lord of lords, and King of kings: and they that are with him are called, and chosen, and faithful.**

Romans 8:33: **Who shall lay any thing to the charge of God's elect? It is God that justifieth.**

Colossians 3:12: **Put on therefore, as the elect of God, holy and beloved, bowels of mercies, kindness, humbleness of mind,** meekness, longsuffering.

Titus 1:1: **Paul, a servant of God, and an apostle of Jesus Christ, according to the faith of God's elect, and the acknowledging of the truth which is after godliness.**

Since the believers are the elect, and since Matthew 24:22 teaches that the tribulation will be shortened for the sake of the elect, we see that the believers will be present through the final tribulation. Thus, on the basis of this verse alone, we have trouble with a doctrine that teaches that the rapture will occur before this final Great Tribulation.

Returning to Matthew 24, we see that God gives us a very careful chronology that covers the relationship of the final Great Tribulation to the return of Christ. In Matthew 24:29-30 God declares:

Immediately after the tribulation of those days shall the sun be darkened, and the moon shall not give her light, and the stars shall fall from heaven, and the powers of the heavens shall be shaken: And then shall appear the sign of the Son of man in heaven: and then shall all the tribes of the earth mourn, and they shall see the Son of man coming in the clouds of heaven with power and great glory.

This tells us emphatically that the last event before the return of Christ is the tribulation spoken of in Matthew 24:21-22. The words "immediately after" do not allow for any passage of time between the tribulation and the events spoken of in verses 29-31.

The events that immediately follow the tribulation, the sun is darkened and the moon does not give its light, indicate that it is the end of time.

From our study of Matthew 24, we see that God's timetable for the rapture of believers is at the end of time. It is immediately after the Great Tribulation and coincides with judgment day. How marvelous God is to give us so many proofs concerning the timing of the rapture!

Thus far we have found five plain and distinctive paths that reveal the rapture will be at the end of time. Let us now look at a sixth path found in the Bible.

The Man of Sin and the Rapture

In II Thessalonians 2 we discover more information that points to the rapture at the end of time. In this passage God teaches us that two events must happen before He will come for His believers. The first is the rebellion and the second is that the man of sin must be revealed. The man of sin will be revealed at the coming of the Lord Jesus Christ, at which time Christ will slay him with the breath of His mouth. That is, the wicked will be cast into hell. Let us read these verses, II Thessalonians 2:1-9:

> **Now we beseech you, brethren, by the coming of our Lord Jesus Christ, and by our gathering together unto him, That ye be not soon shaken in mind, or be troubled, neither by spirit, nor by word, nor by letter as from us, as that the day of Christ is at hand. Let no man deceive you by any means: for that day shall not come, except there come a falling away first, and that man of sin be revealed, the son of perdition; Who opposeth and exalteth himself above all that is called God, or that is worshipped; so that he as God sitteth in the temple of God, shewing himself that he is God. Remember ye not, that, when I was yet with you, I told you these things? And now ye know what withholdeth that he might be revealed in his time. For the mystery of iniquity doth already work: only he who now letteth will let, until he be taken out of the way. And then shall that Wicked be revealed, whom the Lord shall consume with the spirit of his mouth, and shall destroy with the brightness of his [Christ's] coming: Even him [Christ], whose coming is after [should be translated "against"] the working of Satan with all power and signs and lying wonders.**

Who is the "man of sin"? If we understand that he is Satan himself, as he works through his emissaries called false prophets or false christs, we will have total Biblical validation. We find in these verses that he is worshipped as God. Revelation 13:4 speaks of the dragon, who is Satan, being worshipped:

> **And they worshipped the dragon which gave power unto the beast: and they worshipped the beast, saying, Who is like unto the beast? who is able to make war with him?**

Thus, the language of II Thessalonians 2, which speaks of the man of sin being worshipped, points to Satan as being the man of sin. How can Satan be called a man? Isn't he a fallen angel? We shall see that he is called a man because he was typified by the king of Babylon who, of course, was a man.

In Isaiah 14 we read of the fall of Lucifer and from the context we know that Lucifer is Satan. God refers to Lucifer as a man in Isaiah 14:16:

They that see thee shall narrowly look upon thee, and consider thee, saying, Is this the man that made the earth to tremble, that did shake kingdoms?

Satan is called a man because this activity was prefigured by the king of Babylon (Isaiah 14:4). As Revelation 18 teaches, Babylon is used often in the Bible as a figure of the kingdom of Satan. Thus, we see the parallelism that exists. On the one hand, we have Babylon, which is ruled over by the king of Babylon. On the other hand, we have Satan's dominion, which is ruled over by Satan. Thus, Satan rules over Babylon.

The man of sin, Satan, takes his seat in the temple. To what does taking one's seat refer? Jesus is seated at the right hand of God and rules over everything (Ephesians 1:20-22). Thus, to take a seat is Biblical language that means to rule or have authority. The man of sin, Satan, takes his seat or rules in the temple.

To what does the "temple" refer? Is there to be a literal reconstruction of the temple? Nowhere in the Bible do we read of a future reconstruction of the temple in Jerusalem. The fact is, since the veil of the temple was rent when Jesus hung on the cross, the temple in Jerusalem ceased to have significance as a holy place. Rather, the Bible speaks of the body of believers as being the temple. We read in Ephesians 2:19-21:

Now therefore ye are no more strangers and foreigners, but fellowcitizens with the saints, and of the household of God; And are built upon the foundation of the apostles and prophets, Jesus Christ himself being the chief corner stone; In whom all the building fitly framed together groweth unto an holy temple in the Lord.

In I Peter 2:5, we read:

Ye also, as lively stones, are built up a spiritual house, an holy priesthood, to offer up spiritual sacrifices, acceptable to God by Jesus Christ.

In I Corinthians 3:16, God emphasizes that the body of believers is the temple. He declares, **"Know ye not that ye are the temple of God, and that the Spirit of God dwelleth in you?"**

Therefore, we see very clearly that the temple consists of the churches which are the external, corporate representation of the kingdom of God. It is here that Satan will operate as the man of sin. We know that before Christ comes again, the man of sin (Satan) must take his seat (rule) in the temple (the church or body of believers) where he will be worshipped as God. Since he is a spirit, he cannot be seen literally to rule amongst the body of believers. He can rule, however, through false prophets and pseudo christs who bring a gospel other than the true Gospel. The Bible speaks of this kind of activity in II Corinthians 11:13-14:

> **For such are false apostles, deceitful workers, transforming themselves into the apostles of Christ. And no marvel; for Satan himself is transformed into an angel of light.**

Similarly, we read in Matthew 24:24:

> **For there shall arise false Christs, and false prophets, and shall shew great signs and wonders; insomuch that, if it were possible, they shall deceive the very elect.**

These verses emphasize the utter deceitfulness of Satan in this effort. The gospel he brings is so much like the true Gospel that even the elect would be deceived if that were possible.

Note in Matthew 24:24 that these false prophets will come with signs and wonders. Satan will come not only with a gospel so closely patterned after the true Gospel that even the elect would be deceived if that were possible, but he will give life and vitality to his gospel with signs and wonders. Even as Jesus came 2,000 years ago with signs and wonders when He brought us the true Gospel, so Satan will attest to the seemingly God-like, Jesus-related character of his gospel by coming with signs and wonders.

The passage we are presently studying, II Thessalonians 2:1, 9, also speaks of signs and wonders. The false prophets who represent Satan will come with signs and wonders, as verse 9 teaches, **"Even him, whose coming is after the working of Satan with all power and signs and lying wonders."**

We must realize, of course, that these false prophets have been so deceived that they are convinced that they are servants of Christ. Satan is the great deceiver, the father of lies (John 8:44). Moreover, II Thessalonians 2:10-11 teaches that God blinds those who come with signs and lying wonders because they refuse to believe the truth.

Thus, we see that God declares in II Thessalonians 2 that before Christ comes there must be specific evidence of the activity of Satan: Those who come with signs and wonders and who in fact are Satan's servants will rule or have authority among the body of believers where the true Gospel ought to be proclaimed. These false prophets will be convinced that they are true prophets of Christ, but because they come with a gospel other than the true Gospel, they will cause people to worship Satan. This is the primary nature of the rebellion that must come before Christ returns. The church, which consists of congregations and denominations all over the world, will be infiltrated and finally overrun by those who bring false gospels. The chief method of recognizing this threat is to look at its focus on signs and wonders.

We will include here a definition of the true Gospel. In Revelation 22:18-19, God declares:

> **For I testify unto every man that heareth the words of the prophecy of this book, If any man shall add unto these things, God shall add unto him the plagues that are written in this book: And if any man shall take away from the words of the book of this prophecy, God shall take away his part out of the book of life, and out of the holy city, and from the things which are written in this book.**

Before these verses were penned, God declared His Word by the Scriptures that were available at that time in history. In addition, He brought His divine Word by special visitation of angels, by dreams, by visions, by voices, and by unknown heavenly languages called tongues. Thus, Peter or Paul or some of the members of the church in Corinth could receive direct revelation from God. But then God came to the last chapter of His revealed Word. When God wrote Revelation 22, utilizing the Apostle John as His scribe, He indicated that His Word had been completed. Never again could there be a vision or a voice or a tongue from God. Thus, the true Gospel is circumscribed by the Bible. It alone and in its entirety is the articulated, verbalized Word of God. Therefore, anyone who comes with a gospel based upon the Bible but to which he has added the idea of the possibility of divine truth from other sources, such as visions, voices, tongues, dreams, or so called infallible utterances of church leaders, comes with what is by definition another gospel.

As we learned earlier in this study, any doctrine held by a church that is not thoroughly founded on the Bible is a doctrine that has come from the minds of men. Obedience to the doctrines of the Bible is our worship of God who has given us His laws. Thus, obedience to a man-made doctrine is tantamount to the worship of someone other than God. Therefore, when a church holds a human-conceived idea or doctrine and teaches it as though God had declared it, effectively, it is worshipping Satan.

The moment we consider anything at all to be as authoritative as the Bible, we have a gospel that consists of the Bible plus the other source of supposed divine truth. The Bible will then be interpreted not only by itself but by these other supposed sources of divine truth. Obviously, doctrines will then be forthcoming that will be different from those that come when the Bible alone is considered the Word of God. In view of the teaching of Revelation 22:18, these supposed extra Biblical sources of divine truth (visions, voices, etc.), cannot be of God. Even though they may be from the recipient's own mind, nevertheless, they are ultimately from Satan. Those who listen to these other sources are unwittingly serving Satan rather than God.

Remember earlier in our study we learned that these man-made doctrines were like the high places where Judah worshipped false gods. While God overlooked this matter of man-made doctrines throughout the church age, we learned that finally, when the work of the season of the church age was finished, He brought judgment on the churches.

Returning to II Thessalonians 2, we read in verse 7, **"For the mystery of iniquity doth already work: only he who now letteth will let, until he be taken out of the way."**

The word "letteth" is an old English word for "restrain." This passage is thus teaching that the one who restrains sin and Satan will be taken out of the way. There are those who teach that the one who restrains sin is the Holy Spirit, and since He indwells the believer, they therefore suggest that this verse must refer to the rapture of the church.

They are correct, of course, in teaching that the one who restrains sin is God Himself. We need only recall the event recorded in Genesis 20 involving Abraham, Sarah, and Abimelech, king of Gerar. Abraham left Canaan to dwell in the land of Gerar to escape a famine. While there, for fear for his life, he told the king of Gerar that Sarah, his wife, was actually his sister. Consequently, the king of Gerar took Sarah into his palace. Then the king was warned of God not to touch Sarah because she was Abraham's wife. The king responded by indicating he had not touched her, and God declared in Genesis 20:6:

Yea, I know that thou didst this in the integrity of thy heart; for I also withheld thee from sinning against me: therefore suffered I thee not to touch her.

From this incident and from what the Bible declares concerning the nature of mankind, we know that God restrains sin. The Bible states that the heart of man is desperately wicked (Jeremiah 17:9). The Bible indicates that out of the heart of man come evil thoughts, murders, adulteries, fornications, thefts, false witness, and blasphemies (Matthew 15:19). Only because man experiences God's restraint is he able to live a reasonable life and manifest some virtues such as love between parents and children, kindness and loyalty between friends, and compassion for the underprivileged.

We must note, however, that this restraint does not take place because of the presence of believers. While God the Holy Spirit does indeed indwell believers, the Holy Spirit is not limited to them. He does His work of restraining sin in the world completely apart from the believers.

Thus, when God speaks in II Thessalonians 2 of taking Him who restrains out of the way (out of the midst), He is not suggesting that the believers will be raptured, for they are not the restraining power. Rather, He is indicating that He will remove His hand of restraint to permit wickedness to multiply. This is indicated by the context, for in these verses God is speaking of rebellion. Matthew 24 speaks of wickedness being multiplied. Revelation 20 speaks of Satan being loosed. All these passages teach one and the same thing: There will come a time when God will allow the world to become desperately sinful. He will accomplish this by removing His restraint on unsaved man and on Satan and his angels. They will be seen to be more wicked than ever.

We must remember, however, that the restraining activity of the Holy Spirit in the churches was also to restrain Satan from being able to frustrate God's plan to save as the Gospel was preached there. Do you recall that in the parable of the sower, we read in Luke 8:12:

> **Those by the way side are they that hear; then cometh the devil, and taketh away the word out of their hearts, lest they should believe and be saved.**

When the Holy Spirit was poured out at Pentecost, about 3,000 were saved. This was possible because Satan was restrained by having been bound (Revelation 20:1-3), and the Holy Spirit was ruling in the church. But when the Holy Spirit is no longer restraining Satan, and indeed, the Holy Spirit no longer rules in the churches, then we know the churches have come under the judgment of God.

Returning to II Thessalonians 2:1-11, we see that before Christ returns to receive His own, the man of sin must first be revealed. God then declares in this passage that when the man of sin is revealed, Jesus will destroy him by the brightness of His coming. That is, Satan and all the wicked who follow him (the unsaved), will be judged and cast into hell when Christ comes, because it is in hell that the wicked are punished by eternal destruction.

Notice that II Thessalonians 2:1-3 speaks of the gathering of the believers to meet the Lord Jesus. God is saying that this gathering together of believers to meet Christ will not take place until the man of sin is revealed. Since verse 8 states that when the man of sin is revealed the wicked will be destroyed (that is, judged and cast into hell), by Christ's coming, we can see the simultaneous timing of the assembling together of the believers to meet Jesus (the rapture) and the destruction of Satan and the wicked (judgment day). Since the assembling of the saints together to meet Jesus must be the same event as the rapture, we see again that the Bible teaches the rapture will coincide with judgment Day.

Therefore, we find total agreement with the other passages that we studied, all of which teach that the rapture comes at the same time as Judgment day and the end of the world.

Conclusion

We have patiently looked at six different paths in the Scriptures that are concerned with the timing of the rapture. Each of them shows us that the rapture of believers occurs simultaneously with judgment day. God has indeed given us ample evidence of this.

Because this truth is so very clearly documented in the Bible, all other teachings that are concerned with the details of our Savior's return should be studied in the light of this truth. The fact is, as we study the Bible to discover aspects of His return, there should be continuous agreement. This is so because the Bible is perfect in its truth and trustworthiness.

The big question we all must face is whether or not we are ready for our Lord's return. Have we seen ourselves as the sinners we are? Have we repented of our sins, believing in the Lord Jesus Christ as our sin bearer? Have we turned away from our sins, earnestly desiring to be obedient to Christ? We know that only God can save us. We know that it is still the day of salvation. The fact is, we know that there is a great multitude which no man can number who are being saved. This is because God is a God of mercy.

We do not know who His elect are, upon whom He will have mercy. We do know that there is nothing we can do to obtain salvation. We do know that faith cometh by hearing and hearing by the Word of God. Therefore, we know that the environment wherein God is saving is the hearing of the Word of God. Therefore, if I am not saved, even though I have no idea whether I am one of God's elect, and even though I know that no activity on my part will assist in my becoming saved, I recognize it is a wise move to place myself in an environment where God can save me if He so desires. Therefore, I will diligently listen to and study the Bible.

Moreover, even though I know that God is infinite God who knows each and every detail of every individual's life, I know I have the luxury of pleading, begging, imploring God for salvation. This activity will not assist me in any way to become saved, but at least I will know that God is hearing of my intense desire for salvation.

May this wonderful salvation be the gift God will give to each one of us.

Scripture Index

Book of the Bible Chapter: Verses	Page No/s.	Book of the Bible Chapter: Verses	Page No/s.
6:7	86, 320	17:34	332
8:31	xvii	18:28-30	272
13	72, 83, 213, 214	19:13	323
		19:31-34	121
13:1-2	215	21	73, 214, 255
13:2	184	21:5-6	214, 215, 216, 217, 222, 230
13:14	213		
13:15	323-324		
13:35	301	21:6	184
14:37	300	21:20	184, 216
15:43	316	21:20-21	67, 212, 213, 222, 241, 253, 255
Luke	174, 253		
4:1-2	158		
4:16-30	49	21:20-22	228
4:28-29	49	21:20-24	259
4:43	134	21:24	255
5:20	53	21:27	255
8:5	107	22:3	95
8:11-12	36-37	22:53	95
8:12	85, 107, 351		
8:24:6-8	xvii	John	167, 174
8:31	34	1:11	27, 49
9:22	50	2:19	124
10:1	87, 320	3	344
10:13-15	135	5:28-29	199, 337-338, 342
10:17	55		
10:18-19	55	5:29	338
11:52	266	6	135, 177, 336, 337, 342
12:3	229		
13:33-34	218	6:2	51
16	5	6:10	51
16:18	279	6:15	13
17	73	6:39	336
17:10	272	6:40	336
17:27	334	6:39-40	340
17:28-37	331-332	6:39, 40, 44, 54	178
17:30	332		
17:31	228-229	6:44	336
17:32	228	6:54	336

About the Author

Harold Camping was born in Colorado, and his family moved to California when he was very young. The family traditionally was of the Reformed faith. Camping has a degree in Civil Engineering from the University of California. In 1959, he sold his successful construction business in order to devote more time to the ministry of Family Radio. In addition to hosting "The Open Forum" program, he has served as President and General Manager for 40 years. He and his wife live in the San Francisco Bay Area. They had seven children and many grandchildren.

About Family Radio

Family Radio (officially Family Stations, Inc.), is a Christ-centered, educational organization whose sole purpose is to broadcast the Gospel of the Lord Jesus Christ. Headquartered in Oakland, California, Family Radio is listener-supported and carries no commercial advertisements. Family Radio was organized in 1958 and began to broadcast from San Francisco in 1959. It now broadcasts over AM and FM stations in major metropolitan areas of the United States, for example, New York, Los Angeles, Chicago, Salt Lake City, Seattle, and Washington, D.C., and it broadcasts worldwide over shortwave radio. Family Radio is dedicated to obeying the Lord's command of Mark 16:15, **"And he said unto them, Go ye into all the world, and preach the gospel to every creature."**

The International Ministry

The Ministry broadcasts the Gospel worldwide over shortwave radio from Okeechobee, Florida, and transmitters in Taiwan. The broadcasts are in twelve languages, including English, Spanish, French, German, Italian, Portuguese, Arabic, Hindi, Russian, Turkish, Mandarin and Cantonese. Please write to Family Radio, Oakland, CA, 94621, for a free shortwave schedule.

The Family Radio School of the Bible

The Family Radio School of the Bible offers in-depth Bible studies to those who have a sincere desire to know more about God's Holy Word, the

Bible. Several certificates and degree programs are available. Family Radio School of the Bible does not charge tuition; it depends upon the generosity of students and friends. The school operates on the principle of Matthew 10:8, **"freely ye have received, freely give."**

Missionary Tours

Family Radio organizes "Missionary Tours" to provide opportunities for staff members and listeners (at their own expense), to help spread the Gospel through Gospel tract distribution. Family Radio ambassadors have visited cities in North America, South America, Europe, Africa, Asia, and Australia.

On the Internet

Family Radio's Bible-based programs are available on the Internet, 24 hours a day, seven days a week. The web site carries a program guide, a shortwave schedule, Bible studies, and audio and text version of the Bible. Visit Family Radio on the Internet at www.familyradio.com. The email address is famradio@familyradio.com.

The Open Forum

The author of this book, Harold Camping, is President and General Manager of Family Radio, and hosts "The Open Forum," a live, call-in program during which he answers questions about salvation and the Bible. "The Open Forum" is heard weekdays, Monday through Friday, 8:30-10:00 PM Eastern time, 5:30-7:00 PM Pacific time. The number is 1-800-322-5385.

Television

Family Stations broadcasts over two television stations, KFTL in San Leandro, California, and WFME in New York.

Family Radio Location and Frequency Guide

Alabama Stations		
Birmingham	89.5 FM	WBFR
Alabama Translators		
Mountain Brook	104.1 FM	WBFR
Notasulga/Auburn		
	90.3 FM	KEAR
Arizona Stations		
Phoenix	88.3 FM	KPHF
Arizona Translators		
Phoenix	88.9 FM	KEAR
Prescott	88.1 FM	KEAR
Arkansas Translators		
Jonesboro	88.3 FM	KEAR
California Stations		
Bakersfield	91.3 FM	KFRB
Chico	89.1 FM	KHAP
El Cajon	910 AM	KECR
Fresno	90.3 FM	KFNO
Le Grand	89.9 FM	KEFR
Long Beach	1280 AM	KFRN
Sacramento	1210 AM	KEBR
	89.3 FM	KEBR
	88.1 FM	KEDR
San Francisco		
	106.9 FM	KEAR
Soledad	89.9 FM	KFRS
Ukiah	89.5 FM	KPRA
California Translators		
Banning	91.3 FM	KEAR

Fairmont/Mojave		
	91.7 FM	KEAR
Fort Bragg	91.9 FM	KEAR
French Gulch		
	96.5 FM	KHAP
Garberville	94.9 FM	KPRA
Gonzales	98.7 FM	KEAR
Grover Beach		
	101.9 FM	KEAR
Helm/Riverdale		
	88.5 FM	KEFR
La Quinta	89.9 FM	KEAR
Laytonville	96.1 FM	KPRA
Palmdale	96.1 FM	KEAR
Palm Springs		
	101.5 FM	KEAR
Paso Robles	106.9 FM	KEAR
Porterville	91.9 FM	KEAR
Redding	101.5 FM	KHAP
Richvale	90.5 FM	KEAR
Ridgecrest	90.5 FM	KEAR
River Pines	93.3 FM	KEDR
Salida	95.5 FM	KEAR
San Luis Obispo		
	89.7 FM	KEAR
Smith River	88.7 FM	KEAR
So. Lake Tahoe		
	92.5 FM	KEAR
Stockton	105.9 FM	KEDR
Colorado Translators		
Grand Junction		
	90.7 FM	KEAR
Pueblo	88.1 FM	KEAR

(Continued)

Connecticut Stations
Vernon   1170 AM   WCTF

Delaware Translators
Dover   103.3 FM   WFSI

Florida Stations
Florida City 88.5 FM   WMFL
Jacksonville 88.7 FM   WJFR
Okeechobee 91.7 FM   WWFR
Okeechobee
          Shortwave   WYFR
St. Petersburg
          91.7 FM   WFTI

Florida Translators
West Palm Beach
          100.3 FM   WWFR

Georgia Stations
Columbus   90.5 FM   WFRC

Georgia Translators
Albany   88.5 FM   KEAR
La Grange   91.9 FM   KEAR

Illinois Stations
Joliet   91.9 FM   WJCH

Illinois Translators
Rockford   94.5 FM   WJCH

Indiana Translators
La Porte   106.9 FM   WJCH

Iowa Stations
Des Moines 91.3 FM   KDFR
Shenandoah 920 AM   KYFR

Iowa Translators
Amana   89.7 FM   KEAR
Ames   89.1 FM   KDFR
Cedar Rapids
          95.1 FM   KEAR
Fort Dodge 89.1 FM   KEAR
Ottumwa   88.9 FM   KEAR

Kansas
Emporia   90.7 FM   KPOR

Louisiana Translators
Lafayette   89.7 FM   KEAR
Lake Charles 98.3 FM   KTXB
New Roads 91.9 FM   KEAR

Maryland Stations
Annapolis   107.9 FM   WFSI

Maryland Translators
Frederick/Middletown
          93.5 FM   WFSI
Paramount/Hagerstown
          93.5 FM   WFSI

Michigan
Schoolcraft 89.5 FM   WOFR

Michigan Translators
Schoolcraft 88.7 FM   KEAR
Wakelee   89.7 FM   KEAR

Minnesota Translators
Duluth   88.5 FM   KEAR

Mississippi Translators
Meridian   89.7 FM   KEAR
Pascagoula 88.9 FM   KEAR

Montana Translators

Billings	99.7 FM	KEAR
Butte	89.9 FM	KEAR
Great Falls	91.3 FM	KEAR
	102.3 FM	KEAR
Shepherd	88.9 FM	KEAR

Nebraska Translators

Grand Island 90.7 FM		KEAR

Nevada Translators

Carson City	89.1 FM	KEAR
Reno	98.7 FM	KEAR

New Jersey Stations

Camden	106.9 FM	WKDN
Newark	94.7 FM	WFME

New Jersey Translators

Brigantine/Atlantic City

	89.3 FM	WKDN
Cape May	92.3 FM	KEAR

New Mexico Translators

Albuquerque 91.9 FM		KEAR

New York Stations

Buffalo	89.9 FM	WFBF
Kingston	91.7 FM	WFRH
Olivebridge	88.3 FM	ᴴWFSO
Smithtown	88.9 FM	WFRS
Webster	88.1 FM	WFRW

New York Translators

Albany	105.3 FM	WFRH
Catskill/Greenville		
	90.7 FM	WFRH
Hudson/Ravena		
	104.9 FM	WFRH

East Windham

	104.3 FM	WFRH
Newburgh	90.5 FM	KEAR
Poughkeepsie/Hyde Park		
	90.5 FM	WFME
Rhinebeck	105.7 FM	WFRH

North Dakota Translators

Bismarck	91.7 FM	KEAR

Ohio Stations

Cuyahoga Falls	1150 AM	WCUE
Toledo	90.3 FM	WOTL
Youngstown	91.7 FM	WYTN

Oklahoma Translators

Enid	88.3 FM	KEAR

Oregon Stations

Springfield	88.9 FM	KQFE

Oregon Translators

Ashland	90.7 FM	KEAR
Cave Junction	88.5 FM	KEAR
Coos Bay	91.7 FM	KEAR
Florence	92.7 FM	KQFE
Newport	89.3 FM	KEAR
Roseburg	88.1 FM	KEAR
Sutherlin/Black Butte		
	100.1 FM	KEAR

Pennsylvania Stations

Erie	88.1 FM	WEFR
Johnstown	88.9 FM	WFRJ

Pennsylvania Translators

Altoona/Bedford		
	90.7 FM	WFRJ
Bellefonte	88.7 FM	KEAR

(Continued)

374

Berwick	90.3 FM	KEAR
East Stroudsburg	97.3 FM	WFME
Emmaus/Allentown	88.7 FM	WKDN
Freeland/Hazleton	89.3 FM	KEAR
Harrisburg/Carlisle	101.7 FM	WKDN
Lebanon/Lancaster	97.7 FM	WKDN
Muncy/Williamsport	90.9 FM	KEAR
Nanticoke/Wilkes-Barre	89.5 FM	KEAR
Reading	89.3 FM	WKDN
Scranton	103.9 FM	KEAR
West View/Pittsburgh	97.7 FM	WFRJ
York	88.7 FM	WKDN

South Carolina Stations

Charleston	88.5 FM	WFCH

South Carolina Translators

Myrtle Beach	95.9 FM	WFCH

South Dakota Translators

Rapid City	90.3 FM	KEAR

Texas Stations

Beaumont	89.7 FM	KTXB

Texas Translators

El Paso	91.7 FM	KEAR
Galveston	91.1 FM	KEAR

Utah Stations

Salt Lake City	91.7 FM	KUFR

Utah Translators

Ogden	91.9 FM	KEAR

Vermont Translators

Burlington	89.3 FM	KEAR

Virginia Translators

Lynchburg	91.7 FM	KEAR
Roanoke	91.9 FM	KEAR
Winchester	91.9 FM	WFSI

Washington Stations

Kirkland	1460 AM	KARR
Longview	89.5 FM	KJVH

Washington Translators

Olympia	90.1 FM	KEAR

Wisconsin Stations

Milwaukee	88.1 FM	WMWK

Wisconsin Translators

Eau Claire	89.1 FM	KEAR

Wyoming Translators

Casper	91.7 FM	KEAR
Cheyenne	90.7 FM	KEAR

Translator: a means by which Family Radio's signal is rebroadcast from an existing station into a new area, either directly from the station or by satellite from KEAR in Oakland, California.